Lardner on Baseball

LARDNER ON BASEBALL

RING LARDNER

Edited and with a Foreword by
JEFF SILVERMAN

THE LYONS PRESS

Guilford, Connecticut

An imprint of The Globe Pequot Press

The Lyons Press is an imprint of The Globe Pequot Press.

10 9 8 7 6 5 4 3 2 1

Printed in the United States of America

ISBN 1-58574-784-X

Library of Congress Cataloging-in-Publication Data is available on file.

To Abby, of course.

Contents

II

Alibi Ike and Friends

III

Reds 5, Black Sox 3

Lardner on Baseball

Introduction

Nineteen fourteen was an auspicious year for baseball. Two men would make debuts that would, over time, rock perceptions of the National Pastime. Each, in his own way with his own tools, would make the game modern. One was Babe Ruth. The other was Ring Lardner.

Ruth was still a kid, of course, when he pitched twenty-one innings for the Red Sox that year, but before he was through, his impact and his legend would so overwhelm the game that language itself would have to stretch for the right word—"Ruthian"—just to encompass them. In a team game, he'd prove bigger than any team. On and off the diamond, his personality and bat would change baseball's nature; they'd make it bigger, louder, more exciting than it had been before. The field was more than a field when he took it. It was a theater.

And the timing of his entrance couldn't have been better. In just five years, the scandals around the 1919 World Series would suck the air out of a disbelieving nation. Ruth's mammoth clouts and outsized character would resuscitate us—and baseball—almost single-handedly with each at-bat. Is that overstatement? Try to imagine baseball's path, and even the first half of America's twentieth century, without him. You can't.

Nor can you imagine the course of the game on the page without Lardner. I don't think it would be inappropriate to call him the game's most Ruthian scribe. He, too, was so big that his achievement outgrew the lexicon; as with Ruth's, an eponymous adjective would be needed to embrace it. Whenever a story or a character is deemed "Lardneresque," generations of appreciative readers have picked up on the connotation straight away.

While Ruth was a raw rookie of nineteen in 1914, Lardner was almost thirty, and a certifiable star of the sporting press. Born to be a writer—after all, his byline had a distinct Ring to it—he was a formidable fixture at the *Chicago Tribune.* As a reporter and a columnist, his Hall-of-Fame *bona fides* were in place. Still, 1914 marked a rookie season for him, too.

On March 7, the *Saturday Evening Post* ran "A Busher's Letters Home," Lardner's first published short story. Introducing the remarkable character of Jack Keefe, it was unlike any baseball story that had come before it, and scorecards of the day recorded it as a solid hit. In his first at-bat, Ring Lardner became a Major League writer of fiction. Before the year was out, the *Post* would publish eight more baseball-themed short stories, and *Redbook* a ninth. All in all, it was a remarkable rookie campaign.

How the *Post* came to publish the stories is a story itself. Originally, Lardner stitched his fictional letters from Keefe—the rude, crude, self-absorbed hayseed from the bushes called up to pitch for the White Sox—for his own meal ticket, the *Tribune.* In the sports editor equivalent to the *Tribune* nabob who was destined to splash "Dewey Defeats Truman" across the front page, his boss promptly rejected them. He'd decided Lardner's verbal sleights were too slangy and his columnist's sardonic, satiric, dyspeptic take on both his main character and the game was inappropriate for the *Tribune*'s readership. The *Post* had no such qualms, and—to Lardner's delight and the delight of his bankbook—a wider circulation and a freer hand with cash.

Ironically, it was precisely what Lardner's editor deemed unfit for his pages that allowed these tales to break new ground. Before them, baseball stories were uplifting efforts written for kids, and their main characters—like Burt Standish's Frank Merriwell and Lester Chadwick's Baseball Joe—were well-scrubbed Golden Boys conceived to speak in platitudes and teach life lessons. They were good characters, to be sure, *all* good, *too* good, sculpted in cardboard rather than born of the blood of the darker side that flesh is heir to.

Lardner's typewriter would eviscerate that; like a later unforgettable voice, he would "tell it like it is." Not only did Lardner see ballplayers as something less than noble, he also saw the National Pastime as a superb arena to explore and amplify the sour notes of the human symphony. What a superb score he composed, and what a stunning orchestra of misfits he conducted. Keefe, "Alibi Ike," and "My Roomy"—you'll meet them all in the following pages—are just the most cacophonous, and memorable, of his soloists; there are plenty more where they came from throughout the first two sections of *Lardner on Baseball.*

The scoundrels in the third were real.

Thankfully, Lardner was still prowling press boxes and covering baseball in what would be the game's darkest hour, and the dispatches he filed from the 1919 World Series for the Bell Syndicate (with the original headlines that ran with them in the *San Francisco Examiner*) make up that section, the only non-fictional entries in the line-up here. Though quite capable of it, Lardner didn't dream up the Black Sox; he didn't have to. That darker side of the flesh that he refused to sugarcoat, personified by greed and a few other deadly sins, was already abroad in the land to do it for him. Lardner was its amanuensis, and if you read between the lines of his coverage, you'll see how suspicious he was, and, given the restraints of his business, how clever he had to be in the implications of his reporting.

As a journalist, Lardner is certainly best known for his baseball, but he wrote about much more. He covered golf, college football, boxing, even political conventions and a World War. Yet, for all the reams of copy that appeared beneath his byline in one of the most successful newspaper and magazine careers of the first quarter of the twentieth century, it's the short stories we truly remember him for. They are unique in American fiction, with a style and tone all their own. Indeed, no American writer ever did what he did in quite the way he did it. His ear for dialogue was sublime, his comic timing was impeccable, his language danced, and his knack for dissecting the human heart was uncanny. Literary lights as diverse as H. L. Mencken, F. Scott Fitzgerald, John O'Hara, and Virginia Woolf were proud and loud charter members of his fan club.

In the end, Lardner left posterity 130 short stories richer. Of that treasure, forty-six had something to do with baseball; thirty-one of them take the field here, a new roster for a new millennium. The first section of *Lardner on Baseball* covers the sweep of the Jack Keefe stories (another series of these tales will appear in the forthcoming *Lardner on War*) from beginning ("A Busher's Letters Home") to end ("The Busher Pulls a Mays"), and includes the original six reissued in 1916 as the epistolary novel *You Know Me Al.* The second section introduces a rogues gallery of All-Stars led by "Alibi Ike" and the roommate from Hell.

Amazingly, though all the stories in *Lardner on Baseball* are more than eighty years old, everything Lardner wrote about seems not only familiar, but oddly contemporary. By refusing to deify ballplayers, Lardner made them seem as fresh, as flawed, as real, and—yes—as modern as the polyester princes who populate today's box scores and police blotters. That his fictional creations rub elbows—and egos—with the real McCoys throughout adds a bonus layer of verisimilitude, a quality that Lardner, who covered zillions of games in his career, knew would be necessary to keep his fiction oiled and humming and truthful. Thus, in "Along Came Ruth," the penultimate Busher saga, the Babe himself would hit one out in a Lardner story, his name forever in lights on the marquee of its title.

How perfectly Ruthian. How positively Lardneresque.

—Jeff Silverman
January 2003

I

You Know Me Al and Other Busher Stories

A Busher's Letters Home

The Saturday Evening Post
MARCH 7, 1914

Terre Haute, Indiana, September 6.

FRIEND AL: Well, Al old pal I suppose you seen in the paper where I been sold to the White Sox. Believe me Al it comes as a surprise to me and I bet it did to all you good old pals down home. You could of knocked me over with a feather when the old man come up to me and says Jack I've sold you to the Chicago Americans.

I didn't have no idea that anything like that was coming off. For five minutes I was just dum and couldn't say a word.

He says We aren't getting what you are worth but I want you to go up to that big league and show those birds that there is a Central League on the map. He says Go and pitch the ball you been pitching down here and there won't be nothing to it. He says All you need is the nerve and Walsh or no one else won't have nothing on you.

So I says I would do the best I could and I thanked him for the treatment I got in Terre Haute. They always was good to me here and though I did more than my share I always felt that my work was appresiated. We are finishing second and I done most of it. I can't help but be proud of my first year's record in professional baseball and you know I am not boasting when I say that Al.

Well Al it will seem funny to be up there in the big show when I never was really in a big city before. But I guess I seen enough of life not to be scared of the high buildings eh Al?

I will just give them what I got and if they don't like it they can send me back to the old Central and I will be perfectly satisfied.

I didn't know anybody was looking me over, but one of the boys told me that Jack Doyle the White Sox scout was down here looking at me when Grand Rapids was here. I beat them twice in that serious. You know Grand Rapids never had a chance with me when I was right. I shut them out in the first game and they got one run in the second on account of Flynn misjuding that fly ball. Anyway Doyle liked my work and he wired Comiskey to buy me. Comiskey come back with an offer and they excepted it. I don't know how much they got but anyway I am sold to the big league and believe me Al I will make good.

Well Al I will be home in a few days and we will have some of the good old times. Regards to all the boys and tell them I am still their pal and not all swelled up over this big league business.

Your pal, JACK.

Chicago, Illinois, December 14.

OLD PAL: Well Al I have not got much to tell you. As you know Comiskey wrote me that if I was up in Chi this month to drop in and see him. So I got here Thursday morning and went to his office in the afternoon. His office is out to the ball park and believe me its some park and some office.

I went in and asked for Comiskey and a young fellow says He is not here now but can I do anything for you? I told him who I am and says I had an engagement to see Comiskey. He says The boss is out of town hunting and did I have to see him personally?

I says I wanted to see about signing a contract. He told me I could sign as well with him as Comiskey and he took me into another office. He says What salary did you think you ought to get? and I says I wouldn't think of playing ball in the big league for less than three thousand dollars per annum. He laughed and says You don't want much. You better stick round town till the boss comes back. So here I am and it is costing me a dollar a day to stay at the hotel on Cottage Grove Avenue and that don't include my meals.

I generally eat at some of the cafes round the hotel but I had supper downtown last night and it cost me fifty-five cents. If Comiskey don't come back soon I won't have no more money left.

Speaking of money I won't sign no contract unless I get the salary you and I talked of, three thousand dollars. You know what I was getting in Terre Haute, a hundred and fifty a month, and I know it's going to cost me a lot more to live here. I made inquiries round here and find I can get board and room for eight dollars a week but I will be out of town half the time and will have to pay for my room when I am away or look up a new one when I come back. Then I will have to buy cloths to wear on the road in places like New York. When Comiskey comes back I will name him three thousand dollars as my lowest figure and I guess he will come through when he sees I am in ernest. I heard that Walsh was getting twice as much as that.

The papers says Comiskey will be back here sometime to-morrow. He has been hunting with the president of the league so he ought to feel pretty good. But I don't care how he feels. I am going to get a contract for three thousand and if he don't want to give it to me he can do the other thing. You know me Al.

Yours truly, JACK.

Chicago, Illinois, December 16.

DEAR FRIEND AL: Well I will be home in a couple of days now but I wanted to write you and let you know how I come out with Comiskey. I signed my contract yesterday afternoon. He is a great old fellow Al and no wonder everybody likes him. He says Young man will you have a drink? But I was to smart and wouldn't take nothing. He says You was with Terre Haute? I says Yes I was. He says Doyle tells me you were pretty wild. I says Oh no I got good control. He says Well do you want to sign? I says Yes if I get my figure. He asks What is my figure and I says three thousand dollars per annum. He says Don't you want the office furniture too? Then he says I thought you was a young ball-player and I didn't know you wanted to buy my park.

We kidded each other back and forth like that a while and then he says You better go out and get the air and come back when you feel better. I says I feel O. K. now and I want to sign a contract because I have got to get back to Bedford. Then he calls the secretary and tells him to make out my contract. He give it to me and it calls for two hundred and fifty a month. He says You know we always have a city serious here in the fall where a fellow picks up a good bunch of money. I hadn't thought of that so I signed up. My yearly salary will be fifteen hundred dollars besides what the city serious brings me. And that is only for the first year. I will demand three thousand or four thousand dollars next year.

I would of started home on the evening train but I ordered a suit of cloths from a tailor over on Cottage Grove and it won't be done till tomorrow. It's going to cost me twenty bucks but it ought to last a long time. Regards to Frank and the bunch.

Your Pal, JACK.

Paso Robles, California, March 2.

OLD PAL AL: Well Al we been in this little berg now a couple of days and its bright and warm all the time just like June. Seems funny to have it so warm this early in March but I guess this California climate is all they said about it and then some.

It would take me a week to tell you about our trip out here. We came on a Special Train De Lukes and it was some train. Every place we stopped there was crowds down to the station to see us go through and all the people looked me over like I was a actor or something. I guess my hight and shoulders attracted their attention. Well Al we finally got to Oakland which is across part of the ocean from Frisco. We will be back there later on for practice games.

We stayed in Oakland a few hours and then took a train for here. It was another night in a sleeper and believe me I was tired of sleepers before we got here. I have road one night at a time but this was four straight nights. You know Al I am not built right for a sleeping car birth.

The hotel here is a great big place and got good eats. We got in at breakfast time and I made a B line for the dining room. Kid Gleason who is a kind of asst. manager to Callahan come in and sat down with me. He says Leave something for the rest of the boys because they will be just as hungry as you. He says Ain't you afraid you will cut your throat with that knife. He says There ain't no extra charge for using the forks. He says You shouldn't ought to eat so much because you're overweight now. I says You may think I am fat, but it's all solid bone and muscle. He says Yes I suppose it's all solid bone from the neck up. I guess he thought I would get sore but I will let them kid me now because they will take off their hats to me when they see me work.

Manager Callahan called us all to his room after breakfast and give us a lecture. He says there would be no work for us the first day but that we must all take a long walk over the hills. He also says we must not take the training trip as a joke. Then the colored trainer give us our suits and I went to my room and tried mine on. I ain't a bad looking guy in the White Sox uniform Al. I will have my picture taken and send you boys some.

My roommate is Allen a lefthander from the Coast League. He

don't look nothing like a pitcher but you can't never tell about them dam left handers. Well I didn't go on the long walk because I was tired out. Walsh stayed at the hotel too and when he seen me he says Why didn't you go with the bunch? I says I was too tired. He says Well when Callahan comes back you better keep out of sight or tell him you are sick. I says I don't care nothing for Callahan. He says No but Callahan is crazy about you. He says You better obey orders and you will git along better. I guess Walsh thinks I am some rube.

When the bunch come back Callahan never said a word to me but Gleason come up and says Where was you? I told him I was too tired to go walking. He says Well I will borrow a wheelbarrow some place and push you round. He says Do you sit down when you pitch? I let him kid me because he has not saw my stuff yet.

Next morning half the bunch mostly vetrans went to the ball park which isn't no better than the one we got at home. Most of them was vetrans as I say but I was in the bunch. That makes things look pretty good for me don't it Al? We tossed the ball round and hit fungos and run round and then Callahan asks Scott and Russell and I to warm up easy and pitch a few to the batters. It was warm and I felt pretty good so I warmed up pretty good. Scott pitched to them first and kept laying them right over with nothing on them. I don't believe a man gets any batting practice that way. So I went in and after I lobbed a few over I cut loose my fast one. Lord was to bat and he ducked out of the way and then throwed his bat to the bench. Callahan says What's the matter Harry? Lord says I forgot to pay up my life insurance. He says I ain't ready for Walter Johnson's July stuff.

Well Al I will make them think I am Walter Johnson before I get through with them. But Callahan come out to me and says What are you trying to do kill somebody? He says Save your smoke because you're going to need it later on. He says Go easy with the boys at first or I won't have no batters. But he was laughing and I guess he was pleased to see the stuff I had.

There is a dance in the hotel to-night and I am up in my room writing this in my underwear while I get my suit pressed. I got it all mussed up coming out here. I don't know what shoes to wear. I asked Gleason and he says Wear your baseball shoes and if any of the girls gets fresh with you spike them. I guess he was kidding me.

Write and tell me all the news about home.

Yours truly, JACK.

Paso Robles, California, March 7.

FRIEND AL: I showed them something out there to-day Al. We had a game between two teams. One team was made up of most of the regulars and the other was made up of recruts. I pitched three innings for the recruts and shut the old birds out. I held them to one hit and that was a ground ball that the recrut shortstop Johnson ought to of ate up. I struck Collins out and he is one of the best batters in the bunch. I used my fast ball most of the while but showed them a few spitters and they missed them a foot. I guess I must of got Walsh's goat with my spitter because him and I walked back to the hotel together and he talked like he was kind of jealous. He says You will have to learn to cover up your spitter. He says I could stand a mile away and tell when you was going to throw it. He says Some of these days I will learn you how to cover it up. I guess Al I know how to cover it up all right without Walsh learning me.

I always sit at the same table in the dining room along with Gleason and Collins and Bodie and Fournier and Allen the young lefthander I told you about. I feel sorry for him because he never says a word. To-night at supper Bodie says How did I look to-day Kid? Gleason says Just like you always do in the spring. You looked like a cow. Gleason seems to have the whole bunch scared of him and they let him say anything he wants to. I let him kid me to but I ain't scared of him. Collins then says to me You got some fast ball there boy. I says I was not as fast today as I am when I am right. He says Well then I don't want to hit against you when you are right. Then Gleason says to Collins Cut that stuff out. Then he says to me Don't believe what he tells you boy. If the pitchers in this league weren't no faster than you I would still be playing ball and I would be the best hitter in the country.

After supper Gleason went out on the porch with me. He says Boy you have got a little stuff but you have got a lot to learn. He says You field your position like a wash woman and you don't hold the runners up. He says When Chase was on second base to-day he got such a lead on you that the little catcher couldn't of shot him out at third with a rifle. I says They all thought I fielded my position all right in the Central League. He says Well if you think you do it all right you better go back to the Central League where you are appresiated. I says You can't send me back there because you could not get waivers. He says Who would claim you? I says St. Louis and Boston and New York.

You know Al what Smith told me this winter. Gleason says Well if you're not willing to learn St. Louis and Boston and New York can have you and the first time you pitch against us we will steal fifty bases. Then he quit kidding and asked me to go to the field with him early to-morrow morning and he would learn me some things. I don't think he can learn me nothing but I promised I would go with him.

There is a little blonde kid in the hotel here who took a shine to me at the dance the other night but I am going to leave the skirts alone. She is real society and a swell dresser and she wants my picture. Regards to all the boys.

Your friend, JACK.

P.S. The boys thought they would be smart to-night and put something over on me. A boy brought me a telegram and I opened it and it said You are sold to Jackson in the Cotton States League. For just a minute they had me going but then I happened to think that Jackson is in Michigan and there's no Cotton States League round there.

Paso Robles, California, March 9.

DEAR FRIEND AL: You have no doubt read the good news in the papers before this reaches you. I have been picked to go to Frisco with the first team. We play practice games up there about two weeks while the second club plays in Los Angeles. Poor Allen had to go with the second club. There's two other recrut pitchers with our part of the team but my name was first on the list so it looks like I had made good. I knowed they would like my stuff when they seen it. We leave here to-night. You got the first team's address so you will know where to send my mail. Callahan goes with us and Gleason goes with the second club. Him and I have got to be pretty good pals and I wish he was going with us even if he don't let me eat like I want to. He told me this morning to remember all he had learned me and to keep working hard. He didn't learn me nothing I didn't know before but I let him think so.

The little blonde don't like to see me leave here. She lives in Detroit and I may see her when I go there. She wants me to write but I guess I better not give her no encouragement.

Well Al I will write you a long letter from Frisco.

Yours truly, JACK.

Oakland, California, March 19.

DEAR OLD PAL: They have gave me plenty of work here all right. I have pitched four times but have not went over five innings yet. I worked against Oakland two times and against Frisco two times and only three runs have been scored off me. They should only ought to of had one but Bodie misjuged a easy fly ball in Frisco and Weaver made a wild peg in Oakland that let in a run. I am not using much but my fast ball but I have got a world of speed and they can't foul me when I am right. I whiffed eight men in five innings in Frisco yesterday and could of did better than that if I had of cut loose.

Manager Callahan is a funny guy and I don't understand him sometimes. I can't figure out if he is kidding or in ernest. We road back to Oakland on the ferry together after yesterday's game and he says Don't you never throw a slow ball? I says I don't need no slow ball with my spitter and my fast one. He says No of course you don't need it but if I was you I would get one of the boys to learn it to me. He says And you better watch the way the boys fields their positions and holds up the runners. He says To see you work a man might think they had a rule in the Central League forbidding a pitcher from leaving the box or looking toward first base.

I told him the Central didn't have no rule like that. He says And I noticed you taking your wind up when What's His Name was on second base there to-day. I says Yes I got more stuff when I wind up. He says Of course you have but if you wind up like that with Cobb on base he will steal your watch and chain. I says Maybe Cobb can't get on base when I work against him. He says That's right and maybe San Francisco Bay is made of grapejuice. Then he walks away from me.

He give one of the youngsters a awful bawling out for something he done in the game at supper last night. If he ever talks to me like he done to him I will take a punch at him. You know me Al.

I come over to Frisco last night with some of the boys and we took in the sights. Frisco is some live town Al. We went all through China Town and the Barbers' Coast. Seen lots of swell dames but they was all painted up. They have beer out here that they call steam beer. I had a few glasses of it and it made me logey. A glass of that Terre Haute beer would go pretty good right now.

We leave here for Los Angeles in a few days and I will write you from there. This is some country Al and I would love to play ball round here.

Your Pal, JACK.

P.S.—I got a letter from the little blonde and I suppose I got to answer it.

Los Angeles, California, March 26.

Friend Al: Only four more days of sunny California and then we start back East. We got exhibition games in Yuma and El Paso, Texas, and Oklahoma City and then we stop over in St. Joe, Missouri, for three days before we go home. You know Al we open the season in Cleveland and we won't be in Chi no more than just passing through. We don't play there till April eighteenth and I guess I will work in that serious all right against Detroit. Then I will be glad to have you and the boys come up and watch me as you suggested in your last letter.

I got another letter from the little blonde. She has went back to Detroit but she give me her address and telephone number and believe me Al I am going to look her up when we get there the twenty-ninth of April.

She is a stenographer and was out here with her uncle and aunt.

I had a run in with Kelly last night and it looked like I would have to take a wallop at him but the other boys separated us. He is a bush outfielder from the New England League. We was playing poker. You know the boys plays poker a good deal but this was the first time I got in. I was having pretty good luck and was about four bucks to the good and I was thinking of quitting because I was tired and sleepy. Then Kelly opened the pot for fifty cents and I stayed. I had three sevens. No one else stayed. Kelly stood pat and I drawed two cards. And I catched my fourth seven. He bet fifty cents but I felt pretty safe even if he did have a pat hand. So I called him. I took the money and told them I was through.

Lord and some of the boys laughed but Kelly got nasty and begun to pan me for quitting and for the way I played. I says Well I won the pot didn't I? He says Yes and he called me something. I says I got a notion to take a punch at you.

He says Oh you have have you? And I come back at him. I says Yes I have have I? I would of busted his jaw if they hadn't stopped me. You know me Al.

I worked here two times once against Los Angeles and once against Venice. I went the full nine innings both times and Venice beat me four to two. I could of beat them easy with any kind of support. I walked a couple of guys in the forth and Chase drops a throw and Collins lets a fly ball get away from him. At that I would of shut them out if I had wanted to cut loose. After the game Callahan says You didn't look so good in there to-day. I says I didn't cut loose. He says Well you been working pretty near three weeks now and you ought to be in shape to cut loose. I says Oh I am in shape all right. He says Well don't work no harder than you have to or you might get hurt and then the league would blow up. I don't know if he was kidding me or not but I guess he thinks pretty well of me because he works me lots oftener than Walsh or Scott or Benz.

I will try to write you from Yuma, Texas, but we don't stay there only a day and I may not have time for a long letter.

Yours truly, JACK.

Yuma, Arizona, April 1.

DEAR OLD AL: Just a line to let you know we are on our way back East. This place is in Arizona and it sure is sandy. They haven't got no regular ball club here and we play a pick-up team this afternoon. Callahan told me I would have to work. He says I am using you because we want to get through early and I know you can beat them quick. That is the first time he has said anything like that and I guess he is wiseing up that I got the goods.

We was talking about the Athaletics this morning and Callahan says None of you fellows pitch right to Baker. I was talking to Lord and Scott afterward and I say to Scott How do you pitch to Baker? He says I use my fadeaway. I says How do you throw it? He says Just like you throw a fast ball to anybody else. I says Why do you call it a fadeaway then? He says Because when I throw it to Baker it fades away over the fence.

This place is full of Indians and I wish you could see them Al. They don't look nothing like the Indians we seen in that show last summer.

Your old pal, JACK.

Oklahoma City, April 4.

FRIEND AL: Coming out of Amarillo last night I and Lord and Weaver was sitting at a table in the dining car with a old lady. None of us were talking to her but she looked me over pretty careful and seemed to kind of like my looks. Finally she says Are you boys with some football club? Lord nor Weaver didn't say nothing so I thought it was up to me and I says No mam this is the Chicago White Sox Ball Club. She says I knew you were athaletes. I says Yes I guess you could spot us for athaletes. She says Yes indeed and specially you. You certainly look healthy. I says You ought to see me stripped. I didn't see nothing funny about that but I thought Lord and Weaver would die laughing. Lord had to get up and leave the table and he told everybody what I said.

All the boys wanted me to play poker on the way here but I told them I didn't feel good. I know enough to quit when I am ahead Al. Callahan and I sat down to breakfast all alone this morning. He says Boy why don't you get to work? I says What do you mean? Ain't I working? He says You ain't improving none. You have got the stuff to make a good pitcher but you don't go after bunts and you don't cover first base and you don't watch the baserunners. He made me kind of sore talking that way and I says Oh I guess I can get along all right.

He says Well I am going to put it up to you. I am going to start you over in St. Joe day after to-morrow and I want you to show me something. I want you to cut loose with all you've got and I want you to get round the infield a little and show them you aren't tied in that box. I says Oh I can field my position if I want to. He says Well you better want to or I will have to ship you back to the sticks. Then he got up and left. He didn't scare me none Al. They won't ship me to no sticks after the way I showed on this trip and even if they did they couldn't get no waivers on me.

Some of the boys have begun to call me Four Sevens but it don't bother me none.

Yours truly, JACK.

St. Joe, Missouri, April 7.

FRIEND AL: It rained yesterday so I worked to-day instead and St. Joe done well to get three hits. They couldn't of scored if we had played all week. I give a couple of passes but I catched a guy flatfooted off of first base and I come up with a couple of bunts and throwed guys out. When the game was over Callahan says That's the way I like to see you work. You looked better to-day than you looked on the whole trip. Just once you wound up with a man on but otherwise you was all O.K. So I guess my job is cinched Al and I won't have to go to New York or St. Louis. I would rather be in Chi anyway because it is near home. I wouldn't care though if they traded me to Detroit. I hear from Violet right along and she says she can't hardly wait till I come to Detroit. She says she is strong for the Tigers but she will pull for me when I work against them. She is nuts over me and I guess she has saw lots of guys to.

I sent her a stickpin from Oklahoma City but I can't spend no more dough on her till after our first payday the fifteenth of the month. I had thirty bucks on me when I left home and I only got about ten left including the five spot I won in the poker game. I have to tip the waiters about thirty cents a day and I seen about twenty picture shows on the coast besides getting my cloths pressed a couple of times.

We leave here to-morrow night and arrive in Chi the next morning. The second club joins us there and then that night we go to Cleveland to open up. I asked one of the reporters if he knowed who was going to pitch the opening game and he says it would be Scott or Walsh but I guess he don't know much about it.

These reporters travel all round the country with the team all season and send in telegrams about the game every night. I ain't seen no Chi papers so I don't know what they been saying about me. But I should worry eh Al? Some of them are pretty nice fellows and some of them got the swell head. They hang round with the old fellows and play poker most of the time.

Will write you from Cleveland. You will see in the paper if I pitch the opening game.

Your old pal, JACK.

Cleveland, Ohio, April 10.

OLD FRIEND AL: Well Al we are all set to open the season this afternoon. I have just ate breakfast and I am sitting in the lobby of the hotel. I eat at a little lunch counter about a block from here and I saved seventy cents on breakfast. You see Al they give us a dollar a meal and if we don't want to spend that much all right. Our rooms at the hotel are paid for.

The Cleveland papers says Walsh or Scott will work for us this afternoon. I asked Callahan if there was any chance of me getting into the first game and he says I hope not. I don't know what he meant but he may surprise these reporters and let me pitch. I will beat them Al. Lajoie and Jackson is supposed to be great batters but the bigger they are the harder they fall.

The second team joined us yesterday in Chi and we practiced a little. Poor Allen was left in Chi last night with four others of the recrut pitchers. Looks pretty good for me eh Al? I only seen Gleason for a few minutes on the train last night. He says, Well you ain't took off much weight. You're hog fat. I says Oh I ain't fat. I didn't need to take off no weight. He says One good thing about it the club don't have to engage no birth for you because you spend all your time in the dining car. We kidded along like that a while and then the trainer rubbed my arm and I went to bed. Well Al I just got time to have my suit pressed before noon.

Yours truly, JACK.

Cleveland, Ohio, April 11.

FRIEND AL: Well Al I suppose you know by this time that I did not pitch and that we got licked. Scott was in there and he didn't have nothing. When they had us beat four to one in the eight inning Callahan told me to go out and warm up and he put a batter in for Scott in our ninth. But Cleveland didn't have to play their ninth so I got no chance to work. But it looks like he means to start me in one of the games here. We got three more to play. Maybe I will pitch this afternoon. I got a postcard from Violet. She says Beat them Naps. I will give them a battle Al if I get a chance.

Glad to hear you boys have fixed it up to come to Chi during the Detroit serious. I will ask Callahan when he is going to pitch me and let you know. Thanks Al for the papers.

Your friend, JACK.

St. Louis, Missouri, April 15.

FRIEND AL: Well Al I guess I showed them. I only worked one inning but I guess them Browns is glad I wasn't in there no longer than that. They had us beat seven to one in the sixth and Callahan pulls Benz out. I honestly felt sorry for him but he didn't have nothing, not a thing. They was hitting him so hard I thought they would score a hundred runs. A righthander name Bumgardner was pitching for them and he didn't look to have nothing either but we ain't got much of a batting team Al. I could hit better than some of them regulars. Anyway Callahan called Benz to the bench and sent for me. I was down in the corner warming up with Kuhn. I wasn't warmed up good but you know I got the nerve Al and I run right out there like I meant business. There was a man on second and nobody out when I come in. I didn't know who was up there but I found out afterward it was Shotten. He's the centerfielder. I was cold and I walked him. Then I got warmed up good and I made Johnston look like a boob. I give him three fast balls and he let two of them go by and missed the other one. I would of handed him a spitter but Schalk kept signing for fast ones and he knows more about them batters than me. Anyway I whiffed Johnston. Then up come Williams and I tried to make him hit at a couple of bad ones. I was in the hole with two balls and nothing and come right across the heart with my fast one. I wish you could of saw the hop on it. Williams hit it right straight up and Lord was camped under it. Then up come Pratt the best hitter on their club. You know what I done to him don't you Al? I give him one spitter and another he didn't strike at that was a ball. Then I come back with two fast ones and Mister Pratt was a dead baby. And you notice they didn't steal no bases neither.

In our half of the seventh inning Weaver and Schalk got on and I was going up there with a stick when Callahan calls me back and sends Easterly up. I don't know what kind of managing you call that. I hit good on the training trip and he must of knew they had no chance to score off me in the innings they had left while they were liable to murder his other pitchers. I come back to the bench pretty hot and I says You're making a mistake. He says If Comiskey had wanted you to manage this team he would of hired you.

Then Easterly pops out and I says Now I guess you're sorry you didn't let me hit. That sent him right up in the air and he bawled me awful. Honest Al I would of cracked him right in the jaw if we hadn't been right out where everybody could of saw us. Well he sent Cicotte in to finish and they didn't score no more and we didn't neither.

I road down in the car with Gleason. He says Boy you shouldn't ought to talk like that to Cal. Some day he will lose his temper and bust you one. I says He won't never bust me. I says He didn't have no right to talk like that to me. Gleason says I suppose you think he's going to laugh and smile when we lost four out of the first five games. He says Wait till to-night and then go up to him and let him know you are sorry you sassed him. I says I didn't sass him and I ain't sorry.

So after supper I seen Callahan sitting in the lobby and I went over and sit down by him. I says When are you going to let me work? He says I wouldn't never let you work only my pitchers are all shot to pieces. Then I told him about you boys coming up from

Bedford to watch me during the Detroit serious and he says Well I will start you in the second game against Detroit. He says But I wouldn't if I had any pitchers. He says A girl could get out there and pitch better than some of them have been doing.

So you see Al I am going to pitch on the nineteenth. I hope you guys can be up there and I will show you something. I know I can beat them Tigers and I will have to do it even if they are Violet's team.

I notice that New York and Boston got trimmed to-day so I suppose they wish Comiskey would ask for waivers on me. No chance Al.

Your old pal, JACK.

P.S.—We play eleven games in Chi and then go to Detroit. So I will see the little girl on the twenty-ninth.

Oh you Violet.

Chicago, Illinois, April 19.

DEAR OLD PAL: Well Al it's just as well you couldn't come. They beat me and I am writing you this so as you will know the truth about the game and not get a bum steer from what you read in the papers.

I had a sore arm when I was warming up and Callahan should never ought to of sent me in there. And Schalk kept signing for my fast ball and I kept giving it to him because I thought he ought to know something about the batters. Weaver and Lord and all of them kept kicking them round the infield and Collins and Bodie couldn't catch nothing.

Callahan ought never to of left me in there when he seen how sore my arm was. Why, I couldn't of threw hard enough to break a pain of glass my arm was so sore.

They sure did run wild on the bases. Cobb stole four and Bush and Crawford and Veach about two apiece. Schalk didn't even make a peg half the time. I guess he was trying to throw me down.

The score was sixteen to two when Callahan finally took me out in the eighth and I don't know how many more they got. I kept telling him to take me out when I seen how bad I was but he wouldn't do it. They started bunting in the fifth and Lord and Chase just stood there and didn't give me no help at all.

I was all O.K. till I had the first two men out in the first inning. Then Crawford come up. I wanted to give him a spitter but Schalk signs me for the fast one and I give it to him. The ball didn't hop much and Crawford happened to catch it just right. At that Collins ought to of catched the ball. Crawford made three bases and up come Cobb. It was the first time I ever seen him. He hollered at me right off the reel. He says You better walk me you busher. I says I will walk you back to the bench. Schalk signs for a spitter and I gives it to him and Cobb misses it.

Then instead of signing for another one Schalk asks for a fast one and I shook my head no but he signed for it again and yells Put something on it. So I throwed a fast one and Cobb hits it right over second base. I don't know what Weaver was doing but he never made a move for the ball. Crawford scored and Cobb was on first base. First thing I knowed he had stole second while I held the ball. Callahan yells Wake up out there and I says Why don't your catcher tell me when they are going to steal. Schalk says Get in there and pitch and shut your mouth. Then I got mad and walked Veach and Moriarty but before I walked Moriarty Cobb and Veach pulled a double steal on Schalk. Gainor lifts a fly and Lord drops it and two more come in. Then Stanage walks and I whiffs their pitcher.

I come in to the bench and Callahan says Are your friends from Bedford up there? I was pretty sore and I says Why don't you get a catcher? He says We don't need no catcher when you're pitching because you can't get nothing past their bats. Then he says You better leave your uniform in here when you go out next inning or Cobb will steal it off your back. I says My arm is sore. He says Use your other one and you'll do just as good.

Gleason says Who do you want to warm up? Callahan says

Nobody. He says Cobb is going to lead the league in batting and basestealing anyway so we might as well give him a good start. I was mad enough to punch his jaw but the boys winked at me not to do nothing.

Well I got some support in the next inning and nobody got on. Between innings I says Well I guess I look better now don't I? Callahan says Yes but you wouldn't look so good if Collins hadn't jumped up on the fence and catched that one off Crawford. That's all the encouragement I got Al.

Cobb come up again to start the third and when Schalk signs me for a fast one I shakes my head. Then Schalk says All right pitch anything you want to. I pitched a spitter and Cobb bunts it right at me. I would of threw him out a block but I stubbed my toe in a rough place and fell down. This is the roughest ground I ever seen Al. Veach bunts and for a wonder Lord throws him out. Cobb goes to second and honest Al I forgot all about him being there and first thing I knowed he had stole third. Then Moriarty hits a fly ball to Bodie and Cobb scores though Bodie ought to of threw him out twenty feet.

They batted all round in the forth inning and scored four or five more. Crawford got the luckiest three-base hit I ever see. He popped one way up in the air and the wind blowed it against the fence. The wind is something fierce here Al. At that Collins ought to of got under it.

I was looking at the bench all the time expecting Callahan to call me in but he kept hollering Go on and pitch. Your friends wants to see you pitch.

Well Al I don't know how they got the rest of their runs but they had more luck than any team I ever seen. And all the time Jennings was on the coaching line yelling like a Indian. Some day Al I'm going to punch his jaw.

After Veach had hit one in the eight Callahan calls me to the bench and says You're through for the day. I says it's about time you found out my arm was sore. He says I ain't worrying about your arm but I'm afraid some of our outfielders will run their legs off and some of them poor infielders will get killed. He says The reporters just sent me a message saying they had run out of paper. Then he says I wish some of the other clubs had pitchers like you so we could hit once in a while. He says Go in the clubhouse and get your arm rubbed off. That's the only way I can get Jennings sore he says.

Well Al that's about all there was to it. It will take two or three stamps to send this but I want you to know the truth about it. The way my arm was I ought never to of went in there.

Yours truly, JACK.

Chicago, Illinois, April 25.

FRIEND AL: Just a line to let you know I am still on earth. My arm feels pretty good again and I guess maybe I will work at Detroit. Violet writes that she can't hardly wait to see me. Looks like I got a regular girl now Al. We go up there the twenty-ninth and maybe I won't be gald to see her. I hope she will be out to the game the day I pitch. I will pitch the way I want to next time and them Tigers won't have such a picnic.

I suppose you seen what the Chicago reporters said about that game. I will punch a couple of their jaws when I see them.

Your pal, JACK.

Chicago, Illinois, April 29.

DEAR OLD AL: Well Al it's all over. The club went to Detroit last night and I didn't go along. Callahan told me to report to Comiskey this morning and I went up to the office at ten o'clock. He give me my pay to date and broke the news. I am sold to Frisco.

I asked him how they got waivers on me and he says Oh there was no trouble about that because they all heard how you tamed the Tigers. Then he patted me on the back and says Go out there and work hard boy and maybe you'll get another chance some day. I was kind of choked up so I walked out of the office.

I ain't had no fair deal Al and I ain't going to no Frisco. I will quit the game first and take that job Charley offered me at the billiard hall.

I expect to be in Bedford in a couple of days. I have got to pack up first and settle with my landlady about my room here which I engaged for all season thinking I would be treated square. I am going to rest and lay round home a while and try to forget this rotten game. Tell the boys about it Al and tell them I never would of got let out if I hadn't worked with a sore arm.

I feel sorry for that little girl up in Detroit Al. She expected me there today.

Your old pal, JACK.

P.S. I suppose you seen where that lucky lefthander Allen shut out Cleveland with two hits yesterday. The lucky stiff.

The Busher Comes Back

The Saturday Evening Post
MAY 23, 1914

San Francisco, California, May 13.

FRIEND AL: I suppose you and the rest of the boys in Bedford will be supprised to learn that I am out here, because I remember telling you when I was sold to San Francisco by the White Sox that not under no circumstances would I report here. I was pretty mad when Comiskey give me my release, because I didn't think I had been given a fair show by Callahan. I don't think so yet Al and I never will but Bill Sullivan the old White Sox catcher talked to me and told me not to pull no boner by refuseing to go where they sent me. He says You're only hurting yourself. He says You must remember that this was your first time up in the big show and very few men no matter how much stuff they got can expect to make good right off the reel. He says All you need is experience and pitching out in the Coast League will be just the thing for you.

So I went in and asked Comiskey for my transportation and he says That's right Boy go out there and work hard and maybe I will want you back. I told him I hoped so but I don't hope nothing of the kind Al. I am going to see if I can't get Detroit to buy me, because I would rather live in Detroit than anywheres else. The little girl who got stuck on me this spring lives there. I guess I told you about her Al. Her name is Violet and she is some queen. And then if I got with the Tigers I wouldn't never have to pitch against Cobb and Crawford, though I believe I could show both of them up if I was right. They ain't got much of a ball club here and hardly any good pitchers outside of me. But I don't care.

I will win some games if they give me any support and I will get back in the big league and show them birds something. You know me, Al.

Your pal, JACK.

Los Angeles, California, May 20.

AL: Well old pal I don't suppose you can find much news of this league in the papers at home so you may not know that I have been standing this league on their heads. I pitched against Oakland up home and shut them out with two hits. I made them look like suckers Al. They hadn't never saw no speed like mine and they was scared to death the minute I cut loose. I could of pitched the last six innings with my foot and trimmed them they was so scared.

Well we come down here for a serious and I worked the second game. They got four hits and one run, and I just give them the one run. Their shortstop Johnson was on the training trip with the White Sox and of course I knowed him pretty well. So I eased up in the last inning and let him hit one. If I had of wanted to let myself out he couldn't of hit me with a board. So I am going along good and Howard our manager says he is going to use me regular. He's a pretty nice manager and not a bit sarkastic like some of them big leaguers. I am fielding my position good and watching the baserunners to. Thank goodness Al they ain't no Cobbs in this league and a man ain't scared of haveing his uniform stole off his back.

But listen Al I don't want to be bought by Detroit no more. It is all off between Violet and I. She wasn't the sort of girl I suspected. She is just like them all Al. No heart. I wrote her a letter from Chicago telling her I was sold to San Francisco and she wrote back a postcard saying something about not haveing no time to waste on bushers. What do you know about that Al? Calling me a busher. I will show them. She wasn't no good Al and I figure I am well rid of her. Good riddance is rubbish as they say.

I will let you know how I get along and if I hear anything about being sold or drafted.

Yours truly, JACK.

San Francisco, California, July 20.

FRIEND AL: You will forgive me for not writeing to you oftener when you hear the news I got for you. Old pal I am engaged to be married. Her name is Hazel Carney and she is some queen, Al—a great big stropping girl that must weigh one hundred and sixty lbs. She is out to every game and she got stuck on me from watching me work.

Then she writes a note to me and makes a date and I meet her down on Market Street one night. We go to a nickel show together and have some time. Since then we been together pretty near every evening except when I was away on the road.

Night before last she asked me if I was married and I tells her No and she says a big handsome man like I ought to have no trouble finding a wife. I tells her I ain't never looked for one and she says Well you wouldn't have to look very far. I asked her if she was married and she said No but she wouldn't mind it. She likes her beer pretty well and her and I had several and I guess I was feeling pretty good. Anyway I guess I asked her if she wouldn't marry me and she says it was O.K. I ain't a bit sorry Al because she is some doll and will make them all sit up back home. She wanted to get married right away but I said No wait till the season is over and maybe I will have more dough. She asked me what I was getting and I told her two hundred dollars a month. She says she didn't think I was getting enough and I don't neither but I will get the money when I get up in the big show again.

Anyway we are going to get married this fall and then I will bring her home and show her to you. She wants to live in Chi or New York but I guess she will like Bedford O.K. when she gets acquainted.

I have made good here all right Al. Up to a week ago Sunday I had won eleven straight. I have lost a couple since then, but one day I wasn't feeling good and the other time they kicked it away behind me.

I had a run in with Howard after Portland had beat me. He says Keep on running round with that skirt and you won't never win another game.

He says Go to bed nights and keep in shape or I will take your money. I told him to mind his own business and then he walked away from me. I guess he was scared I was going to smash him. No manager ain't going to bluff me Al.

So I went to bed early last night and didn't keep my date with the kid. She was pretty sore about it but business before pleasure Al. Don't tell the boys nothing about me being engaged. I want to surprise them.

Your pal, JACK.

Sacramento, California, August 16.

FRIEND AL: Well Al I got the surprise of my life last night. Howard called me up after I got to my room and tells me I am going back to the White Sox. Come to find out, when they sold me out here they kept a option on me and yesterday they exercised it. He told me I would have to report at once. So I packed up as quick as I could and then went down to say good-by to the kid. She was all broke up and wanted to go along with me but I told her I didn't have enough dough to get married. She said she would come anyway and we could get married in Chi but I told her she better wait. She cried all over my sleeve. She sure is gone on me Al and I couldn't help feeling sorry for her but I promised to send for her in October and then everything will be all O.K. She asked me how much I was going to get in the big league and I told her I would get a lot more money than out here because I wouldn't play if I didn't. You know me Al.

I come over here to Sacramento with the club this morning and I am leaveing to-night for Chi. I will get there next Tuesday and I guess Callahan will work me right away because he must of seen his mistake in letting me go by now. I will show them Al.

I looked up the skedule and I seen where we play in Detroit the fifth and sixth of September. I hope they will let me pitch there Al. Violet goes to the games and I will make her sorry she give me that kind of treatment. And I will make them Tigers sorry they kidded me last spring. I ain't afraid of Cobb or none of them now, Al.

Your pal, JACK.

Chicago, Illinois, August 27.

AL: Well old pal I guess I busted in right. Did you notice what I done to them Athaletics, the best ball club in the country? I bet Violet wishes she hadn't called me no busher.

I got here last Tuesday and set up in the stand and watched the game that afternoon. Washington was playing here and Johnson pitched. I was anxious to watch him because I had heard so much about him. Honest Al he ain't as fast as me. He shut them out, but they never was much of a hitting club. I went to the clubhouse after the game and shook hands with the bunch. Kid Gleason the assistant manager seemed pretty glad to see me and he says Well have you learned something? I says Yes I guess I have. He says Did you see the game this afternoon? I says I had and he asked me what I thought of Johnson. I says I don't think so much of him. He says

Well I guess you ain't learned nothing then. He says What was the matter with Johnson's work? I says He ain't got nothing but a fast ball. Then he says Yes and Rockefeller ain't got nothing but a hundred million bucks.

Well I asked Callahan if he was going to give me a chance to work and he says he was. But I sat on the bench a couple of days and he didn't ask me to do nothing. Finally I asked him why not and he says I am saving you to work against a good club, the Athaletics. Well the Athaletics come and I guess you know by this time what I done to them. And I had to work against Bender at that but I ain't afraid of none of them now Al.

Baker didn't hit one hard all afternoon and I didn't have no trouble with Collins neither. I let them down with five blows all though the papers give them seven. Them reporters here don't no more about scoreing than some old woman. They give Barry a hit on a fly ball that Bodie ought to of eat up, only he stumbled or something and they handed Oldring a two base hit on a ball that Weaver had to duck to get out of the way from. But I don't care nothing about reporters. I beat them Athaletics and beat them good, five to one. Gleason slapped me on the back after the game and says Well you learned something after all. Rub some arnicky on your head to keep the swelling down and you may be a real pitcher yet. I says I ain't got no swell head. He says No. If I hated myself like you do I would be a moveing picture actor.

Well I asked Callahan would he let me pitch up to Detroit and he says Sure. He says Do you want to get revenge on them? I says, Yes I did. He says Well you have certainly got some comeing. He says I never seen no man get worse treatment than them Tigers give you last spring. I says Well they won't do it this time because I will know how to pitch to them. He says How are you going to pitch to Cobb? I says I am going to feed him on my slow one. He says Well Cobb had ought to make a good meal off of that. Then we quit jokeing and he says You have improved a hole lot and I am going to work you right along regular and if you can stand the gaff I may be able to use you in the city serious. You know Al the White Sox plays a city serious every fall with the Cubs and the players makes quite a lot of money. The winners gets about eight hundred dollars a peace and the losers about five hundred. We will be the winners if I have anything to say about it.

I am tickled to death at the chance of working in Detroit and I can't hardly wait till we get there. Watch my smoke Al.

Your pal, JACK.

P.S. I am going over to Allen's flat to play cards a while to-night. Allen is the left-hander that was on the training trip with us. He ain't got a thing, Al, and I don't see how he gets by. He is married and his wife's sister is visiting them. She wants to meet me but it won't do her much good. I seen her out to the game today and she ain't much for looks.

Detroit, Mich., September 6.

FRIEND AL: I got a hole lot to write but I ain't got much time because we are going over to Cleveland on the boat at ten P.M. I made them Tigers like it Al just like I said I would. And what do you think, Al, Violet called me up after the game and wanted to see me but I will tell you about the game first.

They got one hit off me and Cobb made it a scratch single that he beat out. If he hadn't of been so dam fast I would of had a no hit game. At that Weaver could of threw him out if he had of started after the ball in time. Crawford didn't get nothing like a hit and I whiffed him once. I give two walks both of them to Bush but he is such a little guy that you can't pitch to him.

When I was warming up before the game Callahan was standing beside me and pretty soon Jennings come over. Jennings says You ain't going to pitch that bird are you? And Callahan said Yes he was. Then Jennings says I wish you wouldn't because my boys is all tired out and can't run the bases. Callahan says They won't get no chance to-day. No, says Jennings I suppose not. I suppose he will walk them all and they won't have to run. Callahan says He won't give no bases on balls, he says. But you better tell your gang that he is liable to bean them and they better stay away from the plate. Jennings says He won't never hurt my boys by beaning them. Than I cut in. Nor you neither, I says. Callahan laughs at that so I guess I must of pulled a pretty good one. Jennings didn't have no comeback so he walks away.

Then Cobb come over and asked if I was going to work. Callahan told him Yes. Cobb says How many innings? Callahan says All the way. Then Cobb says Be a good fellow Cal and take him out early. I am lame and can't run. I butts in then and said Don't worry, Cobb. You won't have to run because we have got a catcher who can hold them third strikes. Callahan laughed again and says to me You sure did learn something out on that Coast.

Well I walked Bush right off the real and they all begun to holler on the Detroit bench There he goes again. Vitt come up and Jennings yells Leave your bat in the bag Osker. He can't get them over. But I got them over for that bird all O.K. and he pops out trying to bunt. And then I whiffed Crawford. He starts off with a foul that had me scared for a minute because it was pretty close to the foul line and it went clear out of the park. But he missed a spitter a foot and then I supprised them Al. I give him a slow ball and I honestly had to laugh to see him lunge for it. I bet he must of strained himself. He throwed his bat way like he was mad and I guess he was. Cobb came prancing up like he always does and yells Give me that slow one Boy. So I says All right. But I fooled him. Instead of giveing him a slow one like I said I was going I handed him a spitter. He hit it all right but it was a line drive right in Chase's hands. He says Pretty lucky Boy but I will get you next time. I come right back at him. I says Yes you will.

Well Al I had them going like that all through. About the sixth inning Callahan yells from the bench to Jennings What do you think of him now? And Jennings didn't say nothing. What could he of said?

Cobb makes their one hit in the eighth. He never would of made it if Schalk had of let me throw him spitters instead of fast ones. At that Weaver ought to of threw him out. Anyway they didn't score and we made a monkey out of Dubuque, or whatever his name is.

Well Al I got back to the hotel and snuck down the street a ways and had a couple of beers before supper. So I come to the supper table late and Walsh tells me they had been several phone calls for me. I go down to the desk and they tell me to call up a certain number. So I called up and they charged me a nickel for it. A girl's voice answers the phone and I says Was they some one there that wanted to talk to Jack Keefe? She says You bet they is. She says Don't you know me, Jack? This is Violet. Well, you could of knocked me down with a peace of bread. I says What do you want? She says Why I want to see you. I says Well you can't see me. She says Why what's the matter, Jack? What have I did that you should be sore at me? I says I guess you know all right. You called me a busher. She says Why I didn't do nothing of the kind. I says Yes you did on that postcard. She says I didn't write you no postcard.

Then we argued along for a while and she swore up and down that she didn't write me no postcard or call me no busher. I says Well then why didn't you write me a letter when I was in Frisco? She says she had lost my address. Well Al I don't know if she was telling me the truth or not but may be she didn't write that postcard after all. She was crying over the telephone so I says Well it is too late for I and you to get together because I am engaged to be married. Then she screamed and I hang up the receiver. She must of called back two or three times because they was calling my name round the hotel but I wouldn't go near the phone. You know me Al.

Well when I hang up and went back to finish my supper the dining room was locked. So I had to go out and buy myself a sandwich. They soaked me fifteen cents for a sandwich and a cup of coffee so with the nickel for the phone I am out twenty cents altogether for nothing. But then I would of had to tip the waiter in the hotel a dime.

Well Al I must close and catch the boat. I expect a letter from Hazel in Cleveland and maybe Violet will write me too. She is stuck on me all right Al. I can see that. And I don't believe she could of wrote that postcard after all.

Yours truly, JACK.

Boston, Massachusetts, September 12.

OLD PAL: Well Al I got a letter from Hazel in Cleveland and she is comeing to Chi in October for the city serious. She asked me to send her a hundred dollars for her fare and to buy some cloths with. I sent her thirty dollars for the fare and told her she could wait till she got to Chi to buy her cloths. She said she would give me the money back as soon as she seen me but she is a little short now because one of her girl friends borrowed fifty off of her. I guess she must be pretty soft-hearted Al. I hope you and Bertha can come up for the wedding because I would like to have you stand up with me.

I all so got a letter from Violet and they was blots all over it like she had been crying. She swore she did not write that postcard and said she would die if I didn't believe her. She wants to know who the lucky girl is who I am engaged to be married to. I believe her Al when she says she did not write that postcard but it is too late now. I will let you know the date of my wedding as soon as I find out.

I guess you seen what I done in Cleveland and here. Allen was going awful bad in Cleveland and I relieved him in the eighth when we had a lead of two runs. I put them out in one-two-three order in the eighth but had hard work in the ninth due to rotten support. I walked Johnston and Chapman and Turner sacrificed them ahead. Jackson come up then and I had two strikes on him. I could of whiffed him but Schalk makes me give him a fast one when I wanted to give him a slow one. He hit it to Berger and Johnston ought to of been threw out at the plate but Berger fumbles and then has to make the play at first base. He got Jackson all O.K. but they was only one run behind then and Chapman was on third base. Lajoie was up next and Callahan sends out word for me to walk him. I thought that was rotten manageing because Lajoie or no one else can hit me when I want to cut loose. So after I give him two bad balls I tried to slip over a strike on him but the lucky stiff hit it on a line to Weaver. Anyway the game was over and I felt pretty good. But Callahan don't appresiate good work Al. He give me a call in the clubhouse and said if I ever disobeyed his orders again he would suspend me without no pay and lick me too. Honest Al it was all I could do to keep from wrapping his jaw but Gleason winks at me not to do nothing.

I worked the second game here and give them three hits two of which was bunts that Lord ought to of eat up. I got better support in Frisco than I been getting here Al. But I don't care. The Boston bunch couldn't of hit me with a shovel and we beat them two to nothing. I worked against Wood at that. They call him Smoky Joe and they say he has got a lot of speed.

Boston is some town, Al, and I wish you and Bertha could come here sometime. I went down to the wharf this morning and seen them unload the fish. They must of been a million of them but I didn't have time to count them. Every one of them was five or six times as big as a blue gill.

Violet asked me what would be my address in New York City so I am dropping her a postcard to let her know all though I don't know what good it will do her. I certainly won't start no correspondents with her now that I am engaged to be married.

Yours truly, JACK.

New York, New York, September 16.

FRIEND AL: I opened the serious here and beat them easy but I know you must of saw about it in the Chi papers. At that they don't give me no fair show in the Chi papers. One of the boys bought one here and I seen in it where I was lucky to win that game in Cleveland. If I knowed which one of them reporters wrote that I would punch his jaw.

Al I told you Boston was some town but this is the real one. I never seen nothing like it and I been going some since we got here. I walked down Broadway the Main Street last night and I run into a couple of the ball players and they took me to what they call the Garden but it ain't like the gardens at home because this one is indoors. We sat down to a table and had several drinks. Pretty soon one of the boys asked me if I was broke and I says No, why? He says You better get some lubricateing oil and loosen up. I don't know what he meant but pretty soon when we had had a lot of drinks the waiter brings a check and hands it to me. It was for one dollar. I says Oh I ain't paying for all of them. The waiter says This is just for that last drink.

I thought the other boys would make a holler but they didn't say nothing. So I give him a dollar bill and even then he didn't act satisfied so I asked him what he was waiting for and he said Oh nothing, kind of sassy. I was going to bust him but the boys give me the sign to shut up and not to say nothing. I excused myself pretty soon because I wanted to get some air. I give my check for my hat to a boy and he brought my hat and I started going and he says Haven't you forgot something? I guess he must of thought I was wearing a overcoat.

Then I went down the Main Street again and some man stopped me and asked me did I want to go to the show. He said he had a ticket. I asked him what show and he said the Follies. I never heard of it but I told him I would go if he had a ticket to spare. He says I will spare you this one for three dollars. I says You must take me for some boob. He says No I wouldn't insult no boob. So I walks on but if he had of insulted me I would of busted him.

I went back to the hotel then and run into Kid Gleason. He asked me to take a walk with him so out I go again. We went to the corner and he bought me a beer. He don't drink nothing but pop himself. The two drinks was only ten cents so I says This is the place for me. He says Where have you been? and I told him about paying one dollar for three drinks. He says I see I will have to take charge of you. Don't go round with them ball players no more. When you want to go out and see the sights come to me and I will stear you. So to-night he is going to stear me. I will write to you from Philadelphia.

Your pal, JACK.

Philadelphia, Pa., September 19.

FRIEND AL: They won't be no game here to-day because it is raining. We all been loafing round the hotel all day and I am glad of it because I got all tired out over in New York City. I and Kid Gleason went round together the last couple of nights over there and he wouldn't let me spend no money. I seen a lot of girls that I would of liked to of got acquainted with but he wouldn't even let me answer them when they spoke to me. We run in to a couple of peaches last night and they had us spotted too. One of them says I'll bet you're a couple of ball players. But Kid says You lose your bet. I am a bell-hop and the big rube with me is nothing but a pitcher.

One of them says What are you trying to do kid somebody? He says Go home and get some soap and remove your disguise from your face. I didn't think he ought to talk like that to them and I called him about it and said maybe they was lonesome and it wouldn't hurt none if we treated them to a soda or something. But he says Lonesome. If I don't get you away from here they will steal everything you got. They won't even leave you your fast ball. So we left them and he took me to a picture show. It was some California pictures and they made me think of Hazel so when I got back to the hotel I sent her three postcards.

Gleason made me go to my room at ten o'clock both nights but I was pretty tired anyway because he had walked me all over town. I guess we must of saw twenty shows. He says I would take you to the grand opera only it would be throwing money away because we can hear Ed Walsh for nothing. Walsh has got some voice Al a loud high tenor.

To-morrow is Sunday and we have a double header Monday on account of the rain to-day. I thought sure I would get another chance to beat the Athaletics and I asked Callahan if he was going to pitch me here but he said he thought he would save me to work against Johnson in Washington. So you see Al he must figure I am about the best he has got. I'll beat him Al if they get a couple of runs behind me.

Yours truly, JACK.

P.S. They was a letter here from Violet and it pretty near made me feel like crying. I wish they was two of me so both them girls could be happy.

Washington, D.C., September 22.

DEAR OLD AL: Well Al here I am in the capital of the old United States. We got in last night and I been walking round town all morning. But I didn't tire myself out because I am going to pitch against Johnson this afternoon.

This is the prettiest town I ever seen but I believe they is more colored people here than they is in Evansville or Chi. I seen the White House and the Monumunt. They say that Bill Sullivan and Gabby St. once catched a baseball that was threw off of the top of the Monumunt but I bet they couldn't catch it if I throwed it.

I was in to breakfast this morning with Gleason and Bodie and Weaver and Fournier. Gleason says I'm surprised that you ain't sick in bed to-day. I says Why?

He says Most of our pitchers get sick when Cal tells them they are going to work against Johnson. He says Here's these other fellows all feeling pretty sick this morning and they ain't even pitchers. All they have to do is hit against him but it looks like as if Cal would have to send substitutes in for them. Bodie is complaining of a sore arm which he must of strained drawing to two card flushes. Fournier and Weaver have strained their legs doing the tango dance. Nothing could cure them except to hear that big Walter had got throwed out of his machine and wouldn't be able to pitch against us in this serious.

I says I feel O.K. and I ain't afraid to pitch against Johnson and I ain't afraid to hit against him neither. Then Weaver says Have you ever saw him work? Yes, I says, I seen him in Chi. Then Weaver says Well if you have saw him work and ain't afraid to hit against him I'll bet you would go down to Wall Street and holler Hurrah for Roosevelt. I says No I wouldn't do that but I ain't afraid of no pitcher and what is more if you get me a couple of runs I'll beat him. Then Fournier says Oh we will get you a couple of runs all right. He says That's just as easy as catching whales with a angleworm.

Well Al I must close and go in and get some lunch. My arm feels great and they will have to go some to beat me Johnson or no Johnson.

Your pal, JACK.

Washington, D.C., September 22.

FRIEND AL: Well I guess you know by this time that they didn't get no two runs for me, only one, but I beat him just the same. I beat him one to nothing and Callahan was so pleased that he give me a ticket to the theater. I just got back from there and it is pretty late and I already have wrote you one letter to-day but I am going to sit up and tell you about it.

It was cloudy before the game started and when I was warming up I made the remark to Callahan that the dark day ought to make my speed good. He says Yes and of course it will handicap Johnson.

While Washington was takeing their practice their two coachers Schaefer and Altrock got out on the infield and cut up and I pretty near busted laughing at them. They certainly is funny Al. Callahan asked me what was I laughing at and I told him and he says That's the first time I ever seen a pitcher laugh when he was going to work against Johnson. He says Griffith is a pretty good fellow to give us something to laugh at before he shoots that guy at us.

I warmed up good and told Schalk not to ask me for my spitter much because my fast one looked faster than I ever seen it. He says it won't make much difference what you pitch to-day. I says Oh, yes, it will because Callahan thinks enough of me to work me against Johnson and I want to show him he didn't make no mistake. Then Gleason says No he didn't make no mistake. Wasteing Cicotte or Scotty would of been a mistake in this game.

Well, Johnson whiffs Weaver and Chase and makes Lord pop out in the first inning. I walked their first guy but I didn't give Milan nothing to bunt and finally he flied out. And then I whiffed the next two. On the bench Callahan says That's the way, boy. Keep that up and we got a chance.

Johnson had fanned four of us when I come up with two out in the third inning and he whiffed me to. I fouled one though that if I had ever got a good hold of I would of knocked out of the park. In the first seven innings we didn't have a hit off of him. They had got five or six lucky ones off of me and I had walked two or three, but I cut loose with all I had when they was men on and they couldn't do nothing with me. The only reason I walked so many was because my fast one was jumping so. Honest Al it was so fast that Evans the umpire couldn't see it half the time and he called a lot of balls that was right over the heart.

Well I come up in the eighth with two out and the score still nothing and nothing. I had whiffed the second time as well as the first but it was account of Evans missing one on me. The eighth started with Shanks muffing a fly ball off of Bodie. It was way out by the fence so he got two bases on it and he went to third while they was throwing Berger out. Then Schalk whiffed.

Callahan says Go up and try to meet one Jack. It might as well be you as anybody else. But your old pal didn't whiff this time Al. He gets two strikes on me with fast ones and then I passed up two bad ones. I took my healthy at the next one and slapped it over first base. I guess I could of made two bases on it but I didn't want to tire myself out. Anyway Bodie scored and I had them beat. And my hit was the only one we got off of him so I guess he is a pretty good pitcher after all Al.

They filled up the bases on me with one out in the ninth but it was pretty dark then and I made McBride and their catcher look like suckers with my speed.

I felt so good after the game that I drunk one of them pink cocktails. I don't know what their name is. And then I sent a postcard to poor little Violet. I don't care nothing about her but it don't hurt me none to try and cheer her up once in a while. We leave here Thursday night for home and they had ought to be two or three letters there for me from Hazel because I haven't heard from her lately. She must of lost my road addresses.

Your pal, JACK.

P.S. I forgot to tell you what Callahan said after the game. He said I was a real pitcher now and he is going to use me in the city serious. If he does Al we will beat them Cubs sure.

Chicago, Illinois, September 27.

FRIEND AL: They wasn't no letter here at all from Hazel and I guess she must of been sick. Or maybe she didn't think it was worth while writeing as long as she is comeing next week.

I want to ask you to do me a favor Al and that is to see if you can find me a house down there. I will want to move in with Mrs. Keefe, don't that sound funny Al? sometime in the week of October twelfth. Old man Cutting's house or that yellow house across from you would be O.K. I would rather have the yellow one so as to be near you. Find out how much rent they want Al and if it is not no more than twelve dollars a month get it for me. We will buy our furniture here in Chi when Hazel comes.

We have a couple of days off now Al and then we play St. Louis two games here. Then Detroit comes to finish the season the third and fourth of October.

Your pal, JACK.

Chicago, Illinois, October 3.

DEAR OLD AL: Thanks Al for getting the house. The one-year lease is O.K. You and Bertha and me and Hazel can have all sorts of good times together. I guess the walk needs repairs but I can fix that up when I come. We can stay at the hotel when we first get there.

I wish you could of came up for the city serious Al but anyway I want you and Bertha to be sure and come up for our wedding. I will let you know the date as soon as Hazel gets here.

The serious starts Tuesday and this town is wild over it. The Cubs finished second in their league and we was fifth in ours but that don't scare me none. We would of finished right on top if I had of been here all season.

Callahan pitched one of the bushers against Detroit this afternoon and they beat him bad. Callahan is saveing up Scott and Allen and Russell and Cicotte and I for the big show. Walsh isn't in no shape and neither is Benz. It looks like I would have a good deal to do because most of them others can't work no more than once in four days and Allen ain't no good at all.

We have a day to rest after to-morrow's game with the Tigers and then we go at them Cubs.

Your pal, JACK.

P.S. I have got it figured that Hazel is fixing to surprise me by dropping in on me because I haven't heard nothing yet.

Chicago, Illinois, October 7.

FRIEND AL: Well Al you know by this time that they beat me today and tied up the serious. But I have still got plenty of time Al and I will get them before it is over. My arm wasn't feeling good Al and my fast ball didn't hop like it had ought to. But it was the rotten support I got that beat me. That lucky stiff Zimmerman was the only guy that got a real hit off of me and he must of shut his eyes and throwed his bat because the ball he hit was a foot over his head. And if they hadn't been makeing all them errors behind me they wouldn't of been nobody on bases when Zimmerman got that lucky scratch. The serious now stands one and one Al and it is a cinch we will beat them even if they are a bunch of lucky stiffs. They has been great big crowds at both games and it looks like as if we should ought to get over eight hundred dollars a peace if we win and we will win sure because I will beat them three straight if necessary.

But Al I have got bigger news than that for you and I am the happyest man in the world. I told you I had not heard from Hazel for a long time. To-night when I got back to my room they was a letter waiting for me from her.

Al she is married. Maybe you don't know why that makes me happy but I will tell you. She is married to Kid Levy the middle weight. I guess my thirty dollars is gone because in her letter she called me a cheap skate and she inclosed one one-cent stamp and two twos and said she was paying me for the glass of beer I once bought her. I bought her more than that Al but I won't make no holler. She all so said not for me to never come near her or her husband would bust my jaw. I ain't afraid of him or no one else Al but they ain't no danger of me ever bothering them. She was no good and I was sorry the minute I agreed to marry her.

But I was going to tell you why I am happy or maybe you can guess. Now I can make Violet my wife and she's got Hazel beat forty ways. She ain't nowheres near as big as Hazel but she's classier Al and she will make me a good wife. She ain't never asked me for no money.

I wrote her a letter the minute I got the good news and told her to come on over here at once at my expense. We will be married right after the serious is over and I want you and Bertha to be sure and stand up with us. I will wire you at my own expense the exact date.

It all seems like a dream now about Violet and I haveing our misunderstanding Al and I don't see how I ever could of accused her of sending me that postcard. You and Bertha will be just as crazy about her as I am when you see her Al. Just think Al I will be married inside of a week and to the only girl I ever could of been happy with instead of the woman I never really cared for except as a passing fancy. My happyness would be complete Al if I had not of let that woman steal thirty dollars off of me.

Your happy pal, JACK.

P.S. Hazel probibly would of insisted on us takeing a trip to Niagara falls or somewheres but I know Violet will be perfectly satisfied if I take her right down to Bedford. Oh you little yellow house.

Chicago, Illinois, October 9.

FRIEND AL: Well Al we have got them beat three games to one now and will wind up the serious to-morrow sure. Callahan sent me in to save poor Allen yesterday and I stopped them dead. But I don't care now Al. I have lost all interest in the game and I don't care if Callahan pitches me to-morrow or not. My heart is just about broke Al and I wouldn't be able to do myself justice feeling the way I do.

I have lost Violet Al and just when I was figureing on being the happyest man in the world. We will get the big money but it won't do me no good. They can keep my share because I won't have no little girl to spend it on.

Her answer to my letter was waiting for me at home to-night. She is engaged to be married to Joe Hill the big lefthander Jennings got from Providence. Honest Al I don't see how he gets by. He ain't got no more curve ball than a rabbit and his fast one floats up there like a big balloon. He beat us the last game of the regular season here but it was because Callahan had a lot of bushers in the game.

I wish I had knew then that he was stealing my girl and I would of made Callahan pitch me against him. And when he come up to bat I would of beaned him. But I don't suppose you could hurt him by hitting him in the head. The big stiff. Their wedding ain't going to come off till next summer and by that time he will be pitching in the Southwestern Texas League for about fifty dollars a month.

Violet wrote that she wished me all the luck and happyness in the world but it is too late for me to be happy Al and I don't care what kind of luck I have now.

Al you will have to get rid of that lease for me. Fix it up the best way you can. Tell the old man I have changed my plans. I don't know just yet what I will do but maybe I will go to Australia with Mike Donlin's team. If I do I won't care if the boat goes down or not. I don't believe I will even come back to Bedford this winter. It would drive me wild to go past that little house every day and think how happy I might of been.

Maybe I will pitch to-morrow Al and if I do the serious will be over to-morrow night. I can beat them Cubs if I get any kind of decent support. But I don't care now Al.

Yours truly, JACK.

Chicago, Illinois, October 12.

AL: Your letter received. If the old man won't call it off I guess I will have to try and rent the house to some one else. Do you know of any couple that wants one Al? It looks like I would have to come down there myself and fix things up someway. He is just mean enough to stick me with the house on my hands when I won't have no use for it.

They beat us the day before yesterday as you probibly know and it rained yesterday and to-day. The papers says it will be all O.K. to-morrow and Callahan tells me I am going to work. The Cub pitchers was all shot to peaces and the bad weather is just nuts for them because it will give Cheney a good rest. But I will beat him Al if they don't kick it away behind me.

I must close because I promised Allen the little lefthander that I would come over to his flat and play cards a while to-night and I must wash up and change my collar. Allen's wife's sister is visiting them again and I would give anything not to have to go over there. I am through with girls and don't want nothing to do with them.

I guess it is maybe a good thing it rained to-day because I dreamt about Violet last night and went out and got a couple of high balls before breakfast this morning. I hadn't never drank nothing before breakfast before and it made me kind of sick. But I am all O.K. now.

Your pal, JACK.

Chicago, Illinois, October 13.

DEAR OLD AL: The serious is all over Al. We are the champions and I done it. I may be home the day after to-morrow or I may not come for a couple of days. I want to see Comiskey before I leave and fix up about my contract for next year. I won't sign for no less than five thousand and if he hands me a contract for less than that I will leave the White Sox flat on their back. I have got over fourteen hundred dollars now Al with the city serious money which was $814.30 and I don't have to worry.

Them reporters will have to give me a square deal this time Al. I had everything and the Cubs done well to score a run. I whiffed Zimmerman three times. Some of the boys say he ain't no hitter but he is a hitter and a good one Al only he could not touch the stuff I got. The umps give them their run because in the fourth inning I had Leach flatfooted off of second base and Weaver tagged him O.K. but the umps wouldn't call it. Then Schulte the lucky stiff happened to get a hold of one and pulled it past first base. I guess Chase must of been asleep. Anyway they scored but I don't care because we piled up six runs on Cheney and I drove in one of them myself with one of the prettiest singles you ever see. It was a spitter and I hit it like a shot. If I had hit it square it would of went out of the park.

Comiskey ought to feel pretty good about me winning and I

guess he will give me a contract for anything I want. He will have to or I will go to the Federal League.

We are all invited to a show to-night and I am going with Allen and his wife and her sister Florence. She is O.K. Al and I guess she thinks the same about me. She must because she was out to the game to-day and seen me hand it to them. She maybe ain't as pretty as Violet and Hazel but as they say beauty isn't only so deep.

Well Al tell the boys I will be with them soon. I have gave up the idea of going to Australia because I would have to buy a evening full-dress suit and they tell me they cost pretty near fifty dollars.

Yours truly, JACK.

Chicago, Illinois, October 14.

FRIEND AL: Never mind about that lease. I want the house after all Al and I have got the supprise of your life for you.

When I come home to Bedford I will bring my wife with me. I and Florence fixed things all up after the show last night and we are going to be married to-morrow morning. I am a busy man to-day Al because I have got to get the license and look round for furniture. And I have also got to buy some new cloths but they are haveing a sale on Cottage Grove Avenue at Clark's store and I know one of the clerks there.

I am the happyest man in the world Al. You and Bertha and I and Florence will have all kinds of good times together this winter because I know Bertha and Florence will like each other. Florence looks something like Bertha at that. I am glad I didn't get tied up with Violet or Hazel even if they was a little bit prettier than Florence.

Florence knows a lot about baseball for a girl and you would be supprised to hear her talk. She says I am the best pitcher in the league and she has saw them all. She all so says I am the best looking ball player she ever seen but you know how girls will kid a guy Al. You will like her O.K. I fell for her the first time I seen her.

Your old pal, Jack.

P.S. I signed up for next year. Comiskey slapped me on the back when I went in to see him and told me I would be a star next year if I took good care of myself. I guess I am a star without waiting for next year Al. My contract calls for twenty-eight hundred a year which is a thousand more than I was getting. And it is pretty near a cinch that I will be in on the World Serious money next season.

P.S. I certainly am relieved about that lease. It would of been fierce to of had that place on my hands all winter and not getting any use out of it. Everything is all O.K. now. Oh you little yellow house.

The Busher's Honeymoon

The Saturday Evening Post
JULY 11, 1914

Chicago, Illinois, October 17.

FRIEND AL: Well Al it looks as if I would not be writeing so much to you now that I am a married man. Yes Al I and Florrie was married the day before yesterday just like I told you we was going to be and Al I am the happyest man in the world though I have spent $30 in the last 3 days incluseive. You was wise Al to get married in Bedford where not nothing is nearly half so dear. My expenses was as follows:

License	$2.00
Preist	3.50
Haircut and shave	.35
Shine	.05
Carfair	.45

New suit	14.50
Show tickets	3.00
Flowers	.50
Candy	.30
Hotel	4.50
Tobacco both kinds	.25

You see Al it costs a hole lot of money to get married here. The sum of what I have wrote down is $29.40 but as I told you I have spent $30 and I do not know what I have did with that other $0.60. My new brother-in-law Allen told me I should ought to give the preist $5 and I thought it should be about $2 the same as the license so I split the difference and give him $3.50. I never seen him before and probily won't never see him again so why should I give him anything at all when it is his business to marry couples? But I like to do the right thing. You know me Al.

I thought we would be in Bedford by this time but Florrie wants to stay here a few more days because she says she wants to be with her sister. Allen and his wife is thinking about takeing a flat for the winter instead of going down to Waco Texas where they live. I don't see no sense in that when it costs so much to live here but it is none of my business if they want to throw their money away. But I am glad I got a wife with some sense though she kicked because I did not get no room with a bath which would cost me $2 a day instead of $1.50. I says I guess the clubhouse is still open yet and if I want a bath I can go over there and take the shower. She says Yes and I suppose I can go and jump in the lake. But she would not do that Al because the lake here is cold at this time of the year.

When I told you about my expenses I did not include in it the meals because we would be eating them if I was getting married or not getting married only I have to pay for six meals a day now instead of three and I didn't used to eat no lunch in the playing season except once in a while when I knowed I was not going to work that afternoon. I had a meal ticket which had not quite ran out over to a resturunt on Indiana Ave and we eat there for the first day except at night when I took Allen and his wife to the show with us and then he took us to a chop suye resturunt. I guess you have not never had no chop suye Al and I am here to tell you you have not missed nothing but when Allen was going to buy the supper what could I say? I could not say nothing.

Well yesterday and to-day we been eating at a resturunt on Cottage Grove Ave near the hotel and at the resturunt on Indiana that I had the meal ticket at only I do not like to buy no new meal ticket when I am not going to be round here no more than a few days. Well Al I guess the meals has cost me all together about $1.50 and I have eat very little myself. Florrie always wants desert ice cream or something and that runs up into money faster than regular stuff like stake and ham and eggs.

Well Al Florrie says it is time for me to keep my promise and take her to the moveing pictures which is $0.20 more because the one she likes round here costs a dime apeace. So I must close for this time and will see you soon.

Your pal, JACK.

Chicago, Illinois, October 22.

AL: Just a note Al to tell you why I have not yet came to Bedford yet where I expected I would be long before this time. Allen and his wife have took a furnished flat for the winter and Allen's wife wants Florrie to stay here untill they get settled. Meentime it is costing me a hole lot of money at the hotel and for meals besides I am paying $10 a month rent for the house you got for me and what good am I getting out of it? But Florrie wants to help her sister and what can I say? Though I did make her promise she would not stay no longer than next Saturday at least. So I guess Al we will be home on the evening train Saturday and then may be I can save some money.

I know Al that you and Bertha will like Florrie when you get acquainted with her spesially Bertha though Florrie dresses pretty swell and spends a hole lot of time fusing with her face and her hair.

She says to me to-night Who are you writeing to and I told her

Al Blanchard who I have told you about a good many times. She says I bet you are writeing to some girl and acted like as though she was kind of jealous. So I thought I would tease her a little and I says I don't know no girls except you and Violet and Hazel. Who is Violet and Hazel? she says. I kind of laughed and says Oh I guess I better not tell you and then she says I guess you will tell me. That made me kind of mad because no girl can't tell me what to do. She says Are you going to tell me? and I says No.

Then she says If you don't tell me I will go over to Marie's that is her sister Allen's wife and stay all night. I says Go on and she went downstairs but I guess she probily went to get a soda because she has some money of her own that I give her. This was about two hours ago and she is probily down in the hotel lobby now trying to scare me by makeing me believe she has went to her sister's. But she can't fool me Al and I am now going out to mail this letter and get a beer. I won't never tell her about Violet and Hazel if she is going to act like that.

Yours truly, JACK.

Chicago, Illinois, October 24.

FRIEND AL: I guess I told you Al that we would be home Saturday evening. I have changed my mind. Allen and his wife has a spair bedroom and wants us to come there and stay a week or two. It won't cost nothing except they will probily want to go out to the moveing pictures nights and we will probily have to go along with them and I am a man Al that wants to pay his share and not be cheap.

I and Florrie had our first quarrle the other night. I guess I told you the start of it but I don't remember. I made some crack about Violet and Hazel just to tease Florrie and she wanted to know who they was and I would not tell her. So she gets sore and goes over to Marie's to stay all night. I was just kidding Al and was willing to tell her about them two poor girls whatever she wanted to know except that I don't like to brag about girls being stuck on me. So I goes over to Marie's after her and tells her all about them except that I turned them down cold at the last minute to marry her because I did not want her to get all swelled up. She made me sware that I did not never care nothing about them and that was easy because it was the truth. So she come back to the hotel with me just like I knowed she would when I ordered her to.

They must not be no mistake about who is the boss in my house. Some men let their wife run all over them but I am not that kind. You know me Al.

I must get busy and pack my suitcase if I am going to move over to Allen's. I sent three collars and a shirt to the laundrey this morning so even if we go over there to-night I will have to take another trip back this way in a day or two. I won't mind Al because they sell my kind of beer down to the corner and I never seen it sold nowheres else in Chi. You know the kind it is, eh Al? I wish I was lifting a few with you to-night.

Your pal, JACK.

Chicago, Illinois, October 28.

DEAR OLD AL: Florrie and Marie has went downtown shopping because Florrie thinks she has got to have a new dress though she has got two changes of cloths now and I don't know what she can do with another one. I hope she don't find none to suit her though it would not hurt none if she got something for next spring at a reduckshon. I guess she must think I am Charles A. Comiskey or somebody. Allen has went to a colledge football game. One of the reporters give him a pass. I don't see nothing in football except a lot of scrapping between little slobs that I could lick the whole bunch of them so I did not care to go. The reporter is one of the guys that travled round with our club all summer. He called up and said he hadn't only the one pass but he was not hurting my feelings none because I would not go to no rotten football game if they payed me.

The flat across the hall from this here one is for rent furnished. They want $40 a month for it and I guess they think they must be lots of suckers running round loose. Marie was talking about it and says Why don't you and Florrie take it and then we can be right together all winter long and have some big times? Florrie says It would be all right with me. What about it Jack? I says What do you think I am? I don't have to live in no high price flat when I got a home in Bedford where they ain't no people trying to hold everybody up all the time. So they did not say no more about it when they seen I was in ernest. Nobody cannot tell me where I am going to live sister-in-law or no sister-in-law. If I was to rent the rotten old flat I would be paying $50 a month rent includeing the house down in Bedford. Fine chance Al.

Well Al I am lonesome and thirsty so more later.

Your pal, JACK.

Chicago, Illinois, November 2.

FRIEND AL: Well Al I got some big news for you. I am not comeing to Bedford this winter after all except to make a visit which I guess will be round Xmas. I changed my mind about that flat across the hall from the Allens and decided to take it after all. The people who was in it and owns the furniture says they would let us have it till the 1 of May if we would pay $42.50 a month which is only $2.50 a month more than they would of let us have it for for a short time. So you see we got a bargain because it is all furnished and everything and we won't have to blow no money on furniture besides the club goes to California the middle of Febuery so Florrie would not have no place to stay while I am away.

The Allens only subleased their flat from some other people till the 2 of Febuery and when I and Allen goes West Marie can come over and stay with Florrie so you see it is best all round. If we should of boughten furniture it would cost us in the neighborhood of $100 even without no piano and they is a piano in this here flat which makes it nice because Florrie plays pretty good with one hand and we can have lots of good times at home without it costing us nothing except just the bear liveing expenses. I consider myself lucky to of found out about this before it was too late and somebody else had of gotten the tip.

Now Al old pal I want to ask a great favor of you Al. I all ready have payed one month rent $10 on the house in Bedford and I want you to see the old man and see if he won't call off that lease. Why should I be paying $10 a month rent down there and $42.50 up here when the house down there is not no good to me because I am liveing up here all winter? See Al? Tell him I will gladly give him another month rent to call off the lease but don't tell him that if you don't have to. I want to be fare with him.

If you will do this favor for me, Al, I won't never forget it. Give my kindest to Bertha and tell her I am sorry I and Florrie won't see her right away but you see how it is Al.

Yours, JACK.

Chicago, Illinois, November 30.

FRIEND AL: I have not wrote for a long time have I Al but I have been very busy. They was not enough furniture in the flat and we have been buying some more. They was enough for some people maybe but I and Florrie is the kind that won't have nothing but the best. The furniture them people had in the liveing room was oak but they had a bookcase bilt in in the flat that was mohoggeny and Florrie would not stand for no joke combination like that so she moved the oak chairs and table in to the spair bedroom and we went downtown to buy some mohoggeny. But it costs too much Al and we was feeling pretty bad about it when we seen some Sir Cashion walnut that was prettier even than the mohoggeny and not near so expensive. It is not no real Sir Cashion walnut but it is just as good and we got it reasonable. Then we got some mission chairs for the dining room because the old ones was just straw and was no good and we got a big lether couch for $9 that somebody can sleep on if we get to much company.

I hope you and Bertha can come up for the holidays and see how comfertible we are fixed. That is all the new furniture we have boughten but Florrie set her heart on some old Rose drapes and a red table lamp that is the biggest you ever seen Al and I did not have the heart to say no. The hole thing cost me in the neighborhood of $110 which is very little for what we got and then it will always be ourn even when we move away from this flat though we will have to leave the furniture that belongs to the other people but their part of it is not no good anyway.

I guess I told you Al how much money I had when the season ended. It was $1400 all told includeing the city serious money. Well Al I got in the neighborhood of $800 left because I give $200 to Florrie to send down to Texas to her other sister who had a bad egg for a husband that managed a club in the Texas Oklahoma League and this was the money she had to pay to get the divorce. I am glad Al that I was lucky enough to marry happy and get a good girl for my wife that has got some sense and besides if I have got $800 left I should not worry as they say.

Your pal, JACK.

Chicago, Illinois, December 7.

DEAR OLD AL: No I was in ernest Al when I says that I wanted you and Bertha to come up here for the holidays. I know I told you that I might come to Bedford for the holidays but that is all off. I have gave up the idea of comeing to Bedford for the holidays and I want you to be sure and come up here for the holidays and I will show you a good time. I would love to have Bertha come to and she can come if she wants to only Florrie don't know if she would have a good time or not and thinks maybe she would rather stay in Bedford and you come alone. But be sure and have Bertha come if she wants to come but maybe she would not injoy it. You know best Al.

I don't think the old man give me no square deal on that lease but if he wants to stick me all right. I am grateful to you Al for trying to fix it up but maybe you could of did better if you had of went at it in a different way. I am not finding no fault with my old pal though. Don't think that. When I have a pal I am the man to stick to him threw thick and thin. If the old man is going to hold me to that lease I guess I will have to stand it and I guess I won't starv to death for no $10 a month because I am going to get $2800 next year besides the city serious money and maybe we will get into the World Serious too. I know we will if Callahan will pitch me every 3d day like I wanted him to last season. But if you had of approached the old man in a different way maybe you could of fixed it up. I wish you would try it again Al if it is not no trouble.

We had Allen and his wife here for thanksgiveing dinner and the dinner cost me better than $5. I thought we had enough to eat to last a week but about six o'clock at night Florrie and Marie said they was hungry and we went downtown and had dinner all over again and I payed for it and it cost me $5 more. Allen was all ready to pay for it when Florrie said No this day's treat is on us so I had to pay for it but I don't see why she did not wait and let me do the talking. I was going to pay for it any way.

Be sure and come and visit us for the holidays Al and of coarse if Bertha wants to come bring her along. We will be glad to see you both. I won't never go back on a friend and pal. You know me Al.

Your old pal, JACK.

Chicago, Illinois, December 20.

FRIEND AL: I don't see what can be the matter with Bertha because you know Al we would not care how she dressed and would not make no kick if she come up here in a night gown. She did not have no license to say we was to swell for her because we did not never think of nothing like that. I wish you would talk to her again Al and tell her she need not get sore on me and that both her and you is welcome at my house any time I ask you to come. See if you can't make her change her mind Al because I feel like as if she must of took offense at something I may of wrote you. I am sorry you and her are not comeing but I suppose you know best. Only we was getting all ready for you and Florrie said only the other day that she wished the holidays was over but that was before she knowed you was not comeing. I hope you can come Al.

Well Al I guess there is not no use talking to the old man no more. You have did the best you could but I wish I could of came down there and talked to him. I will pay him his rotten old $10 a month and the next time I come to Bedford and meet him on the street I will bust his jaw. I know he is a old man Al but I don't like to see nobody get the best of me and I am sorry I ever asked him to let me off. Some of them old skinflints has no heart Al but why should I fight with a old man over chicken feed like $10? Florrie says a star pitcher like I should not ought never to scrap about little things and I guess she is right Al so I will pay the old man his $10 a month if I have to.

Florrie says she is jealous of me writeing to you so much and she says she would like to meet this great old pal of mine. I would like to have her meet you to Al and I would like to have you change your mind and come and visit us and I am sorry you can't come Al.

Yours truly, JACK.

Chicago, Illinois, December 27.

OLD PAL: I guess all these lefthanders is alike though I thought this Allen had some sense. I thought he was different from the most and was not no rummy but they are all alike Al and they are all lucky that somebody don't hit them over the head with a ax and kill them but I guess at that you could not hurt no lefthanders by hitting them over the head. We was all down on State St. the day before Xmas and the girls was all tired out and ready to go home but Allen says No I guess we better stick down a while because now the crowds is out and it will be fun to watch them. So we walked up and down State St. about a hour longer and finally we come in front of a big jewlry store window and in it was a swell dimond ring that was marked $100. It was a ladies' ring so Marie says to Allen Why don't you buy that for me? And Allen says Do you really want it? And she says she did.

So we tells the girls to wait and we goes over to a salloon where Allen has got a friend and gets a check cashed and we come back and he bought the ring. Then Florrie looks like as though she was getting all ready to cry and I asked her what was the matter and she says I had not boughten her no ring not even when we was engaged. So I and Allen goes back to the salloon and I gets a check cashed and we come back and bought another ring but I did not think the ring Allen had boughten was worth no $100 so I gets one for $75. Now Al you know I am not makeing no kick on spending a little money for a present for my own wife but I had allready boughten her a rist watch for $15 and a rist watch was just what she had wanted. I was willing to give her the ring if she had not of wanted the rist watch more than the ring but when I give her the ring I kept the rist watch and did not tell her nothing about it.

Well I come downtown alone the day after Xmas and they would not take the rist watch back in the store where I got it. So I am going to give it to her for a New Year's present and I guess that will make Allen feel like a dirty doose. But I guess you cannot hurt no lefthander's feelings at that. They are all alike. But Allen has not got nothing but a dinky curve ball and a fast ball that looks like my slow one. If Comiskey was not good hearted he would of sold him long ago.

I sent you and Bertha a cut glass dish Al which was the best I could get for the money and it was pretty high pricet at that. We was glad to get the pretty pincushions from you and Bertha and Florrie says to tell you that we are well supplied with pincushions now because the ones you sent makes a even half dozen. Thanks Al for remembering us and thank Bertha too though I guess you paid for them.

Your pal, JACK.

Chicago, Illinois, Januery 3.

OLD PAL: Al I been pretty sick ever since New Year's eve. We had a table at 1 of the swell resturunts downtown and I never seen so much wine drank in my life. I would rather of had beer but they would not sell us none so I found out that they was a certain kind that you can get for $1 a bottle and it is just as good as the kind that has got all them fancy names but this left-hander starts ordering some other kind about 11 oclock and it was $5 a bottle and the girls both says they liked it better. I could not see a hole lot of difference myself and I would of gave $0.20 for a big stine of my kind of beer. You know me Al. Well Al you know they is not nobody that can drink more than your old pal and I was all O.K. at one oclock but I seen the girls was getting kind of sleepy so I says we better go home.

Then Marie says Oh, shut up and don't be no quiter. I says You better shut up yourself and not be telling me to shut up, and she says What will you do if I don't shut up? And I says I would bust her in the jaw. But you know Al I would not think of busting no girl. Then Florrie says You better not start nothing because you had to much to drink or you would not be talking about busting girls in the jaw. Then I says I don't care if it is a girl I bust or a lefthander. I did not mean nothing at all Al but Marie says I had insulted Allen and he gets up and slaps my face. Well Al I am not going to stand that from nobody not even if he is my brother-in-law and a lefthander that has not got enough speed to brake a pain of glass.

So I give him a good beating and the waiters butts in and puts us all out for fighting and I and Florrie comes home in a taxi and Allen and his wife don't get in till about 5 oclock so I guess she must of had to of took him to a doctor to get fixed up. I been in bed ever since till just this morning kind of sick to my stumach. I guess I must of eat something that did not agree with me. Allen come over after breakfast this morning and asked me was I all right so I guess he is not sore over the beating I give him or else he wants to make friends because he has saw that I am a bad guy to monkey with.

Florrie tells me a little while ago that she paid the hole bill at the resturunt with my money because Allen was broke so you see what kind of a cheap skate he is Al and some day I am going to bust his jaw. She won't tell me how much the bill was and I won't ask her to no more because we had a good time outside of the fight and what do I care if we spent a little money?

Yours truly, JACK.

Chicago, Illinois, Januery 20.

FRIEND AL: Allen and his wife have gave up the flat across the hall from us and come over to live with us because we got a spair bedroom and why should they not have the bennifit of it? But it is pretty hard for the girls to have to cook and do the work when they is four of us so I have a hired girl who does it all for $7 a week. It is great stuff Al because now we can go round as we please and don't have to wait for no dishes to be washed or nothing. We generally almost always has dinner downtown in the evening so it is pretty soft for the girl too. She don't generally have no more than one meal to get because we generally run round downtown till late and don't get up till about noon.

That sounds funny don't it Al, when I used to get up at 5 every morning down home. Well Al I can tell you something else that may sound funny and that is that I lost my taste for beer. I don't seem to care for it no more and I found I can stand allmost as many drinks of other stuff as I could of beer. I guess Al they is not nobody ever lived can drink more and stand up better under it than me. I make the girls and Allen quit every night.

I only got just time to write you this short note because Florrie and Marie is giving a big party to-night and I and Allen have got to beat it out of the house and stay out of the way till they get things ready. It is Marie's berthday and she says she is 22 but say Al if she is 22 Kid Gleason is 30. Well Al the girls says we must blow so I will run out and mail this letter.

Yours truly, JACK.

Chicago, Illinois, Januery 31.

AL: Allen is going to take Marie with him on the training trip to California and of course Florrie has been at me to take her along. I told her postivly that she can't go. I can't afford no stunt like that but still I am up against it to know what to do with her while we are on the trip because Marie won't be here to stay with her. I don't like to leave her here all alone but they is nothing to it Al I can't afford to take her along. She says I don't see why you can't take me if Allen takes Marie. And I says That stuff is all O.K. for Allen because him and Marie has been grafting off of us all winter. And then she gets mad and tells me I should not ought to say her sister was no grafter. I did not mean nothing like that Al but you don't never know when a woman is going to take offense.

If our furniture was down in Bedford everything would be all O.K. because I could leave her there and I would feel all O.K. because I would know that you and Bertha would see that she was getting along O.K. But they would not be no sense in sending her down to a house that has not no furniture in it. I wish I knowed somewheres where she could visit Al. I would be willing to pay her bord even.

Well Al enough for this time.

Your old pal, JACK.

Chicago, Illinois, Febuery 4.

FRIEND AL: You are a real old pal Al and I certainly am greatful to you for the invatation. I have not told Florrie about it yet but I am sure she will be tickled to death and it is certainly kind of you old pal. I did not never dream of nothing like that. I note what you say Al about not excepting no bord but I think it would be better and I would feel better if you would take something say about $2 a week.

I know Bertha will like Florrie and that they will get along O.K. together because Florrie can learn her how to make her cloths look good and fix her hair and fix up her face. I feel like as if you had took a big load off of me Al and I won't never forget it.

If you don't think I should pay no bord for Florrie all right. Suit yourself about that old pal.

We are leaveing here the 20 of Febuery and if you don't mind I will bring Florrie down to you about the 18. I would like to see the old bunch again and spesially you and Bertha.

Yours, JACK.

P.S. We will only be away till April 14 and that is just a nice visit. I wish we did not have no flat on our hands.

Chicago, Illinois, Febuery 9.

OLD PAL: I want to thank you for asking Florrie to come down there and visit you Al but I find she can't get away. I did not know she had no engagements but she says she may go down to her folks in Texas and she don't want to say that she will come to visit you when it is so indefanate. So thank you just the same Al and thank Bertha too.

Florrie is still at me to take her along to California but honest Al I can't do it. I am right down to my last $50 and I have not payed no rent for this month. I owe the hired girl 2 weeks' salery and both I and Florrie needs some new cloths.

Florrie has just came in since I started writeing this letter and we have been talking some more about California and she says maybe if I would ask Comiskey he would take her along as the club's guest. I had not never thought of that Al and maybe he would because he is a pretty good scout and I guess I will go and see him about it. The league has its skedule meeting here to-morrow and may be I can see him down to the hotel where they meet at. I am so worried Al that I can't write no more but I will tell you how I come out with Comiskey.

Your pal, JACK.

Chicago, Illinois, Febuery 11.

Friend Al: I am up against it right Al and I don't know where I am going to head in at. I went down to the hotel where the league was holding its skedule meeting at and I seen Comiskey and got some money off of the club but I owe all the money I got off of them and I am still wondering what to do about Florrie.

Comiskey was busy in the meeting when I went down there and they was not no chance to see him for a while so I and Allen and some of the boys hung round and had a few drinks and fanned. This here Joe Hill the busher that Detroit has got that Violet is hooked up to was round the hotel. I don't know what for but I felt like busting his jaw only the boys told me I had better not do nothing because I might kill him and any way he probily won't be in the league much longer. Well finally Comiskey got threw the meeting and I seen him and he says Hello young man what can I do for you? And I says I would like to get $100 advance money. He says Have you been takeing care of yourself down in Bedford? And I told him I had been liveing here all winter and it did not seem to make no hit with him though I don't see what business it is of hisn where I live.

So I says I had been takeing good care of myself. And I have Al. You know that. So he says I should come to the ball park the next day which is to-day and he would have the secretary take care of me but I says I could not wait and so he give me $100 out of his pocket and says he would have it charged against my salery. I was just going to brace him about the California trip when he got away and went back to the meeting.

Well Al I hung round with the bunch waiting for him to get threw again and we had some more drinks and finally Comiskey was threw again and I braced him in the lobby and asked him if it was all right to take my wife along to California. He says Sure they would be glad to have her along. And then I says Would the club pay her fair? He says I guess you must of spent that $100 buying some nerve. He says Have you not got no sisters that would like to go along to? He says Does your wife insist on the drawing room or will she take a lower birth? He says Is my special train good enough for her?

Then he turns away from me and I guess some of the boys must of heard the stuff he pulled because they was laughing when he went away but I did not see nothing to laugh at. But I guess he ment that I would have to pay her fair if she goes along and that is out of the question Al. I am up against it and I don't know where I am going to head in at.

Your pal, JACK.

Chicago, Illinois, Febuery 12.

DEAR OLD AL: I guess everything will be all O.K. now at least I am hopeing it will. When I told Florrie about how I come out with Comiskey she bawled her head off and I thought for a while I was going to have to call a doctor or something but pretty soon she cut it out and we sat there a while without saying nothing. Then she says If you could get your salery razed a couple of hundred dollars a year would you borrow the money ahead somewheres and take me along to California? I says Yes I would if I could get a couple hundred dollars more salery but how could I do that when I had signed a contract for $2800 last fall allready? She says Don't you think you are worth more than $2800? And I says Yes of coarse I was worth more than $2800. She says Well if you will go and talk the right way to Comiskey I believe he will give you $3000 but you must be sure you go at it the right way and don't go and ball it all up.

Well we argude about it a while because I don't want to hold nobody up Al but finally I says I would. It would not be holding nobody up anyway because I am worth $3000 to the club if I am worth a nichol. The papers is all saying that the club has got a good chance to win the pennant this year and talking about the pitching staff and I guess they would not be no pitching staff much if it was not for I and one or two others—about one other I guess.

So it looks like as if everything will be all O.K. now Al. I am going to the office over to the park to see him the first thing in the morning and I am pretty sure that I will get what I am after because if I do not he will see that I am going to quit and then he will see what he is up against and not let me get away.

I will let you know how I come out.

Your pal, JACK.

Chicago, Illinois, Febuery 14.

FRIEND AL: Al old pal I have got a big supprise for you. I am going to the Federal League. I had a run in with Comiskey yesterday and I guess I told him a thing or 2. I guess he would of been glad to sign me at my own figure before I got threw but I was so mad I would not give him no chance to offer me another contract.

I got out to the park at 9 oclock yesterday morning and it was a hour before he showed up and then he kept me waiting another hour so I was pretty sore when I finally went in to see him. He says Well young man what can I do for you? I says I come to see about my contract. He says Do you want to sign up for next year all ready? I says No I am talking about this year. He says I thought I and you talked business last fall. And I says Yes but now I think I am worth more money and I want to sign a contract for $3000. He says If you behave yourself and work good this year I will see that you are took care of. But I says That won't do because I have got to be sure I am going to get $3000.

Then he says I am not sure you are going to get anything. I says What do you mean? And he says I have gave you a very fare contract and if you don't want to live up to it that is your own business. So I give him a awful call Al and told him I would jump to the Federal League. He says Oh, I would not do that if I was you. They are haveing a hard enough time as it is. So I says something back to him and he did not say nothing to me and I beat it out of the office.

I have not told Florrie about the Federal League business yet as I am going to give her a big suppprise. I bet they will take her along with me on the training trip and pay her fair but even if they don't I should not worry because I will make them give me a contract for $4000 a year and then I can afford to take her with me on all the trips.

I will go down and see Tinker to-morrow morning and I will write you to-morrow night Al how much salery they are going to give me. But I won't sign for no less than $4000. You know me Al.

Yours, JACK.

Chicago, Illinois, Febuery 15.

OLD PAL: It is pretty near midnight Al but I been to bed a couple of times and I can't get no sleep. I am worried to death Al and I don't know where I am going to head in at. Maybe I will go out and buy a gun Al and end it all and I guess it would be better for everybody. But I cannot do that Al because I have not got the money to buy a gun with.

I went down to see Tinker about signing up with the Federal League and he was busy in the office when I come in. Pretty soon Buck Perry the pitcher that was with Boston last year come out and seen me and as Tinker was still busy we went out and had a drink together. Buck shows me a contract for $5000 a year and Tinker had allso gave him a $500 bonus. So pretty soon I went up to the office and pretty soon Tinker seen me and called me into his private office and asked what did I want. I says I was ready to jump for $4000 and a bonus. He says I thought you was signed up with the White Sox. I says Yes I was but I was not satisfied. He says That does not make no difference to me if you are satisfied or not. You ought to of came to me before you signed a contract. I says I did not know enough but I know better now. He says Well it is to late now. We cannot have nothing to do with you because you have went and signed a contract with the White Sox. I argude with him a while and asked him to come out and have a drink so we could talk it over but he said he was busy so they was nothing for me to do but blow.

So I am not going to the Federal League Al and I will not go with the White Sox because I have got a raw deal. Comiskey will be sorry for what he done when his team starts the season and is up against it for good pitchers and then he will probily be willing to give me anything I ask for but that don't do me no good now Al. I am way in debt and no chance to get no money from nobody. I wish I had of stayed with Terre Haute Al and never saw this league.

Your pal, JACK.

Chicago, Illinois, Febuery 17.

FRIEND AL: Al don't never let nobody tell you that these here left-handers is right. This Allen my own brother-in-law who married sisters has been grafting and spongeing on me all winter Al. Look what he done to me now Al. You know how hard I been up against it for money and I know he has got plenty of it because I seen it on him. Well Al I was scared to tell Florrie I was cleaned out and so I went to Allen yesterday and says I had to have $100 right away because I owed the rent and owed the hired girl's salery and could not even pay no grocery bill. And he says No he could not let me have none because he has got to save all his money to take his wife on the trip to California. And here he has been liveing on me all winter and maybe I could of took my wife to California if I had not of spent all my money takeing care of this no good lefthander and his wife. And Al honest he has not got a thing and ought not to be in the league. He gets by with a dinky curve ball and has not got no more smoke than a rabbit or something.

Well Al I felt like busting him in the jaw but then I thought No I might kill him and then I would have Marie and Florrie both to take care of and God knows one of them is enough besides paying his funeral expenses. So I walked away from him without takeing a crack at him and went into the other room where Florrie and Marie was at. I says to Marie I says Marie I wish you would go in the other room a minute because I want to talk to Florrie. So Marie beats it into the other room and then I tells Florrie all about what Comiskey and the Federal League done to me. She bawled something awful and then she says I was no good and she wished she had not never married me. I says I wisht it too and then she says Do you mean that and starts to cry.

I told her I was sorry I says that because they is not no use fussing with girls Al specially when they is your wife. She says No California trip for me and then she says What are you going to do? And I says I did not know. She says Well if I was a man I would do something. So then I got mad and I says I will do something. So I went down to the corner salloon and started in to get good and drunk but I could not do it Al because I did not have the money.

Well old pal I am going to ask you a big favor and it is this. I want you to send me $100 Al for just a few days till I can get on my feet. I do not know when I can pay it back Al but I guess you know the money is good and I know you have got it. Who would not have it when they live in Bedford? And besides I let you take $20 in June 4 years ago Al and you give it back but I would not have said nothing to you if you had of kept it. Let me hear from you right away old pal.

Yours truly, JACK.

Chicago, Illinois, Febuery 19.

AL: I am certainly greatful to you Al for the $100 which come just a little while ago. I will pay the rent with it and part of the grocery bill and I guess the hired girl will have to wait a while for hern but she is sure to get it because I don't never forget my debts. I have changed my mind about the White Sox and I am going to go on the trip and take Florrie along because I don't think it would not be right to leave her here alone in Chi when her sister and all of us is going.

I am going over to the ball park and up in the office pretty soon to see about it. I will tell Comiskey I changed my mind and he will be glad to get me back because the club has not got no chance to finish nowheres without me. But I won't go on no trip or give the club my services without them giveing me some more advance money so as I can take Florrie along with me because Al I would not go without her.

Maybe Comiskey will make my salery $3000 like I wanted him to when he sees I am willing to be a good fellow and go along with him and when he knows that the Federal League would of gladly gave me $4000 if I had not of signed no contract with the White Sox.

I think I will ask him for $200 advance money Al and if I get it may be I can send part of your $100 back to you but I know you cannot be in no hurry Al though you says you wanted it back as soon as possible. You could not be very hard up Al because it don't cost near so much to live in Bedford as it does up here.

Anyway I will let you know how I come out with Comiskey and I will write you as soon as I get out to Paso Robles if I don't get no time to write you before I leave.

Your pal, JACK.

P.S. I have took good care of myself all winter Al and I guess I ought to have a great season.

P.S. Florrie is tickled to death about going along and her and I will have some time together out there on the Coast if I can get some money somewheres.

Chicago, Illinois, Febuery 21.

FRIEND AL: I have not got the heart to write this letter to you Al. I am up here in my $42.50 a month flat and the club has went to California and Florrie has went too. I am flat broke Al and all I am asking you is to send me enough money to pay my fair to Bedford and they and all their leagues can go to hell Al.

I was out to the ball park early yesterday morning and some of the boys was there allready fanning and kidding each other. They tried to kid me to when I come in but I guess I give them as good as they give me. I was not in no mind for kidding Al because I was there on business and I wanted to see Comiskey and get it done with.

Well the secretary come in finally and I went up to him and says I wanted to see Comiskey right away. He says The boss was busy and what did I want to see him about and I says I wanted to get some advance money because I was going to take my wife on the trip. He says This would be a fine time to be telling us about it even if you was going on that trip.

And I says What do you mean? And he says You are not going on no trip with us because we have got wavers on you and you are sold to Milwaukee.

Honest Al I thought he was kidding at first and I was waiting for him to laugh but he did not laugh and finally I says What do you mean? And he says Cannot you understand no English? You are sold to Milwaukee. Then I says I want to see the boss. He says It won't do you no good to see the boss and he is to busy to see you. I says I want to get some money. And he says You cannot get no money from this club and all you get is your fair to Milwaukee. I says I am not going to no Milwaukee anyway and he says I should not worry about that. Suit yourself.

Well Al I told some of the boys about it and they was pretty sore and says I ought to bust the secretary in the jaw and I was going to do it when I thought No I better not because he is a little guy and I might kill him.

I looked all over for Kid Gleason but he was not nowheres round and they told me he would not get into town till late in the afternoon. If I could of saw him Al he would of fixed me all up. I asked 3 or 4 of the boys for some money but they says they was all broke.

But I have not told you the worst of it yet Al. When I come back to the flat Allen and Marie and Florrie was busy packing up and they asked me how I come out. I told them and Allen just stood there stareing like a big rummy but Marie and Florrie both begin to cry and I almost felt like as if I would like to cry to only I am not no baby Al.

Well Al I told Florrie she might just as well quit packing and make up her mind that she was not going nowheres till I got money enough to go to Bedford where I belong. She kept right on crying and it got so I could not stand it no more so I went out to get a drink because I still had just about a dollar left yet.

It was about 2 oclock when I left the flat and pretty near 5 when I come back because I had ran in to some fans that knowed who I was and would not let me get away and besides I did not want to see no more of Allen and Marie till they was out of the house and on their way.

But when I come in Al they was nobody there. They was not nothing there except the furniture and a few of my things scattered round. I sit down for a few minutes because I guess I must of had to much to drink but finally I seen a note on the table addressed to me and I seen it was Florrie's writeing.

I do not remember just what was there in the note Al because I tore it up the minute I read it but it was something about I could not support no wife and Allen had gave her enough money to go back to Texas and she was going on the 6 oclock train and it would not do me no good to try and stop her.

Well Al they was not no danger of me trying to stop her. She was not no good Al and I wisht I had not of never saw either she or her sister or my brother-in-law.

For a minute I thought I would follow Allen and his wife down to the deepo where the special train was to pull out of and wait till I see him and punch his jaw but I seen that would not get me nothing.

So here I am all alone Al and I will have to stay here till you send me the money to come home. You better send me $25 because I have got a few little debts I should ought to pay before I leave town.

I am not going to Milwaukee Al because I did not get no decent deal and nobody cannot make no sucker out of me.

Please hurry up with the $25 Al old friend because I am sick and tired of Chi and want to get back there with my old pal.

Yours, JACK.

P.S. Al I wish I had of took poor little Violet when she was so stuck on me.

A New Busher Breaks In

The Saturday Evening Post
SEPTEMBER 12, 1914

Chicago, Illinois, March 2.

FRIEND AL: Al that peace in the paper was all O.K. and the right dope just like you said. I seen president Johnson the president of the league to-day and he told me the peace in the papers was the right dope and Comiskey did not have no right to sell me to Milwaukee because the Detroit Club had never gave no wavers on me. He says the Detroit Club was late in fileing their claim and Comiskey must of tooken it for granted that they was going to wave but president Johnson was pretty sore about it at that and says Comiskey did not have no right to sell me till he was positive that they was not no team that wanted me.

It will probily cost Comiskey some money for acting like he done and not paying no attention to the rules and I would not be supprised if president Johnson had him throwed out of the league.

Well I asked president Johnson should I report at once to the Detroit Club down south and he says No you better wait till you hear from Comiskey and I says What has Comiskey got to do with it now? And he says Comiskey will own you till he sells you to Detroit or somewheres else. So I will have to go out to the ball park tomorrow and see is they any mail for me there because I probily will get a letter from Comiskey telling me I am sold to Detroit.

If I had of thought at the time I would of knew that Detroit never would give no wavers on me after the way I showed Cobb and Crawford up last fall and I might of knew too that Detroit is in the market for good pitchers because they got a rotten pitching staff but they won't have no rotten staff when I get with them.

If necessary I will pitch every other day for Jennings and if I do we will win the pennant sure because Detroit has got a club that can get 2 or 3 runs every day and all as I need to win most of my games is 1 run. I can't hardly wait till Jennings works me against the White Sox and what I will do to them will be a plenty. It don't take no pitching to bear them anyway and when they get up against a pitcher like I they might as well leave their bats in the bag for all the good their bats will do them.

I guess Cobb and Crawford will be glad to have me on the Detroit Club because then they won't never have to hit against me except in practice and I won't pitch my best in practice because they will be teammates of mine and I don't never like to show none of my teammates up. At that though I don't suppose Jennings will let me do much pitching in practice because when he gets a hold of a good pitcher he won't want me to take no chances of throwing my arm away in practice.

Al just think how funny it will be to have me pitching for the Tigers in the same town where Violet lives and pitching on the same club with her husband. It will not be so funny for Violet and her husband though because when she has a chance to see me work regular she will find out what a mistake she made takeing that left-hander instead of a man that has got some future and soon will be makeing 5 or $6000 a year because I won't sign with Detroit for no less than $5000 at most. Of coarse I could of had her if I had of wanted to but still and all it will make her feel pretty sick to see me winning games for Detroit while her husband is batting fungos and getting splinters in his unie from slideing up and down the bench.

As for her husband the first time he opens his clam to me I will haul off and bust him one in the jaw but I guess he will know more than to start trouble with a man of my size and who is going to be one of their stars while he is just holding down a job because they feel sorry for him. I wish he could of got the girl I married instead of the one he got and I bet she would of drove him crazy. But I guess you can't drive a left-hander crazyer than he is to begin with.

I have not heard nothing from Florrie Al and I don't want to hear nothing. I and her is better apart and I wish she would sew me for a bill of divorce so she could not go round claiming she is my wife and disgraceing my name. If she would consent to sew me for a bill of divorce I would gladly pay all the expenses and settle with her for any sum of money she wants say about $75.00 or $100.00 and they is no reason I should give her a nichol after the way her and her sister Marie and her brother-in-law Allen grafted off of me. Probily I could sew her for a bill of divorce but they tell me it costs money to sew and if you just lay low and let the other side do the sewing it don't cost you a nichol.

It is pretty late Al and I have got to get up early to-morrow and go to the ball park and see is they any mail for me. I will let you know what I hear old pal.

Your old pal, JACK.

Chicago, Illinois, March 4.

AL: I am up against it again. I went out to the ball park office yesterday and they was nobody there except John somebody who is asst secretary and all the rest of them is out on the Coast with the team. Maybe this here John was trying to kid me but this is what he told me. First I says Is they a letter here for me? And he says No. And I says I was expecting word from Comiskey that I should join the Detroit Club and he says What makes you think you are going to Detroit? I says Comiskey asked wavers on me and Detroit did not give no wavers. He says Well that is not no sign that you are going to Detroit. If Comiskey can't get you out of the league he will probily keep you himself and it is a cinch he is not going to give no pitcher to Detroit no matter how rotten he is.

I says What do you mean? And he says You just stick round town till you hear from Comiskey and I guess you will hear pretty soon because he is comeing back from the Coast next Saturday. I says Well the only thing he can tell me is to report to Detroit because I won't never pitch again for the White Sox. Then John gets fresh and says I suppose you will quit the game and live on your saveings and then I blowed out of the office because I was scared I would loose my temper and break something.

So you see Al what I am up against. I won't never pitch for the White Sox again and I want to get with the Detroit Club but how can I if Comiskey won't let me go? All I can do is stick round till next Saturday and then I will see Comiskey and I guess when I tell him what I think of him he will be glad to let me go to Detroit or anywheres else. I will have something on him this time because I know that he did not pay no attention to the rules when he told me I was sold to Milwaukee and if he tries to slip something over on me I will tell president Johnson of the league all about it and then you will see where Comiskey heads in at.

Al old pal that $25.00 you give me at the station the other day is all shot to peaces and I must ask you to let me have $25.00 more which will make $75.00 all together includeing the $25.00 you sent me before I come home. I hate to ask you this favor old pal but I know you have got the money. If I am sold to Detroit I will get some advance money and pay up all my dedts incluseive.

If he don't let me go to Detroit I will make him come across with part of my salery for this year even if I don't pitch for him because I signed a contract and was ready to do my end of it and would of if he had not of been nasty and tried to slip something over on me. If he refuses to come across I will hire a attorney at law and he will get it all. So Al you see you have got a cinch on getting back what you lone me but I guess you know that Al without all this talk because you have been my old pal for a good many years and I have allways treated you square and tried to make you feel that I and you was equals and that my success was not going to make me forget my old friends.

Wherever I pitch this year I will insist on a salery of 5 or $6000 a year. So you see on my first pay day I will have enough to pay you up and settle the rest of my dedts but I am not going to pay no more rent for this rotten flat because they tell me if a man don't pay no rent for a while they will put him out. Let them put me out. I should not worry but will go and rent my old room that I had before I met Florrie and got into all this trouble.

The sooner you can send me that $35.00 the better and then I will owe you $85.00 incluseive and I will write and let you now how I come out with Comiskey.

Your pal, JACK.

Chicago, Illinois, March 12.

FRIEND AL: I got another big supprise for you and this is it I am going to pitch for the White Sox after all. If Comiskey was not a old man I guess I would of lost my temper and beat him up but I am glad now that I kept my temper and did not loose it because I forced him to make a lot of consessions and now it looks like as though I would have a big year both pitching and money.

He got back to town yesterday morning and showed up to his office in the afternoon and I was there waiting for him. He would not see me for a while but finally I acted like as though I was getting tired of waiting and I guess the secretary got scared that I would beat it out of the office and leave them all in the lerch. Anyway he went in and spoke to Comiskey and then come out and says the boss was ready to see me. When I went into the office where he was at he says Well young man what can I do for you? And I says I want you to give me my release so as I can join the Detroit Club down South and get in shape. Then he says What makes you think you are going to join the Detroit Club? Because we need you here. I says Then why did you try to sell me to Milwaukee? But you could not because you could not get no wavers.

Then he says I thought I was doing you a favor by sending you to Milwaukee because they make a lot of beer up there. I says What do you mean? He says You been keeping in shape all this winter by trying to drink this town dry and besides that you tried to hold me up for more money when you allready had signed a contract allready and so I was going to send you to Milwaukee and learn you something and besides you tried to go with the Federal League but they would not take you because they was scared to.

I don't know where he found out all that stuff at Al and besides he was wrong when he says I was drinking to much because they is not nobody that can drink more than me and not be effected. But I did not say nothing because I was scared I would forget myself and call him some name and he is a old man. Yes I did say something. I says Well I guess you found out that you could not get me out of the league and then he says Don't never think I could not get you out of the league. If you think I can't send you to Milwaukee I will prove it to you that I can. I says You can't because Detroit won't give no wavers on me. He says Detroit will give wavers on you quick enough if I ask them.

Then he says Now you can take your choice you can stay here and pitch for me at the salery you signed up for and you can cut out the monkey business and drink water when you are thirsty or else you can go up to Milwaukee and drownd yourself in one of them brewrys. Which shall it be? I says How can you keep me or send me to Milwaukee when Detroit has allready claimed my services? He says Detroit has claimed a lot of things and they have even claimed the pennant but that is not no sign they will win it. He says And besides you would not want to pitch for Detroit because then you would not never have no chance to pitch against Cobb and show him up.

Well Al when he says that I knowed he appresiated what a pitcher I am even if he did try to sell me to Milwaukee or he would not of made that remark about the way I can show Cobb and Crawford up. So I says Well if you need me that bad I will pitch for you but I must have a new contract. He says Oh I guess we can fix that up O.K. and he steps out in the next room a while and then he comes back with a new contract. And what do you think it was Al? It was a contract for 3 years so you see I am sure of my job here for 3 years and everything is all O.K.

The contract calls for the same salery a year for 3 years that I was going to get before for only 1 year which is $2800.00 a year and then I will get in on the city serious money too and the Detroit Club don't have no city serious and have no chance to get into the World's Serious with the rotten pitching staff they got. So you see Al he fixed me up good and that shows that he must think a hole lot of me or he would of sent me to Detroit or maybe to Milwaukee but I don't see how he could of did that without no wavers.

Well Al I allmost forgot to tell you that he has gave me a ticket to Los Angeles where the 2d team are practicing at now but where the 1st team will be at in about a week. I am leaveing to-night and I guess before I go I will go down to president Johnson and tell him that I am fixed up all O.K. and have not got no kick comeing so that president Johnson will not fine Comiskey for not paying no attention to the rules or get him fired out of the league because I guess Comiskey must be all O.K. and good hearted after all.

I won't pay no attention to what he says about me drinking this town dry because he is all wrong in regards to that. He must of been jokeing I guess because nobody but some boob would think he could drink this town dry but at that I guess I can hold more than anybody and not be effected. But I guess I will cut it out for a while at that because I don't want to get them sore at me after the contract they give me.

I will write to you from Los Angeles Al and let you know what the boys says when they see me and I will bet that they will be tickled to death. The rent man was round to-day but I seen him comeing and he did not find me. I am going to leave the furniture that belongs in the flat in the flat and allso the furniture I bought which don't amount to much because it was not no real Sir Cashion walnut and besides I don't want nothing round me to remind me of Florrie because the sooner her and I forget each other the better.

Tell the boys about my good luck Al but it is not no luck neither because it was comeing to me.

Yours truly, JACK.

Los Angeles, California, March 16

AL: Here I am back with the White Sox again and it seems to good to be true because just like I told you they are all tickled to death to see me. Kid Gleason is here in charge of the 2d team and when he seen me come into the hotel he jumped up and hit me in the stumach but he acts like that whenever he feels good so I could not get sore at him though he had no right to hit me in the stumach. If he had of did it in ernest I would of walloped him in the jaw.

He says Well if here ain't the old lady killer. He ment Al that I am strong with the girls but I am all threw with them now but he don't know nothing about the troubles I had. He says Are you in shape? And I told him Yes I am. He says Yes you look in shape like a barrel. I says They is not no fat on me and if I am a little bit bigger than last year it is because my mussels is bigger. He says Yes your stumach mussels is emense and you must of gave them plenty of exercise. Wait till Bodie sees you and he will want to stick round you all the time because you make him look like a broom straw or something. I let him kid me along because what is the use of getting mad at him? And besides he is all O.K. even if he is a little rough.

I says to him A little work will fix me up all O.K. and he says You bet you are going to get some work because I am going to see to it myself. I says You will have to hurry because you will be going up to Frisco in a few days and I am going to stay here and join the 1st club. Then he says You are not going to do no such a thing. You are going right along with me. I knowed he was kidding me then because Callahan would not never leave me with the 2d team no more after what I done for him last year and besides most of the stars generally allways goes with the 1st team on the training trip.

Well I seen all the rest of the boys that is here with the 2d team and they all acted like as if they was glad to see me and why should not they be when they know that me being here with the White Sox and not with Detroit means that Callahan won't have to do no worrying about his pitching staff? But they is four or 5 young recrut pitchers with the team here and I bet they is not so glad to see me because what chance have they got?

If I was Comiskey and Callahan I would not spend no money on new pitchers because with me and 1 or 2 of the other boys we got the best pitching staff in the league. And instead of spending the money for new pitching recruts I would put it all in a lump and buy Ty Cobb or Sam Crawford off of Detroit or somebody else who can hit and Cobb and Crawford is both real hitters Al even if I did make them look like suckers. Who wouldn't?

Well Al to-morrow A.M. I am going out and work a little and in the P.M. I will watch the game between we and the Venice Club but I won't pitch none because Gleason would not dare take no chances of me hurting my arm. I will write to you in a few days from here because no matter what Gleason says I am going to stick here with the 1st team because I know Callahan will want me along with him for a attraction.

Your pal, JACK.

San Francisco, California, March 20.

FRIEND AL: Well Al here I am back in old Frisco with the 2d team but I will tell you how it happened Al. Yesterday Gleason told me to pack up and get ready to leave Los Angeles with him and I says No I am going to stick here and wait for the 1st team and then he says I guess I must of overlooked something in the papers because I did not see nothing about you being appointed manager of the club. I says No I am not manager but Callahan is manager and he will want to keep me with him. He says I got a wire from Callahan telling me to keep you with my club but of coarse if you know what Callahan wants better than he knows it himself why then go ahead and stay here or go jump in the Pacific Ocean.

Then he says I know why you don't want to go with me and I says Why? And he says Because you know I will make you work and won't let you eat everything on the bill of fair includeing the name of the hotel at which we are stopping at. That made me sore and I was just going to call him when he says Did not you marry Mrs. Allen's sister? And I says Yes but that is not none of your business. Then he says Well I don't want to butt into your business but I heard you and your wife had some kind of a argument and she beat it. I says Yes she give me a rotten deal. He says Well then I don't see where it is going to be very pleasant for you traveling round with the 1st club because Allen and his wife is both with that club and what do you want to be mixed up with them for? I says I am not scared of Allen or his wife or no other old hen.

So here I am Al with the 2d team but it is only for a while till Callahan gets sick of some of them pitchers he has got and sends for me so as he can see some real pitching. And besides I am glad to be here in Frisco where I made so many friends when I was pitching here for a short time till Callahan heard about my work and called me back to the big show where I belong at and nowheres else.

Yours truly, JACK.

San Francisco, California, March 25.

OLD PAL: Al I got a supprise for you. Who do you think I seen last night? Nobody but Hazel. Her name now is Hazel Levy because you know Al she married Kid Levy the middleweight and I wish he was champion of the world Al because then it would not take me more than about a minute to be champion of the world myself. I have not got nothing against him though because he married her and if he had not of I probily would of married her myself but at that she could not of treated me no worse than Florrie. Well they was setting at a table in the cafe where her and I use to go pretty near every night. She spotted me when I first come in and sends a waiter over to ask me to come and have a drink with them. I went over because they was no use being nasty and let bygones be bygones.

She interduced me to her husband and he asked me what was I drinking. Then she butts in and says Oh you must let Mr. Keefe buy the drinks because it hurts his feelings to have somebody else buy the drinks. Then Levy says Oh he is one of these here spendrifts is he? and she says Yes he don't care no more about a nichol than his right eye does. I says I guess you have got no holler comeing on the way I spend my money. I don't steal no money anyway. She says What do you mean? and I says I guess you know what I mean. How about that $30.00 that you borrowed off of me and never give it back? Then her husband cuts in and says You cut that line of talk out or I will bust you. I says Yes you will. And he says Yes I will.

Well Al what was the use of me starting trouble with him when he has got enough trouble right to home and besides as I say I have not got nothing against him. So I got up and blowed away from the table and I bet he was relieved when he seen I was not going to start nothing. I beat it out of there a while afterward because I was not drinking nothing and I don't have no fun setting round a place and lapping up ginger ail or something. And besides the music was rotten.

Al I am certainly glad I throwed Hazel over because she has grew to be as big as a horse and is all painted up. I don't care nothing about them big dolls no more or about no other kind neither. I am off of them all. They can all of them die and I should not worry.

Well Al I done my first pitching of the year this P.M. and I guess I showed them that I was in just as good a shape as some of them birds that has been working a month. I worked 4 innings against my old team the San Francisco Club and I give them nothing but fast ones but they sure was fast ones and you could hear them zip. Charlie O'Leary was trying to get out of the way of one of them and it hit his bat and went over first base for a base hit but at that Fournier would of eat it up if it had of been Chase playing first base instead of Fournier.

That was the only hit they got off of me and they ought to of been ashamed to of tooken that one. But Gleason don't appresiate my work and him and I allmost come to blows at supper. I was pretty hungry and I ordered some stake and some eggs and some pie and some ice cream and some coffee and a glass of milk but Gleason would not let me have the pie or the milk and would not let me eat more than ½ the stake. And it is a wonder I did not bust him and tell him to mind his own business. I says What right have you got to tell me what to eat? And he says You don't need nobody to tell you what to eat you need somebody to keep you from floundering yourself. I says Why can't I eat what I want to when I have worked good?

He says Who told you you worked good and I says I did not need nobody to tell me. I know I worked good because they could not do nothing with me. He says Well it is a good thing for you that they did not start bunting because if you had of went to stoop over and pick up the ball you would of busted wide open. I says Why? and he says because you are hog fat and if you don't let up on the stable and fancy groceries we will have to pay 2 fairs to get you back to Chi. I don't remember now what I says to him but I says something you can bet on that. You know me Al.

I wish Al that Callahan would hurry up and order me to join the 1st team. If he don't Al I believe Gleason will starve me to death. A little slob like him don't realize that a big man like I needs good food and plenty of it.

Your pal, JACK.

Salt Lake City, Utah, April 1.

AL: Well Al we are on our way East and I am still with the 2d team and I don't understand why Callahan don't order me to join the 1st team but maybe it is because he knows that I am all right and have got the stuff and he wants to keep them other guys round where he can see if they have got anything.

The recrut pitchers that is along with our club have not got nothing and the scout that reckommended them must of been full of hops or something. It is not no common thing for a club to pick up a man that has got the stuff to make him a star up here and the White Sox was pretty lucky to land me but I don't understand why they throw their money away on new pitchers when none of them is no good and besides who would want a better pitching staff than we got right now without no raw recruts and bushers.

I worked in Oakland the day before yesterday but he only let me go the 1st 4 innings. I bet them Oakland birds was glad when he took me out. When I was in that league I use to just throw my glove in the box and them Oakland birds was licked and honest Al some of them turned white when they seen I was going to pitch the other day.

I felt kind of sorry for them and I did not give them all I had so they got 5 or 6 hits and scored a couple of runs. I was not feeling very good at that and besides we got some awful excuses for a ball player on this club and the support they give me was the rottenest I ever seen gave anybody. But some of them won't be in this league more than about 10 minutes more so I should not fret as they say.

We play here this afternoon and I don't believe I will work because the team they got here is not worth wasteing nobody on. They must be a lot of boobs in this town Al because they tell me that some of them has got ½ a dozen wives or so. And what a man wants with 1 wife is a misery to me let alone a ½ dozen.

I will probily work against Denver because they got a good club and was champions of the Western League last year. I will make them think they are champions of the Epworth League or something.

Yours truly, JACK.

Des Moines, Iowa, April 10.

FRIEND AL: We got here this A.M. and this is our last stop and we will be in old Chi to-morrow to open the season. The 1st team gets home to-day and I would be there with them if Callahan was a real manager who knowed something about manageing because if I am going to open the season I should ought to have 1 day of rest at home so I would have all my strength to open the season. The Cleveland Club will be there to open against us and Callahan must know that I have got them licked any time I start against them.

As soon as my name is announced to pitch the Cleveland Club is licked or any other club when I am right and they don't kick the game away behind me.

Gleason told me on the train last night that I was going to pitch here to-day but I bet by this time he has got orders from Callahan to let me rest and to not give me no more work because suppose even if I did not start the game to-morrow I probily will have to finish it.

Gleason has been sticking round me like as if I had a million bucks or something. I can't even sit down and smoke a cigar but what he is there to knock the ashes off of it. He is O.K. and good-hearted if he is a little rough and keeps hitting me in the stumach but I wish he would leave me alone sometimes espesially at meals. He was in to breakfast with me this A.M. and after I got threw I snuck off down the street and got something to eat. This is not right because it costs me money when I have to go away from the hotel and eat and what right has he got to try and help me order my meals? Because he don't know what I want and what my stumach wants.

My stumach don't want to have him punching it all the time but he keeps on doing it. So that shows he don't know what is good for me. But he is a old man Al otherwise I would not stand for the stuff he pulls. The 1st thing I am going to do when we get to Chi is I am going to a resturunt somewheres and get a good meal where Gleason or no one else can't get at me. I know allready what I am going to eat and that is a big stake and a apple pie and that is not all.

Well Al watch the papers and you will see what I done to that Cleveland Club and I hope Lajoie and Jackson is both in good shape because I don't want to pick on no cripples.

Your pal, JACK.

Chicago, Illinois, April 16.

OLD PAL: Yesterday was the 1st pay day old pal and I know I promised to pay you what I owe you and it is $75.00 because when I asked you for $35.00 before I went West you only sent me $25.00 which makes the hole sum $75.00. Well Al I can't pay you now because the pay we drawed was only for 4 days and did not amount to nothing and I had to buy a meal ticket and fix up about my room rent.

And then they is another thing Al which I will tell you about. I come into the clubhouse the day the season opened and the 1st guy I seen was Allen. I was going to bust him but he come up and held his hand out and what was they for me to do but shake hands with him if he is going to be yellow like that? He says Well Jack I am glad they did not send you to Milwaukee and I bet you will have a big year. I says Yes I will have a big year O.K. if you don't sick another 1 of your sister-in-laws on to me. He says Oh don't let they be no hard feelings about that. You know it was not no fault of mine and I bet if you was to write to Florrie everything could be fixed up O.K.

I says I don't want to write to Florrie but I will get a attorney at law to write to her. He says You don't even know where she is at and

I says I don't care where she is at. Where is she? He says She is down to her home in Waco, Texas, and if I was you I would write to her myself and not let no attorney at law write to her because that would get her mad and besides what do you want a attorney at law to write to her about? I says I am going to sew her for a bill of divorce.

The he says On what grounds? and I says Dessertion. He says You better not do no such thing or she will sew you for a bill of divorce for none support and then you will look like a cheap guy. I says I don't care what I look like. So you see Al I had to send Florrie $10.00 or maybe she would be mean enough to sew me for a bill of divorce on the ground of none suport and that would make me look bad.

Well Al, Allen told me his wife wanted to talk to me and try and fix things up between I and Florrie but I give him to understand that I would not stand for no meeting with his wife and he says Well suit yourself about that but they is no reason you and I should quarrel.

You see Al he don't want no mix-up with me because he knows he could not get nothing but the worst of it. I will be friends with him but I won't have nothing to do with Marie because if it had not of been for she and Florrie I would have money in the bank besides not being in no danger of getting sewed for none support.

I guess you must of read about Joe Benz getting married and I guess he must of got a good wife and 1 that don't bother him all the time because he pitched the opening game and shut Cleveland out with 2 hits. He was pretty good Al, better than I ever seen him and they was a couple of times when his fast ball was pretty near as fast as mine.

I have not worked yet Al and I asked Callahan to-day what was the matter and he says I was waiting for you to get in shape. I says I am in shape now and I notice that when I was pitching in practice this A.M. they did not hit nothing out of the infield. He says That was because you are so spread out that they could not get nothing past you. He says The way you are now you cover more ground than the grand stand. I says Is that so? And he walked away.

We go out on a trip to Cleveland and Detroit and St. Louis in a few days and maybe I will take my regular turn then because the other pitchers has been getting away lucky because most of the hitters has not got their batting eye as yet but wait till they begin hitting and then it will take a man like I to stop them.

The 1st of May is our next pay day Al and then I will have enough money so as I can send you the $75.00.

Your pal, JACK.

Detroit, Michigan, April 28.

FRIEND AL: What do you think of a rotten manager that bawls me out and fines me $50.00 for loosing a 1 to 0 game in 10 innings when it was my 1st start this season? And no wonder I was a little wild in the 10th when I had not had no chance to work and get control. I got a good notion to quit this rotten club and jump to the Federals where a man gets some kind of treatment. Callahan says I throwed the game away on purpose but I did not do no such a thing Al because when I throwed that ball at Joe Hill's head I forgot that the bases was full and besides if Gleason had not of starved me to death the ball that hit him in the head would of killed him.

And how could a man go to 1st base and the winning run be forced in if he was dead which he should ought to of been the lucky left handed stiff if I had of had my full strenth to put on my fast one instead of being ½ starved to death and weak. But I guess I better tell you how it come off. The papers will get it all wrong like they generally allways does.

Callahan asked me this A.M. if I thought I was hard enough to work and I was tickled to death, because I seen he was going to give me a chance. I told him Sure I was in good shape and if them Tigers scored a run off me he could keep me setting on the bench the rest of the summer. So he says All right I am going to start you and if you go good maybe Gleason will let you eat some supper.

Well Al when I begin warming up I happened to look up in the grand stand and who do you think I seen? Nobody but Violet. She smiled when she seen me but I bet she felt more like crying. Well I smiled back at her because she probily would of broke down and made a seen or something if I had not of. They was not nobody warming up for Detroit when I begin warming up but pretty soon I looked over to their bench and Joe Hill Violet's husband was warming up. I says to myself Well here is where I show that bird up if they got nerve enough to start him against me but probily Jennings don't want to waste no real pitcher on this game which he knows we got cinched and we would of had it cinched Al if they had of got a couple of runs or even 1 run for me.

Well, Jennings come passed our bench just like he allways does and tried to pull some of his funny stuff. He says Hello are you still in the league? I says Yes but I come pretty near not being. I came pretty near being with Detroit. I wish you could of heard Gleason and Callahan laugh when I pulled that one on him. He says something back but it was not no hot comeback like mine.

Well Al if I had of had any work and my regular control I guess I would of pitched a 0 hit game because the only time they could touch me was when I had to ease up to get them over. Cobb was out of the game and they told me he was sick but I guess the truth is that he knowed I was going to pitch. Crawford got a couple of lucky scratch hits off of me because I got in the hole to him and had to let up. But the way that lucky left handed Hill got by was something awful and if I was as lucky as him I would quit pitching and shoot craps or something.

Our club can't hit nothing anyway. But batting against this bird was just like hitting fungos. His curve ball broke about ½ a inch and you could of wrote your name and address on his fast one while it was comeing up there. He had good control but who would not when they put nothing on the ball?

Well Al we could not get started against the lucky stiff and they could not do nothing with me even if my suport was rotten and I give a couple or 3 or 4 bases on balls but when they was men waiting to score I zipped them threw there so as they could not see them let alone hit them. Every time I come to the bench between innings I looked up to where Violet was setting and give her a smile and she smiled back and once I seen her clapping her hands at me after I had made Moriarty pop up in the pinch.

Well we come along to the 10th inning, 0 and 0, and all of a sudden we got after him. Bodie hits one and Schalk gets 2 strikes and 2 balls and then singles. Callahan tells Alcock to bunt and he does it but Hill sprawls all over himself like the big boob he is and the bases is full with nobody down. Well Gleason and Callahan argude about should they send somebody up for me or let me go up there and I says Let me go up there because I can murder this bird and Callahan says Well they is nobody out so go up and take a wallop.

Honest Al if this guy had of had anything at all I would of hit 1 out of the park, but he did not have even a glove. And how can a man hit pitching which is not no pitching at all but just slopping them up? When I went up there I hollered to him and says Stick 1 over here now you yellow stiff. And he says Yes I can stick them over allright and that is where I got something on you.

Well Al I hit a foul off of him that would of been a fare ball and broke up the game if the wind had not of been against it. Then I swung and missed a curve that I don't see how I missed it. The next 1 was a yard outside and this Evans calls it a strike. He has had it in for me ever since last year when he tried to get funny with me and I says something back to him that stung him. So he calls this 3d strike on me and I felt like murdering him. But what is the use?

I throwed down my bat and come back to the bench and I was glad Callahan and Gleason was out on the coaching line or they probily would of said something to me and I would of cut loose and beat them up. Well Al Weaver and Blackburne looked like a couple of rums up there and we don't score where we ought to of had 3 or 4 runs with any kind of hitting.

I would of been all O.K. in spite of that peace of rotten luck if this big Hill had of walked to the bench and not said nothing like a real pitcher. But what does he do but wait out there till I start for the box and I says Get on to the bench you lucky stiff or do you want me to hand you something? He says I don't want nothing more of yourn. I allready got your girl and your goat.

Well Al what do you think of a man that would say a thing like that? And nobody but a left hander could of. If I had of had a gun I would of killed him deader than a doornail or something. He starts for the bench and I hollered at him Wait till you get up to that plate and then I am going to bean you.

Honest Al I was so mad I could not see the plate or nothing. I don't even know who it was come up to bat 1st but whoever it was I hit him in the arm and he walks to first base. The next guy bunts and Chase tries to pull off 1 of them plays of hisn instead of playing safe and he don't get nobody. Well I kept getting madder and madder and I walks Stanage who if I had of been myself would not foul me.

Callahan has Scotty warming up and Gleason runs out from the bench and tells me I am threw but Callahan says Wait a minute he is going to let Hill hit and this big stiff ought to be able to get him out of the way and that will give Scotty a chance to get warm. Gleason says You better not take a chance because the big busher is hogwild, and they kept argueing till I got sick of listening to them and I went back to the box and got ready to pitch. But when I seen this Hill up there I forgot all about the ball game and I cut loose at his bean.

Well Al my control was all O.K. this time and I catched him square on the fourhead and he dropped like as if he had been shot. But pretty soon he gets up and gives me the laugh and runs to first base. I did not know the game was over till Weaver came up and pulled me off the field. But if I had not of been ½ starved to death and weak so as I could not put all my stuff on the ball you can bet that Hill never would of ran to first base and Violet would of been a widow and probily a lot better off than she is now. At that I never should ought to of tried to kill a left-hander by hitting him in the head.

Well Al they jumped all over me in the clubhouse and I had to hold myself back or I would of gave somebody the beating of their life. Callahan tells me I am fined $50.00 and suspended without no pay. I asked him What for and he says They would not be no use in telling you because you have not got no brains. I says Yes I have to got some brains and he says Yes but they is in your stumach. And then he says I wish we had of sent you to Milwaukee and I come back at him. I says I wish you had of.

Well Al I guess they is no chance of getting square treatment on this club and you won't be supprised if you hear of me jumping to the Federals where a man is treated like a man and not like no white slave.

Yours truly, JACK.

Chicago, Illinois, May 2.

AL: I have got to disappoint you again Al. When I got up to get my pay yesterday they held out $150.00 on me. $50.00 of it is what I was fined for loosing a 1 to 0 10-inning game in Detroit when I was so weak that I should ought never to of been sent in there and the $100.00 is the advance money that I drawed last winter and which I had forgot all about and the club would of forgot about it to if they was not so tight fisted.

So you see all I get for 2 weeks' pay is about $80.00 and I sent $25.00 to Florrie so she can't come no none support business on me.

I am still suspended Al and not drawing no pay now and I got a notion to hire a attorney at law and force them to pay my salery or else jump to the Federals where a man gets good treatment.

Allen is still after me to come over to his flat some night and see his wife and let her talk to me about Florrie but what do I want to talk about Florrie for or talk about nothing to a nut left hander's wife?

The Detroit Club is here and Cobb is playing because he knows I am suspended but I wish Callahan would call it off and let me work against them and I would certainly love to work against this Joe Hill again and I bet they would be a different story this time because I been getting something to eat since we been home and I got back most of my strenth.

Your old pal, JACK.

Chicago, Illinois, May 5.

FRIEND AL: Well Al if you been reading the papers you will know before this letter is received what I done. Before the Detroit Club come here Joe Hill had win 4 strate but he has not win no 5 strate or won't neither Al because I put a crimp in his winning streek just like I knowed I would do if I got a chance when I was feeling good and had all my strenth. Callahan asked me yesterday A.M. if I thought I had enough rest and I says Sure because I did not need no rest in the 1st place. Well, he says, I thought maybe if I layed you off a few days you would do some thinking and if you done some thinking once in a while you would be a better pitcher.

Well anyway I worked and I wish you could of saw them Tigers trying to hit me Cobb and Crawford incluseive. The 1st time Cobb come up Weaver catched a lucky line drive off of him and the next time I eased up a little and Collins run back and took a fly ball off of the fence. But the other times he come up he looked like a sucker except when he come up in the 8th and then he beat out a bunt but allmost anybody is liable to do that once in a while.

Crawford got a scratch hit between Chase and Blackburne in the 2d inning and in the 4th he was gave a three-base hit by this Evans who should ought to be writeing for the papers instead of trying to umpire. The ball was 2 feet foul and I bet Crawford will tell you the same thing if you ask him. But what I done to this Hill was awful. I give him my curve twice when he was up there in the 3d and he missed it a foot. Then I come with my fast ball right past his nose and I bet if he had not of ducked it would of drove that big horn of hisn clear up in the press box where them rotten reporters sits and smokes their hops. Then when he was looking for another fast one I slopped up my slow one and he is still swinging at it yet.

But the best of it was that I practally won my own game. Bodie and Schalk was on when I come up in the 5th and Hill hollers to me and says I guess this is where I shoot one of them bean balls. I says Go ahead and shoot and if you hit me in the head and I ever find it out I will write and tell your wife what happened to you. You see what I was getting at Al. I was insinuateing that if he beaned me with his fast one I would not never know nothing about it if somebody did not tell me because his fast one is not fast enough to hurt nobody even if it should hit them in the head. So I says to him Go ahead and shoot and if you hit me in the head and I ever find it out I will write and tell your wife what happened to you. See, Al?

Of coarse you could not hire me to write to Violet but I did not mean that part of it in ernest. Well sure enough he shot at my bean and I ducked out of the way though if it had of hit me it could not of did no more than tickle. He takes 2 more shots and misses me and then Jennings hollers from the bench What are you doing pitching or trying to win a cigar? So then Hill sees what a monkey he is makeing out of himself and tries to get one over, but I have him 3 balls and nothing and what I done to that groover was a plenty. She went over Bush's head like a bullet and got between Cobb and Veach and goes clear to the fence. Bodie and Schalk scores and I would of scored to if anybody else besides Cobb had of been chaseing the ball. I got 2 bases and Weaver scores me with another wallop.

Say, I wish I could of heard what they said to that baby on the bench. Callahan was tickled to death and he says Maybe I will give you back that $50.00 if you keep that stuff up. I guess I will get that $50.00 back next pay day and if I do Al I will pay you the hole $75.00.

Well Al I beat them 5 to 4 and with good support I would of held them to 1 run but what do I care as long as I beat them? I wish though that Violet could of been there and saw it.

Yours truly, JACK.

Chicago, Illinois, May 29.

OLD PAL: Well Al I have not wrote to you for a long while but it is not because I have forgot you and to show I have not forgot you I am incloseing the $75.00 which I owe you. It is a money order Al and you can get it cashed by takeing it to Joe Higgins at the P.O.

Since I wrote to you Al I been East with the club and I guess you know what I done in the East. The Athaletics did not have no right to win that 1 game off of me and I will get them when they come here the week after next. I beat Boston and just as good as beat New York twice because I beat them 1 game all alone and then saved the other for Eddie Cicotte in the 9th inning and shut out the Washington Club and would of did the same thing if Johnson had of been working against me instead of this left handed stiff Boehling.

Speaking of left handers Allen has been going rotten and I would not be supprised if they sent him to Milwaukee or Frisco or somewheres.

But I got bigger news than that for you Al. Florrie is back and we are liveing together in the spair room at Allen's flat so I hope they don't send him to Milwaukee or nowheres else because it is not costing us nothing for room rent and this is no more than right after the way the Allens grafted off of us all last winter.

I bet you will be supprised to know that I and Florrie has made it up and they is a secret about it Al which I can't tell you now but maybe next month I will tell you and then you will be more supprised than ever. But that is all I can tell you now.

We got in this A.M. Al and when I got to my room they was a slip of paper there telling me to call up a phone number so I called it up and it was Allen's flat and Marie answered the phone. And when I reckonized her voice I was going to hang up the phone but she says Wait a minute somebody wants to talk with you. And then Florrie come to the phone and I was going to hang up the phone again when she pulled this secret on me that I was telling you about.

So it is all fixed up between us Al and I wish I could tell you the secret but that will come later. I have tooken my baggage over to

Allen's and I am there now writeing to you while Florrie is asleep. And after a while I am going out and mail this letter and get a glass of beer because I think I have got 1 comeing now on account of this secret. Florrie says she is sorry for the way she treated me and she cried when she seen me. So what is the use of me being nasty Al? And let bygones be bygones.

Your pal, JACK.

Chicago, Illinois, June 16.

FRIEND AL: Al I beat the Athaletics 2 to 1 to-day but I am writeing to you to give you the supprise of your life. Old pal I got a baby and he is a boy and we are going to name him Allen which Florrie thinks is after his uncle and aunt Allen but which is after you old pal. And she can call him Allen but I will call him Al because I don't never go back on my old pals. The baby was born over to the hospital and it is going to cost me a bunch of money but I should not worry. This is the secret I was going to tell you Al and I am the happyest man in the world and I bet you are most as tickled to death to hear about it as I am.

The baby was born just about the time I was makeing McInnis look like a sucker in the pinch but they did not tell me nothing about it till after the game and then they give me a phone messige in the clubhouse. I went right over there and everything was all O.K. Little Al is a homely little skate but I guess all babys is homely and don't have no looks till they get older and maybe he will look like Florrie or I then I won't have no kick comeing.

Be sure and tell Bertha the good news and tell her everything has came out all right except that the rent man is still after me about that flat I had last winter. And I am still paying the old man $10.00 a month for that house you got for me and which has not never done me no good. But I should not worry about money when I got a real family. Do you get that Al, a real family?

Well Al I am to happy to do no more writeing to-night but I

wanted you to be the 1st to get the news and I would of sent you a telegram only I did not want to scare you.

Your pal, JACK.

Chicago, Illinois, July 2.

OLD PAL: Well old pal I just come back from St. Louis this A.M. and found things in pretty fare shape. Florrie and the baby is out to Allen's and we will stay there till I can find another place. The Dr. was out to look at the baby this A.M. and the baby was waveing his arm round in the air. And Florrie asked was they something the matter with him that he kept waveing his arm. And the Dr. says No he was just getting his exercise.

Well Al I noticed that he never waved his right arm but kept waveing his left arm and I asked the Dr. why was that. Then the Dr. says I guess he must be left handed. That made me sore and I says I guess you doctors don't know it all. And then I turned round and beat it out of the room.

Well Al it would be just my luck to have him left handed and Florrie should ought to of knew better than to name him after Allen. I am going to hire another Dr. and see what he has to say because they must be some way of fixing babys so as they won't be left handed. And if nessary I will cut his left arm off of him. Of coarse I would not do that Al. But how would I feel if a boy of mine turned out like Allen and Joe Hill and some of them other nuts?

We have a game with St. Louis to-morrow and a double header on the 4th of July. I guess probily Callahan will work me in one of the 4th of July games on account of the holiday crowd.

Your pal, JACK.

P.S. Maybe I should ought to leave the kid left handed so as he can have some of their luck. The lucky stiffs.

The Busher's Kid

The Saturday Evening Post
October 3, 1914

Chicago, Illinois, July 31.

FRIEND AL: Well Al what do you think of little Al now? But I guess I better tell you first what he done. Maybe you won't believe what I am telling you but did you ever catch me telling you a lie? I guess you know you did not Al. Well we got back from the East this A.M. and I don't have to tell you we had a rotten trip and if it had not of been for me beating Boston once and the Athaletics two times we would of been ashamed to come home.

I guess these here other pitchers thought we was haveing a vacation and when they go up in the office to-morrow to get there checks they should ought to be arrested if they take them. I would not go nowheres near Comiskey if I had not of did better than them others but I can go and get my pay and feel all O.K. about it because I done something to ern it.

Me loseing that game in Washington was a crime and Callahan says so himself. This here Weaver throwed it away for me and I would not be surprised if he done it from spitework because him and Scott is pals and probily he did not want to see me winning all them games when Scott was getting knocked out of the box. And no wonder when he has not got no stuff. I wish I knowed for sure that Weaver was throwing me down and if I knowed for sure I would put him in a hospital or somewheres.

But I was going to tell you what the kid done Al. So here goes. We are still liveing at Allen's and his wife. So I and him come home together from the train. Well Florrie and Marie was both up and the baby was up too—that is he was not up but he was woke up. I beat it right into the room where he was at and Florrie come in with me. I says Hello Al and what do you suppose he done. Well Al he did not say Hello pa or nothing like that because he is not only one month old. But he smiled at me just like as if he was glad to see me and I guess maybe he was at that.

I was tickled to death and I says to Florrie Did you see that. And she says See what. I says The baby smiled at me. Then she says They is something the matter with his stumach. I says I suppose because a baby smiles that is a sign they is something the matter with his stumach and if he had the toothacke he would laugh. She says You think your smart but I am telling you that he was not smileing at all but he was makeing a face because they is something the matter with his stumach. I says I guess I know the difference if somebody is smileing or makeing a face. And she says I guess you don't know nothing about babys because you never had none before. I says How many have you had. And then she got sore and beat it out of the room.

I did not care because I wanted to be in there alone with him and see would he smile at me again. And sure enough Al he did. Then I called Allen in and when the baby seen him he begin to cry. It don't take a man no time at all to get wise to these babys and it don't take them long to know if a man is there father or there uncle.

When he begin to cry I chased Allen out of the room and called Florrie because she should ought to know by this time how to make him stop crying. But she was still sore and she says Let him cry or if you know so much about babys make him stop yourself. I says Maybe he is sick. And she says I was just telling you that he had a pane in his stumach or he would not of made that face that you said was smileing at you.

I says Do you think we should ought to call the doctor but she says No if you call the doctor every time he has the stumach acke you might just as well tell him he should bring his trunk along and stay here. She says All babys have collect and they is not no use fussing about it but come and get your breakfast.

Well Al I did not injoy my breakfast because the baby was crying all the time and I knowed he probily wanted I should come in and visit with him. So I just eat the prunes and drunk a little coffee and did not wait for the rest of it and sure enough when I went back in our room and started talking to him he started smileing again and pretty soon he went to sleep so you see Al he was smileing and not makeing no face and that was a hole lot of bunk about him haveing the collect. But I don't suppose I should ought to find fault with Florrie for not knowing no better because she has not never had no babys before but still and all I should think she should ought to of learned something about them by this time or ask somebody.

Well Al little Al is woke up again and is crying and I just about got time to fix him up and get him asleep again and then I will have to go to the ball park because we got a poseponed game to play with Detroit and Callahan will probily want me to work though I pitched the next to the last game in New York and would of gave them a good beating except for Schalk dropping that ball at the plate but I got it on these Detroit babys and when my name is announced to pitch they feel like forfiting the game. I won't try for no strike out record because I want them to hit the first ball and get the game over with quick so as I can get back here and take care of little Al.

Your pal, JACK.

P.S. Babys is great stuff Al and if I was you I would not wait no longer but would hurry up and adopt 1 somewheres.

Chicago, Illinois, August 15.

Old Pal: What do you think Al. Kid Gleason is comeing over to the flat and look at the baby the day after to-morrow when we don't have no game skeduled but we have to practice in the A.M. because we been going so rotten. I had a hard time makeing him promise to come but he is comeing and I bet he will be glad he come when he has came. I says to him in the clubhouse Do you want to see a real baby? And he says You're real enough for me Boy.

I says No I am talking about babys. He says Oh I thought you was talking about ice cream soda or something. I says No I want you to come over to the flat to-morrow and take a look at my kid and tell me what you think of him. He says I can tell you what I think of him without takeing no look at him. I think he is out of luck. I says What do you mean out of luck. But he just laughed and would not say no more.

I asked him again would he come over to the flat and look at the baby and he says he had troubles enough without that and kidded along for a while but finally he seen I was in ernest and then he says he would come if I would keep the missus out of the room while he was there because he says if she seen him she would probily be sorry she married me.

He was just jokeing and I did not take no excepshun to his remarks because Florrie could not never fall for him after seeing me because he is not no big stropping man like I am but a little runt and look at how old he is. But I am glad he is comeing because he will think more of me when he sees what a fine baby I got though he thinks a hole lot of me now because look what I done for the club and where would they be at if I had jumped to the Federal like I once thought I would. I will tell you what he says about little Al and I bet he will say he never seen no prettyer baby but even if he don't say nothing at all I will know he is kidding.

The Boston Club comes here to-morrow and plays 4 days includeing the day after to-morrow when they is not no game. So on account of the off day maybe I will work twice against them and if I do they will wish the grounds had of burned down.

Yours truly, JACK.

Chicago, Illinois, August 17.

AL: Well old pal what did I tell you about what I would do to that Boston Club? And now Al I have beat every club in the league this year because yesterday was the first time I beat the Boston Club this year but now I have beat all of them and most of them several times.

This should ought to of gave me a record of 16 wins and 0 defeats because the only games I lost was throwed away behind me but instead of that my record is 10 games win and 6 defeats and that don't include the games I finished up and helped the other boys win which is about 6 more alltogether but what do I care about my record Al? because I am not the kind of man that is allways thinking about there record and playing for there record while I am satisfied if I give the club the best I got and if I win all O.K. And if I lose who's fault is it. Not mine Al.

I asked Callahan would he let me work against the Boston Club again before they go away and he says I guess I will have to because you are going better than anybody else on the club. So you see Al he is beginning to appresiate my work and from now on I will pitch in my regular turn and a hole lot offtener then that and probily Comiskey will see the stuff I am made from and will raise my salery next year even if he has got me signed for 3 years and for the same salery I am getting now.

But all that is not what I was going to tell you Al and what I was going to tell you was about Gleason comeing to see the baby and what he thought about him. I sent Florrie and Marie downtown and says I would take care of little Al and they was glad to go because

Florrie says she should ought to buy some new shoes though I don't see what she wants of no new shoes when she is going to be tied up in the flat for a long time yet on account of the baby and nobody cares if she wears shoes in the flat or goes round in her bear feet. But I was glad to get rid of the both of them for a while because little Al acts better when they is not no women round and you can't blame him.

The baby was woke up when Gleason come in and I and him went right in the room where he was laying. Gleason takes a look at him and says Well that is a mighty fine baby and you must of boughten him. I says What do you mean? And he says I don't believe he is your own baby because he looks humaner than most babys. And I says Why should not he look human. And he says Why should he.

Then he goes to work and picks the baby right up and I was a-scared he would drop him because even I have not never picked him up though I am his father and would be a-scared of hurting him. I says Here, don't pick him up and he says Why not? He says Are you going to leave him on that there bed the rest of his life? I says No but you don't know how to handle him. He says I have handled a hole lot bigger babys than him or else Callahan would not keep me.

Then he starts patting the baby's head and I says Here, don't do that because he has got a soft spot in his head and you might hit it. He says I thought he was your baby and I says Well he is my baby and he says Well then they can't be no soft spot in his head. Then he lays little Al down because he seen I was in ernest and as soon as he lays him down the baby begins to cry. Then Gleason says See he don't want me to lay him down and I says Maybe he has got a pane in his stumach and he says I would not be supprised because he just took a good look at his father.

But little Al did not act like as if he had a pane in his stumach and he kept sticking his finger in his mouth and crying. And Gleason says He acts like as if he had a toothacke. I says How could he have a toothacke when he has not got no teeth? He says That is easy. I have saw a lot of pitchers complane that there arm was sore when they did not have no arm.

Then he asked me what was the baby's name and I told him Allen but that he was not named after my brother-in-law Allen. And Gleason says I should hope not. I should hope you would have better sense than to name him after a left hander. So you see Al he don't like them no better then I do even if he does jolly Allen and Russell along and make them think they can pitch.

Pretty soon he says What are you going to make out of him, a ball player? I says Yes I am going to make a hitter out of him so as he can join the White Sox and then maybe they will get a couple of runs once in a while. He says If I was you I would let him pitch and then you won't have to give him no educasion. Besides, he says, he looks now like he would divellop into a grate spitter.

Well I happened to look out of the window and seen Florrie and Marie comeing acrost Indiana Avenue and I told Gleason about it. And you ought to of seen him run. I asked him what was his hurry and he says it was in his contract that he was not to talk to no women but I knowed he was kidding because I allready seen him talking to severel of the players' wifes when they was on trips with us and they acted like as if they thought he was a regular comeedion though they really is not nothing funny about what he says only it is easy to make women laugh when they have not got no grouch on about something.

Well Al I am glad Gleason has saw the baby and maybe he will fix it with Callahan so as I won't have to go to morning practice every A.M. because I should ought to be home takeing care of little Al when Florrie is washing the dishs or helping Marie round the house. And besides why should I wear myself all out in practice because I don't need to practice pitching and I could hit as well as the rest of the men on our club if I never seen no practice.

After we get threw with Boston, Washington comes here and then we go to St. Louis and Cleveland and then come home and then go East again. And after that we are pretty near threw except the city serious. Callahan is not going to work me no more after I beat Boston again till it is this here Johnson's turn to pitch for Washington. And I hope it is not his turn to work the 1st game of the serious because then I would not have no rest between the last game against Boston and the 1st game against Washington.

But rest or no rest I will work against this here Johnson and show him up for giveing me that trimming in Washington, the lucky stiff. I wish I had a team like the Athaletics behind me and I would loose about 1 game every 6 years and then they would have to get all the best of it from these rotten umpires.

Your pal, JACK.

New York, New York, September 16.

FRIEND AL: Al it is not no fun running round the country no more and I wish this dam trip was over so as I could go home and see how little Al is getting along because Florrie has not wrote since we was in Philly which was the first stop on this trip. I am a-scared they is something the matter with the little fellow or else she would of wrote but then if they was something the matter with him she would of sent me a telegram or something and let me know.

So I guess they can't be nothing the matter with him. Still and all I don't see why she has not wrote when she knows or should ought to know that I would be worrying about the baby. If I don't get no letter to-morrow I am going to send her a telegram and ask her what is the matter with him because I am positive she would of wrote if they was not something the matter with him.

The boys has been trying to get me to go out nights and see a show or something but I have not got no heart to go to shows. And besides Callahan has not gave us no pass to no show on this trip. I guess probily he is sore on account of the rotten way the club has been going but still he should ought not to be sore on me because I have win 3 out of my last 4 games and would of win the other if he had not of started me against them with only 1 day's rest and the Athaletics at that, who a man should ought not to pitch against if he don't feel good.

I asked Allen if he had heard from Marie and he says Yes he did but she did not say nothing about little Al except that he was keeping her awake nights balling. So maybe Al if little Al is balling they is something wrong with him. I am going to send Florrie a telegram to-morrow—that is if I don't get no letter.

If they is something the matter with him I will ask Callahan to send me home and he won't want to do it neither because who else has he got that is a regular winner. But if little Al is sick and Callahan won't let me go home I will go home anyway. You know me Al.

Yours truly, JACK.

Boston, Massachusetts, September 24.

AL: I bet if Florrie was a man she would be a left hander. What do you think she done now Al? I sent her a telegram from New York when I did not get no letter from her and she did not pay no atension to the telegram. Then when we got up here I sent her another telegram and it was not more then five minutes after I sent the 2d telegram till I got a letter from her. And it said the baby was all O.K. but she had been so busy takeing care of him that she had not had no time to write.

Well when I got the letter I chased out to see if I could catch the boy who had took my telegram but he had went allready so I was spending $.60 for nothing. Then what does Florrie do but send me a telegram after she got my second telegram and tell me that little Al is all O. K., which I knowed all about then because I had just got her letter. And she sent her telegram c. o. d. and I had to pay for it at this end because she had not paid for it and that was $.60 more but I bet if I had of knew what was in the telegram before I read it I would of told the boy to keep it and would not of gave him no $.60

but how did I know if little Al might not of tooken sick after Florrie had wrote the letter?

I am going to write and ask her if she is trying to send us both to the Poor House or somewheres with her telegrams. I don't care nothing about the $.60 but I like to see a woman use a little judgement though I guess that is impossable.

It is my turn to work to-day and to-night we start West but we have got to stop off at Cleveland on the way. I have got a nosion to ask Callahan to let me go right on threw to Chi if I win to-day and not stop off at no Cleveland but I guess they would not be no use because I have got that Cleveland Club licked the minute I put on my glove. So probily Callahan will want me with him though it don't make no difference if we win or lose now because we have not got no chance for the pennant. One man can't win no pennant Al I don't care who he is.

Your pal, JACK.

Chicago, Illinois, October 2.

FRIEND AL: Well old pal I am all threw till the city serious and it is all fixed up that I am going to open the serious and pitch 3 of the games if nessary. The club has went to Detroit to wind up the season and Callahan did not take me along but left me here with a couple other pitchers and Billy Sullivan and told me all as I would have to do was go over to the park the next 3 days and warm up a little so as to keep in shape. But I don't need to be in no shape to beat them Cubs Al. But it is a good thing Al that Allen was tooken on the trip to Detroit or I guess I would of killed him. He has not been going good and he has been acting and talking nasty to everybody because he can't win no games.

Well the 1st night we was home after the trip little Al was haveing a bad night and was balling pretty hard and they could not nobody in the flat get no sleep. Florrie says he was haveing the collect and I says Why should he have the collect all the time when he did not drink nothing but milk? She says she guessed the milk did not agree with him and upsetted his stumach. I says Well he must take after his mother if his stumach gets upsetted every time he takes a drink because if he took after his father he could drink a hole lot and not never be effected. She says You should ought to remember he has only got a little stumach and not a great big resservoire. I says Well if the milk don't agree with him why don't you give him something else? She says Yes I suppose I should ought to give him weeny worst or something.

Allen must of heard us talking because he hollered something and I did not hear what it was so I told him to say it over and he says Give the little X-eyed brat poison and we would all be better off. I says You better take poison yourself because maybe a rotten pitcher like you could get by in the league where you're going when you die. Then I says Besides I would rather my baby was X-eyed then to have him left handed. He says It is better for him that he is X-eyed or else he might get a good look at you and then he would shoot himself. I says Is that so? and he shut up. Little Al is not no more X-eyed than you or I are Al and that was what made me sore because what right did Allen have to talk like that when he knowed he was lying?

Well the next morning Allen nor I did not speak to each other and I seen he was sorry for the way he had talked and I was willing to fix things up because what is the use of staying sore at a man that don't know no better.

But all of a sudden he says When are you going to pay me what you owe me? I says What do you mean? And he says You been live-ing here all summer and I been paying all the bills. I says Did not you and Marie ask us to come here and stay with you and it would not cost us nothing. He says Yes but we did not mean it was a life sentence. You are getting more money than me and you don't never spend a nichol. All I have to do is pay the rent and buy your food and it would take a millionare or something to feed you.

Then he says I would not make no holler about you grafting off of me if that brat would shut up nights and give somebody a chance to sleep. I says You should ought to get all the sleep you need on the bench. Besides, I says, who done the grafting all last winter and without no invatation? If he had of said another word I was going to bust him but just then Marie come in and he shut up.

The more I thought about what he said and him a rotten left hander that should ought to be hussling freiht the more madder I got and if he had of opened his head to me the last day or 2 before he went to Detroit I guess I would of finished him. But Marie stuck pretty close to the both of us when we was together and I guess she knowed they was something in the air and did not want to see her husband get the worst of it though if he was my husband and I was a woman I would push him under a st. car.

But Al I won't even stand for him saying that I am grafting off of him and I and Florrie will get away from here and get a flat of our own as soon as the city serious is over. I would like to bring her and the kid down to Bedford for the winter but she wont listen to that.

I allmost forgot Al to tell you to be sure and thank Bertha for the little dress she made for little Al. I don't know if it will fit him or not because Florrie has not yet tried it on him yet and she says she is going to use it for a dishrag but I guess she is just kidding.

I suppose you seen where Callahan took me out of that game down to Cleveland but it was not because I was not going good Al but it was because Callahan seen he was makeing a mistake wasteing me on that bunch who allmost any pitcher could beat. They beat us that game at that but only by one run and it was not no fault of mine because I was tooken out before they got the run that give them the game.

Your old pal, JACK.

Chicago, Illinois, October 4.

FRIEND AL: Well Al the club winds up the season at Detroit tomorrow and the serious starts the day after to-morrow and I will be in there giveing them a battle. I wish I did not have nobody but the Cubs to pitch against all season and you bet I would have a record that would make Johnson and Mathewson and some of them other swell heads look like a dirty doose.

I and Florrie and Marie has been haveing a argument about how could Florrie go and see the city serious games when they is not nobody here that can take care of the baby because Marie wants to go and see the games to even though they is not no more chance of Callahan starting Allen than a rabbit or something.

Florrie and Marie says I should ought to hire a nurse to take care of little Al and Florrie got pretty sore when I told her nothing doing because in the first place I can't afford to pay no nurse a salary and in the second place I would not trust no nurse to take care of the baby because how do I know the nurse is not nothing but a grafter or a dope fiend maybe and should ought not to be left with the baby?

Of coarse Florrie wants to see me pitch and a man can't blame her for that but I won't leave my baby with no nurse Al and Florrie will have to stay home and I will tell her what I done when I get there. I might of gave my consent to haveing a nurse at that if it had not of been for the baby getting so sick last night when I was takeing care of him while Florrie and Marie and Allen was out to a show and if I had not of been home they is no telling what would of happened. It is a cinch that none of them bonehead nurses would of knew what to do.

Allen must of been out of his head because right after supper he says he would take the 2 girls to a show. I says All right go on and I will take care of the baby. Then Florrie says Do you think you can take care of him all O. K.? And I says Have not I tooken care of him before allready? Well, she says, I will leave him with you only don't run in to him every time he cries. I says Why not? And she says Because it is good for him to cry. I says You have not got no heart or you would not talk that way.

They all give me the laugh but I let them get away with it

because I am not picking no fights with girls and why should I bust this Allen when he don't know no better and has not got no baby himself. And I did not want to do nothing that would stop him take-ing the girls to a show because it is time he spent a peace of money on somebody.

Well they all went out and I went in on the bed and played with the baby. I wish you could of saw him Al because he is old enough now to do stunts and he smiled up at me and waved his arms and legs round and made a noise like as if he was trying to say Pa. I did not think Florrie had gave him enough covers so I rapped him up in some more and took a blanket off of the big bed and stuck it round him so as he could not kick his feet out and catch cold.

I thought once or twice he was going off to sleep but all of a sudden he begin to cry and I seen they was something wrong with him. I gave him some hot water but that made him cry again and I thought maybe he was to cold yet so I took another blanket off of Allen's bed and wrapped that round him but he kept on crying and trying to kick inside the blankets. And I seen then that he must have collect or something.

So pretty soon I went to the phone and called up our regular Dr. and it took him pretty near a hour to get there and the baby balling all the time. And when he come he says they was nothing the matter except that the baby was to hot and told me to take all them blankets off of him and then soaked me 2 dollars. I had a nosion to bust his jaw. Well pretty soon he beat it and then little Al begin crying again and kept getting worse and worse so finally I got a-scared and run down to the corner where another Dr. is at and I brung him up to see what was the matter but he did not charge me a cent so I thought he was not no robber like our regular doctor even if he was just as much of a boob.

The baby did not cry none while he was there but the minute he had went he started crying and balling again and I seen they was not no use of fooling no longer so I looked around the house and found the medicine the doctor left for Allen when he had a stumach acke once and I give the baby a little of it in a spoon but I guess he did not like the taste because he hollered like a Indian and finally I could not stand it no longer so I called that second Dr. back again and this time he seen that the baby was sick and asked me what I had gave it and I told him some stumach medicine and he says I was a fool and should ought not to of gave the baby nothing. But while he was talking the baby stopped crying and went off to sleep so you see what I done for him was the right thing to do and them doctors was both off of there nut.

This second Dr. soaked me 2 dollars the 2d time though he had not did no more than when he was there the 1st time and charged me nothing but they is all a bunch of robbers Al and I would just as leave trust a policeman.

Right after the baby went to sleep Florrie and Marie and Allen come home and I told Florrie what had come off but instead of giveing me credit she says If you want to kill him why don't you take a ax? Then Allen butts in and says Why don't you take a ball and throw it at him? Then I got sore and I says Well if I did hit him with a ball I would kill him while if you was to throw that fast ball of yours at him and hit him in the head he would think the musketoes was biteing him and brush them off. But at that, I says, you could not hit him with a ball except you was aiming at something else.

I guess they was no comeback to that so him and Marie went to there room. Allen should ought to know better than to try and get the best of me by this time and I would shut up anyway if I was him after getting sent home from Detroit with some of the rest of them when he only worked 3 innings up there and they had to take him out or play the rest of the game by electrick lights.

I wish you could be here for the serious Al but you would have to stay at a hotel because we have not got no spair room and it would cost you a hole lot of money. But you can watch the papers and you will see what I done.

Yours truly, JACK.

Chicago, Illinois, October 6.

DEAR OLD PAL: Probily before you get this letter you will of saw by the paper that we was licked in the first game and that I was tooken out but the papers don't know what really come off so I am going to tell you and you can see for yourself if it was my fault.

I did not never have no more stuff in my life then when I was warming up and I seen the Cubs looking over to our bench and shakeing there heads like they knowed they did not have no chance. O'Day was going to start Cheney who is there best bet and had him warming up but when he seen the smoke I had when I and Schalk was warming up he changed his mind because what was the use of useing his best pitcher when I had all that stuff and it was a cinch that no club in the world could score a run off of me when I had all that stuff?

So he told a couple others to warm up to and when my name was announced to pitch Cheney went and set on the bench and this here lefthander Pierce was announced for them.

Well Al you will see by the paper where I sent there 1st 3 batters back to the bench to get a drink of water and all 3 of them good hitters Leach and Good and this here Saier that hits a hole lot of home runs but would not never hit one off of me if I was O. K. Well we scored a couple in our half and the boys on the bench all says Now you got enough to win easy because they won't never score none off of you.

And they was right to because what chance did they have if this thing that I am going to tell you about had not of happened? We goes along seven innings and only 2 of there men had got to 1st base one of them on a bad peg of Weaver's and the other one I walked because this blind Evans don't know a ball from a strike. We had not did no more scoreing off of Pierce not because he had no stuff but because our club could not take a ball in there hands and hit it out of the infield.

Well Al I did not tell you that before I come out to the park I kissed little Al and Florrie good by and Marie says she was going to stay home to and keep Florrie Co. and they was not no reason for Marie to come to the game anyway because they was not a chance in the world for Allen to do nothing but hit fungos. Well while I was doing all this here swell pitching and makeing them Cubs look like a lot of rummys I was thinking about little Al and Florrie and how glad they would be when I come home and told them what I done though of coarse little Al is not only a little over 3 months of age and how could he appresiate what I done? But Florrie would.

Well Al when I come in to the bench after there ½ of the 7th I happened to look up to the press box to see if the reporters had gave Schulte a hit on that one Weaver throwed away and who do you think I seen in a box right alongside of the press box? It was Florrie and Marie and both of them claping there hands and hollering with the rest of the bugs.

Well old pal I was never so surprised in my life and it just took all the heart out of me. What was they doing there and what had they did with the baby? How did I know that little Al was not sick or maybe dead and balling his head off and nobody round to hear him?

I tried to catch Florrie's eyes but she would not look at me. I hollered her name and the bugs looked at me like as if I was crazy and I was to Al. Well I seen they was not no use of standing out there in front of the stand so I come into the bench and Allen was setting there and I says Did you know your wife and Florrie was up there in the stand? He says No and I says What are they doing here? And he says What would they be doing here—mending there stockings? I felt like busting him and I guess he seen I was mad because he got up off of the bench and beat it down to the corner of the field where some of the others was getting warmed up though why should they have anybody warming up when I was going so good?

Well Al I made up my mind that ball game or no ball game I was not going to have little Al left alone no longer and I seen they was not no use of sending word to Florrie to go home because they was a big crowd and it would take maybe 15 or 20 minutes for somebody to get up to where she was at. So I says to Callahan You have got to take me out. He says What is the matter? Is your arm gone? I says No my arm is not gone but my baby is sick and home all alone. He says Where is your wife? And I says She is setting up there in the stand.

Then he says How do you know your baby is sick? And I says I don't know if he is sick or not but he is left home all alone. He says Why don't you send your wife home? And I says I could not get word to her in time. He says Well you have only got two innings to go and the way your going the game will be over in 10 minutes. I says Yes and before 10 minutes is up my baby might die and are you going to take me out or not? He says Get in there and pitch you yellow dog and if you don't I will take your share of the serious money away from you.

By this time our part of the inning was over and I had to go out there and pitch some more because he would not take me out and he has not got no heart Al. Well Al how could I pitch when I kept thinking maybe the baby was dying right now and maybe if I was home I could do something? And instead of paying attension to what I was doing I was thinking about little Al and looking up there to where Florrie and Marie was setting and before I knowed what come off they had the bases full and Callahan took me out.

Well Al I run to the clubhouse and changed my cloths and beat it for home and I did not even hear what Callahan and Gleason says to me when I went by them but I found out after the game that Scott went in and finished up and they batted him pretty hard and we was licked 3 and 2.

When I got home the baby was crying but he was not all alone after all Al because they was a little girl about 14 years of age there watching him and Florrie had hired her to take care of him so as her and Marie could go and see the game. But just think Al of leaveing little Al with a girl 14 years of age that did not never have no babys of her own! And what did she know about takeing care of him? Nothing Al.

You should ought to of heard me ball Florrie out when she got home and I bet she cried pretty near enough to flood the basemunt.

We had it hot and heavy and the Allens butted in but I soon showed them where they was at and made them shut there mouth.

I had a good nosion to go out and get a hole lot of drinks and was just going to put on my hat when the doorbell rung and there was Kid Gleason. I thought he would be sore and probily try to ball me out and I was not going to stand for nothing but instead of balling me out he come and shook hands with me and interduced himself to Florrie and asked how was little Al.

Well we all set down and Gleason says the club was depending on me to win the serious because I was in the best shape of all the pitchers. And besides the Cubs could not never hit me when I was right and he was telling the truth to.

So he asked me if I would stand for the club hireing a train nurse to stay with the baby the rest of the serious so as Florrie could go and see her husband win the serious but I says No I would not stand for that and Florrie's place was with the baby.

So Gleason and Florrie goes out in the other room and talks a while and I guess he was persuadeing her to stay home because pretty soon they come back in the room and says it was all fixed up and I would not have to worry about little Al the rest of the serious but could give the club the best I got. Gleason just left here a little while ago and I won't work to-morrow Al but I will work the day after and you will see what I can do when I don't have nothing to worry me.

Your pal, JACK.

Chicago, Illinois, October 8.

OLD PAL: Well old pal we got them 2 games to one now and the serious is sure to be over in three more days because I can pitch 2 games in that time if nessary. I shut them out to-day and they should ought not to of had four hits but should ought to of had only 2 but Bodie don't cover no ground and 2 fly balls that he should ought to of eat up fell safe.

But I beat them anyway and Benz beat them yesterday but why

should he not beat them when the club made 6 runs for him? All they made for me was three but all I needed was one because they could not hit me with a shuvvel. When I come to the bench after the 5th inning they was a note there from the boy that answers the phone at the ball park and it says that somebody just called up from the flat and says the baby was asleep and getting along fine. So I felt good Al and I was better than ever in the 6th.

When I got home Florrie and Marie was both there and asked me how did the game come out because I beat Allen home and I told them all about what I done and I bet Florrie was proud of me but I supose Marie is a little jellus because how could she help it when Callahan is depending on me to win the serious and her husband is wearing out the wood on the bench? But why should she be sore when it is me that is winning the serious for them? And if it was not for me Allen and all the rest of them would get about $500.00 apeace instead of the winners' share which is about $750.00 apeace.

Cicotte is going to work to-morrow and if he is lucky maybe he can get away with the game and that will leave me to finish up the day after to-morrow but if nessary I can go in to-morrow when they get to hitting Cicotte and stop them and then come back the following day and beat them again. Where would this club be at Al if I had of jumped to the Federal?

Yours truly, JACK.

Chicago, Illinois, October 11.

FRIEND AL: We done it again Al and I guess the Cubs won't never want to play us again not so long as I am with the club. Before you get this letter you will know what we done and who done it but probily you could of guessed that Al without seeing no paper.

I got 2 more of them phone messiges about the baby dureing the game and I guess that was what made me so good because I knowed then that Florrie was takeing care of him but I could not help feeling sorry for Florrie because she is a bug herself and it must of been pretty hard for her to stay away from the game espesially when she knowed I was going to pitch and she has been pretty good to sacrifice her own plesure for little Al.

Cicotte was knocked out of the box the day before yesterday and then they give this here Faber a good beating but I wish you could of saw what they done to Allen when Callahan sent him in after the game was gone allready. Honest Al if he had not of been my brother in law I would of felt like laughing at him because it looked like as if they would have to call the fire department to put the side out. They had Bodie and Collins hollering for help and with there tongue hanging out from running back to the fence.

Anyway the serious is all over and I won't have nothing to do but stay home and play with little Al but I don't know yet where my home is going to be at because it is a cinch I won't stay with Allen no longer. He has not come home since the game and I suppose he is out somewheres lapping up some beer and spending some of the winner's share of the money which he would not of had no chance to get in on if it had not of been for me.

I will write and let you know my plans for the winter and I wish Florrie would agree to come to Bedford but nothing doing Al and after her staying home and takeing care of the baby instead of watching me pitch I can't be too hard on her but must leave her have her own way about something.

Your pal, JACK.

Chicago, Illinois, October 13.

AL: I am all threw with Florrie Al and I bet when you hear about it you won't say it was not no fault of mine but no man liveing who is any kind of a man would act different from how I am acting if he had of been decieved like I been.

Al Florrie and Marie was out to all them games and was not home takeing care of the baby at all and it is not her fault that little Al is not dead and that he was not killed by the nurse they hired to take care of him while they went to the games when I thought they was home takeing care of the baby. And all them phone messiges was just fakes and maybe the baby was sick all the time I was winning them games and balling his head off instead of being asleep like they said he was.

Allen did not never come home at all the night before last and when he come in yesterday he was a sight and I says to him Where have you been? And he says I have been down to the Y. M. C. A. but that is not none of your business. I says Yes you look like as if you had been to the Y. M. C. A. and I know where you have been and you have been out lushing beer. And he says Suppose I have and what are you going to do about it? And I says Nothing but you should ought to be ashamed of yourself and leaveing Marie here while you was out lapping up beer.

Then he says Did you not leave Florrie home while you was getting away with them games, you lucky stiff? And I says Yes but Florrie had to stay home and take care of the baby but Marie don't never have to stay home because where is your baby? You have not got no baby. He says I would not want no X-eyed baby like yourn. Then he says So you think Florrie stayed to home and took care of the baby do you? And I says What do you mean? And he says You better ask her.

So when Florrie come in and heard us talking she busted out crying and then I found out what they put over on me. It is a wonder Al that I did not take some of that cheap furniture them Allens got and bust it over there heads, Allen and Florrie. This is what they done Al. The club give Florrie $50.00 to stay home and take care of the baby and she said she would and she was to call up every so often and tell me the baby was all O. K. But this here Marie told her she was a sucker so she hired a nurse for part of the $50.00 and then her and Marie went to the games and beat it out quick after the games was over and come home in a taxicab and chased the nurse out before I got home.

Well Al when I found out what they done I grabbed my hat and goes out and got some drinks and I was so mad I did not know where I was at or what come off and I did not get home till this A.M. And they was all asleep and I been asleep all day and when I woke up Marie and Allen was out but Florrie and I have not spoke to each other and I won't never speak to her again.

But I know now what I am going to do Al and I am going to take little Al and beat it out of here and she can sew me for a bill of divorce and I should not worry because I will have little Al and I will see that he is tooken care of because I guess I can hire a nurse as well as they can and I will pick out a train nurse that knows something. Maybe I and him and the nurse will come to Bedford Al but I don't know yet and I will write and tell you as soon as I make up my mind. Did you ever hear of a man getting a rottener deal Al? And after what I done in the serious too.

Your pal, JACK.

Chicago, Illinois, October 17.

OLD PAL: I and Florrie has made it up Al but we are threw with Marie and Allen and I and Florrie and the baby is staying at a hotel here on Cottage Grove Avenue the same hotel we was at when we got married only of coarse they was only the 2 of us then.

And now Al I want to ask you a favor and that is for you to go and see old man Cutting and tell him I want to ree-new the lease on that house for another year because I and Florrie has decided to spend the winter in Bedford and she will want to stay there and take care of little Al while I am away on trips next summer and not stay in no high-price flat up here. And may be you and Bertha can help her round the house when I am not there.

I will tell you how we come to fix things up Al and you will see that I made her apollojize to me and after this she will do what I tell her to and won't never try to put nothing over. We was eating breakfast—I and Florrie and Marie. Allen was still asleep yet because I guess he must of had a bad night and he was snoreing so as you could hear him in the next st. I was not saying nothing to nobody but pretty soon Florrie says to Marie I don't think you and Allen should ought to kick on the baby crying when Allen's snoreing makes more noise than a hole wagonlode of babys. And Marie got sore and says I guess a man has got a right to snore in his own house and you and Jack has been grafting off of us long enough.

Then Florrie says What did Allen do to help win the serious and get that $750.00? Nothing but set on the bench except when they was makeing him look like a sucker the 1 inning he pitched. The trouble with you and Allen is you are jellous of what Jack has did and you know he will be a star up here in the big league when Allen is tending bar which is what he should ought to be doing because then he could get stewed for nothing.

Marie says Take your brat and get out of the house. And Florrie says Don't you worry because we would not stay here no longer if you hired us. So Florrie went in her room and I followed her in and she says Let's pack up and get out.

Then I says Yes but we won't go nowheres together after what you done to me but you can go where you dam please and I and little Al will go to Bedford. Then she says You can't take the baby because he is mine and if you was to take him I would have you arrested for kidnaping. Besides, she says, what would you feed him and who would take care of him?

I says I would find somebody to take care of him and I would get him food from a resturunt. She says He can't eat nothing but milk and I says Well he has the collect all the time when he is eating milk and he would not be no worse off if he was eating watermelon. Well, she says, if you take him I will have you arrested and sew you for a bill of divorce for dessertion.

Then she says Jack you should not ought to find no fault with me for going to them games because when a woman has a husband that can pitch like you can do you think she wants to stay home and not see her husband pitch when a lot of other women is cheering him and makeing her feel proud because she is his wife?

Well Al as I said right along it was pretty hard on Florrie to have to stay home and I could not hardly blame her for wanting to be out there where she could see what I done so what was the use of argueing?

So I told her I would think it over and then I went out and I went and seen a attorney at law and asked him could I take little Al away and he says No I did not have no right to take him away from his mother and besides it would probily kill him to be tooken away from her and then he soaked me $10.00 the robber.

Then I went back and told Florrie I would give her another chance and then her and I packed up and took little Al in a taxicab over to this hotel. We are threw with the Allens Al and let me know right away if I can get that lease for another year because Florrie has gave up and will go to Bedford or anywheres else with me now.

Yours truly, JACK.

Chicago, Illinois, October 20.

FRIEND AL: Old pal I won't never forget your kindnus and this is to tell you that I and Florrie except your kind invatation to come and stay with you till we can find a house and I guess you won't regret it none because Florrie will livun things up for Bertha and Bertha will be crazy about the baby because you should ought to see how cute he is now Al and not yet four months old. But I bet he will be talking before we know it.

We are comeing on the train that leaves here at noon Saturday Al and the train leaves here about 12 o'clock and I don't know what time it gets to Bedford but it leaves here at noon so we shall be there probily in time for supper.

I wish you would ask Ben Smith will he have a hack down to the deepo to meet us but I won't pay no more than $.25 and I should think he should ought to be glad to take us from the deepo to your house for nothing.

Your pal, JACK.

P.S. The train we are comeing on leaves here at noon Al and will probily get us there in time for a late supper and I wonder if Bertha would have spair ribs and crout for supper. You know me Al.

The Busher Beats It Hence

The Saturday Evening Post
NOVEMBER 7, 1914

Chicago, Ill., Oct. 18.

FRIEND AL: I guess may be you will begin to think I dont never do what I am going to do and that I change my mind a hole lot because I wrote and told you that I and Florrie and little Al would be in Bedford to-day and here we are in Chi yet on the day when I told you we would get to Bedford and I bet Bertha and you and the rest of the boys will be dissapointed but Al I dont feel like as if I should ought to leave the White Sox in a hole and that is why I am here yet and I will tell you how it come off but in the 1st place I want to tell you that it wont make a diffrence of more than 5 or 6 or may be 7 days at least and we will be down there and see you and Bertha and the rest of the boys just as soon as the N. Y. giants and the White Sox leaves here and starts a round the world. All so I remember I told you to fix it up so as a hack would be down to the deepo to meet us to-night and you wont get this letter in time to tell them not to send no hack so I supose the hack will be there but may be they will be some body else that gets off of the train that will want the hack and then every thing will be all O. K. but if they is not nobody else that wants the hack I will pay them ½ of what they was going to charge me if I had of came and road in the hack though I dont have to pay them nothing because I am not going to ride in the hack but I want to do the right thing and besides I will want a hack at the deepo when I do come so they will get a peace of money out of me any way so I dont see where they got no kick comeing even if I dont give them a nichol now.

I will tell you why I am still here and you will see where I am trying to do the right thing. You knowed of coarse that the White Sox and the N. Y. giants was going to make a trip a round the world and they been after me for a long time to go a long with them but I says No I would not leave Florrie and the kid because that would not be fare and besides I would be paying rent and grocerys for them some wheres and me not getting nothing out of it and besides I would probily be spending a hole lot of money on the trip because though the clubs pays all of our regular expences they would be a hole lot of times when I felt like blowing my self and buying some thing to send home to the Mrs and to good old friends of mine like you and Bertha so I turned them down and Callahan acted like he was sore at me but I dont care nothing for that because I got other people to think a bout and not Callahan and besides if I was to go a long the fans in the towns where we play at would want to see me work and I would have to do a hole lot of pitching which I would not be getting nothing for it and it would not count in no standing because the games is to be just for fun and what good would it do me and besides Florrie says I was not under no circumstance to go and of coarse I would go if I wanted to go no matter what ever she says but all and all I turned them down and says I would stay here all winter or rather I would not stay here but in Bedford. Then Callahan says All right but you know before we start on the trip the giants and us is going to play a game right here in Chi next Sunday and after what you done in the city serious the fans would be sore if they did not get no more chance to look at you so will you stay and pitch part of the game here and I says I would think it over and I come home to the hotel where we are staying at and asked Florrie did she care if we did not go to Bedford for an other week and she says No she did not care if we dont go for 6 years so I called Callahan up and says I would stay and he says Thats the boy and now the fans will have an other treat so you see Al he appresiates what I done and wants to give the fans fare treatment because this town is nuts over me after what I done to them Cubs but I could do it just the same to the Athaletics or any body else if it would of been them in stead of the Cubs. May be we will leave here the A.M. after the game that is Monday and I will let you know so as you can order an other hack and tell Bertha I hope she did not go to no extra trouble a bout getting ready for us and did not order no spair ribs and crout but you can eat them up if she all ready got them and may be she can order some more for us when we come but tell her it dont make no diffrence and not to go to no trouble because most anything she has is O. K. for I and Florrie accept of coarse we would not want to make no meal off of sardeens or something.

Well Al I bet them N. Y. giants will wish I would of went home before they come for this here exibishun game because my arm feels grate and I will show them where they would be at if they had to play ball in our league all the time though I supose they is some pitchers in our league that they would hit good against them if they can hit at all but not me. You will see in the papers how I come out and I will write and tell you a bout it.

Your pal, JACK.

Chicago, Ill., Oct. 25.

OLD PAL: I have not only got a little time but I have got some news for you and I knowed you would want to hear all a bout it so I am writeing this letter and then I am going to catch the train. I would be saying good by to little Al instead of writeing this letter only Florrie wont let me wake him up and he is a sleep but may be by the time I get this letter wrote he will be a wake again and I can say good by to him. I am going with the White Sox and giants as far as San Francisco or may be Van Coover where they take the boat at but I am not going a round the world with them but only just out to the coast to help them out because they is a couple of men going to join them out there and untill them men join them they will be short of men and they got a hole lot of exibishun games to play before they get out there so I am going to help them out. It all come off in the club house after the game to-day and I will tell you how it come off but 1st I want to tell you a bout the game and honest Al them giants is the luckyest team in the world and it is not no wonder they keep wining the penant in that league because a club that has got there luck could win ball games with out sending no team on the field at all but staying down to the hotel.

They was a big crowd out to the park so Callahan says to me I did not know if I was going to pitch you or not but the crowd is out here to see you so I will have to let you work so I warmed up but I knowed the minute I throwed the 1st ball warming up that I was not right and I says to Callahan I did not feel good but he says You wont need to feel good to beat this bunch because they heard a hole lot a bout you and you would have them beat if you just throwed your glove out there in the box. So I went in and tried to pitch but my arm was so lame it pretty near killed me every ball I throwed and I bet if I was some other pitchers they would not never of tried to work with my arm so sore but I am not like some of them yellow dogs and quit because I would not dissapoint the crowd or throw Callahan down when he wanted me to pitch and was depending on me. You know me Al. So I went in there but I did not have nothing and if them giants could of hit at all in stead of like a lot of girls they would of knock down the fence because I was not my self. At that they should not ought to of had only the 1 run off of me if Weaver and them had not of begin kicking the ball a round like it was a foot ball or something. Well Al what with dropping fly balls and booting them a round and this in that the giants was gave 5 runs in the 1st 3 innings and they should ought to of had just the 1 run or may be not that and that ball Merkle hit in to the seats I was trying to waist it and a man that is a good hitter would not never of hit at it and if I was right this here Merkle could not foul me in 9 years. When I was comeing into the bench after the 3th inning this here smart alex Mcgraw come passed me from the 3 base coaching line and he says Are you going on the trip and I says No I am not going on no trip and he says That is to bad because if you was going we would win a hole lot of games and I give him a hot come back and he did not say nothing so I went in to the bench and Callahan says Them giants is not such rotten hitters is they and I says No they hit pretty good when a man has got a sore arm against them and he says Why did not you tell me your arm was sore and I says I did not want to dissapoint no crowd that come out here to see me and he says Well I guess you need not pitch no more because if I left you in there the crowd might begin to get tired of watching you a bout 10 oclock to-night and I says What do you mean and he did not say nothing more so I set there a while and then went to the club house. Well Al after the game Callahan come in to the club house and I was still in there yet talking to the trainer and getting my arm rubbed and Callahan says Are you getting your arm in shape for next year and I says No but it give me so much pane I could not stand it and he says I bet if you was feeling good you could make them giants look like a sucker and I says You know I could make them look like a sucker and he says Well why dont you come a long with us and you will get an other chance at them when you feel good and I says I would like to get an other crack at them but I could not go a way on no trip and leave the Mrs and the baby and then he says he would not ask me to make the hole trip a round the world but he wisht I would go out to the coast with them because they was hard up for pitchers and he says

Mathewson of the giants was not only going as far as the coast so if the giants had there star pitcher that far the White Sox should ought to have theren and then some of the other boys coaxed me would I go so finely I says I would think it over and I went home and seen Florrie and she says How long would it be for and I says a bout 3 or 4 weeks and she says If you dont go will we start for Bedford right a way and I says Yes and then she says All right go a head and go but if they was any thing should happen to the baby while I was gone what would they do if I was not a round to tell them what to do and I says Call a Dr. in but dont call no Dr. if you dont have to and besides you should ought to know by this time what to do for the baby when he got sick and she says Of course I know a little but not as much as you do because you know it all. Then I says No I dont know it all but I will tell you some things before I go and you should not ought to have no trouble so we fixed it up and her and little Al is to stay here in the hotel untill I come back which will be a bout the 20 of Nov. and then we will come down home and tell Bertha not to get to in patient and we will get there some time. It is going to cost me $6.00 a week at the hotel for a room for she and the baby besides there meals but the babys meals dont cost nothing yet and Florrie should not ought to be very hungry because we been liveing good and besides she will get all she can eat when we come to Bedford and it wont cost me nothing for meals on the trip out to the coast because Comiskey and Mcgraw pays for that.

I have not even had no time to look up where we play at but we stop off at a hole lot of places on the way and I will get a chance to make them giants look like a sucker before I get threw and Mcgraw wont be so sorry I am not going to make the hole trip. You will see by the papers what I done to them before we get threw and I will write as soon as we stop some wheres long enough so as I can write and now I am going to say good by to little Al if he is a wake or not a wake and wake him up and say good by to him because even if he is not only 5 months old he is old enough to think a hole lot of me and why not. I all so got to say good by to Florrie and fix it up with the hotel clerk a bout she and the baby staying here a while and catch the train. You will hear from me soon old pal.

Your pal, JACK.

St. Joe, Miss., Oct. 29.

FRIEND AL: Well Al we are on our way to the coast and they is quite a party of us though it is not no real White Sox and giants at all but some players from off of both clubs and then some others that is from other clubs a round the 2 leagues to fill up. We got Speaker from the Boston club and Crawford from the Detroit club and if we had them with us all the time Al I would not never loose a game because one or the other of them 2 is good for a couple of runs every game and that is all I need to win my games is a couple of runs or only 1 run and I would win all my games and would not never loose a game.

I did not pitch to-day and I guess the giants was glad of it because no matter what Mcgraw says he must of saw from watching me Sunday that I was a real pitcher though my arm was so sore I could not hardly raze it over my sholder so no wonder I did not have no stuff but at that I could of beat his gang with out no stuff if I had of had some kind of decent suport. I will pitch against them may be tomorrow or may be some day soon and my arm is all O. K. again now so I will show them up and make them wish Callahan had of left me to home. Some of the men has brung there wife a long and besides that there is some other men and there wife that is not no ball players but are going a long for the trip and some more will join the party out the coast before they get a bord the boat but of coarse I and Mathewson will drop out of the party then because why should I or him go a round the world and throw our arms out pitching games that dont count in no standing and that we dont get no money for pitching them out side of just our bare expences. The people in the towns we played at so far has all wanted to shake hands with Mathewson and I so I guess they know who is the real pitchers on these here 2 clubs no matter what them reporters says and the stars is all ways the men that the people wants to shake there hands with and make friends with them but Al this here Mathewson pitched to-day and honest Al I dont see how he gets by and either the batters in the National league dont know nothing a bout hitting or else he is such a old man that they feel sorry for him and may be when he was a bout 10 years younger than he is may be then he had some thing and was a pretty fare pitcher but all he does now is stick the 1st ball right over with 0 on it and pray that they dont hit it out of the park. If a pitcher like he can get by in the National league and fool them batters they is not nothing I would like better then to pitch in the National league and I bet I would not get scored on in 2 to 3 years. I heard a hole lot a bout this here fade a way that he is suposed to pitch and it is a ball that is throwed out between 2 fingers and falls in at a right hand batter and they is not no body cant hit it but if he throwed 1 of them things to-day he done it while I was a sleep and they was not no time when I was not wide a wake and looking right at him and after the game was over I says to him Where is that there fade a way I heard so much a bout and he says O I did not have to use none of my regular stuff against your club and I says Well you would have to use all you got if I was working against you and he says Yes if you worked like you done Sunday I would have to do some pitching or they would not never finish the game. Then I says a bout me haveing a sore arm Sunday and he says I wisht I had a sore arm like yourn and a little sence with it and was your age and I would not never loose a game so you see Al he has heard a bout me and is jellus because he has not got my stuff but they cant every body expect to have the stuff that I got or ½ as much stuff. This smart alex Mcgraw was trying to kid me to-day and says Why did not I make friends with Mathewson and let him learn me some thing a bout pitching and I says Mathewson could not learn me nothing and he says I guess thats right and I guess they is not nobody could learn you nothing a bout nothing and if you was to stay in the league 20 years probily you would not be no better than you are now so you see he had to add mit that I am good Al even if he has not saw me work when my arm was O. K.

Mcgraw says to me to-night he says I wisht you was going all the way and I says Yes you do. I says Your club would look like a sucker after I had worked against them a few times and he says May be thats right to because they would not know how to hit against a regular pitcher after that. Then he says But I dont care nothing a bout that but I wisht you was going to make the hole trip so as we could have a good time. He says We got Steve Evans and Dutch Schaefer going a long and they is both of them funny but I like to be a round with boys that is funny and dont know nothing a bout it. I says Well I would go a long only for my wife and baby and he says Yes it would be pretty tough on your wife to have you a way that long but still and all think how glad she would be to see you when you come back again and besides them dolls acrost the ocean will be pretty sore at I and Callahan if we tell them we left you to home. I says Do you supose the people over there has heard a bout me and he says Sure because they have wrote a lot of letters asking me to be sure and bring you and Mathewson a long. Then he says I guess Mathewson is not going so if you was to go and him left here to home they would not be nothing to it. You could have things all your own way and probily could marry the Queen of europe if you was not all ready married. He was giveing me the strate dope this time Al because he did not crack a smile and I wisht I could go a long but it would not be fare to Florrie but still and all did not she leave me and beat it for Texas last winter and why should not I do the same thing to her only I am not that kind of a man. You know me Al.

We play in Kansas city to-morrow and may be I will work there because it is a big town and I have got to close now and write to Florrie.

Your old pal, JACK.

Abilene, Texas, Nov. 4.

AL: Well Al I guess you know by this time that I have worked against them 2 times since I wrote to you last time and I beat them both times and Mcgraw knows now what kind of a pitcher I am and

I will tell you how I know because after the game yesterday he road down to the place we dressed at a long with me and all the way in the automobile he was after me to say I would go all the way a round the world and finely it come out that he wants I should go a long and pitch for his club and not pitch for the White Sox. He says his club is up against it for pitchers because Mathewson is not going and all they got left is a man named Hern that is a young man and not got no experiense and Wiltse that is a left hander. So he says I have talked it over with Callahan and he says if I could get you to go a along it was all O. K. with him and you could pitch for us only I must not work you to hard because he is depending on you to win the penant for him next year. I says Did not none of the other White Sox make no holler because may be they might have to bat against me and he says Yes Crawford and Speaker says they would not make the trip if you was a long and pitching against them but Callahan showed them where it would be good for them next year because if they hit against you all winter the pitchers they hit against next year will look easy to them. He was crazy to have me go a long on the hole trip but of coarse Al they is not no chance of me going on acct. of Florrie and little Al but you see Mcgraw has cut out his trying to kid me and is treating me now like a man should ought to be treated that has did what I done.

They was not no game here to-day on acct. of it raining and the people here was sore because they did not see no game but they all come a round to look at us and says they must have some speechs from the most prommerent men in the party so I and Comiskey and Mcgraw and Callahan and Mathewson and Ted Sullivan that I guess is putting up the money for the trip made speechs and they clapped there hands harder when I was makeing my speech then when any 1 of the others was makeing there speech. You did not know I was a speech maker did you Al and I did not know it neither untill to-day but I guess they is not nothing I can do if I make up my mind and 1 of the boys says that I done just as well as Dummy Taylor could of.

I have not heard nothing from Florrie but I guess may be she is to busy takeing care of little Al to write no letters and I am not worring none because she give me her word she would let me know was they some thing the matter.

Yours truly, JACK.

San Dago, Cal, Nov. 9.

FRIEND AL: Al some times I wisht I was not married at all and if it was not for Florrie and little Al I would go a round the world on this here trip and I guess the boys in Bedford would not be jellus if I was to go a round the world and see every thing they is to be saw and some of the boys down home has not never been no futher a way then Terre Haute and I dont mean you Al but some of the other boys. But of coarse Al when a man has got a wife and a baby they is not no chance for him to go a way on 1 of these here trips and leave them a lone so they is not no use I should even think a bout it but I cant help thinking a bout it because the boys keeps after me all the time to go. Callahan was talking a bout it to me to-day and he says he knowed that if I was to pitch for the giants on the trip his club would not have no chance of wining the most of the games on the trip but still and all he wisht I would go a long because he was a scared the people over in Rome and Paris and Africa and them other countrys would be awful sore if the 2 clubs come over there with out bringing none of there star pitchers along. He says We got Speaker and Crawford and Doyle and Thorp and some of them other real stars in all the positions accept pitcher and it will make us look bad if you and Mathewson dont neither 1 of you come a long. I says What is the matter with Scott and Benz and this here left hander Wiltse and he says They is not nothing the matter with none of them accept they is not no real stars like you and Mathewson and if we cant show them forreners 1 of you 2 we will feel like as if we was cheating them. I says You would not want me to pitch my best against your club would you and he says

O no I would not want you to pitch your best or get your self all wore out for next year but I would want you to let up enough so as we could make a run oncet in a while so the games would not be to 1 sided. I says Well they is not no use talking a bout it because I could not leave my wife and baby and he says Why dont you write and ask your wife and tell her how it is and can you go. I says No because she would make a big holler and besides of coarse I would go any way if I wanted to go with out no I yes or no from her only I am not the kind of a man that runs off and leaves his family and besides they is not nobody to leave her with because her and her sister Allens wife has had a quarrle. Then Callahan says Where is Allen at now is he still in Chi. I says I dont know where is he at and I dont care where he is at because I am threw with him. Then Callahan says I asked him would he go on the trip before the season was over but he says he could not and if I knowed where was he I would wire a telegram to him and ask him again. I says What would you want him a long for and he says Because Mcgraw is shy of pitchers and I says I would try and help him find 1. I says Well you should ought not to have no trouble finding a man like Allen to go along because his wife probily would be glad to get rid of him. Then Callahan says Well I wisht you would get a hold of where Allen is at and let me know so as I can wire him a telegram. Well Al I know where Allen is at all O. K. but I am not going to give his adress to Callahan because Mcgraw has treated me all O. K. and why should I wish a man like Allen on to him and besides I am not going to give Allen no chance to go a round the world or no wheres else after the way he acted a bout I and Florrie haveing a room in his flat and asking me to pay for it when he give me a invatation to come there and stay. Well Al it is to late now to cry in the sour milk but I wisht I had not never saw Florrie untill next year and then I and her could get married just like we done last year only I dont know would I do it again or not but I guess I would on acct. of little Al.

Your pal, JACK.

San Francisco; Cal., Nov. 14.

OLD PAL: Well old pal what do you know a bout me being back here in San Francisco where I give the fans such a treat 2 years ago and then I was not nothing but a busher and now I am with a team that is going a round the world and are crazy to have me go a long only I cant because of my wife and baby. Callahan wired a telegram to the reporters here from Los Angeles telling them I would pitch here and I guess they is going to be 20 or 25000 out to the park and I will give them the best I got.

But what do you think Florrie has did Al. Her and the Allens has made it up there quarrle and is friends again and Marie told Florrie to write and tell me she was sorry we had that there argument and let by gones be by gones. Well Al it is all O. K. with me because I cant help not feeling sorry for Allen because I dont beleive he will be in the league next year and I feel sorry for Marie to because it must be pretty tough on her to see how well her sister done and what a misstake she made when she went and fell for a left hander that could not fool a blind man with his curve ball and if he was to hit a man in the head with his fast ball they would think there nose iched. In Florries letter she says she thinks us and the Allens could find an other flat like the 1 we had last winter and all live in it to gether in stead of going to Bedford but I have wrote to her before I started writeing this letter all ready and told her that her and I is going to Bedford and the Allens can go where they feel like and they can go and stay on a boat on Michigan lake all winter if they want to but I and Florrie is comeing to Bedford. Down to the bottom of her letter she says Allen wants to know if Callahan or Mcgraw is shy of pitchers and may be he would change his mind and go a long on the trip. Well Al I did not ask either Callahan nor Mcgraw nothing a bout it because I knowed they was looking for a star and not for no left hander that could not brake a pane of glass with his fast 1 so I wrote and told Florrie to tell Allen they was all filled up and would not have no room for no more men.

It is pretty near time to go out to the ball park and I wisht you could be here Al and hear them San Francisco fans go crazy when they hear my name anounced to pitch. I bet they wish they had of had me here this last year.

Yours truly, JACK.

Medford, Organ, Nov. 16.

FRIEND AL: Well Al you know by this time that I did not pitch the hole game in San Francisco but I was not tooken out because they was hitting me Al but because my arm went back on me all of a sudden and it was the change in the clime it that done it to me and they could not hire me to try and pitch another game in San Francisco. They was the biggest crowd there that I ever seen in San Francisco and I guess they must of been 40000 people there and I wisht you could of heard them yell when my name was anounced to pitch. But Al I would not never of went in there but for the crowd. My arm felt like a wet rag or some thing and I knowed I would not have nothing and besides the people was packed in a round the field and they had to have ground rules so when a man hit a pop fly it went in to the crowd some wheres and was a 2 bagger and all them giants could do against me was pop my fast ball up in the air and then the wind took a hold of it and dropped it in to the crowd the lucky stiffs. Doyle hit 3 of them pop ups in to the crowd so when you see them 3 2 base hits oposit his name in the score you will know they was not no real 2 base hits and the infielders would of catched them had it not of been for the wind. This here Doyle takes a awful wallop at a ball but if I was right and he swang at a ball the way he done in San Francisco the catcher would all ready be throwing me back the ball a bout the time this here Doyle was swinging at it. I can make him look like a sucker and I done it both in Kansas city and Bonham and if he will get up there and bat against me when I feel good and when they is not no wind blowing I will bet him a $25.00 suit of cloths that he cant foul 1 off of me. Well when Callahan seen how bad my arm was he says I guess I should ought to take you out and not run no chance of you getting killed in there and so I quit and Faber went in to finnish it up because it dont make no diffrence if he hurts his arm or dont. But I guess Mcgraw knowed my arm was sore to because he did not try and kid me like he done that day in Chi because he has saw enough of me since then to know I can make his club look rotten when I am O.K. and my arm is good. On the train that night he come up and says to me Well Jack we catched you off your strid to-day or you would of gave us a beating and then he says What your arm needs is more work and you should ought to make the hole trip with us and then you would be in fine shape for next year but I says You cant get me to make no trip so you might is well not do no more talking a bout it and then he says Well I am sorry and the girls over to Paris will be sorry to but I guess he was just jokeing a bout the last part of it.

Well Al we go to 1 more town in Organ and then to Washington but of coarse it is not the same Washington we play at in the summer but this is the state Washington and have not got no big league club and the boys gets there boat in 4 more days and I will quit them and then I will come strate back to Chi and from there to Bedford.

Your pal, JACK.

Portland, Organ, Nov. 17.

FRIEND AL: I have just wrote a long letter to Florrie but I feel like as if I should ought to write to you because I wont have no more chance for a long while that is I wont have no more chance to male a letter because I will be on the pacific Ocean and un less we should run passed a boat that was comeing the other way they would not be no chance of getting no letter maled. Old pal I am going to make the hole trip clear a round the world and back and so I wont see you this winter after all but when I do see you Al I will have a lot to tell you a bout my trip and besides I will write you a letter a bout it from every place we head in at.

I guess you will be surprised a bout me changeing my mind and makeing the hole trip but they was not no way for me to get out of it and I will tell you how it all come off. While we was still in that there Medford yesterday Mcgraw and Callahan come up to me and says was they not no chance of me changeing my mind a bout makeing the hole trip. I says No they was not. Then Callahan says Well I dont know what we are going to do then and I says Why and he says Comiskey just got a letter from president Wilson the President of the united states and in the letter president Wilson says he had got an other letter from the king of Japan who says that they would not stand for the White Sox and giants comeing to Japan un less they brought all there stars a long and president Wilson says they would have to take there stars a long because he was a scared if they did not take there stars a long Japan would get mad at the united states and start a war and then where would we be at. So Comiskey wired a telegram to president Wilson and says Mathewson could not make the trip because he was so old but would everything be all O.K. if I was to go a long and president Wilson wired a telegram back and says Yes he had been talking to the priest from Japan and he says Yes it would be all O.K. I asked them would they show me the letter from president Wilson because I thought may be they might be kiding me and they says they could not show me no letter because when Comiskey got the letter he got so mad that he tore it up. Well Al I finely says I did not want to brake up there trip but I knowed Florrie would not stand for letting me go so Callahan says All right I will wire a telegram to a friend of mine in Chi and have him get a hold of Allen and send him out here and we will take him a long and I says It is to late for Allen to get here in time and Mcgraw says No they was a train that only took 2 days from Chi to where ever it was the boat is going to sale from because the train come a round threw canada and it was down hill all the way. Then I says Well if you will wire a telegram to my wife and fix things up with her I will go a long with you but if she is going to make a holler it is all off. So we all 3 went to the telegram office to gether and we wired Florrie a telegram that must of cost $2.00 but Callahan and Mcgraw payed for it out of there own pocket and then we waited a round a long time and the anser come back and the anser was longer than the telegram we wired and it says it would not make no difference to her but she did not know if the baby would make a holler but he was hollering most of the time any way so that would not make no diffrence but if she let me go it was on condishon that her and the Allens could get a flat to gether and stay in Chi all winter and not go to no Bedford and hire a nurse to take care of the baby and if I would send her a check for the money I had in the bank so as she could put it in her name and draw it out when she need it. Well I says at 1st I would not stand for nothing like that but Callahan and Mcgraw showed me where I was makeing a mistake not going when I could see all them diffrent countrys and tell Florrie all a bout the trip when I come back and then in a year or 2 when the baby was a little older I could make an other trip and take little Al and Florrie a long so I finely says O.K. I would go and we wires still an other telegram to Florrie and told her O.K. and then I set down and wrote her a check for ½ the money I got in the bank and I got $500.00 all together there so I wrote her a check for ½ of that or $250.00 and maled it to her and if she cant get a long on that she would be a awfull spendrift because I am not only going to be a way untill March. You should ought to of heard the boys cheer when Callahan tells them I am going to make the hole trip but when he tells them I am going to pitch for the giants and not for the White Sox I bet Crawford and Speaker and them wisht I was going to stay to home but it is just like Callahan says if they bat against me all winter the pitchers they bat against next season will look easy to them and you wont be surprised Al if Crawford and Speaker hits a bout 500 next year and if they hit good you will know why it is. Steve Evans asked me was I all fixed up with cloths and I says No but I was going out and buy some cloths includeing a full dress suit of evening cloths and he says You dont need no full dress suit of evening cloths because you look funny enough with out them. This Evans is a great kidder Al and no body never gets sore at the stuff he pulls some thing like Kid Gleason. I wisht Kid Gleason was going on the trip Al but I will tell him all a bout it when I come back.

Well Al old pal I wisht you was going a long to and I bet we could have the time of our life but I will write to you right a long Al and I will send Bertha some post cards from the diffrent places we head in at. I will try and write you a letter on the boat and male it as soon as we get to the 1st station which is either Japan or Yokohama I forgot which. Good by Al and say good by to Bertha for me and tell her how sorry I and Florrie is that we cant come to Bedford this winter but we will spend all the rest of the winters there and her and Florrie will have a plenty of time to get acquainted. Good by old pal.

Your pal, JACK.

Seattle, Wash., Nov. 18.

AL: Well Al it is all off and I am not going on no trip a round the world and back and I been looking for Callahan or Mcgraw for the last ½ hour to tell them I have changed my mind and am not going to make no trip because it would not be fare to Florrie and besides that I think I should ought to stay home and take care of little Al and not leave him to be tooken care of by no train nurse because how do I know what would she do to him and I am not going to tell Florrie nothing a bout it but I am going to take the train to-morrow night right back to Chi and supprise her when I get there and I bet both her and little Al will be tickled to death to see me. I supose Mcgraw and Callahan will be sore at me for a while but when I tell them I want to do the right thing and not give my famly no raw deal I guess they will see where I am right.

We was to play 2 games here and was to play 1 of them in Tacoma and the other here but it rained and so we did not play neither 1 and the people was pretty mad a bout it because I was announced to pitch and they figured probily this would be there only chance to see me in axion and they made a awful holler but Comiskey says No they would not be no game because the field neither here or in Tacoma was in no shape for a game and he would not take no chance of me pitching and may be slipping in the mud and straneing myself and then where would the White Sox be at next season. So we been laying a round all the P.M. and I and Dutch Schaefer had a long talk to gether while some of the rest of the boys was out buying some cloths to take on the trip and Al I bought a full dress suit of evening cloths at Portland yesterday and now I owe Callahan the money for them and am not going on no trip so probily I wont never get to ware them and it is just $45.00 throwed a way but I would rather throw $45.00 a way then go on a trip a round the world and leave my family all winter.

Well Al I and Schaefer was talking to gether and he says Well may be this is the last time we will ever see the good old US and I says What do you mean and he says People that gos acrost the pacific Ocean most generally all ways has there ship recked and then they is not no more never heard from them. Then he asked me was I a good swimmer and I says Yes I had swam a good deal in the river and he says Yes you have swam in the river but that is not nothing like swimming in the pacific Ocean because when you swim in the pacific Ocean you cant move your feet because if you move your feet the sharks comes up to the top of the water and bites at them and even if they did not bite your feet clean off there bite is poison and gives you the hiderofobeya and when you get that you start barking like a dog and the water runs in to your mouth and chokes you to death. Then he says Of coarse if you can swim with out useing your feet you are all O.K. but they is very few can do that and especially in the pacific Ocean because they got to keep useing there hands all the time to scare the sord fish a way so when you dont dare use your feet and your hands is busy you got nothing left to swim with but your stumach mussles. Then he says You should ought to get a long all O.K. because your stumach muscles should ought to be strong from the exercise they get so I guess they is not no danger from a man like you but men like Wiltse and Mike Donlin that is not hog fat like you has not got no chance. Then he says

Of course they have been times when the boats got acrost all O.K. and only a few lives lost but it dont offten happen and the time the old Minneapolis club made the trip the boat went down and the only thing that was saved was the catchers protector that was full of air and could not do nothing else but flote. Then he says May be you would flote to if you did not say nothing for a few days.

I asked him how far would a man got to swim if some thing went wrong with the boat and he says O not far because they is a hole lot of ilands a long the way that a man could swim to but it would not do a man no good to swim to these here ilands because they dont have nothing to eat on them and a man would probily starve to death un less he happened to swim to the sandwich islands. Then he says But by the time you been out on the pacific Ocean a few months you wont care if you get any thing to eat or not. I says Why not and he says the pacific Ocean is so ruff that not nothing can set still not even the stuff you eat. I asked him how long did it take to make the trip acrost if they was not no ship reck and he says they should ought to get acrost a long in febuery if the weather was good. I says Well if we dont get there until febuery we wont have no time to train for next season and he says You wont need to do no training because this trip will take all the weight off of you and every thing else you got. Then he says But you should not ought to be scared of getting sea sick because they is 1 way you can get a way from it and that is to not eat nothing at all while you are on the boat and they tell me you dont eat hardly nothing any way so you wont miss it. Then he says Of coarse if we should have good luck and not get in to no ship reck and not get shot by 1 of them war ships we will have a grate time when we get acrost because all the girls in europe and them places is nuts over ball players and especially stars. I asked what did he mean saying we might get shot by 1 of them war ships and he says we would have to pass by Swittserland and the Swittserland war ships was all the time shooting all over the ocean and of coarse they was not trying to hit no body but they was as wild as most of them left handers and how could you tell what was they going to do next.

Well Al after I got threw talking to Schaefer I run in to Jack Sheridan the umpire and I says I did not think I would go on no trip and I told him some of the things Schaefer was telling me and Sheridan says Schaefer was kidding me and they was not no danger at all and of coarse Al I did not believe ½ of what Schaefer was telling me and that has not got nothing to do with me changeing my mind but I don't think it is not hardly fare for me to go a way on a trip like that and leave Florrie and the baby and suppose some of them things really did happen like Schaefer said though of coarse he was kidding me but if 1 of them things really did happen they would not be no body left to take care of Florrie and little Al and I got a $1000.00 insurence policy but how do I know after I am dead if the insurence co. comes acrost and gives my famly the money.

Well Al I will male this letter and then try again and find Mcgraw and Callahan and then I will look up a time table and see what train can I get to Chi. I dont know yet when I will be in Bedford and may be Florrie has hired a flat all ready but the Allens can live in it by them self and if Allen says any thing a bout I paying for ½ of the rent I will bust his jaw.

Your pal, JACK.

Victoria, Can., Nov. 19.

DEAR OLD AL: Well old pal the boat goes to-night I am going a long and I would not be takeing no time to write this letter only I wrote to you yesterday and says I was not going and you probily would be expecting to see me blow in to Bedford in a few days and besides Al I got a hole lot of things to ask you to do for me if any thing happens and I want to tell you how it come a bout that I changed my mind and am going on the trip. I am glad now that I did not write Florrie no letter yesterday and tell her I was not going because now I would have to write her an other letter and tell her I was going and she would be expecting to see me the day after she got the 1st letter and in stead of seeing me she would get this 2nd. letter and not me at all. I have all ready wrote her a good by letter to-day though and while I was writeing it Al I all most broke down and cried and especially when I thought a bout leaveing little Al so long and may be when I see him again he wont be no baby no more or may be some thing will of happened to him or that train nurse did some thing to him or may be I wont never see him again no more because it is pretty near a cinch that some thing will either happen to I or him. I would give all most any thing I got Al to be back in Chi with little Al and Florrie and I wisht she had not of never wired that telegram telling me I could make the trip and if some thing happens to me think how she will feel when ever she thinks a bout wireing me that telegram and she will feel all most like as if she was a murder.

Well Al after I had wrote you that letter yesterday I found Callahan and Mcgraw and I tell them I have changed my mind and am not going on no trip. Callahan says Whats the matter and I says I dont think it would be fare to my wife and baby and Callahan says Your wife says it would be all O.K. because I seen the telegram my self. I says Yes but she dont know how dangerus the trip is and he says Whos been kiding you and I says They has not no body been kiding me. I says Dutch Schaefer told me a hole lot of stuff but I did not believe none of it and that has not got nothing to do with it. I says I am not a scared of nothing but supose some thing should happen and then where would my wife and my baby be at. Then Callahan says Schaefer has been giveing you a lot of hot air and they is not no more danger on this trip than they is in bed. You been in a hole lot more danger when you was pitching some of them days when you had a sore arm and you would be takeing more chances of getting killed in Chi by 1 of them taxi cabs or the dog catcher then on the Ocean. This here boat we are going on is the Umpires of Japan and it has went acrost the Ocean a million times with out nothing happening and they could not nothing happen to a boat that the N. Y. giants was rideing on because they is to lucky. Then I says Well I have made up my mind to not go on no trip and he says All right then I guess we might is well call the trip off and I says Why and he says You know what president Wilson says a bout Japan and they wont stand for us comeing over there with out you a long and then Mcgraw says Yes it looks like as if the trip was off because we dont want to take no chance of starting no war between Japan and the united states. Then Callahan says You will be in fine with Comiskey if he has to call the trip off because you are a scared of getting hit by a fish. Well Al we talked and argude for a hour or a hour and ½ and some of the rest of the boys come a round and took Callahan and Mcgraw side and finely Callahan says it looked like as if they would have to posepone the trip a few days untill he could get a hold of Allen or some body and then get them to take my place so finely I says I would go because I would not want to brake up no trip after they had made all there plans and some of the players wifes was all ready to go and would be dissapointed if they was not no trip. So Mcgraw and Callahan says Thats the way to talk and so I am going Al and we are leaveing to-night and may be this is the last letter you will ever get from me but if they does not nothing happen Al I will write to you a lot of letters and tell you all a bout the trip but you must not be looking for no more letters for a while untill we get to Japan where I can male a letter and may be its likely as not we wont never get to Japan.

Here is the things I want to ask you to try and do Al and I am not asking you to do nothing if we get threw the trip but if some thing happens and I should be drowned here is what I am asking you to do for me and that is to see that the insurence co. dont skin Florrie out of that $1000.00 policy and see that she all so gets that other $250.00 out of the bank and find her some place down in Bedford to live if she is willing to live down there because she can live there a hole lot cheaper than she can live in Chi and besides I know Bertha would treat her right and help her out all she could. All so Al I want you and Bertha to help take care of little Al untill he grows up big enough to take care of him self and if he looks like as if he was going to be left handed dont let him Al but make him use his right hand for every thing. Well Al they is 1 good thing and that is if I get drowned Florrie wont have to buy no lot in no cemetary and hire no herse.

Well Al old pal you all ways been a good friend of mine and I all ways tried to be a good friend of yourn and if they was ever any thing I done to you that was not O.K. remember by gones is by gones. I want you to all ways think of me as your best old pal. Good by old pal.

Your old pal, JACK.

P.S. Al if they should not nothing happen and if we was to get acrost the Ocean all O.K. I am going to ask Mcgraw to let me work the 1st game against the White Sox in Japan because I should certainly ought to be right after giveing my arm a rest and not doing nothing at all on the trip acrost and I bet if Mcgraw lets me work Crawford and Speaker will wish the boat had of sank. You know me Al.

Call for Mr. Keefe!

The Saturday Evening Post
MARCH 9, 1918

St. Louis, April 10.

FRIEND AL: Well Al the training trips over and we open up the season here tomorrow and I suppose the boys back home is all anxious to know about our chances and what shape the boys is in. Well old pal you can tell them we are out after that old flag this year and the club that beats us will know they have been in a battle. I'll say they will.

Speaking for myself personly I never felt better in my life and you know what that means Al. It means I will make a monkey out of this league and not only that but the boys will all have more confidence in themself and play better baseball when they know my arms right and that I can give them the best I got and if Rowland handles the club right and don't play no favorites like last season we will be so far out in front by the middle of July that Boston and the rest of them will think we have jumped to some other league.

Well I suppose the old towns all excited about Uncle Sam declairing war on Germany. Personly I am glad we are in it but between you and I Al I figure we ought to of been in it a long time ago right after the Louisiana was sank. I often say alls fair in love and war but that don't mean the Germans or no one else has got a right to murder American citizens but thats about all you can expect from a German and anybody that expects a square deal from them is a sucker. You don't see none of them umpireing in our league but at that they couldn't be no worse than the ones we got. Some of ours is so crooked they can't lay in a birth only when the trains making a curve.

But speaking about the war Al you couldn't keep me out of it only for Florrie and little Al depending on me for sport and of course theys the ball club to and I would feel like a trader if I quit them now when it looks like this is our year. So I might just as well make up my mind to whats got to be and not mop over it but I like to kid the rest of the boys and make them think I'm going to enlist to see their face fall and tonight at supper I told Gleason I thought I would quit the club and join the army. He tried to laugh it off with some of his funny stuff. He says "They wouldn't take you." "No," I said. "I suppose Uncle Sam is turning down men with a perfect physic." So he says "They don't want a man that if a shell would hit him in the head it would explode all over the trench and raise havioc." I forget what I said back to him.

Well Al I don't know if I will pitch in this serious or not but if I do I will give them a touch of high life but maybe Rowland will save me to open up at Detroit where a mans got to have something besides their glove. It takes more than camel flags to beat that bunch. I'll say it does.

Your pal, Jack.

Chicago, April 15.

FRIEND AL: Well Al here I am home again and Rowland sent some of us home from St. Louis instead of takeing us along to Detroit and

I suppose he is figureing on saveing me to open up the home season next Thursday against St. Louis because they always want a big crowd on opening day and St. Louis don't draw very good unless theys some extra attraction to bring the crowd out. But anyway I was glad to get home and see Florrie and little Al and honest Al he is cuter than ever and when he seen me he says "Who are you?" Hows that for a 3 year old?

Well things has been going along pretty good at home while I was away only it will take me all summer to pay the bills Florrie has ran up on me and you ought to be thankfull that Bertha aint 1 of these Apollos thats got to keep everybody looking at them or they can't eat. Honest Al to look at the clothes Florrie has boughten you would think we was planning to spend the summer at Newport News or somewhere. And she went and got herself a hired girl that sticks us for $8.00 per week and all as she does is cook up the meals and take care of little Al and run wild with a carpet sweeper and dust rag every time you set down to read the paper. I says to Florrie "What is the idea? The 3 of us use to get along O.K. without no help from Norway." So she says "I got sick in tired of staying home all the time or dragging the baby along with me when I went out." So I said I remembered when she wouldn't leave no one else take care of the kid only herself and she says "Yes but that was when I didn't know nothing about babys and every time he cried I thought he had lumbago or something but now I know he has got no intentions of dying so I quit worring about him."

So I said "Yes but I can't afford no high price servants to say nothing about dressing you like an actor and if you think I am going to spend all my salary on silks and satans and etc. you will get a big surprise." So she says "You might as well spend your money on me as leave the ball players take it away from you in the poker game and show their own wives a good time with it. But if you don't want me to spend your money I will go out and get some of my own to spend." Then I said "What will you do teach school?" And she says "No and I won't teach school either." So I said "No I guess you won't. But if you think you want to try standing up behind a cigar counter or something all day why go ahead and try it and we'll see how long you will last." So she says "I don't have to stand behind no counter but I can go in business for myself and make more than you do." So I said "Yes you can" and she didn't have no come back.

Imagine Al a girl saying she could make more money then a big league pitcher. Probably theys a few of them that does but they are movie actors or something and I would like to see Florrie try to be a movie actor because they got to look pleasant all the time and Florrie would strain herself.

Well Al the ski jumper has got dinner pretty near ready and after dinner I am going over North and see what the Cubs look like and I wish I pitched in that league Al and the only trouble is that I would feel ashamed when I went after my pay check.

Your old pal, Jack.

Chicago, May 19.

Dear Friend Al: Well old pal if we wasn't married we would all have to go to war now and I mean all of us thats between 21 and 30. I suppose you seen about the Govt. passing the draft law and a whole lot of the baseball players will have to go but our club won't loose nobody except 1 or 2 bushers that don't count because all as they do any way is take up room on the bench and laugh when Rowland springs a joke.

When I first seen it in the paper this morning I thought it meant everybody that wasn't crippled up or something but Gleason explained it to me that if you got somebody to sport they leave you home and thats fair enough but he also says they won't take no left handers on acct. of the guns all being made for right handed men and thats just like the lucky stiffs to set in a rocking chair and take it easy while the regular fellows has got to go over there and get shot up but anyway the yellow stiffs would make a fine lot of soldiers because the first time a German looked X eyed at them they would wave a flag of truants.

But I can't help from wishing this thing had of come off before I see Florrie or little Al and if I had money enough saved up so as they wouldn't have to worry I would go any way but I wouldn't wait for no draft. Gleason says I will have to register family or no family when the time comes but as soon as I tell them about Florrie they will give me an excuse. I asked him what they would do with the boys that wasn't excused and if they would send them right over to France and he says No they would keep them here till they learned to talk German. He says, "You can't fight nobody without a quarrel and you can't quarrel with a man unless they can understand what you are calling them." So I asked him how about the aviators because their machines would be makeing so much noise that they couldn't tell if the other one was talking German or rag time and he said "Well if you are in an areoplane and you see a German areoplane coming tords you you can pretty near guess that he don't want to spoon with you."

That's what I would like to be Al is an aviator and I think Gleasons afraid I'm going to bust into that end of the game though he pretends like he don't take me in ernest. "Why don't you?" he said "You could make good there all right because the less sense they got the better. But I wish you would quit practiceing till you get away from here." I asked him what he meant quit practiceing. "Well" he said "you was up in the air all last Tuesday afternoon."

He was refering to that game I worked against the Phila. club but honest Al my old souper was so sore I couldn't cut loose. Well Al a mans got a fine chance to save money when they are married to a girl like Florrie. When I got paid Tuesday the first thing when I come home she wanted to borrow $200.00 and that was all I had comeing so I said "What am I going to do the next 2 weeks walk back and forth to the ball park and back?" I said "What and the hell do you want with $200.00?" So then she begin to cry so I split it with her and give her a $100.00 and she wouldn't tell me what she wanted it for but she says she was going to supprise me. Well Al I will be supprised if she don't land us all out to the county farm but you can't do nothing with them when they cry.

Your pal, Jack.

Chicago, May 24.

FRIEND AL: What do you think Florrie has pulled off now? I told you she was fixing to land us in the poor house and I had the right dope. With the money I give her and some she got somewheres else she has opened up a beauty parlor on 43th St. right off of Michigan. Her and a girl that worked in a place like it down town.

Well Al when she sprung it on me you couldn't of knocked me down with a feather. I always figured girls was kind of crazy but I never seen one loose her mind as quick as that and I don't know if I ought to have them take her to some home or leave her learn her lesson and get over it.

I know you ain't got no beauty parlor in Bedford so I might as well tell you what they are. They are for women only and the women goes to them when they need something done to their hair or their face or their nails before a wedding or a eucher party or something. For inst. you and Bertha was up here and you wanted to take her to a show and she would have to get fixed up so she would go to this place and tell them to give her the whole treatment and first they would wash the grime out of her hair and then comb it up fluffy and then they would clean up her complexion with buttermilk and either get rid of the moles or else paint them white and then they would put some eyebrows on her with a pencil and red up her lips and polish her teeth and pair her finger nails and etc. till she looked as good as she could and it would cost her $5.00 or $10.00 according to what they do to her and if they would give her a bath and a massage I suppose its extra.

Well theys plenty of high class beauty parlors down town where women can go and know they will get good service but Florrie thinks she can make it pay out here with women that maybe haven't time to go clear down town because their husband or their friend might loose his mind in the middle of the afternoon and phone home that he had tickets for the Majestic or something and then of course they would have to rush over to some place in the neighborhood for repairs.

I didn't know Florrie was wise to the game but it seems she has been takeing some lessons down town without telling me nothing about it and this Miss Nevins thats in partners with her says Florrie is a darb. Well I wouldn't have no objections if I thought they was a chance for them to make good because she acts like she liked the work and its right close to where we live but it looks to me like their expenses would eat them up. I was in the joint this morning and the different smells alone must of cost them $100.00 to say nothing about all the bottles and cans and tools and brushs and the rent and furniture besides. I told Florrie I said "You got everything here but patients." She says "Don't worry about them. They will come when they find out about us." She says they have sent their cards to all the South Side 400.

"Well" I said "If they don't none of them show up in a couple of months I suppose you will call on the old meal ticket." So she says "You should worry." So I come away and went over to the ball park.

When I seen Kid Gleason I told him about it and he asked me where Florrie got the money to start up so I told him I give it to her. "You" he says "where did you get it?" So just jokeing I said "Where do you suppose I got it? I stole it." So he says "You did if you got it from this ball club." But he was kidding Al because of course he knows I'm no thief. But I got the laugh on him this afternoon when Silk O'Loughlin chased him out of the ball park. Johnson was working against us and they was two out and Collins on second base and Silk called a third strike on Gandil that was down by his corns. So Gleason hollered "All right Silk you won't have to go to war. You couldn't pass the eye test." So Silk told him to get off the field. So then I hollered something at Silk and he hollered back at me "That will be all from you you big busher." So I said "You are a busher yourself you busher." So he said:

"Get off the bench and let one of the ball players set down."

So I and Gleason stalled a while and finely come into the club house and I said "Well Kid I guess we told him something that time." "Yes" says Gleason "you certainly burned him up but the trouble with me is I can't never think of nothing to say till it's too late." So I said "When a man gets past sixty you can't expect their brain to act quick." And he didn't say nothing back.

Well we win the ball game any way because Cicotte shut them out. The way some of the ball players was patting him on the back afterwards you would have thought it was the 1st. time anybody had ever pitched a shut out against the Washington club but I don't see no reason to swell a man up over it. If you shut out Detroit or Cleveland you are doing something but this here Washington club gets a bonus every time they score a run.

But it does look like we was going to cop that old flag and play the Giants for the big dough and it will sure be the Giants we will have to play against though some of the boys seem to think the Cubs have got a chance on acct. of them just winning 10 straight on their eastren trip but as Gleason says how can a club help from winning 10 straight in that league?

Your pal, Jack.

Chicago, June 6.

FRIEND AL: Well Al the clubs east and Rowland left me home because my old souper is sore again and besides I had to register yesterday for the draft. They was a big crowd down to the place we registered and you ought to seen them when I come in. They was all trying to get up close to me and I was afraid some of them would get hurt in the jam. All of them says "Hello Jack" and I give them a smile and shook hands with about a dozen of them. A man hates to have everybody stareing at you but you got to be pleasant or they will think you are swelled up and besides a man can afford to put themself out a little if its going to give the boys any pleasure.

I don't know how they done with you Al but up here they give us a card to fill out and then they give us another one to carry around with us to show that we been registered and what our number is. I had to put down my name on the first card and my age and where I live and the day I was born and what month and etc. Some of the questions was crazy like "Was I a natural born citizen?" I wonder what they think I am. Maybe they think I fell out of a tree or something. Then I had to tell them I was born in Bedford, Ind. and it asked what I done for a liveing and I put down that I was a pitcher but the man made me change it to ball player and then I had to give Comiskey's name and address and then name the people that was dependent on me so I put down a wife and one child.

And the next question was if I was married or single. I supposed they would know enough to know that a man with a wife dependent on him was probably married. Then it says what race and I had a notion to put down "pennant" for a joke but the man says to put down white. Then it asked what military service had I had and of course I says none and then come the last question Did I claim exemption and what grounds so the man told me to write down married with dependents.

Then the man turned over to the back of the card and wrote down about my looks. Just that I was tall and medium build and brown eyes and brown hair. And the last question was if I had lost an arm or leg or hand or foot or both eyes or was I other wise disabled so I told him about my arm being sore and thats why I wasn't east with the club but he didn't put it down. So that's all they was to it except the card he give me with my number which is 3403.

It looks to me like it was waisting a mans time to make you go down there and wait for your turn when they know you are married and got a kid or if they don't know if they could call up your home or the ball park and find it out but of course if they called up my flat when I or Florrie wasn't there they wouldn't get nothing but a bunch of Swede talk that they couldn't nobody understand and I don't believe the girl knows herself what she is talking about over the phone. She can talk english pretty good when shes just talking to you but she must think all the phone calls is long distance from Norway because the minute she gets that reciever up to her ear you can't hardly tell the difference between she and Hughey Jennings on the coaching line.

I told Florrie I said "This girl could make more than $8.00 per week if she would get a job out to some ball park as announcer and announce the batterys and etc. She has got the voice for it and she would be right in a class with the rest of them because nobody could make heads or tales out of what she was trying to get at."

Speaking about Florrie what do you think Al? They have had enough suckers to pay expenses and also pay up some of the money they borrowed and Florrie says if their business gets much bigger they will have to hire more help. How would you like a job Al white washing some dames nose or leveling off their face with a steam roller? Of course I am just jokeing Al because they won't allow no men around the joint but wouldn't it be some job Al? I'll say so.

Your old pal, Jack.

Chicago, June 21.

DEAR AL: Well Al I suppose you read in the paper the kind of luck I had yesterday but of course you can't tell nothing from what them dam reporters write and if they know how to play ball why aint they playing it instead of trying to write funny stuff about the ball game but at that some of it is funny Al because its so rotten its good. For inst. one of them had it in the paper this morning that I flied out to Speaker in the seventh inning. Well listen Al I hit that ball right on the pick and it went past that shortstop so fast that he didn't even have time to wave at it and if Speaker had of been playing where he belongs that ball would of went between he and Graney and bumped against the wall. But no. Speakers laying about ten feet back of second base and over to the left and of course the ball rides right to him and there was the whole ball game because that would of drove in 2 runs and made them play different then they did in the eigth. If a man is supposed to be playing center field why don't he play center field and of course I thought he was where he ought to been or I would of swung different.

Well the eigth opened up with the score 1 to 1 and I get 2 of them out but I got so much stuff I can't stick it just where I want to and I give Chapman a base on balls. At that the last one cut the heart of the plate but Evans called it a ball. Evans lives in Cleveland. Well I said "All right Bill you won't have to go to war. You couldn't pass the eye test." So he says "You must of read that one in a book." "No" I said "I didn't read it in no book either."

So up comes this Speaker and I says "What do you think you are going to do you lucky stiff?" So he says "I'm going to hit one where theys nobody standing in the way of it." I said "Yes you are." But I had to hold Chapman up at first base and Schalk made me waist 2 thinking Chapman was going and then of course I had to ease up and Speaker cracked one down the first base line but Gandil got his glove on it and if he hadn't of messed it all up he could of beat Speaker to the bag himself but instead of that they all started to ball me out for not covering. I told them to shut their mouth. Then Roth come up and I took a half wind up because of course I didn't think Chapman would be enough of a bone head to steal third with 2 out but him and Speaker pulled a double steal and then Rowland and all of them begin to yell at me and they got my mind off of what I was doing and then Schalk asked for a fast one though he said afterwards he didn't but I would of made him let me curve the ball if they hadn't got me all nervous yelling at me. So Roth hit one to left field that Jackson could of caught in his hip pocket if he had been playing right. So 2 runs come in and then Rowland takes me out and I would of busted him only for makeing a seen on the field.

I said to him "How can you expect a man to be at his best when I have not worked for a month?" So he said "Well it will be more than a month before you will work for me again." "Yes" I said "because I am going to work for Uncle Sam and join the army." "Well," he says "you won't need no steel helmet." "No" I said "and you wouldn't either." Then he says "I'm afraid you won't last long over there because the first time they give you a hand grenade to throw you will take your wind up and loose a hand." So I said "If Chapman is a smart ball player why and the hell did he steal third base with 2 out?" He couldn't answer that but he says "What was you doing all alone out in No Mans Land on that ball of Speakers to Gandil?" So I told him to shut up and I went in the club house and when he come in I didn't speak to him or to none of the rest of them either.

Well Al I would quit right now and go up to Fort Sheridan and try for a captain only for Florrie and little Al and of course if it come to a show down Comiskey would ask me to stick on acct. of the club being in the race and it wouldn't be the square thing for me to walk out on him and when he has got his heart set on the pennant.

Your pal, Jack.

Chicago, July 5.

FRIEND AL: Just a few lines Al to tell you how Florrie is getting along and I bet you will be surprised to hear about it. Well Al she paid me back my $100.00 day before yesterday and she showed me their figures for the month of June and I don't know if you will believe it or not but she and Miss Nevins cleared $400.00 for the month or $200.00 a peace over and above all expenses and she says the business will be even better in the fall and winter time on acct. of more people going to partys and theaters then. How is that for the kind of a wife to have Al and the best part of it is that she is stuck on the work and a whole lot happier then when she wasn't doing nothing. They got 2 girls working besides themself and they are talking about moveing into a bigger store somewheres and she says we will have to find a bigger flat so as we can have a nurse and a hired girl instead of just the one.

Tell Bertha about it Al and tell her that when she comes up to Chi she can get all prettied up and I will see they don't charge her nothing for it.

The clubs over in Detroit but it was only a 5 day trip so Rowland left me home to rest up my arm for the eastren clubs and Phila. is due here the day after tomorrow and all as I ask is a chance at them. My arm don't feel exactly right but I could roll the ball up to the plate and beat that club.

Its a cinch now that the Giants is comeing through in the other league and if we can keep going it will be some worlds serious between the 2 biggest towns in the country and the club that wins ought to grab off about $4500.00 a peace per man. Is that worth going after Al? I'll say so.

Your old pal, Jack.

Chicago, July 20.

FRIEND AL: Well Al I don't suppose you remember my draft number and I don't remember if I told it to you or not. It was 3403 Al. And it was the 5th number drawed at Washington.

Well old pal they can wipe the town of Washington off of the map and you won't hear no holler from me. The day before yesterday Rowland sends me in against the Washington club and of course it had to be Johnson for them. And I get beat 3 and 2 and I guess its the only time this season that Washington scored 3 runs in 1 day. And the next thing they announce the way the draft come out and I'm No. 5 and its a misery to me why my number wasn't the 1st. they drawed out instead of the 5th.

Well Al of course it don't mean I got to go if I don't want to. I can get out of it easy enough by telling them about Florrie and little Al and besides Gleason says they have promised Ban Johnson that they won't take no baseball stars till the seasons over and maybe not then and besides theys probably some White Sox fans that will go to the front for me and get me off on acct. of the club being in the fight for the pennant and they can't nobody say I'm trying to get excused because I said all season that I would go in a minute if it wasn't for my family and the club being in the race and I give $50.00 last week for a liberty bond that will only bring me in $1.75 per annum which is nothing you might say. You couldn't sport a flee on $1.75 per annum.

Florrie wanted I should go right down to the City Hall or where ever it is you go and get myself excused but Gleason says the only thing to do is just wait till they call me and then claim exemptions. I read somewheres a while ago that President Wilson wanted base-ball kept up because the people would need amusement and I asked Gleason if he had read about that and he says "Yes but that won't get you nothing because the rest of the soldiers will need amusement even more than the people."

Well Al I don't know what your number was or how you come out but I hope you had better luck but if you did get drawed you will probably have a hard time getting out of it because you don't make no big salary and you got no children and Bertha could live with your mother and pick up a few dollars sowing. Enough to pay for her board and clothes. Of course they might excuse you for flat feet which they say you can't get in if you have them. But if I was you Al I would be tickled to death to get in because it would give you a chance to see something outside of Bedford and if your feet gets by you ought to be O. K.

I guess they won't find fault with my feet or anything about me as far physical goes. Hey Al?

I will write as soon as I learn anything.

Your pal, Jack.

Chicago, Aug. 6.

FRIEND AL: Well Al I got notice last Friday that I was to show up right away over to Wendell Phllips high school where No. 5 board of exemptions was setting but when I got over there it was jamed so I went back there today and I have just come home from there now.

The 1st. man I seen was the doctor and he took my name and number and then he asked me if my health was O. K. and I told him it was only I don't feel good after meals. Then he asked me if I was all sound and well right now so I told him my pitching arm was awful lame and that was the reason I hadn't went east with the club. Then he says "Do you understand that if a man don't tell the truth about themself here they are libel to prison?" So I said he didn't have to worry about that.

So then he made me strip bear and I wish you had seen his eyes pop out when he got a look at my shoulders and chest. I stepped on the scales and tipped the bean at 194 and he measured me at 6 ft. 1 and a half. Then he went all over me and poked me with his finger and counted my teeth and finely he made me tell him what different letters was that he held up like I didn't know the alphabet or something. So when he was through he says "Well I guess you ain't going to die right away." He signed the paper and sent me to the room where the rest of the board was setting.

Well 1 of them looked up my number and then asked me did I claim exemptions. I told him yes and he asked me what grounds so I said "I sport a wife and baby and besides I don't feel like it would be a square deal to Comiskey for me to walk out on him now." So he says "Have you got an affidavit from your wife that you sport her?" So I told him no and he says "Go and get one and bring it back here tomorrow but you don't need to bring none from Comiskey." So you see Comiskey must stand pretty good with them.

So he give me a blank for Florrie to fill out and when she gets home we will go to a notary and tend to it and tomorrow they will fix up my excuse and then I won't have nothing to think about only to get the old souper in shape for the big finish.

Your pal, Jack.

Chicago, Aug. 8.

DEAR OLD PAL: Well old pal it would seem like the best way to get along in this world is to not try and get nowheres because the minute a man gets somewheres they's people that can't hardly wait to bite your back.

The 1st. thing yesterday I went over to No. 5 board and was going to show them Florrie's affidavit but while I was pulling it out of my pocket the man I seen the day before called me over to 1 side and says "Listen Keefe I am a White Sox fan and don't want to see you get none the worst of it and if I was you I would keep a hold of that paper." So I asked him what for and he says "Do you know what the law is about telling the truth and not telling the truth and if you turn in an affidavit thats false and we find it out you and who ever made the affidavit is both libel to prison?" So I said what was he trying to get at and he says "We got informations that your wife is in business for herself and makeing as high as $250.00 per month which is plenty for she and your boy to get along on." "Yes" I said "but who pays for the rent of our flat and the hired girl and what we eat?" So he says "That don't make no difference. Your wife could pay for them and that settles it."

Well Al I didn't know what to say for a minute but finely I asked him where the information come from and he says he was tipped off in a letter that who ever wrote it didn't sign their name the sneaks and I asked him how he knowed that they was telling the truth. So he says "Its our business to look them things up. If I was you I wouldn't make no claim for exemptions but just lay quiet and take a chance."

Then all of a sudden I had an idea Al and I will tell you about it but 1st. as soon as it come to me I asked the man if this here board was all the board they was and he says no that if they would not excuse me I could appeal to the Dist. board but if he was me he wouldn't do it because it wouldn't do no good and might get me in trouble. So I said "I won't get in no trouble" and he says "All right suit yourself." So I said I would take the affadavit and go to the Dist. board but he says no that I would have to get passed on 1st. by his board and then I could appeal if I wanted to.

So I left the affadavit and he says they would notify me how I come out so then I beat it home and called up Florrie and told her they was something important and for her to come up to the flat.

Well Al here was the idea. I had been thinking for a long time that while it was all O. K. for Florrie to earn a little money in the summer when I was tied up with the club it would be a whole lot better if we was both free after the season so as we could take little Al and go on a trip somewheres or maybe spend the winter in the south but of course if she kept a hold of her share in the business she couldn't get away so the best thing would be to sell out to Miss Nevins for a good peace of money and we could maybe buy us a winter home somewheres with what she got and whats comeing to me in the worlds serious.

So when Florrie got home I put it up to her. I said "Florrie I'm sick in tired of haveing you tied up in business because it don't seem right for a married woman to be in business when their husbands in the big league and besides a womans place is home especially when they got a baby so I want you to sell out and when I get my split of the worlds serious we will go south somewheres and buy a home."

Well she asked me how did I come out with the affadavit. So I said "The affadavit is either here nor there. I am talking about something else" and she says "Yes you are." And she says "I been worring all day about that affadavit because if they find out about it what will they do to us." So I said "You should worry because if this board won't excuse me I will go to the Dist. board and mean while you won't be earning nothing because you will be out of business." Well Al she had a better idea then that. She says "No I will hold on to the business till you go to the Dist. board and then if they act like they wouldn't excuse you you can tell them I am going to sell out. And if they say all right I will sell out. But if they say its to late why then I will still have something to live on if you have to go."

So when she said that about me haveing to go we both choked up a little but pretty soon I was O. K. and now Al it looks like a cinch I would get my exemptions from the Dist. board because if Florrie says she wants to sell out they can't stop her.

Your pal, Jack.

Chicago, Aug. 22.

FRIEND AL: Well Al its all over. The Dist. board won't let me off and between you and I Al I am glad of it and I only hope I won't have to go before I have had a chance at the worlds serious.

My case came up about noon. One of the men asked me my name and then looked over what they had wrote down about me. Then he says "Theys an affadavit here that says your wife and child depends on you. Is that true?" So I said yes it was and he asked me if my wife was in business and I said yes but she was thinking about selling out. So he asked me how much money she made in her business. I said "You can't never tell. Some times its so much and other times different." So he asked me what the average was and I said it was about $250.00 per month. Then he says "Why is she going to sell out?" I said "Because we don't want to live in Chi all winter" and he said "You needn't to worry." Then he said "If she makes $250.00 per month how do you figure she is dependent on you?" So I said "Because she is because I pay for the rent and everything." And he asked me what she done with the $250.00 and I told him she spent it on clothes.

So he says "$250.00 per month on clothes. How does she keep warm this weather?" I said "I guess they don't nobody have no trouble keeping warm in August. Then he says "Look here Keefe this affadavit mitigates against you. We will have to turn down your appeal and I guess your wife can take care of herself and the boy." I said "She can't when she sells out." "Well" he said "you tell her not to sell out. It may be hard for her at first to sport herself and the boy on $250.00 but if the worst comes to the worst she can wear the same shoes twice and she will find them a whole lot more comfortable the second time." So I said "She don't never have no trouble with her feet and if she did I guess she knows how to fix them."

Florrie was waiting for me when I got home. "Well" I said "now you see what your dam beauty parlor has done for us." And then she seen what had happened and begin to cry and of course I couldn't find no more fault with her and I called up the ball park and told them I was sick and wouldn't show up this P.M. and I and Florrie and little Al stayed home together and talked. That is little Al done all the talking. I and Florrie didn't seem to have nothing to say.

Tomorrow I am going to tell them about it over to the ball park. If they can get me off till after the worlds serious all right. And if they can't all right to.

Your old pal, Jack.

P.S. Washington comes tomorrow and I am going to ask Rowland to leave me pitch. The worst I can get is a tie. They scored a run in St. Louis yesterday and that means they are through for the week.

Chicago, Aug. 23.

DEAR AL: Well Al the one that laughs last gets all the best of it. Wait till you hear what come off today.

When I come in the club house Rowland and Gleason was there all alone. I told them hello and was going to spring the news on them but when Rowland seen me he says "Jack I got some bad news for you." So I said what was it. So he says "The boss sold you to Washington this morning."

Well Al at first I couldn't say nothing and I forgot all about that I wanted to tell them. But then I remembered it again and here is what I pulled. I said "Listen Manager I beat the boss to it." "What do you mean?" he said so I said "I'm signed up with Washington all ready only I ain't signed with Griffith but with Uncle Sam." That's what I pulled on them Al and they both got it right away. Gleason jumped up and shook hands with me and so did Rowland and then Rowland said he would have to hurry up in the office and tell the Old Man. "But wait a minute" I said. "I am going to quit you after this game because I don't know when I will be called and theys lots of things I got to fix up." So I stopped and Rowland asked me what I wanted and I said "Let me pitch this game and I will give them the beating of their life."

So him and Gleason looked at each other and then Rowland says "You know we can't afford to loose no ball games now. But if you think you can beat them I will start you."

So then he blowed and I and Gleason was alone.

"Well kid" he says "you make the rest of us look like a monkey. This game ain't nothing compared to what you are going to do. And when you come back they won't be nothing to good for you and your kid will be proud of you because you went while a whole lot of other kids dads stayed home."

So he patted me on the back and I kind of choked up and then the trainer come in and I had him do a little work on my arm.

Well Al you will see in the paper what I done to them. Before the game the boss had told Griffith about me and called the deal off. So while I was warming up Griffith come over and shook hands. He says "I would of like to had you but I am a good looser." So I says "You ought to be." So he couldn't help from laughing but he says "When you come back I will go after you again." I said "Well if you don't get somebody on the club between now and then that can hit something besides fouls I won't come back." So he kind of laughed again and walked away and then it was time for the game.

Well Al the official scorer give them 3 hits but he must be McMullins brother in law or something because McMullin ought to of throwed Milan out from here to Berlin on that bunt. But any way 3 hits and no runs is pretty good for a finish and between you and I Al I feel like I got the last laugh on Washington and Rowland to.

Your pal, Jack.

Chicago, Sept. 18.

Friend Al: Just time for a few lines while Florrie finishs packing up my stuff. I leave with the bunch tomorrow A.M. for Camp Grant at

Rockford. I don't know how long we will stay there but I suppose long enough to learn to talk German and shoot and etc.

We just put little Al to bed and tonight was the first time we told him I was going to war. He says "Can I go to daddy?" Hows that for a 3 year old Al?

Well he will be proud of me when I come back and he will be proud of me if I don't come back and when he gets older he can go up to the kids that belong to some of these left handers and say "Where and the hell was your father when the war come off?"

Good by Al and say good by to Bertha for me.

Your Pal, Jack.

P.S. I won't be in the serious against New York but how about the real worlds serious Al? Won't I be in that? I'll say so.

The Battle of Texas

The Saturday Evening Post
MAY 24, 1919

On the Rattler, March 22.

FRIEND AL: Well Al I am writeing this on the old rattler bound for sunny Texas and a man has got to write letters or something or you would gap yourself to death. They don't have no more poker game Al but just some baby game like rummy that may be O. K. for birds that has spent all their life at some X roads but take a man like I that was over in France and played in the big game and it kind of sets up a man's stomach to watch a bunch of growed up men popping their eyes out for the fear that they might maybe have a picture card left in their hand when some other bird lays down their cards. So about all they's left for a real man to do is write letters or read the paper or look out at the scenery and I all ready read the papers and as for the scenery we been going through Kas. most of the day and you could pull down the shade most any minute and feel pretty sure you wasn't going to miss nothing.

Well Al we left Chi last night and the 1st. thing Kid Gleason come through the car and asked everybody if they had any bottle goods hid in their grips as he says they are getting strick and if they catch a bird carring anything in to dry territory they send you to Siberia or somewheres. So when he come along to me he said "Well you big busher I don't half to ask you if you are bringing anything along with you as my nose knows but is any of it in bottles?" So I said "No all I have got with me they would half to operate to find it."

So he said "Well you want to be sure as they are libel to go through everybody's baggage." So I said "I would like to see some fresh Alex make a move to serch my baggage and I would knock him for a gool."

Well they's 2 or 3 of the other boys besides myself that was in the service or that is they call it being in the service though I was the only 1 that got acrost the old pond outside of Joe Jenkins 1 of the catchers that's still over there yet, but Red Faber was in the navy up to Great Lakes and Ed Collins was in the marines and 1 of the young fellows is wearing a aviation uniform and I suppose he seen the war from Texas and maybe got up so high that the 1st. baseman had to jump for him. But for a wile last night they was all asking me questions about what I seen over there and this in that but every time I would tell them something Collins or 1 of the other smart Alex would say he read about it in the papers and it was different so I said "All right if you seen it in the papers that way it must be so only I kind of figured that me being right up to the front I might be in a position to know something about the war where you take the most of these here reporters and for all they seen of it they might as well of been on Pikes Peek with a pair of opera glasses looking west." So that shut them up.

Well Al we are supposed to get to Mineral Wells tomorrow noon and they can't get us there to soon to suit me as I am wild to get out there in the old ball yard and show Gleason that I have got something left and he was telling me this A.M. that he had picked up a lot of good looking young right handers and I would half to step along to hold a job or the next thing I knowed I would be up to

Minneapolis wearing a white beard and pitching for Joe Cantillon. But the new recruits that I have met on the train so far that thinks they are pitchers couldn't pass the physical examination for the Portugal army so it looks like I wouldn't have much trouble if I get a square deal and if I don't I will knock somebody for a gool.

Your pal, JACK

Mineral Wells, March 24.

FRIEND AL: Well Al we landed here yesterday noon and it was raining when we got here and still raining and don't look like it would ever stop and a man might almost think we had came to France by a mistake. And the only differents is that the harder it rained in France why they would see that we was all out in it wile here they's nothing to do only lay around the hotel. Well Al I don't know how many people they have got in Texas but they are all stopping at this hotel and on a rainy day it would take Houdini to get through the lobby. They call this hotel the Crazy Wells on acct. of 1 of the wells that they say it cures crazy people but it would half to be some well to cure some of the birds on our club a specially after they been jammed up together in this hotel a couple of rainy days with nothing to do only gap at each other.

Well we got in to Ft. Worth yesterday A.M. and they switched us on to the R. R. that runs over here at lease they call it a R. R. and its the Weatherford Mineral Wells and North Western but Buck Weaver says the letters stands for Whoa Mule Whoa now Whoa. So I said if you think this R. R. balks you should ought to ride around France in some of them horse cars so Buck said "I wished I was a extra catcher so as I could set down in the bull pen with you all summer and learn all about France." He said "You boys that went to France thinks you had a tough time of it but what about we birds that has to listen to it all the rest of our life." So I said shut your mouth. But any way Al this R. R. isn't only 28 miles long from 1 end to the other so even if the trains do run like old Cy Young was pace-ing them you get to where you was going some time, where the roads we was on in France never seemed to know where to leave off.

Well we couldn't of done no work yesterday any way on acct. of just getting in and unpacking and getting our uniforms and everything but Gleason was certainly sore when we woke up this A.M. and it was still poring rain and I set with him at the breakfast table and the waiter said this rain was makeing a big hit with the people in Texas as they hadn't had no rain for so long that pretty near everything was drying up so Gleason said "Well you better make it unanimous." He meant for the waiter to dry up to and shut his mouth.

Well Gleason said we would half to go out and work tomorrow rain or shine and he said after this everybody would half to be down for breakfast at 8 bells or they wouldn't get no breakfast and if they didn't get down for breakfast he would go up to their rooms and use his razor strap on them. That's the way he generally always does Al on the new recruits is go after them with his razor strap to show them he is in ernest but of course he wouldn't dast do that on 1 of we old timers and if he ever tried it on me I would knock him for a gool.

I told him that this A.M. and he said "Well they's no danger of you ever comeing late to a meal and the only thing I am a scared of is that you will get here before they open up the dining rm. and bust down the door and get us put out of the hotel."

Well Al I am glad of 1 thing and that is most of the people stopping at the hotel is men and very few gals not that the gals would make any differents in my young life only in most of these southern hotels they's generally always a flock of gals that wants to make a fuss over the ball players and usually 1 of them takes a kind of a shine to me but this time I have made it up in my mind to tend to business and show Gleason that he didn't make no mistake in meeting my terms so I am glad I won't have nothing to take my mind off of my work though they's 1 little gal stopping here that the boys says she is a swell heiress from St. Louis that's here with her mother that's got rheumatism and I noticed she give me a long look when I come in the dining rm. this noon but I looked straight ahead and pretended like I didn't notice it. Her name is Miss Krug and she is some looker but she is certainly wasteing them goggly eyes on me as I am down here to get my arm in shape to pitch and not hold hands or something.

The clerk tells me that she has got a big car that she drives around in it all the wile her mother is takeing the treatments but as far as I am conserned if she gets lonesome driveing she will half to talk to the spare tire.

Your pal, JACK.

Mineral Wells, March 26.

FRIEND AL: Well Al if nerve was all that a bird needed to make good in the big league they's 1 bird down here trying to be a pitcher on our club that has all ready made good. But it takes something besides nerve Al but listen to what come off today and you will say this bird is chesty enough if he only had something to go with it.

Well this bird's name is Belden and he was a semi pro up in Chi but he got catched in the draft and went to France and he just got back from over there last month and somebody recomended him to Comiskey and so he is down here on the trip. Well he is a right hander so he is a rival of mine you might say but to look at him I guess they's no hurry about me packing up my grip and go home.

Well the rain had stopped this A.M. and Gleason said everybody must be out to the pk. at 10 bells so we started out about 9:30 and I was walking with Buck Weaver and Eddie Cicotte and this here Belden. They was about a ft. of mud on the road and Cicotte made some remark about the mud and Belden said "This isn't nothing to what it was in France and over there we would think this was a drout." Well they's a cemetery on the way out to the pk. and wile we was going past it Buck Weaver made the remark that that was where we left most of the young pitchers every spring so Belden said "You can't scare me with no stuff about cemeterys as I seen to many of them in France." So then Buck says "Is they any subject we can talk about that won't remind you of something you seen in France?" So that shut him up for a wile but after a wile Cicotte asked him what battles he was in over there and he said he was in the Marne and the Oregon forest and Bellow Woods. So Cicotte says "Its no wonder the Germans took such a licking in them places as the whole American army was there." So Belden said oh no they wasn't and what made him think that. So Cicotte said "Because every soldier I have seen that's came back from France was in the Oregon forest and Bellow Woods."

Well we finely got out to the pk. and they wasn't no chance for a real practice on acct. of the mud but Gleason found a dry spot over in 1 corner and marked off the pitching distants and had us all throw a few and honest Al my old super never felt better in my life and I cut loose a couple that pretty near knocked Schalk for a gool but Gleason finely come up and stopped me and told me to not go to strong the 1st. day. Well I watched this Belden wile he throwed a few and I was standing along side of Cicotte and he was watching him to so I asked him what he thought of him. So Cicotte said "He looks like he will make a mighty valuable man for us as when he is in there pitching Schalk can set on the bench and rest as he won't never get nothing past the batter."

Well we finely come out of the pk. and started back towards the hotel and the 1st. thing you know they was a machine come hunking up behind us and it was Miss Krug the St. Louis heiress that's stopping at the hotel and she slowed up and asked if anybody wanted a ride. Well Al she was looking right at me but I pretended like I didn't understand but I just give her a kind of a smile and the next thing you know Belden had ran out and jumped in the drivers seat with her and away they went.

How is that for nerve Al when it was me she was looking at and this other bird that's been in the league about 5 minutes you might say jumps in and rides with her and I bet the little gal felt pretty sick when she seen what she had got wished on to and she didn't come in for supper tonight as I suppose she thought some of the boys would make fun of her though she needn't have no fears on that score as if any of them tried it I would knock them for a gool.

Your pal, JACK.

Mineral Wells, March 29.

FRIEND AL: Well old pal I guess they's no more question about me makeing good and sticking with the club and you will say the same thing when I tell you what Gleason said yesterday. We played a game out to the pk. between the 1st. and 2d. clubs and the game was to go 7 innings and Gleason told me I could pitch a part of it for the 2d. club so my arm was feeling so good that I asked him to let me work 4 of the 7 innings. Well Al when I got through the 1st. club had 1 hit and never found out where 2d. base was located. So when it was over Gleason come up to me and said "Well Jack I don't know what the war done to you but I never seen you look better then that in the spring and right now you look like the best man I have got down here pitching." He said "Now don't go and swell up but keep working hard and do like I tell you and you may turn out to be the bird I need to round out my pitching staff." Well the club was going over to play Ft. Worth and Dallas Saturday and Sunday and I thought of course we would all go along but after my showing yesterday Gleason figured he wouldn't take no chances so he left me here to work out with Faber and Wolfgang wile the rest of the boys is gone. He said "I wouldn't pitch you in either of them games after working you yesterday and I want you to do a little work here with these other 2 boys and behave just like I was here watching you." So I said "What and the he—ll could a man do only behave himself in this town?" Well he said "I mean for you to not try and eat for the whole club just because they are not here to eat for themself."

So you see Al it looks like I had made good right from the start this time and that means they will half to come acrost with more jack before long as Gleason promised before I come south that he would give me more then my contract calls for if I show him the right kind of stuff.

Well the bunch went away early this A.M. and was gone before I got up and I had breakfast with Faber and Wolfgang and we decided to go out and work about 11 o'clock so I and the other 2 went out to the pk. and throwed the ball around a wile and done some running but I got tired pretty quick on acct. of pitching yesterday so pretty soon I said I thought I would call it a day so I started back to the hotel and I hadn't no sooner then got outside of the pk. and all of a sudden along come Miss Krug in her machine.

Well they wasn't no getting away from her this time without turning her down cold so I kind of waved to her and she stopped the machine and I got in and we drove back to the hotel.

Well Al she is some gal and it is a pleasure to talk to a gal like she as you take most gals and they can't kid along with a man but about all as they can do is giggle and act silly but this baby can give you as good as you send.

Well I said "You must be pretty lonesome today with Belden gone." So she said "Oh I don't know." So then I said "He is sure some lady killer." So she said "I'll say so. But you notice I am still alive." So after a wile she said "Belden tells me you was in France too." So I said "You and Belden seems to of talked together a whole lot." "Well" she said "I haven't had no one else to talk to." So I said "Well you have got some one else to talk to now." "Yes" she says "but you always run away from me. I suppose you real stars gets tired of haveing girls run after you." So I said "Oh I don't know."

Well we kidded back and 4th. like that till we come to the hotel and then I asked her was she doing anything this P.M. and she said she had a date with her mother but I took her to the picture show tonight and tomorrow she is going to take me for another ride. Well Al it does a man good to be around with a gal like that that keeps a man on edge what to say next as she always gives you as good as you send and from what she said she must be kind of tired of hearing Belden tell how he win the battle of Bellow Woods and etc. and any way I feel like a little rest would be the best thing for me after pitching them 4 innings yesterday. So I will play around with her tomorrow and then forget her when the bunch gets back Monday

A.M. and go to work in ernest but if a man works to hard right at the start you are libel to go stale.

Well Al I had a letter from Florrie today and little Florrie has got 1 tooth and another 1 showing and she says little Al misses me pretty bad and asks every day why daddy don't hurry up and come home. Well they will all be proud of daddy before this season is over eh Al.

Your pal, JACK.

Mineral Wells, March 31.

FRIEND AL: Well Al the boys is back from Ft. Worth and Dallas and I guess they didn't show up any to good over there and any way Gleason don't look like he enjoyed the trip and he told the boys out to the pk. this P.M. that they would half to show a whole lot more pep or he would leave some of them in Texas all summer to graze.

Well he give us a long work out and he stood behind me wile I throwed a few to Schalkie and he said I didn't look as fast as when I pitched them 4 innings last Friday but he wasn't throwing no boquets at any of the boys today so I didn't pay no tension. But I couldn't help from laughing at 1 of the young catchers name Cosgrove that was standing up there catching in the batting practice and Joe Jackson hit a foul ball straight up and Cosgrove throwed off his mask and begin running a mile around a 4 ft. track and finely the ball came down and hit him in the cheek bone and knocked him for a gool. Well he layed there and the trainer come running out to tend to him but Gleason says "Get away from him as he is just as good laying there as standing up and maybe after this he will know enough to keep his mask on after a high foul ball."

Well it was pretty near supper time when he let us off and I tried to be 1 of the 1st. out of the pk. but they was a whole bunch out ahead of me and when Miss Krug come along with her car they all seen me jump in and you ought to of seen Belden when he seen us drive away together and all the boys yelled their head off.

Well I come back here to the hotel and got dressed and come down for supper and after a wile Gleason come in and I was setting with 3 of the other boys but he made 1 of them get up and give him his seat so as he could set down and kid me.

"Well Jack" he says "I hear you worked pretty hard wile we was gone and I suppose you can pretty near run the car by this time."

Well I knew he wasn't sore at me but just sore on acct. of how rotten the young fellows was showing up so I just give him a smile.

"After this" he says "you and all the whole rest of the club will ride back and 4th between the ball pk. and back on your own dogs. They's to much rideing on this club but after this I will do all of it and everybody on this club will get rode to death if they don't quit loafing on me. So remember every one of you will stay out of machines going to the ball pk. and comeing back and besides that when you go up to your rms. you can use the stairs and take a load off the elevator."

Well Al he may be my mgr. out on the old ball field but he can't tell me how to get upstairs or from 1 place to another but I left him get away with it rather then start trouble in the dining rm. of the hotel in front of the other boys to say nothing of the guests.

But I wonder what he would say if he knew how I spent Sunday. Well old pal I had some time. Miss Krug knows all the roads and we drove pretty near all day and she is some gal Al and smart as a whip. Everything you say to her she has got a come back and for inst. wile we was driveing yesterday she happened to ask me where I come from and I told her Indiana and she said "That's a good place to come from." She meant it was a good place to get away from. So I said "I guess it hasn't got nothing on St. Louis at that." "Oh I don't know" she said.

Well it looks like I had Belden's time beat and I suppose I ought to of left him a clear field on acct. of him being single but the gal says herself that she can't stand him on acct. of him talking about himself all the wile and besides his looks is against him and besides a man has got to amuse themself some way in a burg like this or it would take more then the crazy wells to stop you from turning in to squirrel meat.

Your pal, JACK.

Mineral Wells, April 3.

FRIEND AL: Well Al tomorrow is the last day here as we leave for Houston and play there Saturday and Sunday and then Austin and Georgetown and after that we go to Dallas for a few days and play a couple games there before we start north. Gleason was kidding me again tonight and said he wanted to apologize for the schedule that takes us away from here so soon and if he had of known how I was going to enjoy Mineral Wells he would of arranged to stay here longer. But he said I was to be sure and start in saying good by soon enough so as I would be through by train time. Well Al I wonder what he would say if I told him Miss Krug is going to be in Dallas wile we are there as she is going to drive over there with her mother. It kind of looks like she hates me eh Al?

Well we played another ball game today between the 1st. and 2d club and I pitched 5 innings for the 1st. club and they got 5 runs off of me but most of them was on acct. of the way Weaver and Collins was kicking the ball around the infield and then when they had filled up the bases on me Shano Collins caught a hold of 1 that was a mile over his head and the wind blowed it down in the right field corner and the right field fence in this pk. is as far as from here to France and the ground was hard and of course the dam ball rolled and Shano could of ran around the bases twice so when the inning was over Gleason said to me "When you are pitching to a man like Collins you want to say to yourself I am pitching to Collins and not be thinking about some garbage contractor's daughter from St. Louis." So I said "He hit a ball that was over his head." So Gleason said "Yes and over Leibold's head to." He says "The next time I pick out a spot to train a ball club it will be in a man's convent where they's no gals." So I walked away from him.

But wait till you hear what this Belden pulled today Al. Dureing the game some of the boys was trying their hit and run signs and etc. and they got them all balled up so Gleason made us stay out there after the game was over and practice up on our signs and wile he was talking to some of the boys this Belden cut in and said he thought it would be a good idear if instead of slideing their hand up and down the bat or pulling their cap or something if they would learn a few French words and give their signs in French out loud and they couldn't none of the other clubs understand them and for inst. if a man was up there hitting and wanted the man on 1st. base to go down on the next ball he would holler allay at him on acct. of that being the French for go. So Cicotte said it was a great idear only about the 9th. or 10th. time we worked it on some club and they seen the man go every time they might maybe suspect what it meant and then we would half to find out the Russian word for go and use that and he thought the only Russian word for go meant go back and the base runner would get mixed up and think the batter meant he was going to hit a foul ball.

Well Miss Krug had some engagement with her mother tonight so I went with some of the boys to a picture show and Belden went along with us an 1 of the pictures was old last yr. stuff that showed a lot of different places in France and etc. and every time they would show a picture Cicotte would ask Belden if he was there and he said yes every time and finely Cicotte asked him how long he was in France all together and he said 4 mos, so Cicotte said "Well if you was only in France 4 mos. and seen all them places its no wonder you wasn't shot as you never stood still a minute."

Well Al this is the last letter you will get from me here as I will be busy packing up tomorrow and saying good by to my friends but I will try and drop you a line from Houston or somewheres along the line and let you know how things is comeing on.

Your pal, JACK.

Georgetown, April 8.

FRIEND AL: Well I guess Gleason won't half to worry no more about at least 1 member of his pitching staff after what I done over in Houston Saturday and here again today. I worked 5 innings against the Houston club Saturday and believe me Al they have got some club but I made them look like they ought to of paid their way in. They was only 1 ball got out of the infield and Weaver could of nailed that only he didn't start in time and the rest of the wile they was popping them up in the air or missing them all together. Well Williams the left hander followed me and he was pretty good to though he didn't have anywheres near the stuff I showed but we trimmed them 6 to 0 and Gleason was all smiles.

Well of course I didn't work there again Sunday or yesterday at Austin and the boys didn't look so good behind the pitching they got but today we was up against a bunch of collegers and Gleason sent me the whole distants to see how I could stand it and I guess I showed him. Well Al I honestly felt sorry for some of these college boys and they couldn't of got a base hit off me with a shovel only their teachers and friends was watching them so I eased up in the last 2 innings and they got a couple of base hits and they felt so good about them that I wished I had of let them get some more.

Well Gleason come to me afterwards and he said "Now Jack you look like that 1st. day at the Wells and if you can just keep going like that I have got the 4 pitchers I want to work regular and you are 1 of them. You showed in Houston and here what you can do when you haven't got your mind on some millionaire janitor's daughter from St. Louis with rheumatism on the mother's side. You had a fast ball in there to-day that looked like Johnson at his best and you have pretty near got where you can slow ball them without everybody in the pk. calling it on you. You just keep pitching that way and I will get you some dough that is some dough."

So it looks like I was all set Al and the only thing now is to keep him from finding out about Miss Krug and her mother comeing to Dallas and I don't care if I see her or not only it wouldn't seem hardly fair to have she and her mother come all the way over there and then me not even take her to a picture show. But what Gleason don't know won't hurt him and that stuff about girls bothering me is all in his eye as I can pitch when my arm feels good and I can't pitch when it don't feel good girls or no girls.

Your pal, JACK.

Fort Worth, April 13.

FRIEND AL: Well Al I don't know whether to quit baseball or not and maybe I won't quit if I can get away to some other club but I can't work no more under Gleason and do myself justice.

Wait till you hear what come off in Dallas yesterday and I bet you will say I would be a sucker to stand for the kind of stuff he is trying to put over.

Well Al the second day we was there I got a phone call and it was Miss Krug and her and her mother was stopping at a certain hotel so I asked her would she like to go to a picture show or somewheres and she said she would so I said I would meet her that night and we would go somewheres and see a show. Well I was in the lobby of our hotel when the phone call come and of course they had to page me and Gleason heard them so after I got through phoneing he come up to me and asked if the bell of St. Louis was folling me around. So I said no I supposed she was in Mineral Wells. So he said where was I going that evening and I said nowheres and he said all right he wanted me to go to a picture show with him. So then I said I had forgot I had a date to go with 1 of the other boys on the club so he said all right he would go along with us. Well Al they wasn't no shakeing lose from him so finely I had to own up that I was going to take Miss Krug to a show so he said he would go along and pay for it. Well he went along all right and it was the worst picture I ever seen and when it was over Gleason asked Miss Krug and I if we wouldn't have a soda or something.

Well they wasn't nothing to do only go with him and we hadn't no sooner then give our order when he said to her "What do you think of big Jack here?" Well she said she thought I was all right. So Gleason said "Well I never thought so myself but I guess he must be or he couldn't of never got such a sweet wife like he's got up in Chi." Well I couldn't say nothing or neither could the gal. So then Gleason asked me did I have the Mrs. picture with me or either 1 of the 2 kids. Well Al they's no use telling you any more about it only we had our soda and took the gal back to her hotel and then I and Gleason come back to our hotel together and he never said a word all the way home or neither did I only just before he left me to go up to his rm. he said "You pitch tomorrow Jack" and that's all he said.

Well of course they won't be no more picture shows for Miss Krug and I and of course it don't make no differents to me as I was going to tell her about me being married and everything and her and I was just good friends and liked to talk to each other but its haveing him cut in on my private affairs and try to run them that makes me sore and he must think this is the army the way he acts.

Well Al I pitched the game in Dallas yesterday and they couldn't do nothing with me but I wouldn't of never pitched it at all only they had me advertised and I have got a whole lot of good friends there that I wouldn't disapoint them. But as for sticking with the club after that kind of business I couldn't do myself justice and as soon as we get home I will put it up to Comiskey and ask him to trade me to some other club or else I will quit and go in to some business where a man does his work and gets through and when he is through the mgr. of the store don't go noseing around in to your private affairs.

Your pal, JACK.

Louisville, April 18.

FRIEND AL: Well Al I have only got time for a few lines as we are leaveing in a little wile for Cincy for games tomorrow and Sunday and I am going to pitch 5 innings Sunday and then rest till Wednesday when we open up the season in St. Louis. Gleason hasn't gave it out to the papers yet Al but between you and I it looks like a cinch I would pitch the opening game in St. Louis. Gleason and all the rest of the boys admits that I have been going better then any other pitcher on the club and you know how crazy every club is to win the opening game and that is why it looks like I would be the man that is chose.

Well Al I will give them everything I have got and if I only feel as good as I felt yesterday in Nashville why the St. Louis boys might just as well leave their bats in the bag.

Well I guess the last time I wrote you I was kind of on the outs with Gleason and I didn't speak to him for pretty near a wk. but a man can't stay sore at him very long on acct. of the stuff he pulls and 1st. thing you know you half to bust right out laughing and then of course its good night.

I guess I told you about Belden the young pitcher from Chi that was in France and tried to get us to give our signs in French. Well he was with the 2d. club that left us before we come away from Texas and they went up north the other way and yesterday I was setting in the hotel at Nashville talking to Felsch and Gleason come along and Felsch asked him if he had heard how Belden was comeing along with the 2d. club. So Gleason said "He got along a whole lot faster then the club he was with as he is all ready back in Chi." He said "I wired to Shano Collins and asked him if they was anybody on his 2d. club that looked like he could get along without them so he wired back that he could rap Belden up and send him home because though they wasn't no doubt that he had beat Germany it didn't look like he would ever last 2 innings vs. Boston and Cleveland." So when Gleason pulled that I couldn't help from laughing and then he kicked me in the shins like old times and now we are pals again.

Well I haven't no more time to write from here but will try and drop you a line from Cincy but in the mean wile you can tell the boys that it looks like a cinch I will open the season in St. Louis and if any of them has a chance to get a bet down on your old pal they can't go wrong. I wasn't never as good as I am this spring Al and I will knock them for a gool.

Your pal, JACK.

Cincy, April 20.

FRIEND AL: Well Al just a few words before we go out to the pk. and this will be my last game before the opening and Gleason says I and Lefty Williams will pitch 5 and 4 innings today for a final work out so it looks like a cinch I will open up Wednesday in St. Louis.

Speaking about St. Louis Al I guess I told you about that Miss Krug that was down to the Wells wile we was there and kind of lost her head over me and finely I had to get Gleason to tell her I was a married man. Well I had forgot all about her but this A.M. when I come down for breakfast they was a letter in my box and it was from this same gal and she is back in St. Louis and wanted to know if maybe I couldn't call her up when I get there just for old time sake and any way she said she would be out to the opening game Wednesday and pulling for us even if she is a St. Louis gal.

Well I was reading the letter at breakfast and Gleason come in and asked me what was the news from home and I said I hadn't heard nothing from home since we was in Memphis so he said who was the letter from then. So I said "You may be the mgr. of this ball club but you are not my mother." So he said "No and if I was I would give you a spanking." He says "You don't half to tell me who the letter is from because I can tell by your rosy cheeks who it is from and I can just about tell what's in it." So then I said "All right if you are such a smart Alex they's no use in me telling you anything." So then he asked me what was my home address in Chi as he said he wanted all the boys addresses and phone numbers. So I give him mine and he walked away.

Well Al I have got to get ready to go out to the pk. and give these National Leaguers a treat and I bet by the time I get through with them they will be thanking god that they don't half to look at this kind of pitching all summer or they would hit about 6 and 7–8.

Your pal, JACK.

St. Louis, April 24.

FRIEND AL: Well old pal I suppose by this time you have got a hold of the Chi papers and seen what I done yesterday and all as I have seen so far is the St. Louis papers and every 1 of them says it was 1 of the best pitched games they ever seen for an opening game.

Well Al they couldn't of nobody beat me yesterday and either 1 of the 2 hits I give them could of been scored either way and a specially Sisler's but I guess he ain't bragging much this A.M. at that as I sent him back twice for a drink of water.

Well old pal I have had lots of big days in my career both in baseball and in Uncle Sam's service but I don't believe I was ever so happy in my life as when Schalkie caught that foul ball off of Gedeon and made the last out and the way Gleason and the rest of the boys slapped me on the back.

But wait till I tell you the funny part of it Al. Gleason sent us all to bed early Tuesday night and before I went to the hay he told me to get plenty of rest as he was going to pitch me if I looked good out there before the game.

So I didn't get up till pretty near 9 o'clock and it was a quarter to 10 when I come down for breakfast and when I got in the lobby who do you think was there waiting for me? Well Al it was Florrie, all dolled up like the state fair.

Well to make a short story out of it it seems like Gleason had wrote her a letter from Cincy and asked her to come down here at the club's expense and watch me open up the season but to not say nothing to me about she was comeing and believe me Al it was some surprise and some pleasant surprise to see her and I never seen her look prettier in her life.

Well Al I guess with the stuff I had I could of beat them without her setting there in the stand but just the same I worked a whole lot harder for knowing she was up there watching me and I guess the club won't grudge the jack they spent getting her down here.

Well when we come back to the hotel for dinner last night Gleason come in the dining rm. with us and insisted on buying us a bottle of wine and I never seen nobody in my life so tickled over winning 1 ball game as him. Well of course he has got a good reason to be tickled as he will need all the pitching he can get and me makeing this showing means about half his worrys is gone.

Well you will read about the game in the papers and they isn't much more to write about only I can't help from kind of wondering if Miss Krug was out there and seen it but after all what and the he—ll do I care if she was or wasn't?

Your pal, JACK.

Along Came Ruth

The Saturday Evening Post
JULY 26, 1919

St. Louis, April 26.

FRIEND AL: Well Al this is our last day here and we win the 1st. 2 games and lose yesterday and have got one more game to play and tonight we leave for Detroit. Well if we lose today we will have a even break on the serious and a club that can't do no better than break even with this St. Louis club better take up some other line of business but Gleason instead of useing a little judgement sent a left hander in against them yesterday and they certainly give him a welcome and the more I see of left handers I am certainly glad I pitch with my right arm the way God intended for a man.

Well the boys on our club was feeling pretty cocky the 1st. 2 days about how they could hit but yesterday they could of played in a 16 ft. ring without no ground rules as the most of the time they was missing the ball all together and when they did hit it it acted like a geyser and it was Bert Gallia pitching against us and they all kept saying he didn't have nothing but when he got through with us we didn't have nothing either and that's the way it always goes when a pitcher makes a sucker out of a club he didn't have nothing but when they knock him out of the park he's pretty good.

Well any way I told Gleason last night that it looked like we wouldn't get no better than a even break here unless he stuck me in there to pitch the last game today. So he says "No I was figureing on you to open up in Detroit Sunday but of course if you are afraid of Detroit I can make different plans." So I said "I am not afraid of Detroit or nobody else and you know yourself that they can't no club beat me the way I am going whether its Detroit or no matter who it is." So he said "All right then keep your mouth shut about who is going to pitch because if you are going to manage the club I won't have no job left." Well let him try and run the ball club the way he wants to but if I was running the ball club and had a pitcher that is going the way I am going I would work him every other day and get a start on the other clubs as the games we win now counts just as much as the games we win in Sept.

Well Al Florrie went back to Chi last night though I wanted her to stick with the club and go on to Detroit with us but she said she had to get back, and tend to business at the beauty parlor so I told Gleason that and he said he was sorry she was going to leave us as it was a releif for him to look at something pretty once in wile when most of the time he had to watch ball players but he admired her for tending to business and he wished it run in the family. He says "You should ought to be thankfull that your Mrs. is what she is as most wifes is a drug on their husband but your Mrs. makes more jack then you and if she give up her business it would keep you hustleing to make both ends meet the other, where if you missed a meal some time and died from it your family would be that much ahead." So I said "Yes and that is because your cheapskate ball club is only paying me a salary of $2400.00 per annum instead of somewheres near what I am worth." So he said "I have all ready told you that if you keep working hard and show me something I will tear up your contract and give you a good one but before I do it I will half to find out if you are going to win ball games for me or just use up 1 lower birth like in old times." So I told him to shut his mouth.

Well Al I thought the war with Germany was all over but Joe Jenkins joined the club here and now the whole war is being played over again. He is 1 of the catchers on the club and he was in France and if they was any battles he wasn't in its because he can't pronounce them but anybody that thinks the U.S. troop movements was slow over there ought to listen to some of these birds that's came back and some of them was at Verdun 1 evening and Flanders the next A.M. then down to Nice the next day for a couple hours rest and up in the Oregon forest the folling afternoon and etc. till its no wonder the Germans was dazzled. If some of these birds that was in the war could get around the bases like they did around the western front all as the catchers would dast do when they started to steal second base would be walk up the base line towards third with the ball in their hand and try to scare them from comeing all the way home.

Well its Detroit tomorrow and 3 more days after that and then home and I haven't been there since the middle of March and I guess they's 2 kids that won't be tickled to death to see somebody eh Al?

Your pal, JACK.

Detroit, April 28.

FRIEND AL: Well old pal I suppose you read in the papers what come off here yesterday and I guess Gleason won't have no more to say after this about me being afraid of Detroit. The shoe points the other way now and Detroit is the one that's afraid of me and no wonder.

I didn't have the stuff that I had down to St. Louis for the opening but I had enough to make a monkey out of Cobb and Veach and I couldn't help from feeling sorry for this new outfielder they have got name Flagstaff or something and I guess he was about half mast before I got through with him.

Well its a cinch now that I will open in Chi Thursday and I will give St. Louis another spanking and then I will make Gleason come acrost with that contract he has been promiseing me and if he trys to stall I will tell him he must either give me the jack or trade me to some other club and he has got good sence even if he don't act like it sometimes and they's a fine chance of him tradeing me though they's 7 other clubs in this league that would jump at it and Detroit is 1 of them though the Detroit club would be takeing a big chance if they got a hold of somebody that could realy pitch as the fans up here would die from surprise.

Well I had a letter from Florrie today and it was just like the most of her letters when you got through reading it you wondered what she had in mind and about all as she said was that she had a surprise to tell me when I got home and I use to get all excited when she wrote about them surprises but now I can guess what it is. She probably seen a roach in the apartment or something and any way I guess I can wait till I get home and not burn up the wires trying to find out before hand.

Your pal, Jack.

Detroit, April 30.

Friend Al: Well Al we leave for home tonight and open up the season in Chi tomorrow but I won't be out there pitching unless Gleason apologizes for what he pulled on me last night. It was more rotten weather yesterday just like we been haveing ever since the 1st. day in St. Louis and I near froze to death setting out there on the bench so when we come back to the hotel they was a friend of mine here in Detroit waiting for me here in the lobby and he come up in the room with me and I was still shivering yet with the cold and he said how would I like something to warm me up. So I said "That's a fine line of talk to hand out in a dry town." So he said I could easy get a hold of some refreshments if I realy wanted some and all as I would half to do would be call a bell hop and tell him what I wanted.

Well I felt like a good shot would just about save my life so I called a boy and told him to go fetch me some bourbon and he said O. K. and he went out and come back in about a half hr. and he had a qt. with him and I asked him how much did we owe him and he said $15.00. How is that for reasonable Al and I guess it was the liquor men themselfs that voted Michigan dry and you can't blame them. Well my friend seemed to of had a stroke in his arm so as he couldn't even begin to reach in his pocket so I dug down and got 15 berrys and handed it to the kid and he still stood there yet like he expected a tip so I told him to beat it or I would tip him 1 in the jaw.

Well I asked my friend would he have a shot and his arm was O. K. again and he took the bottle and went to it without waiting for no glass or nothing but he got the neck of the bottle caught in his teeth and before he could pry it loose they was about a quarter of the bourbon gone.

Well I was just going to pore some of it out for myself and all of a sudden they come a rap at the door and I said come in and who walked in but Gleason. So I asked him what did he want.

So he said "Well you wasn't the 1st. one in the dinning rm. so I thought you must be pretty sick so I come up to see what was the matter." Well it was to late to hide the bottle and he come over to the table where I was setting and picked it up and looked at it and then he pored out a couple drops in the glass and tasted it and said it tastes like pretty good stuff. So I said it ought to be pretty good stuff as it cost enough jack so he asked me how much and I told him $15.00.

So he said "Well they's some of the newspaper boys has been asking me to try and get a hold of some stuff for them so I will just take this along."

So I said I guest the newspaper boys could write crazy enough without no help from the Michigan boot legs and besides the bottle belongs to me as I payed good money for it. So Gleason said "Oh I wouldn't think of stealing it off of you but I will take it and pay you for it. You say it cost $15.00 but they's only about $11.00 and a half worth of it left so I will settle with you for $11.00 and a half." Well I didn't want to quarrel with him in the front of a outsider so I didn't say nothing and he took the bottle and started out of the rm. and I said hold on a minute where is my $11.00 and a half? So he said "Oh I am going to fine you $11.00 and a half for haveing liquor in your rm. but instead of takeing the fine out of your check I will take what's left in the bottle and that makes us even." So he walked out.

Well Al only for my friend being here in the rm. I would of took the bottle away from Gleason and cracked his head open with it but I didn't want to make no seen before a outsider as he might tell it around and people would say the White Sox players was fighting with their mgr. So I left Gleason get away with $11.00 and a half worth of bourbon that I payed $15.00 for it and never tasted it and don't know now if it was bourbon or cat nip.

Well my friend said "What kind of a bird are you to let a little scrimp like that make a monkey out of you?" So I said I didn't want to make no seen in the hotel. So he said "Well if it had of been me I would of made a seen even if it was in church." So I says "Well they's no danger of you ever havening a chance to make a seen in church and a specialy with Gleason but if you did make a seen with Gleason you would be in church 3 days later and have a box right up close to the front."

Well Al I have told Gleason before this all ready that I would stand for him manageing me out on the old ball field but I wouldn't stand for him trying to run my private affairs and this time I mean it and if he don't apologize this P.M. or tonight on the train he will be shy of a pitcher tomorrow and will half to open up the home season with 1 of them other 4 flushers that claims they are pitchers but if Jackson and Collins didn't hit in 7 or 8 runs every day they would be beating rugs in the stead of ball clubs.

Well any way we go home tonight and tomorrow I will be where it don't cost no $15.00 per qt. and if Gleason walks in on me he can't only rob me of $.20 worth at a time unless he operates.

Your pal, JACK.

Chi, May 3.

FRIEND AL: Well Al I have just now came back from the ball pk. and will set down and write you a few lines before supper. I give the St. Louis club another good trimming today Al and that is 3 games I have pitched and win them all and only 1 run scored off of me in all 3 games together and that was the 1 the St. Louis club got today and they wouldn't of never had that if Felsch had of been playing right for Tobin. But 1 run off of me in 3 games is going some and I should worry how many runs they scratch in as long as I win the ball game.

Well you know we was to open up here Thursday and it rained and we opened yesterday and I was waiting for Gleason to tell me I was going to pitch and then I was going to tell him I would pitch if he would apologize to me for what he done in Detroit but instead of picking me to pitch he picked Lefty Williams and the crowd was sore at him for not picking me and before the 1st inning was over he was sore at himself and Lefty was enjoying the shower bath. Gallia give us another beating and after it was over Gleason come up to me in the club house and said he was going to start me today. So I said "How about what you pulled on me in Detroit?" So he says "Do you mean about grabbing that bottle off of you?" So I said yes and he says "Look at here Jack you have got a great chance to get somewheres this yr. and if you keep on pitching like the way you started you will make a name for yourself and I will see that you get the jack. But you can't do it and be stewed all the wile so that is the reason I took that bottle off of you." So I said "They's no danger of me being stewed all the wile or any part of the wile when bourbon is $15.00 per qt. and me getting a bat boy's salery." So he said "Well you lay off the old burb and pitch baseball and you won't be getting no bat boy's salery. And besides I have told the newspaper boys that you are going to pitch and it will be in the morning papers and if you don't pitch the bugs will jump out of the stand and knock me for a gool." So as long as he put it up to me that way I couldn't do nothing only say all right.

So sure enough it come out in the papers this A.M. that I was going to pitch and you ought to seen the crowd out there today Al and you ought to heard them when my name was gave out to pitch and when I walked out there on the field. Well I got away to a bad start you might say as Felsch wasn't laying right for Tobin and he got a two base hit on a ball that Felsch ought to of caught in his eye and then after I got rid of Gedeon this Sisler hit at a ball he couldn't hardly reach and it dropped over third base and Tobin scored and after that I made a monkey out of them and the 1st. time I come up to bat the fans give me a traveling bag and I suppose they think I have been running around the country all these yrs. with my night gown in a peach basket but I suppose we can give it to 1 of Florrie's friends next xmas and besides it shows the fans of old Chi have got a warm spot for old Jack.

Speaking about Florrie Al when we was in Detroit she wrote and said she had a surprise for me and I thought little Al had picked up a couple hives or something but no it seems like wile I was on the road she met some partys that runs a beauty parlor down town and they wanted she should sell her interest in the one out south and go in pardners with them and they would give her a third interest for $3000.00 and pay her a salery of $300.00 per mo. and a share of the receits and she could pay for her interest on payments. So she asked me what I thought about it and I said if I was her I would stick to what she had where she was makeing so good but no matter what I thought she would do like she felt like so what was the use of asking me so she said she didn't like to make a move without consulting me. That's a good one Al as the only move she ever made and did consult me about it was when we got married and then it wouldn't of made no differents to her what I said.

Well she will do as she pleases and if she goes into this here down town parlor and gets stung we should worry as I will soon be getting real jack and it looks like a cinch we would be in the world serious besides, and besides that the kids would be better off if she was out of business and could be home with them more as the way it is now they don't hardly ever see anybody only the Swede nurse and 1st. thing as we know they will be saying I ban this and I ban that and staying away from the bldg. all the wile like the janitor.

Your pal, JACK.

Chi, May 6.

FRIEND AL: 4 straight now Al. How is that for a way to start out the season? It was Detroit again today and that is twice I have beat them and twice I have beat St. Louis and it don't look like I was never going to stop. They got 2 runs off of me today but it was after we had 7 and had them licked and I kind of eased up to save the old souper for the Cleveland serious. But I wished you could of heard the 1 I pulled on Cobb. You know I have always kind of had him on the run ever since I come in the league and he would as leaf have falling arches as see me walk out there to pitch.

Well the 1st. time he come up they was 2 out and no one on and I had him 2 strikes and nothing and in place of monking with him I stuck a fast one right through the groove and he took it for a third strike. Well he come up again in the 4th. inning and little Bush was on third base and 1 out and Cobb hit the 1st. ball and hit it pretty good towards left field but Weaver jumped up and stabbed it with his glove hand and then stepped on third base and the side was out. Well Cobb hollered at me and said "You didn't put that strike acrost on me." So I said "No why should I put strikes acrost on you when I can hit your bat and get 2 out at a time?" You ought to of heard the boys give him the laugh.

Well he hit one for 3 bases in the 7th. inning with Bush and Ellison both on and that's how they got their 2 runs but he wouldn't of never hit the ball only I eased up on acct. of the lead we had and besides I felt sorry for him on acct. of the way the crowd was rideing him. So wile he was standing over there on third base I said "You wouldn't of hit that one Ty only I eased up." So he said "Yes I knew you was easeing up and I wouldn't take adantage of you so that's why I bunted."

Well 1 more game with Detroit and then we go down to Cleveland and visit Mr. Speaker and the rest of the boys and Speaker hasn't been going any to good against them barbers that's supposed to pitch for Detroit and St. Louis so God help him when he runs up against Williams and Cicotte and I.

Your pal, JACK.

Cleveland, May 9.

FRIEND AL: Well Gleason told me today he wasn't going to pitch me here till the Sunday game to get the crowd. We have broke even on the 2 games so far and ought to of win them both only for bad pitching but we can't expect to win them all and you really can't blame the boys for not pitching baseball when we run into weather like we have got down here and it seems like every place we go its colder then where we just come from and I have heard about people going crazy with the heat but we will all be crazy with the cold if it keeps up like this way and Speaker was down to our hotel last night and said the Cleveland club had a couple of bushers from the Southren league that's all ready lost their mind and he told us what they pulled off wile the St. Louis club was here.

Well it seems like Cleveland was beat to death 1 day and they thought they would give some of the regulars a rest and they put in a young catcher name Drew and the 1st. time he come up to bat they was men on first and second and 1 out and Sothoron was pitching for St. Louis and 1 of the St. Louis infielders yelled at him "Don't worry about this bird as he will hit into a double play." Well Drew stood up there and took 3 strikes without never takeing the bat off his shoulder so then he come back to the bench and said "Well I crossed them on their double play."

Well in another game Bagby was pitching and he had them licked 8 to 1 in the 7th inning and he had a bad finger so they took him out and sent in a busher name Francis to finish the game. Well he got through 1 inning and when he come up to hit they was a man on 3d. base and 2 out and Davenport was pitching for St. Louis and he was kind of wild and he throwed 3 balls to Francis. So then he throwed a strike and Francis took it and then he throwed one that was over the kid's head but he took a cut at it and hit it over Tobin's head and made 3 bases on it. So when the inning was over Larry Gardner heard him calling himself names and balling himself out and Larry asked him what was the matter and he said he was just thinking that if he had of left that ball go by he would of had a base on balls.

Well I had a letter from Florrie today and she has closed up that deal and sold out her interest in the place out near home and went in pardners in that place down town and she said she thought it was a wise move and she would clean up a big bunch of jack and it won't only take her a little wile to pay for her interest in the new parlor as with what she had saved up and what she got out of the other joint she had over $2000.00 cash to start in with.

Well I don't know who her new pardners is but between you and I it looks to me like she was pulling a boner to leave a place where she knew her pardners was friends and go into pardners with a couple women that's probably old hands at the game and maybe wanted some new capital or something and are libel to get her role and then can her out of the firm but as I say they's no use me trying to tell her what to do and I might just is well tell Gleason to take Collins off of second base and send for Jakey Atz.

Well Al nothing to do till Sunday and if I beat them it will make me 5 straight and you can bet I will beat them Al as I am going like a crazy man and they can't no club stop me.

Your pal, JACK.

Chi, May 12.

Friend Al: Well old pal its kind of late to be setting up writeing a letter but I had a little run in with Florrie tonight and I don't feel like I could go to sleep and besides I don't half to work tomorrow as I win yesterday's game in Cleveland and Gleason is saveing me for the Boston serious.

Well we got in from Cleveland early this A.M. and of course I hurried right home and I was here before 8 o'clock but the Swede said Florrie had left home before 7 as she didn't want to be late on the new job and she would call me up dureing the forenoon. Well it got pretty near time to start over to the ball pk. before the phone rung and it was Florrie and I asked her if she wasn't going to congratulate me and she says what for and I said for what I done in Cleveland yesterday and she said she hadn't had time to look at the paper. So I told her I had win my 5th straight game and she acted about as interested as if I said we had a new mail man so I got kind of sore and told her I would half to hang up and go over to the ball pk. She said she would see me at supper and we hung up.

Well we had a long game this P.M. and it seemed longer on acct. of how anxious I was to get back home and when I finely got here it was half past 6 and no Florrie. Well the Swede said she had called up and said she had to stay down town and have supper with some business friends and she would try and be home early this evening.

Well the kids was put in bed and I tried to set down and eat supper alone and they didn't nothing taste right and finaly I give it up and put on my hat and went out and went in a picture show but it was as old as Pat and Mike so I blew it and went in Kramer's to get a couple drinks but I had kind of promised Gleason to lay off of the hard stuff and you take the beer you get now days and its cheaper to stay home and draw it out of the sink so I come back here and it was 8 bells and still no Florrie.

Well I set down and picked up the evening paper and all of a sudden the phone rung and it was a man's voice and he wanted to know if Mrs. Keefe had got home. So I done some quick thinking and I said "Yes she is here who wants her?" So he said "That's all right. I just wanted to know if she got home O. K." So I said who is it but he had hung up. Well I rung central right back and asked her where that party had called from and she said she didn't know and I asked her what and the he—ll she did know and she begun to play some jazz on my ear drum so I hung up.

Well in about 10 minutes more Florrie come in and come running over to give me a smack like usual when I get back off a trip. But she didn't get by with it. So she asked what was the matter. So I said "They's nothing the matter only they was a bird called up here a wile ago and wanted to know if you was home." So she says "Well what of it?" So I said "I suppose he was 1 of them business friends that you had to stay down town to supper with them." So she said "Maybe he was." So I said "Well you ought to know if he was or not." So she says "Do you think I can tell you who all the people are that calls me up when I haven't even heard their voice? I don't even know a one of the girls that keeps calling up and asking for you." So I said "They don't no gals call up here and ask for me because they have got better sence but even if they did I couldn't help it as they see me out there on the ball field and want to get aquainted."

Then she swelled up and says "It may be hard for you to believe but there is actually men that want to get aquainted with me even if they never did see me out there on the ball field." So I said "You tell me who this bird is that called up on the phone." So she said "I thought they was only the 2 babys in this apartment but it seems like there is 3." So then she went in her rm. and shut the door.

Well Al that's the way it stands and if it wasn't for the kiddies I would pack up and move somewheres else but kiddies or no kiddies she has got to explain herself tomorrow morning and meanwile Al you should ought to thank God that you married a woman that isn't flighty and what if a wife ain't the best looker in the world if she has got something under her hat besides marcel wavers?

Your pal, JACK.

Chi, May 14.

FRIEND AL: Well old pal it looks like your old pal was through working for nothing you might say and by tomorrow night I will be signed up to a new contract calling for a $600.00 raise or $3000.00 per annum. I guess I have all ready told you that Gleason promised to see that I got real jack provide it I showed I wasn't no flash out of the pan and this noon we come to a definite understanding.

We was to open against the Boston club and I called him to 1 side in the club house and asked him if I was to pitch the game. So he says you can suit yourself. So I asked him what he meant and he said "I am going to give you a chance to get real money. If you win your game against the Boston club I will tear up your old contract and give you a contract for $3000.00. And you can pick your own spot. You can work against them today or you can work against them tomorrow just as you feel like. They will probably pitch Mays against us today and Ruth tomorrow and you can take your choice." Well Al Mays has always been good against our club and besides my old souper is better this kind of weather the longer I give it a rest so after I though it over I said I would wait and pitch against Ruth tomorrow. So tomorrow is my big day and you know what I will do to them old pal and if the boys only gets 1 run behind me that is all as I ask.

That's all we got today Al was 1 run but Eddie Cicotte was in there with everything and the 1 run was a plenty. They was only 1 time when they had a chance and it looked that time like they couldn't hardly help from scoreing but Eddie hates to beat this Boston club on acct. they canned him once and he certainly give a exhibition in there that I would of been proud of myself. This inning I am speaking of Scott got on and Schang layed down a bunt and Eddie tried to force Scott at second base but he throwed bad and the ball went to center field and Scott got around to third and Schang to second and they wasn't nobody out. Well Mays hit a fly ball to Jackson but it was so short that Scott didn't dast go in. Then Hooper popped up to Collins and Barry hit the 1st. ball and fouled out to Schalkie. Some pitching eh Al and that is the kind I will show them tomorrow. And another thing Eddie done was make a monkey out of Ruth and struck him out twice and they claim he is a great hitter Al but all you half to do is pitch right to him and pitch the ball anywheres but where he can get a good cut at it.

Well they never had another look in against Eddie and we got a run when Barry booted one on Collins and Jackson plastered one out between Ruth and Strunk for 2 bases.

Well Al I am feeling pretty good again as I and Florrie kind of made up our quarrel last night. She come home to supper and I was still acting kind of cross and she asked me if I was still mopping over that bird that called her up and I didn't say nothing so she said "Well that was a man that was the husband of 1 of the girls I had supper with and he was there to and him and his wife wanted to bring me home but I told them I didn't want nobody to bring me home so his wife probably told him to call up and see if I got home all right as they was worried." So she asked me if I was satisfied and I said I guessed I was but why couldn't she of told me that in the 1st. place and she said because she liked to see me jealous. Well I left her think I was jealous but between you and I it was just a kind of a kid on my part as of course I knew all the wile that she was O.K. only I wanted to make her give in and I knew she would if I just held out and pretended like I was sore. Make them come to you Al is the way to get along with them.

I haven't told Florrie what this game tomorrow means to us as I want to surprise her and if I win I will take her out somewheres on a party tomorrow night. And now old pal I must get to bed as I want to get a good rest before I tackle those birds. Oh you $600.00 baseball game.

Your pal, JACK.

Chi, May 16.

FRIEND AL: Well Al I don't care if school keeps or not and all as I wish is that I could get the flu or something and make a end out of it. I have quit the ball club Al and I have quit home and if I ever go back again to baseball it depends on whether I will have my kiddies to work for or whether they will be warded to her.

It all happened yesterday Al and I better start at the start and tell you what come off. Florrie had eat her breakfast and went down town before I got up but she left word with the ski jumper that she was going to try and get out to the ball game and maybe bring the rest of her pardners with her and show me off to them.

Well to make it a short story I was out to the pk. early and Gleason asked me how I felt and I told him fine and I certainly did Al and Danforth was working against us in batting practice to get us use to a left hander and I was certainly slapping the ball on the pick and Gleason said it looked like I was figureing on winning my own game. Well we got through our batting practice and I looked up to where Florrie usualy sets right in back of our bench but she wasn't there but after a wile it come time for me to warm up and I looked over and Ruth was warming up for them so then I looked up in the stand again and there was Florrie. She was just setting down Al and she wasn't alone.

Well Al I had to look up there twice to make sure I wasn't looking cock eyed. But no I was seeing just what was there and what I seen was she and a man with her if that's what you want to call him.

Well I guess I couldn't of throwed more than 4 or 5 balls when I couldn't stand it no more so I told Lynn to wait a minute and Gleason was busy hitting to the infield so I snuck out under the bench and under the stand and I seen 1 of the ushers and sent word up to Florrie to come down a minute as I wanted to see her. Well I waited and finely she come down and we come to the pt. without waisting no time. I asked her to explain herself and do it quick. So she said "You needn't act so crazy as they's nothing to explain. I said I was going to bring my pardner out here and the gentleman with me is him." "Your pardner" I said "What does a man do in a beauty parlor?" "Well" she said "This man happens to do a whole lot.

"Besides owning two thirds of the business he is 1 of the best artists in the world on quaffs." Well I asked her what and the he—ll was quaffs and she said it meant fixing lady's hair.

Well by this time Gleason had found out I wasn't warming up and sent out to find me. So all as I had time to say was to tell her she better get that bird out of the stand before I come up there and quaffed him in the jaw. Then I had to leave her and go back on the field.

Well I throwed about a dozen more balls to Lynn and then I couldn't throw no more and Gleason come over and asked me what was the matter and I told him nothing so he said "Are you warmed up enough?" and I said "I should say I am."

Well Al to make it a short story pretty soon our names was announced to pitch and I walked out there on the field.

Well when I was throwing them practice balls to Schalk I didn't know if he was behind the plate or up in Comiskey's office and when Hooper stepped in the batters box I seen a dozen of him. Well I don't know what was signed for but I throwed something up there and Hooper hit it to right field for 2 bases. Then I throwed something else to Barry and he cracked it out to Jackson on the 1st. hop so fast that Hooper couldn't only get to third base. Well wile Strunk was up there I guess I must of looked up in the stand again and any way the ball I pitched come closer to the barber then it did to Strunk and before they got it back in the game Hooper had scored and Barry was on third base.

Then Schalkie come running out and asked me what was the matter so I said I didn't know but I thought they was getting our signs. "Well" he said "you certainly crossed them on that one as I didn't sign you for no bench ball." Then he looked over at Gleason to have me took out but Gleason hollered "Let him stay in there and see what kind of a money pitcher he is."

Well Al I didn't get one anywheres near close for Strunk and walked him and it was Ruth's turn. The next thing I seen of the ball it was sailing into the right field bleachers where the black birds sets. And that's all I seen of the ball game.

Well old pal I didn't stop to look up in the stand on the way out and I don't remember changing clothes or nothing but I know I must of rode straight down town and when I woke up this A.M. I was still down town and I haven't called up home or the ball pk. or nowheres else and as far is I am concerned I am through with the both of them as a man can't pitch baseball and have any home life and a man can't have the kind of home life I have got and pitch baseball.

All that worrys me is the kiddies and what will become of them if they don't ward them to me. And another thing I would like to know is who put me to bed in this hotel last night as who ever undressed me forgot to take off my clothes.

Your pal, JACK.

Chi, May 20.

FRIEND AL: Well Al I am writeing this from home and that means that everything is O. K. again as I decided to give in and let bygones be bygones for the kiddies sake and besides I found out that this bird that Florrie is pardners with him is O. K. and got a Mrs. of his own and she works down there with him and Florrie is cleaning up more jack then she could of ever made in the old parlor out south so as long as she is makeing good and everything is O. K. why they would be no sence in me makeing things unpleasant.

Well I told you about me staying down town 1 night and I stayed down till late the next P.M. and finely I called up the Swede and told her to pack up my things as I was comeing out there the next day and get thern. Well the Swede said that Gleason had been there the night before looking for me and he left word that I was to call him up at the ball pk. So I thought maybe he might have a letter out there for me or something or maybe I could persuade him to trade me to some other club so I called him up and just got him before he left the pk. and he asked me where I was at and said he wanted to see me so I give him the name of the hotel where I was stopping and he come down and met me there at 6 o'clock that night.

"Well" he says "I was over to see your little wife last night and I have got a notion to bust you in the jaw." So I asked him what he meant and he said "She sported your kids wile you was in the war and she is doing more than you to sport them now and she goes in pardners with a man that's O. K. and has got a wife of his own that works with him and you act like a big sap and make her cry and pretty near force her out of a good business and all for nothing except that you was born a busher and can't get over it."

So I said to him "You mind your own business and keep out of my business and trade me to some ball club where I can get a square deal and we will all get along a hole lot better." So he said where did I want to be traded and I said Boston. "Oh no" he said. "I would trade you to Boston in a minute only Babe Ruth wouldn't stand for it as he likes to have you on our club." But he said "The 1st. thing is what are you going to do about your family?" So I said I would go back to my family if Florrie would get out of that down town barber shop. So Gleason said "Now listen you are going back home right now tonight and your Mrs. isn't going to sacrifice her business neither." So I said "You can't make me do nothing I don't want to do." So he says "No I can't make you but I can tell your Mrs. about that St. Louis janitor's daughter that was down in Texas and then if she wants to get rid of you she can do it and be better off."

Well Al I thought as long as Florrie was all rapped up in this new business it wasn't right to make her drop it and pull out and besides there was the kiddies to be considered so I decided to not make no trouble. So I promised Gleason to go home that night.

So then I asked him about the ball club. "Well," he said "you still belong to us." "Yes" I said "but I can't work for no $2400.00"

"Well" he said "we are scheduled against a club now that hasn't no Ruths on it and its a club that even you should ought to beat and if you want to try it again why I will leave you pick your day to work against the Philadelphia club and the same bet goes."

So yesterday was the day I picked Al and Roth got a base hit and Burns got a base hit and that's all the base hits they got and the only 2 runs we got I drove in myself. But they was worth $600.00 to me Al and I guess Gleason knows now what kind of a money pitcher I am.

Your pal, JACK.

The Busher Pulls a Mays

The Saturday Evening Post
OCTOBER 18, 1919

N. Y., July 29.

FRIEND AL: Well old pal here we are on the gay white way but they don't nobody on this ball club feel gay and no wonder. In the 1st. place to look at our club you would think we had just came back from the Marne as Gandil was left home in a hospital with appendix and Felsch is so lame that he can't cover no more ground then where his dogs is parked and Cracker Schalk has to be wheeled up to the plate and back you might say and to cap off the climax I got stomach trouble from something I eat or something and wile I don't pitch with my stomach a man can't do themself justice when the old feed bag acts up.

To make it worse Detroit has got a hold of a couple pitchers that can do something besides make 9 men on the field and Jennings club is comeing like a house on fire and all and all it looks like we was a bad bet and will be mighty lucky to get back off of this trip in 1st. place. For inst. Cicotte pitched a nice game today and lose it because they was a couple fly balls hit to center field that Felsch only had to take 3 or 4 steps to get under them but his sick dog layed down on him and wouldn't buge and zowey they went for 3 base hits. So as I say they can call this the gay white way but they can't hardily call us the gay White Sox eh Al.

Well I suppose you seen in the paper what Carl Mays the Boston pitcher pulled off and you will half to hand it to him. He walked out on the Boston club wile they was playing us out in Chi and said he wouldn't pitch no more for the pennant though when the season opened up and they had all their men back from the service we all of us thought they would be the club we would half to beat as they had 2 stars for every position you might say and they could stick 1 club in the field 1 day and a whole different club the next day and 1 of them as good is the other but any way they blowed up like Willard and it got so as they felt cocky when they only lose 1 game per day so Mays said he was through and instead of the club suspending him why they pretty near kissed him you might say and all the other clubs in the league begun biding for him.

Well we would of had him only I guess the Boston club insisted on Gleason giveing them Cocky Collins or Schalk or myself or somebody so of course Gleason give them the razz and finely Huggins got him for the N. Y. club for 4 or 5 ball players and the liberty loan and now Mr. Mays is with a club that has got a chance to get in the world serious and it shows what a sucker a ball player is to stick with a club where you can't get nothing only the worst of it.

Well Al I guess if I was to have a run in now with Gleason or something I will know what to do as the minute he looks X eyed at me I will Mays him and I guess they wouldn't some clubs jump at the chance to get a hold of me and specially Detroit as Jennings is makeing a great fight for the old rag without hardily any pitching at all you might say and what would he do with a man like I on the club to go in there every 3d. day and take my own turn besides helping the other birds out when they begin to weaken.

Well old N. Y. is some dry town since the 1 of July and the only way a man can get a drink here is go in a saloon and the only differents between old times is what they soak you for it now which is plenty but when a man has got to have it he has got to have like today after the game for inst. my old stomach was freting pretty bad and I got myself 6 high balls on the way back from the pk. and it set me back $2.40 but as I say what is $2.40 compared to a man's health.

Your pal, Jack

Boston, Aug. 2.

FRIEND AL: Well Al we are haveing a fine trip and the way we been going you would think we must of clumb in to 1st. place some night after dark but we won't be there long if Gleason don't wake up and use his pitchers right. He acts like Cicotte and Williams was Adam and Eve and they wasn't nobody else in the world and he keeps yelping about what tough shape he is in on acct. of not only haveing 2 pitchers and as far is the rest of us is conserned we might as well be takeing tickets.

Well a man can't hardily blame him for going slow with birds like Kerr and Faber and Lowdermilk that when they do throw a ball somewheres close to the plate somebody's bat gets in the way but just because I lose them games to the St. Louis and N. Y. clubs in Chi with my stomach why that isn't no reason I should spend August with my feet on the water cooler and as I said to Gleason today he might as well of left me home and he says yes and the rest of the club to.

Well you don't see Jennings trying to cop the old rag with 2 pitchers but he works his staff in turn like a mgr. should and some A.M. we will wake up and find ourself a few laps behind Detroit instead of leading them and all because Jennings gives his pitchers a chance but instead of Gleason giveing me a chance he sets around and mones about what tough shape we are in and if he could only get a hold of some pitcher like Page with the Phila. club but it looks to me like if Page was so dam good the Athaletics would get rid of him. We have all ready signed up Pat Ragan that every club in the National League tried him and I don't know what and the he—ll they can expect him to do here where a man has got to have something besides acquaintences in all the big citys and it looks to me like Gleason has went plain cuckoo and it wouldn't surprise me to see him bark like a dog.

Well I suppose you seen where Ban Johnson stepped in and suspend it Mays after it come out that the N. Y. club had boughten him and I don't see what Ban has got to say about it now and I suppose we will be reading pretty soon where he has plastered a $5.00 fine on Hap Felsch for limping.

Ban said a few yrs. ago that Ty Cobb wouldn't never play another game in this league but the last time we played the Detroit club they had somebody in center field that looked a whole lot like Cobb and Jennings and the rest of the boys called him Ty.

Well this old burg isn't running as wide open as N. Y. and if a man wants a little refreshmunts they have got to go out and hunt for it like tonight I and 1 of the boys thought we better lay in a qt. to last over the sabath and 1 of the boys on the Boston club told us where to go get it so we got a qt. of it and it cost $7.00 and that means $7.00 a drink as they couldn't nobody in the world take more then 1 swallow and I wouldn't be surprised if that is what ails the Boston club. They are poisoned. Well the qt. all but 2 drinks is standing on my burro and that is where it is going to spend the sabath and when we leave here I will give it to the chamber horse for a tip and tell her what it cost and she will know she died a high price death. In the old days when we was here on a Sunday they closed up the bars but you could walk in the hotel cafe and order up a drink as long is you ordered sandwichs with it and if they knowed you they would bring you the same sandwichs every trip.

Well 1 more game here Monday and then we go to Philly and

maybe we will win 1 there as we have got 4 to play and if Mack ever win 4 in a row he would put on a auction sale.

Your pal, Jack.

Phila., Aug. 4.

FRIEND AL: Well Al just a line to let you know I am here in Philly and the club still up in Boston yet and don't get here till tomorrow. Well that means that I am going to take my regular turn from now on and will start against this club either tomorrow or the next day and Gleason sent me on ahead to rest up along with Cicotte. You see in the old days the ball clubs use to get a party rate on the R. R. and it saved them money to all travel together from town to town but now everybody has got to pay full fare so if a mgr. wants to send a couple of his star pitchers a day or 2 ahead to the next town to rest them up why it don't cost nothing so that is how it come that I and Cicotte is here in Phila.

I didn't have no idear I was comeing on ahead till yesterday A.M. when I run in to Gleason in the hotel dinning rm. up in Boston and he motioned me to come and set down with him. Well he said how is your heart so I asked him what did he mean. "Well" he says "in them last 2 games you pitched vs. St. Louis and N. Y. out in Chi it looked to me like you was missing." So I said I guest my heart was O. K. but my stomach had been freting me on acct. of something I eat. I said "I would of made them 2 clubs look like a bum only a man can't work when your stomach aint right." "No" he says "and your stomach won't never get right on that liquid diet." So I asked him what he meant and he says you know what I mean and I should think you would get wise to yourself. So I says I guest I was wise enough so he says "Well if your wise you will cut out the rough stuff and get to work." So I asked him how could I get to work when he wouldn't give me no chance and he said "I will tell you what I will do with you. Cicotte is going over to Phila. tonight to rest up and you can go along with him and rest up includeing your stomach and if you aint in shape to pitch when I call on you it won't be nobody's fault only your own. And remember they won't be nobody over there watching you and you can behave yourself or not just as you feel like but when I get there I will know if you been behaveing."

So he had Joe O'Neill buy me a ticket and birth and I and Cicotte got here this A.M. and have the whole day to ourself and maybe we will go out this P.M. and see the game as the St. Louis club is playing here and besides we will have a chance to study Mack's batters. They are some study Al but maybe we can set where we can watch foxy Connie waggle his score card and maybe get his signs though it looks to me like he would do a whole lot better if he give up his score card long enough to have a few good ball players names printed on it.

Well 1 of the waiters here in the hotel tells me a man can get all they want to drink here in Phila. if they go at it right but nothing doing Al as I am going to be in shape to give Gleason the best I got though 3 or 4 wouldn't hurt me and what Gleason don't know won't hurt him.

Your pal, Jack.

Phila., Aug. 6.

FRIEND AL: Well Al I guess they's no use of a man trying to go along with a mgr. that has went cuckoo and if it wasn't for the rest of the boys on the club I would pull a Mays and walk out on the club and go to some club where a man can get a square deal but if I done that it might maybe cost this club the pennant and it wouldn't be the right thing towards the rest of the boys.

Well I guess I told you that I and Cicotte was sent on here ahead of the rest of the club to rest up so as we would be in good shape for the serious here and we layed around the hotel here all Monday A.M. and after lunch Eddie said he was going out to the ball pk. and did I want to go along. Well I said I guest I seen enough of baseball without spending 2 P.M. looking at a couple clubs like Burke and

Mack has got a hold of and the more a man seen of Mack's club why the lest he would know about how to pitch to them and besides the best thing for me would be to get my mind off of baseball. So Eddie went out to the game and pretty soon I got kind of lonesome so I called up a friend of mine that is quite a fan and we found a place where you can still get it and we histed a few and then he said how about running down to Atlantic City.

Well Al we went down there and seen the sights and took a dip and my friend says he wondered why all the queens was giveing us the double O as they didn't never pay no tension to him when he was alone so I just laughed and didn't say nothing and didn't even look X eyed at 1 of them as I leave the flirting game to birds that hasn't no wife or no respect for the ones they have got so we got a dinj to dig us up a qt. and we was comeing back here at 11 P.M. but they must of been sleeping powders or something in that stuff we got and any way we layed down on the beach to rest for a few minutes after supper and the both of us overslept ourselfs and missed the train. Well Al we finely got back here at 9 o'clock yesterday A.M. and the club was all ready here and Gleason was setting in the lobby when I come in. Well he said where have you been. So I told him I had been out for a walk and he didn't say nothing so I come up to my rm. and layed down.

Well when we got out to the ball pk. he had both Cicotte and I take our turn in batting practice and when it come time to warm up he said it would be me. Well I didn't feel any to good but I warmed up pretty good and finely the game started and I hadn't pitched for pretty near 2 wks. and no wonder I couldn't start right out as good as ever but instead of giveing me a chance to get started he halls me out of there after I walked the 1st. 2 men. Well Cicotte went in and I come in to the bench and Gleason begin to rave and I said how can a man pitch when you don't even leave him get started. "Well" he says "you was out for 1 walk this morning and you was out for 2 walks this afternoon and I thought 3 walks a day would be enough for you." "Where was you last night?" he says and I told him nowheres. So he said "Yes you was. You was out for a board walk down to Atlantic City and I have got a notion to board walk you 1 in the jaw."

Well Al I don't know how he could of knew where I had been but I am not the kind that trys to lie out of something so I says yes I went down to Atlantic City and took a dip. So he says you mean you took a dipper. Well they's no use argueing with a crazy man Al so all as I could do was walk away from him before my temper got the best of me so I went in the club house and dressed and went up in the stand and watched the rest of the game. Well they didn't score off of Cicotte and we got 1 run in the 11th. off of Page and beat them 1 to 0 but I might of shut them out just the way Cicotte done if he had of left me in there but he has went cuckoo Al and to show you how bad he is he has signed up Mayer that has been in the National League 20 or 30 yrs. and the next thing you know he will be sending for Geo. Van Haltren or somebody. Well I only wished I was off this club and I would walk out on them in a minute only for the rest of the boys that has got their heart set on winning.

Your pal, Jack

Washington, Aug. 9.

FRIEND AL: Well old pal don't be surprised if you pick up a paper some A.M. and see where I have walked out on this bunch of cuckoos and pulled a Mays on them only it won't be no 2 or 3 wks. before I land somewheres else as they's a certain club in this league that would give their eye to get a hold of me as it would mean the pennant. Don't think I am bosting Al as I am just giveing you the facts and when I tell you what come off yesterday you will know who I refer. Even if the deal don't come off I can give Gleason a good scare and maybe come to some kind of a understanding with him.

Well yesterday was our last day in Philly and the Detroit club had finished up their serious in Washington the day before and their whole bunch was over in Philly yesterday and out to see our game. Well afterwards we seen the whole bunch of them and Jennings kind of smiled at me like he wanted to see me alone so I give him the chance and he says what was on my mind. So I seen he was trying to give me a opening so I said I was tired of pitching for Gleason. So he says "Well I been watching the box scores where you pitched lately and it didn't look to me like you was pitching for Gleason." He is a great kidder Al but that is just his way.

Well he humed and haud and finely he says they was no use him talking to me as Gleason wouldn't trade no pitcher to a club that was fighting him for the pennant. So I said maybe he wouldn't trade me but suppose I walked out on him like Mays done on Boston why then maybe he would give me to the club that made the best offer.

So Jennings said "Yes but we tried to get Mays but all as we could offer for him was jack and we couldn't offer nothing else for you and when a club offers money to Comiskey why it is like takeing coal to a castle."

So I said "Well it looks to me like it would be to your int. to offer something besides jack as Gleason could use a couple of your ball players." Yes said Jennings but when you begin talking trade to Gleason he can't only talk in words of 1 sylable Cobb and Bush. Well I said if I make up my mind to walk out on him Cleveland or N. Y. will get me either 1 and you know what that means. So he says "I guess you won't go to neither 1 of them clubs." That is what he said Al and they's only 1 way to take it but at that it wasn't so much what he said as how he looked when he said it. He kind of half smiled and give me a kind of a wink and walked away from me and besides he was scared to make it to strong as a mgr. of a club is not supposed to temper with a player on another club. But last night just before we left for here I seen Bush of the Detroit club and I told him what had came off and he says why didn't I go ahead and pull a Mays and see what happened. He says "We are going to win the pennant any way so you better take a chance of getting on a live 1."

Well old pal I am not going to do nothing I will be sorry for and if our club wakes up and begins to show something I won't leave them in the lerch but Gleason better get help to himself or he will wake up some A.M. and I won't be around for him to snarl at me.

Well comeing over on the train I set with 1 of the reporters that travels with the club and he told me that Gleason had been trying to get this here Page that pitched the 11 innings game vs. Cicotte and Gleason wanted to pay cash for him but Mack must of been unconscious or something and any way he turned it down so it looks like Gleason would half to struggle along without Mr. Page and I guess we will get along just as good without him as from what I seen of him you could write up the game on his fast ball wile its comeing up there but maybe he would bring us luck as a bird that can make us go 11 innings for 1 run must have god with him.

Well I asked this reporter if Gleason had said anything about me lately and he said nothing that could be printed so I said well maybe I will have a story for you 1 of these mornings so he asked me what I meant and I said well if Gleason didn't give me a square deal I would maybe pull a Mays on him and go to some club where I can get fair treatmunt. "Well" he says "if I was you I would cut out that line of talk as it may get back to Gleason and he will beat you to it." Well Al I should worry if it gets back to Gleason or not as it might give him a scare but I don't want him to know nothing about it yet a wile till I see how things comes along so I haven't told nobody about my plans only a couple of the boys on the club that knows enough to keep their mouth shut and in the mean wile mum is the word till we see how matters comes along.

Your pal, Jack.

On Train, Aug 12.

FRIEND AL: Well old pal we are on our way back to old Chi and everybody is happy even the Washington club though we took 2 out of 3 from them but they made more jack out of our serious then they ever seen before and what is 2 or 3 ball games to them you might say. Well Gleason didn't start me but you notice he stuck me in there yesterday in the 8th inning when Lefty Williams begin to wilt and put the brakes on them and that ball Judge hit would have been nuts for Gandil only for him being weak on acct. of his appendix.

Well when Gleason 1st. told me to go in there I had a notion to go in there and dink the ball up there and let the Washington boys get their name in the averages for once in their life and show Gleason I didn't give a dam but then I thought of the rest of the boys and it wasn't square to them to not give them the best I got so I cut loose and you see what happened.

Well Gleason patted me on the back when it was over and tried to give me the old oil but I just kind of smiled and pertended like I fell for it but that is the way he is Al when you win you are aces but when you have a bad day your as welcome is a gangrene.

Well it looks now like we would go right through and win the old rag as everybody has got so as they can waggle their legs without groaning and Gandil will soon have his strength back and then look out as about all as we half to do is break even and Detroit will have 1 he—ll of a time catching up with us so it looks like your old pal will get in once on the world serious dough and about time after all I have did for this club and would of been in on it in 1917 only I give up everything for my country wile the rest of the boys stayed home and made nasty remarks about the Kaiser.

Speaking about the world serious Al it looks now like Cincinnati would give the Giants some battle in the other league and if Moran can keep his club going they have got a good chance and I guess that old burg wouldn't go cuckoo if they win a championship. Well I guess the ball pk. down there can't handle the crowd that we would draw in the Polo Grounds but even if we can't make as much jack out of a serious down there all the boys on our club would about as leaf play them as it would save us time as we can get it over in 4 days if we play them where it would probably take 5 days vs. N. Y. on acct. of 1 day to make the jump. The boys was talking this

A.M. about what Cicotte and Williams should ought to do to Moran's club and they would make a bum out of them and etc. but I guess after what I showed in Washington Gleason can't do no lest then start me in 1 game at the outside and then we will see if Roush and Groh is such wales when they get up vs. real pitching after the dead arm Dicks they been looking at all season.

Well old pal it is pretty near time to stick the old nose in the old feed bag and we land in old Chi this P.M. and no game tomorrow but Thursday we open up vs. Boston and I suppose it will be Cicotte as Gleason sent him on ahead to get ready. Well if he can't cut her they's others on the old pitching staff that can and 1 of them is

Your pal, Jack.

Chi, Aug 15.

FRIEND AL: Well Al I suppose you seen what the Boston club done to Cicotte yesterday and Gleason had to take him out so as Felsch and Liebold could stand still and rest a minute but when he come in to the bench all as Gleason said to him was better luck next time Ed instead of fuming at the mouth like he done to me in Philly. So I said to Gleason I says "You send this bird on ahead of the club to be ready for this game and they make a bum out of him and all as you say to him is better luck next time Ed and the same thing came off in Philly the day I started and you went cuckoo and barked like a dog." So Gleason says "Yes you big stiff but the reason they got to Eddie was because he didn't have no stuff when he got in there but your trouble was that you had to much stuff before you ever went in." So I just laughed at him.

Well it looks more then ever like Pat Moran was going to cop in the other league the way his club made a bum out of the Giants in the serious down there and I was just thinking tonight if the big show comes off in Cincinnati why couldn't you hop on a train and breeze down there for the 1st. game that is scheduled down there and maybe that will be the game I pitch or 1 of them and it would tickle me to death to know my old pal was up there in the stand pulling for me and I promise you won't be ashamed of saying your my friend when you see me out there. It wouldn't only cost you about $6.00 or $7.00 R. R. fare and you wouldn't half to bother about no ticket to the game as the boys on our club can get 2 of them a peace to every game at the regular prices and I would leave you use 1 of mine 1 day and it wouldn't only cost you $2.00 or $3.00 and after the game we could go somewheres and hist a few as its a cinch they have still got some tucked away somewheres in that old burg as even the babys would die down there without their beer.

Maybe you will think you shouldn't ought to take no trip like that and leave Bertha home but between you and I Al the ladys is a nusance when it comes to a trip like that and besides no matter how good a man and their wife gets along when you have lived with them a few yrs. its like a sweet dream to be away from them a day or 2. Think it over Al and leave me know how you feel about it and I would say come up to 1 of the games here only what with the Swede and the 2 kids we wouldn't have no place to park you and besides we could have a better time somewheres where Florrie wasn't folling us around all the wile like a caboose.

Speaking about Florrie we had a long talk last night and it seems like she is about ready to sell out her share in the beauty parlor as she don't get along very good with the Dumonts and besides as I always say a womans place is home so I guess she is about through pairing finger nails and etc. and I am glad of it as with my salery and what I pick up in the world serious and etc. I guess they won't be no over the hills to the poor house for Mr. and Mrs. Keefe yet a wile.

Your pal, Jack.

Chi, Aug. 20.

FRIEND AL: Well Al I and Gleason had some words today and I guess he knows now where I stand and if he don't why it is his own look out. We was playing the Washington club and Nick Altrock was out on the coaching line and I begin to kid him from the bench and I hollered hello handsome at him. So he turned around and hollered why hello Carl I didn't know you was still with us. So Gleason says why is he calling you Carl and I said I didn't know so Gleason says "Yes you do he is calling you Carl after Carl Mays because you told some of the boys you was going to Mays me and walk out on the club and Nick has heard about it." So I said "Well maybe I did say that in a jokeing way." So Gleason says "What was the joke." So I said "Well maybe they wasn't no joke but I just made the remark to some of the boys that I liked to pitch and it looked like they wasn't no chance for me to pitch here so I wished I was somewheres where I could pitch." So Gleason said "Well I will send you somewheres where you can pitch." So I said "I can pitch here if you will give me a chance." "Well" Gleason says "I am not running this club to muse you but I am trying to win a pennant and I can't take no chances with a bird that has only turned out 2 good innings for me in a month." So I said "Well I can't turn out no more good innings till you stick me in there." So Gleason said "Well I will stick you in there when I get good in ready and if you want to walk out on me why walk as far is you like." So I says "I don't half to walk as the Michigan Central will take me as far is I want to go." So that shut him up Al as he knows now that if I jumped I would have a place to light and he can't afford to strengthen a club that is right on our tail you might say.

You have got to hand it to Jennings for the race they are makeing Al though we been going good to thanks to a whole lot of luck like today for inst. Cicotte was in there against a Swede name Erickson that the Washington club got from Detroit and the boys went out and got 10 runs for Eddie and a man that can't win with 10 runs better study for a janitor or something and a specially vs. the Washington club that if they ever scored 10 runs in 1 day the other clubs would ask for a recount. Well this Erickson certainly was good and the only boys on our club that could hit him was those that batted against him. Well Al you never see them pile up 10 runs behind me when I am in there pitching and about the only way as we can score at all with me in there is 3 bases on balls and a balk.

Well Al Florrie told the Dumonts today that she was going to quit them and sell out her share of the business and they wasn't no tears shed on neither side. She hasn't only payed in about $250.00 for the stock they was going to sell her so she will have that comeing besides a few dollars salery as she had drew ahead. Any way I am glad she is out of it and can stay home and pay a little tension to the kiddies and we are going to throw a party. Sat. night to celebrate and as long is you can't be here Al why I suppose I will half to hist a couple for you.

Your pal, Jack.

Chi, Aug. 25.

FRIEND AL: Well Al I am through. Not through with pitching baseball but through working for a cuckoo that treats a man like a dog. They's only I condition that I will go back to him Al and that is a contract calling for more money or a bonus or something and he has got to understand that I work in my regular turn which is the only way a pitcher can do themself justice. But he won't agree to my turns Al as trying to manage a ball club has went to his head and his brains has been A. W. O. L. for the last 2 mos. you might say. So it's going to be moveing day pretty soon for your old pal and I guess you know where I am going to move without me telling you. I have all ready wired a telegram to Jennings telling him what come off and things ought to begin to pop by tomorrow at lease.

Well Al I will tell you what come off and you can judge for yourself what kind of a cuckoo this bird is. Well the last half of last wk. he had me down in the bull pen every day warming up though he didn't have no intentions of sticking me in there and God knows I was warm enough without going out and looking for it but every time I would ease up a little and try and rest he would look down there from the bench and motion to me to get busy and by the time the game was over Sat. P.M. my old souper squeeked like a rat every time I throwed a ball.

Well Sat. night we throwed a party over to the house in honor of Florrie retireing from business and I had 4 qts. of the old hard stuff layed away and I and a couple of Florrie's friends husbands finished 1 of them before supper and after supper we turned on the jazz and triped the life fantastic and I half to be oiled or I can't dance so by 11 o'clock the serch and sieze her birds could of had the run of the house and welcome. Well 1 of the husbands said he knowed a place where they had escaped from the epidemic so we went down there and they served us rat poison in tea cups and I only histed a couple to be polite but I eat something that didn't set right and when I finely got home and put on my night gown I wished it was a sroud.

Well Al I couldn't eat nothing when I got up and whatever it was I had eat the night before had gave me a fever and Florrie wanted I should call up the ball pk. and tell them I was sick but it was Williams's turn to pitch and I thought all as I would half to do would be get down in the bull pen and go through the motions but when I get to the pk. what does this cuckoo do but tell me to take my turn in the batting practice as I am going to work. So I asked him what was the matter with Williams and Gleason said he don't feel good. "Well" I said "if he felt like I do his family would be out shopping for 1 left handed casket." So Gleason said what and the he—ll is the matter with you now. So I told him my stomach. "Well" said Gleason "get in there and give them your fast one and curve and I will tell Schalk not to sign for your stomach." So that was all as I could get out of him Al and they wasn't nothing to do only grip my teeth and try and make the best of it.

Well Al to make a short story out of it I went in there so dizzy that Vick of the N. Y. club looked like he was hitting from both sides of the plate and I tried to throw a ball between him. Well I seen him fall over but he couldn't get out of the way as I catched him right over the ear and if I had of had my regular stuff on the ball they would of been brains splashing clear up in the grand stand. Well I got 1 over for Peck and he past it up and then Schalk thought they was going to hit and run so he signed me to waist 1 and I waisted 4 and then up come Baker and I had 2 balls and nothing on him and I looked in to the bench but Gleason wasn't looking at me and I looked out to the bull pen and they wasn't nobody warming up so I pitched again and got 1 over the plate. Well I don't know what kind of baseball it is for a man to hit with 2 and 0 with birds on 1st. and 2d. and nobody out and the pitcher hog wild but that is what this bird done Al is take a lunge at the ball and Liebold couldn't of catched it without a pass out check.

Well I looked in to the bench again and Gleason didn't say I yes or no but I wasn't going to stay out there and faint away for him or no other cuckoo. So I walked in to the dug out and said I'm through. "Through with what" Gleason says. "Through with a mgr. like you that makes a man go in there and try to pitch when I am so sick I don't know what I am doing." So Gleason said "That is the way you have always pitched." So I said "Well I am not going to pitch that way or no other way for you no more but I am going to pitch for a mgr. that don't ask a man to work when he is only 2 laps this side of a corps." Who are you going to pitch for? I am going to pitch for Detroit. "Well" says Gleason "that puts them out of the race as Jennings is so crazy now that he eats grass and when you get there he will start in on his ball club." Well I said something back to him and went in the club house.

That is what come off Al and I will leave it to you if I didn't do right as how can a man work for a cuckoo that makes a bench lizard out of you for a mo. and then pitchs you 64 innings in 3 days in the bull pen and then when your sick and wore out and your souper whines every time you raise it.

Well he as much is said he wished I would go to Detroit so he can't go back on that Al or try and block the deal so as I say I wired a telegram to Jennings that I am through here and for him to hurry up with his offer.

Well Gleason and the club leaves to-night for St. Louis and I have been kind of expecting that he would call up and try and square things with me but not a peep out of him and as I say he is so cuckoo that he probably won't come down off of his horse. But I should worry Al as I will soon be with a club that can win the pennant with a little help and I am the bird that can give them the kind of help they need.

I will keep you posted Al and let you know the minute I hear news. In the mean wile come on you Tigers.

Your pal, Jack.

Chi, Aug. 29.

FRIEND AL: Well Al no news yet and I called up the ball pk. today to see if maybe they wasn't a telegram there for me though I wired Jennings my home address. They wasn't no telegram there and I don't know what to think only it may be that Jennings is wireing back and 4th. to Gleason trying to make the trade and they can't agree on turns. Well Gleason is not a sucker enough to not make some kind of a deal when he knows that I won't never work for him again but or course its natural for him to hold out for the best man he can get and its natural for Jennings to not give more for me than he has to. But if it comes to a show down you can bet that Jennings will give up anybody he has to outside of Cobb or maybe Bush and I wouldn't be surprised if the final deal was me for Bob Veach and no money on the side. The White Sox has got room for another outfielder God knows wile on the other hand Veach's strength is hitting which is waisted in Detroit as they can all hit up there but dam few of them can pitch.

Of course Veach is in the game every day where most pitchers don't only work about every 4th. day but for a man like Jennings I would go in there every day the rest of the season if he asked me and work my head off to bring the old flag home to Detroit.

In the mean wile I should worry as news is sure to come sooner or later and I and Florrie is enjoying ourselfs and getting acquainted with the kiddies and still got enough jack to keep the wolfs from the door a couple of wks. at the outside.

Your pal, Jack.

Chi, Aug. 31.

FRIEND AL: Well Al I suppose you seen the news in the paper Sat. and I am leaveing for the east tonight to join my new pals. Don't never get it in your head Al that I am not tickled to death to play for Connie Mack as he has always had my respect even if the Athaletics has been tail enders for the last few yrs. He has got the right idear Al and that is to build up a young ball club and learn them the game and by the time they are ready they are still young enough to play their best baseball and when they get good they don't win 1 championship and then crall back in their hole to die but they win 3 or 4 in a row and get enough jack to live in ease and luxery the rest of their life. Besides Al a man that plays ball for Mack knows that he will be treated like a gentleman and not barked at like a dog when things goes wrong.

Well Al the news come to me in a funny way. I was out late Friday night and overslept myself and when I woke up Florrie was up and dressed and I heard her in the next rm. and it sounded like she was sobing. Well I couldn't figure what and the he—ll she had to whine about so I hollered to her and she come in with the morning paper in 1 hand and her nose in the other. "Oh Jack" she says "its in the paper." So I said what was in the paper and she says "They have traded you to Philadelphia you and $5000.00 for Page."

Well for a minute I felt kind of stuned and then I snatched the paper out of her hand and read it over and over again and finely I got it through my head that it was true and Florrie was still snuffleing and I guess maybe I snuffled a little to.

Well finely I seen they wasn't no use makeing a baby out of ourselfs so I griped my teeth and I says "Well lets cut out the sob stuff as this here story don't mean nothing in our young life. They can trade me to Philadelphia for all the Pages in the book but I won't go." So Florrie spruced up to and she says "That's right you just tell them they can either send you to some decent club or you will quit the game for good."

So for a wile we talked along that line Al but Sat. P.M. I said something about going down town for supper and take in a picture show and Florrie begin to snuffle again. We can't afford no partys now she said. She says "You haven't no job and I haven't and we have got less then $200.00 to our name and what is going to become of us."

Well we stayed home and we talked things over and to make a short story out of it we seen where we was makeing a sucker out of ourselfs as when you come to think of it they's no better town in the league to live in then Phila. and its near Atlantic City so as Florrie and the kids can be down there all summer you might say and I can go down nights when the club is playing at home and Florrie thinks maybe she can get in a beauty parlor there and make enough jack to help out this winter.

So all and all Al I am tickled to death the way things has came along and wile I won't get in the world serious this yr. its the long run that counts after all and when we do get going in Philly it will still be a young ball club yet that can stand the pace and cop the old rag 2 or 3 seasons in a row. And about that time Gleason's club and Jennings's to will be in the old folks home lapping up gruel.

Well I have looked up the schedule and Detroit comes to Philly the 9 of Sept. and the White Sox the 13 and I am going to ask Connie to let me work twice against the both of them and then I will show Gleason and Jennings what a fool they made out of themself and what kind of a pitcher old Jack Keefe is when I am working for a man that can talk to you without barking like a dog.

Your pal, Jack.

II

Alibi Ike and Friends

Alibi Ike

Saturday Evening Post
JULY 31, 1915

I

HIS RIGHT NAME WAS Frank X. Farrell, and I guess the X stood for "Excuse me." Because he never pulled a play, good or bad, on or off the field, without apologizin' for it.

"Alibi Ike" was the name Carey wished on him the first day he reported down South. O' course we all cut out the "Alibi" part of it right away for the fear he would overhear it and bust somebody. But we called him "Ike" right to his face and the rest of it was understood by everybody on the club except Ike himself.

He ast me one time, he says:

"What do you all call me Ike for? I ain't no Yid."

"Carey give you the name," I says. "It's his nickname for everybody he takes a likin' to."

"He mustn't have only a few friends then," says Ike. "I never heard him say 'Ike' to nobody else."

But I was goin' to tell you about Carey namin' him. We'd been workin' out two weeks and the pitchers was showin' somethin' when this bird joined us. His first day out he stood up there so good and took such a reef at the old pill that he had everyone lookin'. Then him and Carey was together in left field, catchin' fungoes, and it was after we was through for the day that Carey told me about him.

"What do you think of Alibi Ike?" ast Carey.

"Who's that?" I says.

"This here Farrell in the outfield," says Carey.

"He looks like he could hit," I says.

"Yes," says Carey, "but he can't hit near as good as he can apologize."

Then Carey went on to tell me what Ike had been pullin' out there. He'd dropped the first fly ball that was hit to him and told Carey his glove wasn't broke in good yet, and Carey says the glove could easy of been Kid Gleason's gran'father. He made a whale of a catch out o' the next one and Carey says "Nice work!" or somethin' like that, but Ike says he could of caught the ball with his back turned only he slipped when he started after it and, besides that, the air currents fooled him.

"I thought you done well to get to the ball," says Carey.

"I ought to been settin' under it," says Ike.

"What did you hit last year?" Carey ast him.

"I had malaria most o' the season," says Ike, "I wound up with .356."

"Where would I have to go to get malaria?" says Carey, but Ike didn't wise up.

I and Carey and him set at the same table together for supper. It took him half an hour longer'n us to eat because he had to excuse himself every time he lifted his fork.

"Doctor told me I needed starch," he'd say, and then toss a

shovelful o' potatoes into him. Or, "They ain't much meat on one o' these chops," he'd tell us, and grab another one. Or he'd say: "Nothin' like onions for a cold," and then he'd dip into the perfumery.

"Better try that apple sauce," says Carey. "It'll help your malaria."

"Whose malaria?" says Ike. He'd forgot already why he didn't only hit .356 last year.

I and Carey begin to lead him on.

"Whereabout did you say your home was?" I ast him.

"I live with my folks," he says. "We live in Kansas City—not right down in the business part—outside a ways."

"How's that come?" says Carey. "I should think you'd get rooms in the post office."

But Ike was too busy curin' his cold to get that one.

"Are you married?" I ast him.

"No," he says. "I never run round much with girls, except to shows onct in a wile and parties and dances and roller skatin'."

"Never take 'em to the prize fights, eh?" says Carey.

"We don't have no real good bouts," says Ike. "Just bush stuff. And I never figured a boxin' match was a place for the ladies."

Well, after supper he pulled a cigar out and lit it. I was just goin' to ask him what he done it for, but he beat me to it.

"Kind o' rests a man to smoke after a good work-out," he says. "Kind o' settles a man's supper, too."

"Looks like a pretty good cigar," says Carey.

"Yes," says Ike. "A friend o' mind give it to me—a fella in Kansas City that runs a billiard room."

"Do you play billiards?" I ast him.

"I used to play a fair game," he says. "I'm all out o' practice now—can't hardly make a shot."

We coaxed him into a four-handed battle, him and Carey against Jack Mack and I. Say, he couldn't play billiards as good as Willie Hoppe; not quite. But to hear him tell it, he didn't make a good shot all evenin'. I'd leave him an awful-lookin' layout and he'd gather 'em up in one try and then run a couple o' hundred, and between every carom he'd say he'd put too much stuff on the ball, or the English didn't take, or the table wasn't true, or his stick was crooked, or somethin'. And all the time he had the balls actin' like they was Dutch soliders and him Kaiser William. We started out to play fifty points, but we had to make it a thousand so as I and Jack and Carey could try the table.

The four of us set round the lobby a wile after we was through playin', and when it got along toward bedtime Carey whispered to me and says:

"Ike'd like to go to bed, but he can't think up no excuse."

Carey hadn't hardly finished whisperin' when Ike got up and pulled it:

"Well, good night, boys," he says. "I ain't sleepy, but I got some gravel in my shoes and it's killin' my feet."

We knowed he hadn't never left the hotel since we'd came in from the grounds and changed our clo'es. So Carey says:

"I should think they'd take them gravel pits out o' the billiard room."

But Ike was already on his way to the elevator, limpin'.

"He's got the world beat," says Carey to Jack and I. "I've knew lots o' guys that had an alibi for every mistake they made; I've heard pitchers say that the ball slipped when somebody cracked one off'n 'em; I've heard infielders complain of a sore arm after heavin' one into the stand, and I've saw outfields tooken sick with a dizzy spell when they've misjudged a fly ball. But this baby can't even go to bed without apologizin', and I bet he excuses himself to the razor when he gets ready to shave."

"And at that," says Jack, "he's goin' to make us a good man."

"Yes," says Carey, "unless rheumatism keeps his battin' average down to .400."

Well, sir, Ike kept whalin' away at the ball all through the trip till everybody knowed he'd won a job. Cap had him in there regular the last few exhibition games and told the newspaper boys a week before the season opened that he was goin' to start him in Kane's place.

"You're there, kid," says Carey to Ike, the night Cap made the 'nnouncement. "They ain't many boys that wins a big league berth their third year out."

"I'd of been up here a year ago," says Ike, "only I was bent over all season with lumbago."

II

IT RAINED DOWN in Cincinnati one day and somebody organized a little game o' cards. They was shy two men to make six and ast I and Carey to play.

"I'm with you if you get Ike and make it seven-handed," says Carey. So they got a hold of Ike and we went up to Smitty's room.

"I pretty near forgot how many you deal," says Ike. "It's been a long wile since I played."

I and Carey give each other the wink, and sure enough, he was just as ig'orant about poker as billiards. About the second hand, the pot was opened two or three ahead of him, and they was three in when it come his turn. It cost a buck, and he throwed in two.

"It's raised, boys," somebody says.

"Gosh, that's right, I did raise it," said Ike.

"Take out a buck if you didn't mean to tilt her," says Carey.

"No," says Ike, "I'll leave it go."

Well, it was raised back at him and then he made another mistake and raised again. They was only three left in when the draw come. Smitty'd opened with a pair o' kings and he didn't help 'em. Ike stood pat. The guy that'd raised him back was flushin' and he didn't fill. So Smitty checked and Ike bet and didn't get no call. He tossed his hand away, but I grabbed it and give it a look. He had king, queen, jack and two tens. Alibi Ike he must have seen me peekin', for he leaned over and whispered to me.

"I overlooked my hand," he says. "I thought all the wile it was a straight."

"Yes," I says, "that's why you raised twice by mistake."

They was another pot that he come into with tens and fours. It was tilted a couple o' times and two o' the strong fellas drawed ahead of Ike. They each drawed one. So Ike throwed away his little pair and come out with four tens. And they was four treys against him. Carey'd looked at Ike's discards and then he says:

"This lucky bum busted two pair."

"No, no, I didn't," says Ike.

"Yes, yes, you did," says Carey, and showed us the two fours.

"What do you know about that?" says Ike. "I'd of swore one was a five spot."

Well, we hadn't had no pay day yet, and after a wile everybody except Ike was goin' shy. I could see him gettin' restless and I was wonderin' how he'd make the get-away. He tried two or three times. "I got to buy some collars before supper," he says.

"No hurry," says Smitty. "The stores here keeps open all night in April."

After a minute he opened up again.

"My uncle out in Nebraska ain't expected to live," he says. "I ought to send a telegram."

"Would that save him?" says Carey.

"No, it sure wouldn't," says Ike, "but I ought to leave my old man know where I'm at."

"When did you hear about your uncle?" says Carey.

"Just this mornin'," says Ike.

"Who told you?" ast Carey.

"I got a wire from my old man," says Ike.

"Well," says Carey, "your old man knows you're still here yet this afternoon if you was here this mornin'. Trains leavin' Cincinnati in the middle o' the day don't carry no ball clubs."

"Yes," says Ike, "that's true. But he don't know where I'm goin' to be next week."

"Ain't he got no schedule?" ast Carey.

"I sent him one openin' day," says Ike, "but it takes mail a long time to get to Idaho."

"I thought your old man lived in Kansas City," says Carey.

"He does when he's home," says Ike.

"But now," says Carey, "I s'pose he's went to Idaho so as he can be near your sick uncle in Nebraska."

"He's visitin' my other uncle in Idaho."

"Then how does he keep posted about your sick uncle?" ast Carey.

"He don't," says Ike. "He don't even know my other uncle's sick. That's why I ought to wire and tell him."

"Good night!" says Carey.

"What town in Idaho is your old man at?" I says.

Ike thought it over.

"No town at all," he says. "But he's near a town."

"Near what town?" I says.

"Yuma," says Ike.

Well, by this time he'd lost two or three pots and he was desperate. We was playin' just as fast as we could, because we seen we couldn't hold him much longer. But he was tryin' so hard to frame an escape that he couldn't pay no attention to the cards, and it looked like we'd get his whole pile away from him if we could make him stick.

The telephone saved him. The minute it begun to ring, five of us jumped for it. But Ike was there first.

"Yes," he says, answerin' it. "This is him. I'll come right down."

And he slammed up the receiver and beat it out o' the door without even sayin' good-by.

"Smitty'd ought to locked the door," says Carey.

"What did he win?" ast Carey.

We figured it up—sixty-odd bucks.

"And the next time we ask him to play," says Carey, "his fingers will be so stiff he can't hold the cards."

Well, we set round a wile talkin' it over, and pretty soon the telephone rung again. Smitty answered it. It was a friend of his'n from Hamilton and he wanted to know why Smitty didn't hurry down. He was the one that had called before and Ike had told him he was Smitty.

"Ike'd ought to split with Smitty's friend," says Carey.

"No," I says, "he'll need all he won. It costs money to buy collars and to send telegrams from Cincinnati to your old man in Texas and keep him posted on the health o' your uncle in Cedar Rapids, D.C."

III

AND YOU OUGHT TO heard him out there on that field! They wasn't a day when he didn't pull six or seven, and it didn't make no difference whether he was goin' good or bad. If he popped up in the pinch he should of made a base hit and the reason he didn't was so-and-so. And if he cracked one for three bases he ought to had a home run, only the ball wasn't lively, or the wind brought it back, or he tripped on a lump o' dirt, roundin' first base.

They was one afternoon in New York when he beat all records. Big Marquard was workin' against us and he was good.

In the first innin' Ike hit one clear over that right field stand, but it was a few feet foul. Then he got another foul and then the count come to two and two. Then Rube slipped one acrost on him and he was called out.

"What do you know about that!" he says afterward on the bench. "I lost count. I thought it was three and one, and I took a strike."

"You took a strike all right," says Carey. "Even the umps knowed it was a strike."

"Yes," says Ike, "but you can bet I wouldn't of took it if I'd knew it was the third one. The score board had it wrong."

"That score board ain't for you to look at," says Cap. "It's for you to hit that old pill against."

"Well," says Ike, "I could of hit that one over the score board if I'd knew it was the third."

"Was it a good ball?" I says.

"Well, no, it wasn't," says Ike. "It was inside."

"How far inside?" says Carey.

"Oh, two or three inches or half a foot," says Ike.

"I guess you wouldn't of threatened the score board with it then," says Cap.

"I'd of pulled it down the right foul line if I hadn't thought he'd call it a ball," says Ike.

Well, in New York's part o' the innin' Doyle cracked one and Ike run back a mile and a half and caught it with one hand. We was all sayin' what a whale of a play it was, but he had to apologize just the same as for gettin' struck out.

"That stand's so high," he says, "that a man don't never see a ball till it's right on top o' you."

"Didn't you see that one?" ast Cap.

"Not at first," says Ike; "not till it raised up above the roof o' the stand."

"Then why did you start back as soon as the ball was hit?" says Cap.

"I knowed by the sound that he'd got a good hold of it," says Ike.

"Yes," says Cap, "but how'd you know what direction to run in?"

"Doyle usually hits 'em that way, the way I run," says Ike.

"Why don't you play blindfolded?" says Carey.

"Might as well, with that big high stand to bother a man," says Ike. "If I could of saw the ball all the time I'd of got it in my hip pocket."

Along in the fifth we was one run to the bad and Ike got on with one out. On the first ball throwed to Smitty, Ike went down. The ball was outside and Meyers throwed Ike out by ten feet.

You could see Ike's lips movin' all the way to the bench and when he got there he had his piece learned.

"Why didn't he swing?" he says.

"Why didn't you wait for his sign?" says Cap.

"He give me his sign," says Ike.

"What is his sign with you?" says Cap.

"Pickin' up some dirt with his right hand," says Ike.

"Well, I didn't see him do it," Cap says.

"He done it all right," says Ike.

Well, Smitty went out and they wasn't no more argument till they come in for the next innin'. Then Cap opened it up.

"You fellas better get your signs straight," he says.

"Do you mean me?" says Smitty.

"Yes," Cap says. "What's your sign with Ike?"

"Slidin my left hand up to the end o' the bat and back," says Smitty.

"Do you hear that, Ike?" ast Cap.

"What of it?" says Ike.

"You says his sign was pickin' up dirt and he says it's slidin his hand. Which is right?"

"I'm right," says Smitty. "But if you're arguin' about him goin' last innin', I didn't give him no sign."

"You pulled your cap down with your right hand, didn't you?" ast Ike.

"Well, s'pose I did," says Smitty. "That don't mean nothin'. I never told you to take that for a sign, did I?"

"I thought maybe you meant to tell me and forgot," says Ike.

They couldn't none of us answer that and they wouldn't of been no more said if Ike had of shut up. But wile we was settin' there Carey got on with two out and stole second clean.

"There!" says Ike. "That's what I was tryin' to do and I'd of got away with it if Smitty'd swang and bothered the Indian."

"Oh!" says Smitty. "You was tryin' to steal then, was you? I thought you claimed I give you the hit and run."

"I didn't claim no such a thing," says Ike. "I thought maybe you might of gave me a sign, but I was goin' anyway because I thought I had a good start."

Cap prob'ly would of hit him with a bat, only just about that time Doyle booted one on Hayes and Carey come acrost with the run that tied.

Well, we go into the ninth finally, one and one, and Marquard walks McDonald with nobody out.

"Lay it down," says Cap to Ike.

And Ike goes up there with orders to bunt and cracks the first ball into that right-field stand! It was fair this time, and we're two ahead, but I didn't think about that at the time. I was too busy watchin' Cap's face. First he turned pale and then he got red as fire and then he got blue and purple, and finally he just laid back and busted out laughin'. So we wasn't afraid to laugh ourselfs when we seen him doin' it, and when Ike come in everybody on the bench was in hysterics.

But instead o' takin' advantage, Ike had to try and excuse himself. His play was to shut up and he didn't know how to make it.

"Well," he says, "if I hadn't hit quite so quick at that one I bet it'd of cleared the center-field fence."

Cap stopped laughin'.

"It'll cost you plain fifty," he says.

"What for?" says Ike.

"When I say 'bunt' I mean 'bunt,'" says Cap.

"You didn't say 'bunt,'" says Ike.

"I says 'Lay it down,'" says Cap. "If that don't mean 'bunt,' what does it mean?"

"'Lay it down' means 'bunt' all right," says Ike, "but I understood you to say 'Lay on it.'"

"All right," says Cap, "and the little misunderstandin' will cost you fifty."

Ike didn't say nothin' for a few minutes. Then he had another bright idear.

"I was just kiddin' about misunderstandin' you," he says. "I knowed you wanted me to bunt."

"Well, then, why didn't you bunt?" ast Cap.

"I was goin' to on the next ball," says Ike. "But I thought if I took a good wallop I'd have 'em all fooled. So I walloped at the first one to fool 'em, and I didn't have no intention o' hittin' it."

"You tried to miss it, did you?" says Cap.

"Yes," says Ike.

"How'd you happen to hit it?" ast Cap.

"Well," Ike says, "I was lookin' for him to throw me a fast one and I was goin' to swing under it. But he come with a hook and I met it right square where I was swingin' to go under the fast one."

"Great!" says Cap. "Boys," he says, "Ike's learned how to hit Marquard's curve. Pretend a fast one's comin' and then try to miss it. It's a good thing to know and Ike'd ought to be willin' to pay for the lesson. So I'm goin' to make it a hundred instead o' fifty."

The game wound up 3 to 1. The fine didn't go, because Ike hit like a wild man all through that trip and we made pretty near a cleanup. The night we went to Philly I got him cornered in the car and I says to him:

"Forget them alibis for a wile and tell me somethin'. What'd you do that for, swing that time against Marquard when you was told to bunt?"

"I'll tell you," he says. "That ball he throwed me looked just like the one I struck out on in the first innin' and I wanted to show Cap what I could of done to that other one if I'd knew it was the third strike."

"But," I says, "the one you struck out on in the first innin' was a fast ball."

"So was the one I cracked in the ninth," says Ike.

IV

You've saw Cap's wife, o' course. Well, her sister's about twict as good-lookin' as her, and that's goin' some.

Cap took his missus down to St. Louis the second trip and the other one come down from St. Joe to visit her. Her name is Dolly, and some doll is right.

Well, Cap was goin' to take the two sisters to a show and he wanted a beau for Dolly. He left it to her and she picked Ike. He'd hit three on the nose that afternoon—off'n Sallee, too.

They fell for each other that first evenin'. Cap told us how it come off. She begin flatterin' Ike for the star game he'd played and o' course he begin excusin' himself for not doin' better. So she thought he was modest and it went strong with her. And she believed everything he said and that made her solid with him—that and her makeup. They was together every mornin' and evenin' for the five days we was there. In the afternoons Ike played the grandest ball you ever see, hittin' and runnin' the bases like a fool and catchin' everything that stayed in the park.

I told Cap, I says: "You'd ought to keep the doll with us and he'd make Cobb's figures look sick."

But Dolly had to go back to St. Joe and we come home for a long serious.

Well, for the next three weeks Ike had a letter to read every day and he'd set in the clubhouse readin' it till mornin' practice was half over. Cap didn't say nothin' to him, because he was goin' so good. But I and Carey wasted a lot of our time tryin' to get him to own up who the letters was from. Fine chanct!

"What are you readin'?" Carey'd say. "A bill?"

"No," Ike'd say, "not exactly a bill. It's a letter from a fella I used to go to school with."

"High school or college?" I'd ask him.

"College," he'd say.

"What college?" I'd say.

Then he'd stall a wile and then he'd say:

"I didn't go to the college myself, but my friend went there."

"How did it happen you didn't go?" Carey'd ask him.

"Well," he'd say, "they wasn't no colleges near where I lived."

"Didn't you live in Kansas City?" I'd say to him.

One time he'd say he did and another time he didn't. One time he says he lived in Michigan.

"Where at?" says Carey.

"Near Detroit," he says.

"Well," I says, "Detroit's near Ann Arbor and that's where they got the university."

"Yes," says Ike, "they got it there now, but they didn't have it there then."

"I come pretty near goin' to Syracuse," I says, "only they wasn't no railroads runnin' through there in them days."

"Where'd this friend o' yours go to college?" says Carey.

"I forget now," says Ike.

"Was it Carlisle?" ast Carey.

"No," says Ike, "his folks wasn't very well off."

"That's what barred me from Smith," I says.

"I was goin' to tackle Cornell's," says Carey, "but the doctor told me I'd have hay fever if I didn't stay up North."

"Your friend writes long letters," I says.

"Yes," says Ike; "he's tellin' me about a ball player."

"Where does he play?" ast Carey.

"Down in the Texas League—Fort Wayne," says Ike.

"It looks like a girl's writin'," Carey says.

"A girl wrote it," says Ike. "That's my friend's sister, writin' for him."

"Didn't they teach writin' at this here college where he went?" says Carey.

"Sure," Ike says, "they taught writin', but he got his hand cut off in a railroad wreck."

"How long ago?" I says.

"Right after he got out o' college," says Ike.

"Well," I says, "I should think he'd of learned to write with his left hand by this time."

"It's his left hand that was cut off," says Ike; "and he was left-handed."

"You get a letter every day," says Carey. "They're all the same writin'. Is he tellin' you about a different ball player every time he writes?"

"No," Ike says. "It's the same ball player. He just tells me what he does every day."

"From the size o' the letters, they don't play nothin' but double-headers down there," says Carey.

We figured that Ike spent most of his evenin's answerin' the letters from his "friend's sister," so we kept tryin' to date him up for shows and parties to see how he'd duck out of 'em. He was bugs over spaghetti, so we told him one day that they was goin' to be a big feed of it over to Joe's that night and he was invited.

"How long'll it last?" he says.

"Well," we says, "we're goin' right over there after the game and stay till they close up."

"I can't go," he says, "unless they leave me come home at eight bells."

"Nothin' doin'," says Carey. "Joe'd get sore."

"I can't go then," says Ike.

"Why not?" I ast him.

"Well," he says, "my landlady locks up the house at eight and I left my key home."

"You can come and stay with me," says Carey.

"No," he says, "I can't sleep in a strange bed."

"How do you get along when we're on the road?" says I.

"I don't never sleep the first night anywheres," he says. "After that I'm all right."

"You'll have time to chase home and get your key right after the game," I told him.

"The key ain't home," says Ike. "I lent it to one o' the other fellas and he's went out o' town and took it with him."

"Couldn't you borry another key off'n the landlady?" Carey ast him.

"No," he says, "that's the only one they is."

Well, the day before we started East again, Ike come into the clubhouse all smiles.

"Your birthday?" I ast him.

"No," he says.

"What do you feel so good about?" I says.

"Got a letter from my old man," he says. "My uncle's goin' to get well."

"Is that the one in Nebraska?" says I.

"Not right in Nebraska," says Ike. "Near there."

But afterwards we got the right dope from Cap. Dolly'd blew in from Missouri and was goin' to make the trip with her sister.

V

Well, I want to alibi Carey and I for what come off in Boston. If we'd of had any idear what we was doin', we'd never did it. They wasn't nobody outside o' maybe Ike and the dame that felt worse over it than I and Carey.

The first two days we didn't see nothin' of Ike and her except out to the park. The rest o' the time they was sight-seein' over to Cambridge and down to Revere and out to Brook-a-line and all the other places where the rubes go.

But when we come into the beanery after the third game Cap's wife called us over.

"If you want to see somethin' pretty," she says, "look at the third finger on Sis's left hand."

Well, o' course we knowed before we looked that it wasn't going' to be no hangnail. Nobody was su'prised when Dolly blew into the dinin' room with it—a rock that Ike'd bought off'n Diamond Joe the first trip to New York. Only o' course it'd been set into a lady's-size ring instead o' the automobile tire he'd been wearin'.

Cap and his missus and Ike and Dolly ett supper together, only Ike didn't eat nothin', but just set there blushin' and spillin' things on the tablecloth. I heard him excusin' himself for not havin' no appetite. He says he couldn't never eat when he was clost to the ocean. He'd forgot about them sixty-five oysters he destroyed the first night o' the trip before.

He was goin' to take her to a show, so after supper he went upstairs to change his collar. She had to doll up, too, and o' course Ike was through long before her.

If you remember the hotel in Boston, they's a little parlor where the piano's at and then they's another little parlor openin' off o' that. Well, when Ike come down Smitty was playin' a few chords and I and Carey was harmonizin'. We seen Ike go up to the desk to leave his key and we called him in. He tried to duck away, but we wouldn't stand for it.

We ast him what he was all duded up for and he says he was goin' to the theayter.

"Goin' alone?" says Carey.

"No," he says, "a friend o' mine's goin' with me."

"What do you say if we go along?" says Carey.

"I ain't only got two tickets," he says.

"Well," says Carey, "we can go down there with you and buy our own seats; maybe we can all get together."

"No," says Ike. "They ain't no more seats. They're all sold out."

"We can buy some off'n the scalpers," says Carey.

"I wouldn't if I was you," says Ike. "They say the show's rotten."

"What are you goin' for, then?" I ast.

"I didn't hear about it bein' rotten till I got the tickets," he says.

"Well," I says, "if you don't want to go I'll buy the tickets from you."

"No," says Ike, "I wouldn't want to cheat you. I'm stung and I'll just have to stand for it."

"What are you goin' to do with the girl, leave her here at the hotel?" I says.

"What girl?" says Ike.

"The girl you ett supper with," I says.

"Oh," he says, "we just happened to go into the dinin' room together, that's all. Cap wanted I should set down with 'em."

"I noticed," says Carey, "that she happened to be wearin' that rock you bought off'n Diamond Joe."

"Yes," says Ike. "I lent it to her for a wile."

"Did you lend her the new ring that goes with it?" I says.

"She had that already," says Ike. "She lost the set out of it."

"I wouldn't trust no strange girl with a rock o' mine," says Carey.

"Oh, I guess she's all right," Ike says. "Besides, I was tired o' the stone. When a girl asks you for somethin', what are you goin' to do?"

He started out toward the desk, but we flagged him.

"Wait a minute!" Carey says. "I got a bet with Sam here, and it's up to you to settle it."

"Well," says Ike, "make it snappy. My friend'll be here any minute."

"I bet," says Carey, "that you and that girl was engaged to be married."

"Nothin' to it," says Ike.

"Now look here," says Carey, "this is goin' to cost me real money if I lose. Cut out the alibi stuff and give it to us straight. Cap's wife just as good as told us you was roped."

Ike blushed like a kid.

"Well, boys," he says, "I may as well own up. You win, Carey."

"Yatta boy!" says Carey. "Congratulations!"

"You got a swell girl, Ike," I says.

"She's a peach," says Smitty.

"Well, I guess she's O.K.," says Ike. "I don't know much about girls."

"Didn't you never run round with 'em?" I says.

"Oh, yes, plenty of 'em," says Ike. "But I never seen none I'd fall for."

"That is, till you seen this one," says Carey.

"Well," says Ike, "this one's O. K., but I wasn't thinkin' about gettin' married yet a wile."

"Who done the askin'—her?" says Carey.

"Oh, no," says Ike, "but sometimes a man don't know what he's gettin' into. Take a good-lookin' girl, and a man gen'ally almost always does about what she wants him to."

"They couldn't no girl lasso me unless I wanted to be lassooed," says Smitty.

"Oh, I don't know," says Ike. "When a fella gets to feelin' sorry for one of 'em it's all off."

Well, we left him go after shakin' hands all round. But he didn't take Dolly to no show that night. Some time while we was talkin' she'd came into that other parlor and she'd stood there and heard us. I don't know how much she heard. But it was enough. Dolly and Cap's missus took the midnight train for New York. And from there Cap's wife sent her on her way back to Missouri.

She'd left the ring and a note for Ike with the clerk. But we didn't ask Ike if the note was from his friend in Fort Wayne, Texas.

VI

WHEN WE'D CAME TO Boston Ike was hittin' plain .397. When we got back home he'd fell off to pretty near nothin'. He hadn't drove one out o' the infield in any o' them other Eastern parks, and he didn't even give no excuse for it.

To show you how bad he was, he struck out three times in Brooklyn one day and never opened his trap when Cap ast him what was the matter. Before, if he'd whiffed oncet in a game he'd of wrote a book tellin' why.

Well, we dropped from first place to fifth in four weeks and we was still goin' down. I and Carey was about the only ones in the club that spoke to each other, and all as we did was remind ourself o' what a boner we'd pulled.

"It's goin' to beat us out o' the big money," says Carey.

"Yes," I says. "I don't want to knock my own ball club, but it looks like a one-man team, and when that one man's dauber's down we couldn't trim our whiskers."

"We ought to knew better," says Carey.

"Yes," I says, "but why should a man pull an alibi for bein' engaged to such a bearcat as she was?"

"He shouldn't," says Carey. "But I and you knowed he would or we'd never started talkin' to him about it. He wasn't no more ashamed o' the girl than I am of a regular base hit. But he just can't come clean on no subjec'."

Cap had the whole story, and I and Carey was as pop'lar with him as an umpire.

"What do you want me to do, Cap?" Carey'd say to him before goin' up to hit.

"Use your own judgment," Cap'd tell him. "We want to lose another game."

But finally, one night in Pittsburgh, Cap had a letter from his missus and he come to us with it.

"You fellas," he says, "is the ones that put us on the bum, and if you're sorry I think they's a chancet for you to make good. The old lady's out to St. Joe and she's been tryin' her hardest to fix things up. She's explained that Ike don't mean nothin' with his talk; I've wrote and explained that to Dolly, too. But the old lady says that Dolly says that she can't believe it. But Dolly's still stuck on this baby, and she's pinin' away just the same as Ike. And the old lady says she thinks if you two fellas would write to the girl and explain how you was always kiddin'; with Ike and leadin' him on, and how the ball club was all shot to pieces since Ike quit hittin', and how he acted like he was goin' to kill himself, and this and that, she'd fall for it and maybe soften down. Dolly, the old lady says, would believe you before she'd believe I and the old lady, because she thinks it's her we're sorry for, and not him."

Well, I and Carey was only too glad to try and see what we could do. But it wasn't no snap. We wrote about eight letters before we got one that looked good. Then we give it to the stenographer and had it wrote out on a typewriter and both of us signed it.

It was Carey's idear that made the letter good. He stuck in somethin' about the world's serious money that our wives wasn't goin' to spend unless she took pity on a "boy who was so shy and modest that he was afraid to come right out and say that he had asked such a beautiful and handsome girl to become his bride."

That's prob'ly what got her, or maybe she couldn't of held out much longer anyway. It was four days after we sent the letter that Cap heard from his missus again. We was in Cincinnati.

"We've won," he says to us. "The old lady says that Dolly says she'll give him another chancet. But the old lady says it won't do no good for Ike to write a letter. He'll have to go out there."

"Send him to-night," says Carey.

"I'll pay half his fare," I says.

"I'll pay the other half," says Carey.

"No," says Cap, "the club'll pay his expenses. I'll send him scoutin'."

"Are you goin' to send him to-night?"

"Sure," says Cap. "But I'm goin' to break the news to him right now. It's time we win a ball game."

So in the clubhouse, just before the game, Cap told him. And I certainly felt sorry for Rube Benton and Red Ames that afternoon! I and Carey was standin' in front o' the hotel that night when Ike come out with his suitcase.

"Sent home?" I says to him.

"No," he says, "I'm goin' scoutin'."

"Where to?" I says. "Fort Wayne?"

"No, not exactly," he says.

"Well," says Carey, "have a good time."

"I ain't lookin' for no good time," says Ike. "I says I was goin' scoutin'."

"Well, then," says Carey, "I hope you see somebody you like."

"And you better have a drink before you go," I says.

"Well," says Ike, "they claim it helps a cold."

My Roomy

The Saturday Evening Post
MAY 9, 1914

I

No—I AIN'T SIGNED for next year; but there won't be no trouble about that. The dough part of it is all fixed up. John and me talked it over and I'll sign as soon as they send me a contract. All I told him was that he'd have to let me pick my own roommate after this and not sic no wild man on to me.

You know I didn't hit much the last two months o' the season. Some o' the boys, I notice, wrote some stuff about me gettin' old and losin' my battin' eye. That's all bunk! The reason I didn't hit was because I wasn't gettin' enough sleep. And the reason for that was Mr. Elliott.

He wasn't with us after the last part o' May, but I roomed with him long enough to get the insomny. I was the only guy in the club game enough to stand for him; but I was sorry afterward that I done it, because it sure did put a crimp in my little old average.

And do you know where he is now? I got a letter today and I'll read it to you. No—I guess I better tell you somethin' about him first. You fellers never got acquainted with him and you ought to hear the dope to understand the letter. I'll make it as short as I can.

He didn't play in no league last year. He was with some semi-pros over in Michigan and somebody writes John about him. So John sends Needham over to look at him. Tom stayed there Saturday and Sunday, and seen him work twice. He was playin' the outfield, but as luck would have it they wasn't a fly ball hit in his direction in both games. A base hit was made out his way and he booted it, and that's the only report Tom could get on his fieldin'. But he wallops two over the wall in one day and they catch two line drives off him. The next day he gets four blows and two o' them is triples.

So Tom comes back and tells John the guy is a whale of a hitter and fast as Cobb, but he don't know nothin' about his fieldin'. Then John signs him to a contract—twelve hundred or somethin' like that. We'd been in Tampa a week before he showed up. Then he comes to the hotel and just sits round all day, without tellin' nobody who he was. Finally the bellhops was going to chase him out and he says he's one o' the ballplayers. Then the clerk gets John to go over and talk to him. He tells John his name and says he hasn't had nothin' to eat for three days, because he was broke. John told me afterward that he'd drew about three hundred in advance—last winter sometime. Well, they took him in the dinin' room and they tell me he inhaled about four meals at once. That night they roomed him with Heine.

Next mornin' Heine and me walks out to the grounds together and Heine tells me about h im. He says:

"Don't never call me a bug again. They got me roomin' with the champion o' the world."

"Who is he?" I says.

"I don't know and I don't want to know," says Heine; "but if they stick him in there with me again I'll jump to the Federals. To start with, he ain't got no baggage. I ast him where his trunk was and he says he didn't have none. Then I ast him if he didn't have no suitcase, and he says: "No. What do you care?' I was goin' to lend him some pajamas, but he put on the shirt o' the uniform John give him last night and slept in that. He was asleep when I got up this mornin'. I seen his collar layin' on the dresser and it looked like he had wore it in Pittsburgh every day for a year. So I throwed it out the window and he comes down to breakfast with no collar. I ast him what size collar he wore and he says he didn't want none, because he wasn't goin' out nowheres. After breakfast he beat it up to the room again and put on his uniform. When I got up there he was lookin' in the glass at himself, and he done it all the time I was dressin'."

When we got out to the park I got my first look at him. Pretty good-lookin' guy, too, in his unie—big shoulders and well put together; built somethin' like Heine himself. He was talkin' to John when I come up.

"What position do you play?" John was askin' him.

"I play anywheres," says Elliott.

"You're the kind I'm lookin' for," says John. Then he says: "You was an outfielder up there in Michigan, wasn't you?" "I don't care where I play," says Elliott.

John sends him to the outfield and forgets all about him for a while. Pretty soon Miller comes in and says:

"I ain't goin' to shag for no bush outfielder!"

John ast him what was the matter, and Miller tells him that Elliott ain't doin' nothin' but just standin' out there; that he ain't makin' no attemp' to catch the fungoes, and that he won't even chase 'em. Then John starts watchin' him, and it was just like Miller said. Larry hit one pretty near in his lap and he stepped out o' the way. John calls him in and ast him:

"Why don't you go after them fly balls?"

"Because I don't want 'em," says Elliott.

John gets sarcastic and says:

"What do you want? Of course we'll see that you get anythin' you want!"

"Give me a ticket back home," says Elliott.

"Don't you want to stick with the club?" says John, and the busher tells him, no, he certainly did not. Then John tells him he'll have to pay his own fare home and Elliott don't get sore at all. He just says:

"Well, I'll have to stick, then—because I'm broke."

We was havin' battin' practice and John tells him to go up and hit a few. And you ought to of seen him bust 'em!

Lavender was in there workin' and he'd been pitchin' a little all winter, so he was in pretty good shape. He lobbed one up to Elliott, and he hit it 'way up in some trees outside the fence—about a mile, I guess. Then John tells Jimmy to put somethin' on the ball. Jim comes through with one of his fast ones and the kid slams it agin the right-field wall on a line.

"Give him your spitter!" yells John, and Jim handed him one. He pulled it over first base so fast that Bert, who was standin' down there, couldn't hardly duck in time. If it'd hit him it'd killed him.

Well, he kep' on hittin' everythin' Jim give him—and Jim had somethin' too. Finally John gets Pierce warmed up and sends him out to pitch, tellin' him to hand Elliott a flock o' curve balls. He wanted to see if lefthanders was goin' to bother him. But he slammed 'em right along, and I don't b'lieve he hit more'n two the whole mornin' that wouldn't of been base hits in a game.

They sent him out to the outfield again in the afternoon, and after a lot o' coaxin' Leach got him to go after fly balls; but that's all he did do—just go after 'em. One hit him on the bean and another on the shoulder. He run back after the short ones and 'way in after the ones that went over his head. He catched just one—a line drive that he couldn't get out o' the way of; and then he acted like it hurt his hands.

I come back to the hotel with John. He ast me what I thought of Elliott.

"Well," I says, "he'd be the greatest ballplayer in the world if he could just play ball. He sure can bust 'em."

John says he was afraid he couldn't never make an outfielder out o' him. He says:

"I'll try him on the infield to-morrow. They must be some place he can play. I never seen a lefthand hitter that looked so good agin lefthand pitchin'—and he's got a great arm; but he acts like he'd never saw a fly ball."

Well, he was just as bad on the infield. They put him at short and he was like a sieve. You could of drove a hearse between him and second base without him gettin' near it. He'd stoop over for a ground ball about the time it was bouncin' up agin the fence; and when he'd try to cover the bag on a peg he'd trip over it.

They tried him at first base and sometimes he'd run 'way over in the coachers' box and sometimes out in right field lookin' for the bag. Once Heine shot one acrost at him on a line and he never touched it with his hands. It went bam! right in the pit of his stomach—and the lunch he'd ate didn't do him no good.

Finally John just give up and says he'd have to keep him on the bench and let him earn his pay by bustin' 'em a couple o' times a week or so. We all agreed with John that this bird would be a whale of a pinch hitter—and we was right too. He was hittin' 'way over five hundred when the blowoff come, along about the last o' May.

II

Before the trainin' trip was over, Elliott had roomed with pretty near everybody in the club. Heine raised an awful holler after the second night down there and John put the bug in with Needham. Tom stood him for three nights. Then he doubled up with Archer, and Schulte, and Miller, and Leach, and Saier—and the whole bunch in turn, averagin' about two nights with each one before they put up a kick. Then John tried him with some o' the youngsters, but they wouldn't stand for him no more'n the others. They all said he was crazy and they was afraid he'd get violent some night and stick a knife in 'em.

He always insisted on havin' the water run in the bathtub all night, because he said it reminded him of the sound of the dam near his home. The fellers might get up four or five times a night and shut off the faucet, but he'd get right up after 'em and turn it on again. Carter, a big bush pitcher from Georgia, started a fight with him about it one night, and Elliott pretty near killed him. So the rest o' the bunch, when they'd saw Carter's map next mornin', didn't have the nerve to do nothin' when it come their turn.

Another o' his habits was the thing that scared 'em, though. He'd brought a razor with him—in his pocket, I guess—and he used to do his shavin' in the middle o' the night. Instead o' doin' it in the bathroom he'd lather his face and then come out and stand in front o' the lookin'-glass on the dresser. Of course he'd have all the lights turned on, and that was bad enough when a feller wanted to sleep; but the worst of it was that he'd stop shavin' every little while and turn round and stare at the guy who was makin' a failure o' tryin' to sleep. Then he'd wave his razor round in the air and laugh, and begin shavin' agin. You can imagine how comf'table his roomies felt!

John had bought him a suitcase and some clothes and things, and charged 'em up to him. He'd drew so much dough in advance that he didn't have nothin' comin' till about June. He never thanked John and he'd wear one shirt and one collar till some one throwed 'em away.

Well, we finally gets to Indianapolis, and we was goin' from there to Cincy to open. The last day in Indianapolis John come and ast me how I'd like to change roomies. I says I was perfectly satisfied with Larry. Then John says:

"I wisht you'd try Elliott. The other boys all kicks on him, but he seems to hang round you a lot and I b'lieve you could get along all right."

"Why don't you room him alone?" I ast.

"The boss or the hotels won't stand for us roomin' alone," says John. "You go ahead and try it, and see how you make out. If he's too much for you let me know; but he likes you and I think he'll be diff'rent with a guy who can talk to him like you can."

So I says I'd tackle it, because I didn't want to throw John down. When we got to Cincy they stuck Elliott and me in one room, and we was together till he quit us.

III

I WENT TO THE ROOM early that night, because we was goin' to open next day and I wanted to feel like somethin'. First thing I done when I got undressed was turn on both faucets in the bathtub. They was makin' an awful racket when Elliott finally come in about midnight. I was layin' awake and I opened right up on him. I says:

"Don't shut off that water, because I like to hear it run."

Then I turned over and pretended to be asleep. The bug got his clothes off, and then what did he do but go in the bathroom and shut off the water! Then he come back in the room and says:

"I guess no one's goin' to tell me what to do in here."

But I kep' right on pretendin' to sleep and didn't pay no attention. When he'd got into his bed I jumped out o' mine and turned on all the lights and begun stroppin' my razor. He says:

"What's comin' off?"

"Some o' my whiskers," I says. "I always shave along about this time."

"No, you don't!" he says. "I was in your room one mornin' down in Louisville and I seen you shavin' then."

"Well," I says, "the boys tell me you shave in the middle o' the night; and I thought if I done all the things you do mebbe I'd get so's I could hit like you."

"You must be superstitious!" he says. And I told him I was. "I'm a good hitter," he says, "and I'd be a good hitter if I never shaved at all. That don't make no diff'rence."

"Yes, it does," I says. "You prob'ly hit good because you shave at night; but you'd be a better fielder if you shaved in the mornin'."

You see, I was tryin' to be just as crazy as him—though that wasn't hardly possible.

"If that's right," says he, "I'll do my shavin' in the mornin'—because I seen in the papers where the boys says that if I could play the outfield like I can hit I'd be as good as Cobb. They tell me Cobb gets twenty thousand a year."

"No," I says; "he don't get that much—but he gets about ten times as much as you do."

"Well," he says, "I'm goin' to be as good as him, because I need the money."

"What do you want with money?" I says.

He just laughed and didn't say nothin'; but from that time on the water didn't run in the bathtub nights and he done his shavin' after breakfast. I didn't notice, though, that he looked any better in fieldin' practice.

IV

It rained one day in Cincy and they trimmed us two out o' the other three; but it wasn't Elliott's fault.

They had Larry beat four to one in the ninth innin' o' the first game. Archer gets on with two out, and John sends my roomy up to hit—though Benton, a lefthander, is workin' for them. The first thing Benton serves up there Elliott cracks it a mile over Hobby's head. It would of been good for three easy—only Archer—playin' safe, o' course—pulls up at third base. Tommy couldn't do nothin' and we was licked.

The next day he hits one out o' the park off the Indian; but we was 'way behind and they was nobody on at the time. We copped the last one without usin' no pinch hitters.

I didn't have no trouble with him nights durin' the whole series. He come to bed pretty late while we was there and I told him he'd better not let John catch him at it.

"What would he do?" he says.

"Fine you fifty," I says.

"He can't fine me a dime," he says, "because I ain't got it."

Then I told him he'd be fined all he had comin' if he didn't get in the hotel before midnight; but he just laughed and says he didn't think John had a kick comin' so long as he kep' bustin' the ball.

"Some day you'll go up there and you won't bust it," I says.

"That'll be an accident," he says.

That stopped me and I didn't say nothin'. What could you say to a guy who hated himself like that?

The "accident" happened in St. Louis the first day. We needed two runs in the eighth and Saier and Brid was on, with two out. John tells Elliott to go up in Pierce's place. The bug goes up and Griner gives him two bad balls—'way outside. I thought they was goin' to walk him—and it looked like good judgment, because they'd heard what he done in Cincy. But no! Griner comes back with a fast one right over and Elliott pulls it down the right foul line, about two foot foul. He hit it so hard you'd of thought they'd sure walk him then; but Griner gives him another fast one. He slammed it again just as hard, but foul. Then Griner gives him one 'way outside and it's two and three. John says, on the bench:

"If they don't walk him now he'll bust that fence down."

I thought the same and I was sure Griner wouldn't give him nothin' to hit; but he come with a curve and Rigler calls Elliott out. From where we sat the last one looked low, and I thought Elliott'd make a kick. He come back to the bench smilin'.

John starts for his position, but stopped and ast the bug what was the matter with that one. Any busher I ever knowed would of said, "It was too low," or "It was outside," or "It was inside." Elliott says:

"Nothin' at all. It was right over the middle."

"Why didn't you bust it, then?" says John.

"I was afraid I'd kill somebody," says Elliott, and laughed like a big boob.

John was pretty near chokin'.

"What are you laughin' at?" he says.

"I was thinkin' of a nickel show I seen in Cincinnati," says the bug.

"Well," says John, so mad he couldn't hardly see, "that show and that laugh'll cost you fifty."

We got beat, and I wouldn't of blamed John if he'd fined him his whole season's pay.

Up 'n the room that night I told him he'd better cut out that laughin' stuff when we was gettin' trimmed or he never would have no pay day. Then he got confidential.

"Pay day wouldn't do me no good," he says. "When I'm all squared up with the club and begin to have a pay day I'll only get a hundred bucks at a time, and I'll owe that to some o' you fellers. I wisht we could win the pennant and get in on that World's Series dough. Then I'd get a bunch at once."

"What would you do with a bunch o' dough?" I ast him.

"Don't tell nobody, sport," he says; "but if I ever get five hundred at once I'm goin' to get married."

"Oh!" I says. "And who's the lucky girl?"

"She's a girl up in Muskegon," says Elliott; "and you're right when you call her lucky."

"You don't like yourself much, do you?" I says.

"I got reason to like myself," says he. "You'd like yourself, too, if you could hit 'em like me."

"Well," I says, "you didn't show me no hittin' to-day."

"I couldn't hit because I was laughin' too hard," says Elliott.

"What was it you was laughin' at?" I says.

"I was laughin' at that pitcher," he says. "He thought he had somethin' and he didn't have nothin'."

"He had enough to whiff you with," I says.

"He didn't have nothin'!" says he again. "I was afraid if I busted one off him they'd can him, and then I couldn't never hit agin him no more."

Naturally I didn't have no comeback to that. I just sort o' gasped and got ready to go to sleep; but he wasn't through.

"I wisht you could see this bird!" he says.

"What bird?" I says.

"This dame that's nuts about me," he says.

"Good-looker?" I ast.

"No," he says; "she ain't no bear for looks. They ain't nothin' about her for a guy to rave over till you hear her sing. She sure can holler some."

"What kind o' voice has she got?" I ast.

"A bear," says he.

"No," I says; "I mean is she a barytone or an air?"

"I don't know," he says; "but she's got the loudest voice I ever hear on a woman. She's pretty near got me beat."

"Can you sing?" I says; and I was sorry right afterward that I ast him that question.

I guess it must of been bad enough to have the water runnin' night after night and to have him wavin' that razor round; but that couldn't of been nothin' to his singin'. Just as soon as I'd pulled that boner he says, "Listen to me!" and starts in on 'Silver Threads Among the Gold.' Mind you, it was after midnight and they was guests all round us tryin' to sleep!

They used to be noise enough in our club when we had Hofman and Sheckard and Richie harmonizin'; but this bug's voice was louder'n all o' theirn combined. We once had a pitcher named Martin Walsh—brother o' Big Ed's—and I thought he could drown out the Subway; but this guy made a boiler factory sound like Dummy

Taylor. If the whole hotel wasn't awake when he'd howled the first line it's a pipe they was when he cut loose, which he done when he come to "Always young and fair to me." Them words could of been heard easy in East St. Louis.

He didn't get no encore from me, but he goes right through it again—or starts to. I knowed somethin' was goin' to happen before he finished—and somethin' did. The night clerk and the house detective come bangin' at the door. I let 'em in and they had plenty to say. If we made another sound the whole club'd be canned out o' the hotel. I tried to salve 'em, and I says:

"He won't sing no more."

But Elliott swelled up like a poisoned pup.

"Won't I?" he says. "I'll sing all I want to."

"You won't sing in here," says the clerk.

"They ain't room for my voice in here anyways," he says. "I'll go outdoors and sing."

And he puts his clothes on and ducks out. I didn't make no attemp' to stop him. I heard him bellowin' 'Silver Threads' down the corridor and down the stairs, with the clerk and the dick chasin' him all the way and tellin' him to shut up.

Well, the guests make a holler the next mornin'; and the hotel people tells Charlie Williams that he'll either have to let Elliott stay somewheres else or the whole club'll have to move. Charlie tells John, and John was thinkin' o' settlin' the question by releasin' Elliott.

I guess he'd about made up his mind to do it; but that afternoon they had us three to one in the ninth, and we got the bases full, with two down and Larry's turn to hit. Elliott had been sittin' on the bench sayin' nothin'.

"Do you think you can hit one today?" says John.

"I can hit one any day," says Elliott.

"Go up and hit that lefthander, then," says John, "and remember there's nothin' to laugh at."

Sallee was workin'—and workin' good; but that didn't bother

the bug. He cut into one, and it went between Oakes and Whitted like a shot. He come into third standin' up and we was a run to the good. Sallee was so sore he kind o' forgot himself and took pretty near his full wind-up pitchin' to Tommy. And what did Elliott do but steal home and get away with it clean!

Well, you couldn't can him after that, could you? Charlie gets him a room somewheres and I was relieved of his company that night. The next evenin' we beat it for Chi to play about two weeks at home. He didn't tell nobody where he roomed there and I didn't see nothin' of him, 'cep' out to the park. I ast him what he did with himself nights and he says:

"Same as I do on the road—borrow some dough some place and go to the nickel shows."

"You must be stuck on 'em," I says.

"Yes," he says; "I like the ones where they kill people—because I want to learn how to do it. I may have that job some day."

"Don't pick on me," I says.

"Oh," says the bug, "you never can tell who I'll pick on."

It seemed as if he just couldn't learn nothin' about fieldin', and finally John told him to keep out o' the practice.

"A ball might hit him in the temple and croak him," says John.

But he busted up a couple o' games for us at home, beatin' Pittsburgh once and Cincy once.

V

They give me a great big room at the hotel in Pittsburgh; so the fellers picked it out for the poker game. We was playin' along about ten o'clock one night when in come Elliott—the earliest he'd showed up since we'd been roomin' together. They was only five of us playin' and Tom ast him to sit in.

"I'm busted," he says.

"Can you play poker?" I ast him.

"They's nothin' I can't do!" he says. "Slip me a couple o' bucks and I'll show you."

So I slipped him a couple o' bucks and honestly hoped he'd win, because I knowed he never had no dough. Well, Tom dealt him a hand and he picks it up and says:

"I only got five cards."

"How many do you want?" I says.

"Oh," he says, "if that's all I get I'll try to make 'em do."

The pot was cracked and raised, and he stood the raise. I says to myself: "There goes my two bucks!" But no—he comes out with three queens and won the dough. It was only about seven bucks; but you'd of thought it was a million to see him grab it. He laughed like a kid.

"Guess I can't play this game!" he says; and he had me fooled for a minute—I thought he must of been kiddin' when he complained of only havin' five cards.

He copped another pot right afterward and was sittin' there with about eleven bucks in front of him when Jim opens a roodle pot for a buck. I stays and so does Elliott. Him and Jim both drawed one card and I took three. I had kings or queens—I forget which. I didn't help 'em none; so when Jim bets a buck I throws my hand away.

"How much can I bet?" says the bug.

"You can raise Jim a buck if you want to," I says.

So he bets two dollars. Jim comes back at him. He comes right back at Jim. Jim raises him again and he tilts Jim right back. Well, when he'd boosted Jim with the last buck he had, Jim says:

"I'm ready to call. I guess you got me beat. What have you got?"

"I know what I've got, all right," says Elliott. "I've got a straight." And he throws his hand down. Sure enough, it was a straight, eight high. Jim pretty near fainted and so did I.

The bug had started pullin' in the dough when Jim stops him.

"Here! Wait a minute!" says Jim. "I thought you had somethin'. I filled up." Then Jim lays down his nine full.

"You beat me, I guess," says Elliott, and he looked like he'd lost his last friend.

"Beat you?" says Jim. "Of course I beat you! What did you think I had?"

"Well," says the bug, "I thought you might have a small flush or somethin'."

When I regained consciousness he was beggin' for two more bucks.

"What for?" I says. "To play poker with? You're barred from the game for life!"

"Well," he says, "if I can't play no more I want to go to sleep, and you fellers will have to get out o' this room."

Did you ever hear o' nerve like that? This was the first night he'd came in before twelve and he orders the bunch out so's he can sleep! We politely suggested to him to go to Brooklyn.

Without sayin' a word he starts in on his 'Silver Threads'; and it wasn't two minutes till the game was busted up and the bunch—all but me—was out o' there. I'd of beat it too, only he stopped yellin' as soon as they'd went.

"You're some buster!" I says. "You bust up ball games in the afternoon and poker games at night."

"Yes," he says; "that's my business—bustin' things."

And before I knowed what he was about he picked up the pitcher of ice-water that was on the floor and throwed it out the window—through the glass and all.

Right then I give him a plain talkin' to. I tells him how near he come to gettin' canned down in St. Louis because he raised so much Cain singin' in the hotel.

"But I had to keep my voice in shape," he says. "If I ever get dough enough to get married the girl and me'll go out singin' together."

"Out where?" I ast.

"Out on the vaudeville circuit," says Elliott.

"Well," I says, "if her voice is like yours you'll be wastin' money if you travel round. Just stay up in Muskegon and we'll hear you, all right!"

I told him he wouldn't never get no dough if he didn't behave himself. That, even if we got in the World's Series, he wouldn't be with us—unless he cut out the foolishness.

"We ain't goin' to get in no World's Series," he says, "and I won't never get a bunch o' money at once; so it looks like I couldn't get married this fall."

Then I told him we played a city series every fall. He'd never thought o' that and it tickled him to death. I told him the losers always got about five hundred apiece and that we were about due to win it and get about eight hundred. "But," I says, "we still got a good chance for the old pennant; and if I was you I wouldn't give up hope o' that yet—not where John can hear you, anyway."

"No," he says, "we won't win no pennant, because he won't let me play reg'lar; but I don't care so long as we're sure o' that city-series dough."

"You ain't sure of it if you don't behave," I says.

"Well," says he, very serious, "I guess I'll behave." And he did—till we made our first Eastern trip.

VI

We went to Boston first, and that crazy bunch goes out and piles up a three-run lead on us in seven innin's the first day. It was the pitcher's turn to lead off in the eighth, so up goes Elliott to bat for him. He kisses the first thing they hands him for three bases; and we says, on the bench: "Now we'll get 'em!"—because, you know, a three-run lead wasn't nothin' in Boston.

"Stay right on that bag!" John hollers to Elliott.

Mebbe if John hadn't said nothin' to him everythin' would of been all right; but when Perdue starts to pitch the first ball to Tommy, Elliott starts to steal home. He's out as far as from here to Seattle.

If I'd been carryin' a gun I'd of shot him right through the heart. As it was, I thought John'd kill him with a bat, because he was standin' there with a couple of 'em, waitin' for his turn; but I guess

John was too stunned to move. He didn't even seem to see Elliott when he went to the bench. After I'd cooled off a little I says:

"Beat it and get into your clothes before John comes in. Then go to the hotel and keep out o' sight."

When I got up in the room afterward, there was Elliott, lookin' as innocent and happy as though he'd won fifty bucks with a pair o' treys.

"I thought you might of killed yourself," I says.

"What for?" he says.

"For that swell play you made," says I.

"What was the matter with the play?" ast Elliott, surprised. "It was all right when I done it in St. Louis."

"Yes," I says; "but they was two out in St. Louis and we wasn't no three runs behind."

"Well," he says, "if it was all right in St. Louis I don't see why it was wrong here."

"It's a diff'rent climate here," I says, too disgusted to argue with him.

"I wonder if they'd let me sing in this climate?" says Elliott.

"No," I says. "Don't sing in this hotel, because we don't want to get fired out o' here—the eats is too good."

"All right," he says. "I won't sing." But when I starts down to supper he says: "I'm li'ble to do somethin' worse'n sing."

He didn't show up in the dinin' room and John went to the boxin' show after supper; so it looked like him and Elliott wouldn't run into each other till the murder had left John's heart. I was glad o' that—because a Mass'chusetts jury might not consider it justifiable hommercide if one guy croaked another for givin' the Boston club a game.

I went down to the corner and had a couple o' beers; and then I come straight back, intendin' to hit the hay. The elevator boy had went for a drink or somethin', and they was two old ladies already waitin' in the car when I stepped in. Right along after me comes Elliott.

"Where's the boy that's supposed to run this car?" he says. I told him the boy'd be right back; but he says: "I can't wait. I'm much too sleepy."

And before I could stop him he'd slammed the door and him and I and the poor old ladies was shootin' up.

"Let us off at the third floor, please!" says one o' the ladies, her voice kind o' shakin'.

"Sorry, madam," says the bug; "but this is a express and we don't stop at no third floor."

I grabbed his arm and tried to get him away from the machinery; but he was as strong as a ox and he throwed me agin the side o' the car like I was a baby. We went to the top faster'n I ever rode in an elevator before. And then we shot down to the bottom, hittin' the bumper down there so hard I thought we'd be smashed to splinters.

The ladies was too scared to make a sound durin' the first trip; but while we was goin' up and down the second time—even faster'n the first—they begun to scream. I was hollerin' my head off at him to quit and he was makin' more noise than the three of us—pretendin' he was the locomotive and the whole crew o' the train.

Don't never ask me how many times we went up and down! The women fainted on the third trip and I guess I was about as near it as I'll ever get. The elevator boy and the bellhops and the waiters and the night clerk and everybody was jumpin' round the lobby screamin'; but no one seemed to know how to stop us.

Finally—on about the tenth trip, I guess—he slowed down and stopped at the fifth floor, where we was roomin'. He opened the door and beat it for the room, while I, though I was tremblin' like a leaf, run the car down to the bottom.

The night clerk knowed me pretty well and knowed I wouldn't do nothin' like that; so him and I didn't argue, but just got to work together to bring the old women to. While we was doin' that Elliott must of run down the stairs and slipped out o' the hotel, because when they sent the officers up to the room after him he'd blowed.

They was goin' to fire the club out; but Charlie had a good standin with Amos, the proprietor, and he fixed it up to let us stay—providin' Elliott kep' away. The bug didn't show up at the ball park next day and we didn't see no more of him till we got on the rattler for New York. Charlie and John both bawled him, but they give him a berth—an upper—and we pulled into the Grand Central Station without him havin' made no effort to wreck the train.

VII

I'D STUDIED THE THING pretty careful, but hadn't come to no conclusion. I was sure he wasn't no stew, because none o' the boys had ever saw him even take a glass o' beer, and I couldn't never detect the odor o' booze on him. And if he'd been a dope I'd of knew about it—roomin' with him.

There wouldn't of been no mystery about it if he'd been a left-hand pitcher—but he wasn't. He wasn't nothin' but a whale of a hitter and he throwed with his right arm. He hit lefthanded, o' course; but so did Saier and Brid and Schulte and me, and John himself; and none of us was violent. I guessed he must of been just a plain nut and li'ble to break out any time.

They was a letter waitin' for him at New York, and I took it, intendin' to give it to him at the park, because I didn't think they'd let him room at the hotel; but after breakfast he come up to the room, with his suitcase. It seems he'd promised John and Charlie to be good, and made it so strong they b'lieved him.

I give him his letter, which was addressed in a girl's writin' and come from Muskegon.

"From the girl?" I says.

"Yes," he says; and, without openin' it, he tore it up and throwed it out the window.

"Had a quarrel?" I ast.

"No, no," he says; "but she can't tell me nothin' I don't know already. Girls always writes the same junk. I got one from her in Pittsburgh, but I didn't read it."

"I guess you ain't so stuck on her," I says.

He swells up and says:

"Of course I'm stuck on her! If I wasn't, do you think I'd be goin' round with this bunch and gettin' insulted all the time? I'm stickin' here because o' that series dough, so's I can get hooked."

"Do you think you'd settle down if you was married?" I ast him.

"Settle down?" he says. "Sure, I'd settle down. I'd be so happy that I wouldn't have to look for no excitement."

Nothin' special happened that night 'cep' that he come in the room about one o'clock and woke me up by pickin' up the foot o' the bed and droppin' it on the floor, sudden-like.

"Give me a key to the room," he says.

"You must of had a key," I says, "or you couldn't of got in."

"That's right!" he says, and beat it to bed.

One o' the reporters must of told Elliott that John had ast for waivers on him and New York had refused to waive, because next mornin' he come to me with that dope.

"New York's goin' to win this pennant!" he says.

"Well," I says, "they will if some one else don't. But what of it?"

"I'm goin' to play with New York," he says, "so's I can get the World's Series dough."

"How you goin' to get away from this club?" I ast.

"Just watch me!" he says. "I'll be with New York before this series is over."

Well, the way he goes after the job was original, anyway. Rube'd had one of his good days the day before and we'd got a trimmin'; but this second day the score was tied up at two runs apiece in the tenth, and Big Jeff'd been wabblin' for two or three innin's.

Well, he walks Saier and me, with one out, and Mac sends for Matty, who was warmed up and ready. John sticks Elliott in in Brid's place and the bug pulls one into the right-field stand.

It's a cinch McGraw thinks well of him then, and might of went after him if he hadn't went crazy the next afternoon. We're tied up in the ninth and Matty's workin'. John sends Elliott up with the bases choked; but he doesn't go right up to the plate. He walks over to their bench and calls McGraw out. Mac tells us about it afterward.

"I can bust up this game right here!" says Elliott.

"Go ahead," says Mac; "but be careful he don't whiff you."

Then the bug pulls it.

"If I whiff," he says, "will you get me on your club?"

"Sure!" says Mac, just as anybody would.

By this time Bill Koem was hollerin' about the delay; so up goes Elliott and gives the worst burlesque on tryin' to hit that you ever see. Matty throws one a mile outside and high, and the bug swings like it was right over the heart. Then Matty throws one at him and he ducks out o' the way—but swings just the same. Matty must of been wise by this time, for he pitches one so far outside that the Chief almost has to go to the coachers' box after it. Elliott takes his third healthy and runs through the field down to the clubhouse.

We got beat in the eleventh; and when we went in to dress he has his street clothes on. Soon as he seen John comin' he says: "I got to see McGraw!" And he beat it.

John was goin' to the fights that night; but before he leaves the hotel he had waivers on Elliott from everybody and had sold him to Atlanta.

"And," says John, "I don't care if they pay for him or not."

My roomy blows in about nine and got the letter from John out of his box. He was goin' to tear it up, but I told him they was news in it. He opens it and reads where he's sold. I was still sore at him; so I says:

"Thought you was goin' to get on the New York club?"

"No," he says. "I got turned down cold. McGraw says he wouldn't have me in his club. He says he'd had Charlie Faust—and that was enough for him."

He had a kind o' crazy look in his eyes; so when he starts up to the room I follows him.

"What are you goin' to do now?" I says.

"I'm goin' to sell this ticket to Atlanta," he says, "and go back to Muskegon, where I belong."

"I'll help you pack," I says.

"No," says the bug. "I come into this league with this suit o'clothes and a collar. They can have the rest of it." Then he sits down on the bed and begins to cry like a baby. "No series dough for me," he blubbers, "and no weddin' bells! My girl'll die when she hears about it!"

Of course that made me feel kind o' rotten, and I says:

"Brace up, boy! The best thing you can do is go to Atlanta and try hard. You'll be up here again next year."

"You can't tell me where to go!" he says, and he wasn't cryin' no more. "I'll go where I please—and I'm li'ble to take you with me."

I didn't want no argument, so I kep' still. Pretty soon he goes up to the lookin'-glass and stares at himself for five minutes. Then, all of a sudden, he hauls off and takes a wallop at his reflection in the glass. Naturally he smashed the glass all to pieces and he cut his hand somethin' awful.

Without lookin' at it he come over to me and says: "Well, good-by, sport!"—and holds out his other hand to shake. When I starts to shake with him he smears his bloody hand all over my map. Then he laughed like a wild man and run out o' the room and out o' the hotel.

VIII

Well boys my sleep was broke up for the rest o' the season. It might of been because I was used to sleepin' in all kinds o' racket and excitement, and couldn't stand for the quiet after he'd went—or it might of been because I kep' thinkin' about him and feelin' sorry for him.

I often wondered if he'd settle down and be somethin' if he could get married; and finally I got to b'lievin' he would. So when we was dividin' the city series dough I was thinkin' of him and the girl. Our share o' the money—the losers', as usual—was twelve thousand seven hundred sixty bucks or somethin' like that. They was twenty-one of us and that meant six hundred seven bucks apiece. We was just goin' to cut it up that way when I says:

"Why not give a divvy to poor old Elliott?"

About fifteen of 'em at once told me that I was crazy. You see, when he got canned he owed everybody in the club. I guess he'd stuck me for the most—about seventy bucks—but I didn't care nothin' about that. I knowed he hadn't never reported to Atlanta, and I thought he was prob'ly busted and a bunch o' money might make things all right for him and the other songbird.

I made quite a speech to the fellers, tellin' 'em how he'd cried when he left us and how his heart'd been set on gettin' married on the series dough. I made it so strong that they finally fell for it. Our shares was cut to five hundred eighty apiece, and John sent him a check for a full share.

For a while I was kind o' worried about what I'd did. I didn't know if I was doin' right by the girl to give him the chance to marry her.

He'd told me she was stuck on him, and that's the only excuse I had for tryin' to fix it up between 'em; but, b'lieve me, if she was my sister or a friend o' mine I'd just as soon of had her manage the Cincinnati Club as marry that bird. I thought to myself:

"If she's all right she'll take acid in a month—and it'll be my fault; but if she's really stuck on him they must be somethin' wrong with her too, so what's the diff'rence?"

Then along comes this letter that I told you about. It's from some friend of hisn up there—and they's a note from him. I'll read 'em to you and then I got to beat it for the station:

> Dear Sir: They have got poor Elliott locked up and they are goin' to take him to the asylum at Kalamazoo. He thanks you for the check, and we will use the money to see that he is made comf'table.
>
> When the poor boy come back here he found that his girl was married to Joe Bishop, who runs a soda fountain. She had wrote to him about it, but he did not read her letters. The news drove him crazy—poor boy—and he went to the place where they was livin' with a baseball bat and very near killed 'em both. Then he marched down the street singin' 'Silver Threads Among the Gold' at the top of his voice. They was goin' to send him to prison for assault with intent to kill, but the jury decided he was crazy.
>
> He wants to thank you again for the money.
>
> Yours truly, Jim——

I can't make out his last name—but it don't make no diff'rence. Now I'll read you his note:

> Old Roomy: I was at bat twice and made two hits; but I guess I did not meet 'em square. They tell me they are both alive yet, which I did not mean 'em to be. I hope they got good curveball pitchers where I am goin'. I sure can bust them curves—can't I, sport?
>
> Yours, B. Elliott.
>
> P.S.—The B stands for Buster.

That's all of it, fellers; and you can see I had some excuse for not hittin'. You can also see why I ain't never goin' to room with no bug again—not for John or nobody else!

Sick 'Em

The Saturday Evening Post
JULY 25, 1914

THIS IS JUST BETWEEN I and you. I don't want it to go no further. In the first place a feller that's had rotten luck as long as Red is entitled to the credit when his club fin'lly comes through and cops. In the second place if I was to tell the newspapers or the public that I was the one that really done it they'd laugh at me. They'd say: "How could you of did it when you was sittin' on the bench all summer?"

But you know I wouldn't lie to you, Jake, and you know I don't care nothin' about the honor or that bunk.

The little old World's Serious check is honor enough for me. So let 'em say that it was Red's managin' and them two guys' pitchin' that won for us, and let it go at that. I'm just tellin' you this to get it offen my chest.

Well, you must of read about Lefty Smith last fall, after we'd grabbed him. He's a wop and Smith ain't his real name, but it's the one he's went under ever since he started pitchin'. I heard his right name oncet, but I ain't got time to tell it to you to-day. It's longer'n Eppa Rixey. Anyway, the papers was full o' what him and Fogarty had did at Fort Wayne; how they'd worked a hundred games between 'em and copped the Central League pennant, and how all the scouts had went after 'em.

Pat had stopped off there when we was goin' West one trip and had saw 'em both work, and they'd looked so good to him that he'd advised Red to buy the both o' them. Well, Red told the big boss and he bought Smitty; paid five thousand for him, they say. They wanted even more for Fogarty; so we just put in a draft for him. But pretty near all the other clubs done the same and the Cubs got him.

Red thought Smitty'd fit in nice with our bunch. We needed all the pitchers we could get after what the Feds done to us. Most o' these guys with all the toutin' turns out to be dubs; but Smitty had a whale of a record, full o' no-hit games and shut-outs. He'd whiffed more guys than Rube Waddell or Johnson, and had tooken part in fifty games. Besides, he had some pitchin' sense, which is more'n you can say for most o' them bushers. Fogarty's record was just as good as Smitty's; but, o' course we wasn't so much interested in him. We figured from what Smitty'd did and from what Pat said about him that he'd come right through from the jump and show enough to make Red stick him in there in his reg'lar turn.

Well, we got down South and had a chancet to look him over. You could spot him right off the reel for a wop, but he was a handsome devil, big as a house, and with black eyes and black hair.

He didn't show nothin' for a couple o' weeks, but nobody lost no sleep over that; we thought he was takin' it easy and was one o' them careful birds that comes slow. Along in the third week we had some practice games between ourselves and Red starts Smitty agin the second club in one o' them. Say, he had a fast one like Waddell's and a cross fire like Sallee's! But he seemed to be afraid he'd show too much. He'd begin an innin' by puttin' more stuff on the ball than I ever seen, but after he'd threw two or three he'd ease up and lob 'em over. Them goofs couldn't see 'em when he was tryin'; but, say, they hit 'em acrost the state line when he let up. That didn't bother us none, neither, for we figured that he had the stuff when he wanted to use it, and when he got in shape he'd burn up the league.

We played a few games with them Southern clubs and Smitty kept on the same way. Maybe he'd pitch hard to one guy in a innin', but then he'd quit workin' and just float 'em up there like a balloon. Red told him one day to cut loose and see if he could go the route. He might just as well of told him to shave himself with a dish o' prunes. He went right along the way he'd been doin', pitchin' like a bear cat oncet in a while and sloppin' 'em over the rest o' the time. We was playin' the Richmond Club and they scored eleven runs, but Red wouldn't take him out.

After the game Red give him a bawlin' and ast him what was the matter. He said, Nothin'; he was doin' the best he knowed how. Red says: "You ain't doin' no such a thing. You've got the stuff, but you won't let go of it. Are you lazy or what?" Smitty didn't say a word. Then Red ast him if he wasn't in shape, and he said, Yes, he guessed he was. "Well," says Red, "you'll have to cut out the monkey business or I'll put the rollers under you!"

We stopped off in Washin'ton for a couple of exhibition games and broke even with 'em. Then we went home and tackled the Athaletics in the spring serious. Alexander trimmed 'em and they licked Mayer. Red sent Smitty at 'em in the third game and he was worse'n ever. I thought he'd be massacreed.

For two innin's they couldn't touch him and then he pulled the old stuff. Cy Young could of run to the plate as fast as the balls this bird throwed. It was just like hittin' fungoes for them Athaletics. A slow ball's all right in its place, but it's got to be mixed up with somethin' else. The way Smitty mixed 'em up was to throw one slow, and then one slower, and then one slower yet. Along in the fourth, before Red took him out, you could of went on one o' them street cars from the hotel to the ball park in St. Louis between the time he let go o' the pill and when one o' them Mackmen kissed it. Pat was crazy. He says:

"I'd give my glove to know what's the matter with him. He was the best pitcher in the world when I looked him over, and now he couldn't hold a job with a high school. He must of been full o' dope at Fort Wayne."

Meantime I got a hold o' one o' the Chi papers and seen where they was pannin' Fogarty. They said he seemed to be as fast as Johnson and to have a lot o' stuff, but he didn't show no more ambish than a horse car. I read the piece to Smitty.

"Your old sidekick don't seem to be cuttin' up much," I says.

"He ain't no sidekick o' mine," Smitty says.

"You and him was together at Fort Wayne, wasn't you?" says I.

"Yes," says Smitty; "and he's a false alarm."

I thought I'd bruise him.

"He ain't got nothin' on you," I says.

But he took it just as calm as though I'd told him his collar was dirty. Then I says:

"You and Fogarty must of pawned your pepper when you left Fort Wayne. Or maybe you can't get along without your Hoosier hops. Somethin's wrong. You couldn't of won all them games if you worked there like you're doin' here. What's the matter?"

"Matter with who?" he says.

"Both o' you—you and Fogarty," I says.

"They's nothin' the matter with me," says Smitty. "I'm all right; but that slob never had no business tryin' to pitch."

"How did he win them games?" I ast.

"I guess they felt sorry for him," says Smitty.

"They'll be feelin' sorry for you if you don't go and get some ginger," says I.

The season opened and we started off like we always do, playin' 'em off their feet and lookin' like champs. Alexander and Rixey was better'n I'd ever saw 'em, and the boys was all hittin'. It was a rotten day when Cravath or Magee or Luderus, or some o' them, didn't pole a couple out o' the park. We didn't get excited about it, though. We'd been May champions too often. We was wonderin' when the Old Jinx was goin' to hit us in the eye, and whether we'd get smashed up in a railroad wreck or have a epidemic o' lepersy. The papers was sayin' that we was up to our old tricks and that we'd blow higher'n a kite when the annual cyclone struck us.

Red had started Smitty just oncet. That was agin the Boston bunch, and he'd tooken him out in the first innin' so's we could finish the game that day. The first ball he throwed made a noise like a cannon when it hit Bill's glove. The rest o' them never got that far. One was all he had the strength to pitch. The first seven guys that come up was expresses—they didn't stop at first or second base. Paskert ast Red to send him a taxi. Smitty fin'lly was invited to the bench and sat there blinkin' while Red sprung a monologue.

"You're layin' down on me," says Red, "and it's goin' to cost you a month's pay. If you're playin' for your release you're wastin' time. I'd get rid o' you if I could, but nobody'll take you. I've ast for waivers and I know what I'm talkin' about. You're wished on to us for the summer, but you ain't goin' to do no more pitchin'. I wouldn't even let you work in battin' practice, 'cause the fellers couldn't see a real pitcher's stuff after lookin' at your'n. You can help the clubhouse boy, and you can hustle out the canvas when it rains, and you can stand and hold the bottle while the real ball players is gettin' rubbed. And you can stick round after the games and hang up the undershirts.

"We'd ought to sue the Fort Wayne club for swindlin' us! I'd like to manage a team in that league if fellers like you can win a pennant there. I'd give the ground keeper a dollar a day extra to do the pitchin' for me, and I'd go in myself when he was too busy. They give you a salary for playin' ball, but they pinch a man for stealin' a loaf o' bread! If you're the best pitcher in the Central League the rest o' them is paralytics. If we'd spent five thousand for the middle of a doughnut we'd have a better chancet o' realizin' on our investment. If pepper was worth a million dollars a ounce you'd be rated at ten cents!"

"Can I go in and dress?" says Smitty.

"I doubt it," says Red. "You better take somebody along to help you." Well, that might of been the end o' the bird if he was with any club but our'n. Red had the waivers all right, but couldn't make no deal that'd bring us within four thousand bucks of even. Still, we wasn't gettin' no service out of him and was payin' him salary all the time.

So Red was just about to sell him to a old-clo'es man when the old hoodoo hit us. Alexander strained his souper and Rixey got a pair o' busted fingers, all in the same serious. We was left with one fair pitcher and a gang o' kids that'd never saw no big-league games till last spring. The bust-up didn't surprise nobody. We figured that we'd been lucky to go till the first o' June without none o' the boys gettin' killed. It was the same old gag with us: Right up near the top and happy for a couple o' months. Then, Blooie!—and the club all shot to pieces.

It wouldn't of been sensible to turn even a rotten pitcher loose at that stage. We had to keep a hold of all o' them, so's when some got their bumps they'd be plenty to take their place. That's how Smitty happened to hang on. Red didn't start him, but he let him finish for some o' the others that wasn't much better. And he kept lookin' worse all the while.

Well, it was the second week in June when Red sent me from Cincy to Dayton to look at a big spitter.

"I ain't strong for the Central League after what they handed me," he says; "but maybe this guy's better'n most o' them, and you can see where we're up agin it. We got to get somebody or we'll go to the bottom so fast they'll pinch us for speedin'. If he's got anything at all and looks like as if he was alive we can use him; but if he's a dope, like this other boob, we don't need him. I don't want to run no lodgin' house for vagrants."

So I beat it over there and seen a double-header between the home club and Evansville. The guy I was sent after worked one game and had about as much action as a soft drink. I voted No! before he'd went two innin's. Evansville had a lefthander who knowed how to pitch, but they told me he'd been in the league six years; and, besides, he was a little feller.

Well, I spotted old Jack Barnett on the Evansville bench, so I waited to shake hands with him when the game was over. You know him and me broke in together at Utica. I found out while we rode downtown that he'd been with the Fort Wayne Club the last year and was traded to Evansville durin' the winter. I'd sort o' lost track of old Jack 'cause he hadn't been playin' enough in recent years to get his name in the book.

"I see your club's still lucky," he says. "We all thought you had a grand chancet till them two fellers got hurt."

"Yes," I says, "but we're gone now. The young guys we got ought to of been dressmakers instead o' pitchers." Then I happened to think o' Smitty. "Maybe you can tell me somethin'," says I. "How did this here Smitty ever win all them games for you?"

Barnett started to laugh.

"What's the matter?" he ast. "Ain't the big wop worth five thousand?"

"He ain't worth a cigar coupon," I says. "He's a big, lazy tramp."

Barnett kept on laughin'.

"I knowed what'd come off," he says, "I told the fellers what'd happen. I bet Punch Knoll fifty bucks that Smitty wouldn't last the season. You guys can talk about McGraw and Mack, and them other big-league managers, all you want to, but it's us fellers down here in the sticks that knows how to get the work out of a man."

I ast him what he meant.

"Well," he says, "we had Smitty two years ago and he was a bum. He was sloppin' along with us like he's doin' with you now. At that time the Grand Rapids Club had Fogarty, the guy the Cubs got now. Fogarty's a big right-hander, with a spitter and a good hook and just as good a fast ball as Smitty. He's a big, handsome brute, too, and maybe he don't know it! Up to Grand Rapids he was doin' nothin' but look pretty and draw his pay. He was just as valuable to them as Smitty was to us; but we used to have all kinds o' fun with 'em both, kiddin' 'em about their looks. We'd say to Smitty: 'You'd be the handsomest guy in this league if it wasn't for Fogarty.' And we'd pull the same stuff on Fogarty when we was playin' Grand Rapids. And the both o' them would get as sore as a boil. I never seen nothin' like it.

"At the schedule meetin' a year ago last winter, our club and Grand Rapids pulled off a trade, Bill Peck comin' to us for Joe Hammond and Bull Harper, a couple of infielders. Jack Burke, our manager, told the owner o' the Grand Rapids Club that it didn't look fair, givin' up two men for one. So he says: 'All right; I'll throw in Fogarty and then you'll have the two handsomest ball players in the business.' Jack thought he was jokin'; but, sure enough, he turned Fogarty over to us.

"We started in on the pair o' them right off the reel, tryin' to make their life miserable. When Smitty was round we'd talk about Fogarty's pretty red hair; and when Fogarty was with us we'd be wishin' we had big black eyes like Smitty's. I done the most of it, but I didn't have no idea what'd happen.

"Well, to make it short, Smitty come up to Jack a week before the season opened and ast if he could pitch the first game. Jack pretty near dropped dead, 'cause it'd been all he could do the year before to get him to put on his uniform. Mind you, we all knowed then that Smitty had the stuff if he'd only use it. Burke told him he'd think it over and was wonderin' whether to turn him down or not, when up come Fogarty and ast the same thing. Burke decided to take a chancet, so he had the two o' them toss a coin, and Smitty won the toss. He opened up for us and shut Terre Haute out with two hits. And the next day Fogarty worked and shut 'em out again, but give 'em one more hit than Smitty. They was nothin' to it after that. We kept up the good work, gettin' 'em madder and madder at each other. And the madder they got the harder they worked. Either one o' them would of pitched every day if Burke had of let 'em. While Fogarty was workin' Smitty'd slide up and down the bench cussin' to himself and pullin' his head off for the other club. And Fogarty'd do the same thing when Smitty was in there.

"Both o' them was strong for the skirts; and, o' course, a pair o' fine-lookin' slobs like them could cop one out in every town. We took up that end of it, too, tellin' Smitty that Fogarty's Marie was prettier than his Julia, and that kind o' stuff.

"You know what they done for us. We'd of finished about sixth without 'em. I never seen such pitchin' in my life, and I never seen two fellers hate each other the way them two done. When you guys bought Smitty and didn't get Fogarty I called the turn. Some o' the boys figured they both might of got the habit o' workin' and might keep it up when they was separated; but I knowed different. And that's why I made the bet with Punch Knoll. Looks like I'll win it easy, don't it?"

"Looks like it," I says. "Alexander and Rixey'd both ought to be ready again in a month and then Smitty'll lose his home sure. And we'll be absolutely last by that time."

We was goin' to Chi that night and I didn't see no use o' stickin' in Dayton when I hadn't had no orders to look at no one else but that one guy. Besides, Barnett told me they wasn't nobody else on neither club worth lampin'. I'd of liked to of listened to some more o' the stuff about the two jealous cats, but I had to beat it back to Cincy.

Well, on the way I done some thinkin'; but I was afraid to spring anything on Red for fear he'd laugh at me. We've all knew o' cases where jealousy'd helped a ball club, and a lot more cases where it'd hurt 'em; but I hadn't never heard o' no case like this here one.

We got to Chi and the Cubs proceeded to murder us. Red was desp'rate and so was the rest o' the gang. We dropped the first three and didn't have no hopes o' winnin' the fourth unless Hank lost his mind and pitched the bat boy agin us.

I hadn't never saw Fogarty. He'd been left to home when the Cubs come East in May. But I spotted him the first day out there to the Cubs' park. He sure was a nice-lookin' devil and big enough to pitch every afternoon and twicet on Sundays. He wasn't doin' no pitchin' for them, though. They was lucky enough to have their reg'lars in shape and wasn't obliged to fill up the box score with ornaments.

Well, I went up to Schulte durin' battin' practice and ast him what was the matter with Fogarty.

"Nothin' at all," says Frank. "I don't figure they can be nothin' the matter with a guy that draws his pay for sittin' on the bench and lookin' beautiful. I wisht I could get away with it."

"Don't he work none?" I ast.

"He pitches to the batters about oncet in two weeks," says Frank. "He does it when Hank can get his consent. And on the days he pitches to us I manage to hide somewheres till the practice is over."

"Why?" I ast.

" 'Cause," says Frank, "I figure that, barrin' accidents, I got many happy years before me. If he was to happen to put all his stuff on the ball oncet and hit me in the head, they wouldn't be nobody to drive the mules on my peach ranch in Georgia."

"He's got a lot o' stuff, then?" I says.

"Yes," says Frank; "and he's savin' it up for somethin'—maybe to give it away for a birthday present. All he does now is sit and wait for everybody to look away from him, so's he can pull out his pocket mirror and enjoy himself."

This dope fit in perfect with what Jack Barnett had been tellin' me. I made up my mind right there that the thing was worth tryin'; but it took all the nerve I had to spring it on Red. My chancet soon come. He was put off the field in the second innin' and I got myself chased right afterward. He was sittin' in the clubhouse with his head in his hands when I come in.

"Red," I says, "we couldn't be worse off'n we are, could we?" He didn't pay no attention. "We'd be better off if we had somebody that could pitch, wouldn't we?" I says.

"What are you drivin' at?" he ast.

"I want you to try a experiment," I says. "It may not do no good, and then again it might. It might pull us through O.K. if you was willin' to take a chancet."

"Shoot," says Red. "I'll try anything oncet."

"Do you think you could get Fogarty offen the Cubs?" I says.

"Could I get him?" says Red. "Sure I could get him! They just give me notice that they'd ast waivers. But what do I want with Fogarty? He's another one just like this Smitty we got. I give him the oncet over to-day on their bench, and if they's anybody in the world that's lazier'n Smitty, he's him. Don't you think we're carryin' enough excess baggage?"

Then I told him what Barnett'd told me, only I made it even stronger. At first he called me a nut, and it took me pretty near till the game was over to coax him into it. He'd just gave up when the gang come in.

"How bad did they trim us?" ast Red.

"I don't know," says Magee; "but I know I chased back to that fence a hundred and sixteen times."

"Better go see Hank," says I to Red.

I had to pretty near drag him to get him out o' the clubhouse. Hank was just goin' in their door.

"Wait a minute, Hank," I says. "Red wants to see you."

"Just heard you was askin' waivers on Fogarty," says Red. "What do want for him?"

"I guess you can get him for the waiver price," says Hank; "but you'll have to see the boss."

So me and Red went up to the office and sprung it on 'em. They seemed surprised, but said Red could have him. So Red wired home and got the deal O.K.'d. And Fogarty went with us to St. Louis.

Before we got on the train, Red told me I'd have to do the funny work. I said I'd tackle it, and then I went to Pat and explained the thing to him and ast for help. He was willin' and we fixed it up that I was to room with Fogarty and Pat with Smitty.

Smitty was in his berth, gettin' his beauty sleep, when Fogarty clumb aboard that night. So they didn't see each other till next mornin'. Smitty nailed me comin' out o' the Union Station in St. Louis.

"What's that guy doin' with us?" he says.

"Who do you mean?" I says.

"That big, ugly Mick," says he.

"Ugly!" I says. "If I was you I wouldn't call him ugly. He's a big, handsome boy, and he looks handsomer'n ever alongside a homely wop like you."

He never said a word. He turned away from me like as if I'd ast him for a hundred bucks. Red told me afterward that he come and sat with him in the dinin' room at the hotel and ast if Fogarty was goin' to be with us.

"Sure!" says Red. "I thought it was about time we was gettin' a pitcher."

"A pitcher!" says Smitty. "If they sold him to you for a pitcher you got cheated. He's only a swell-headed pup that don't think about nothin' but the part in his hair."

"Well," says Red, "if I had hair as pretty as his'n I'd be proud of it too."

That shut up Smitty and he left the table without finishin' his Java; but he come to Red in the lobby an hour later and ast if he could work that afternoon! It took Red five minutes to come to. He hadn't had no such request as that from nobody for pretty near three weeks, and Smitty was the last guy on earth he expected it from. You can bet he give his consent.

When our grips come I went to my room to take a nap and a shave; but I didn't get no nap. My new roomy, Fogarty, followed me in and begin talkin' right away.

"What kind o' burg is Philly?" he says.

"Swell!" says I. "You can get anything you want there."

"How about the female population?" he ast. "Lots o' good lookers?"

"Well," I says, "I guess there's plenty o' pretty girls; but I'm a married man and I ain't got no time for 'em. If you're after information on that subject you better ast Smitty."

"Smitty!" he says. "What does he know about girls?"

"He must know how to grab 'em," says I. "All the real dolls in the burg is bugs over him."

"They must be a fine bunch!" says Fogarty. "It must be they never seen nobody."

"Well," I says, "they ain't looked at nobody since they seen him."

"I can't figure it out," he says.

"That's easy," says I. "In the first place he's a fine-lookin' boy, and in the second place he's a swell pitcher."

"Where do you get that stuff?" says Fogarty. "Don't you think I know nothin'? If he's fine-lookin' I'm a snake. And if he's a swell pitcher, why don't they never start him?"

"He's had a sore arm," I says; "but he's all O.K. now and Red's goin' to work him to-day."

He left the room right after that and I didn't see no more of him till we got out to the park; but Red tipped me that he'd came to him and ast if he could work the game. Red told him he was goin' to start Smitty.

"Good night!" says Fogarty. "They'll get a hundred runs."

But, say, I never seen such a change in a man as they was in Smitty that afternoon. He warmed up with Pat first and was so fast that Pat couldn't hardly keep his glove on. Then Red took him a while and was so pleased that he forgot to get sore when he catched one right on the meat hand.

Well, he didn't shut 'em out—he hadn't had no real work for a long time and he was hog wild; but, say, they couldn't hit him with a shovel! Two blows was what they got, an' we licked 'em, five to two. It was the first game we'd win since we left home; and all through it Fogarty was frothin' at the mouth. Every little while he'd say: "He can't keep it up—the lucky bum! He's slippin'. Better let me warm up!" But Red didn't pay no attention to him.

Maybe you think we didn't feel good in that clubhouse—'specially me and Pat and Red! We was the only ones in on the secret. We'd decided not to ask no help from the other boys for fear they'd make it too raw. I felt the best of anybody, 'cause it was my scheme and I'd been scared that it wouldn't work. It made me look good to myself and to Red too. Before we was dressed, Fogarty'd drew Red aside and got him to promise to pitch him next day.

I wasn't sure yet that success was goin' to be permanent. Still, it was up to I and Pat to go through with our end of it, and my job was to stick close to Fogarty all that evenin' and keep goadin' him. I braced him outside o' the hotel after supper and ast him to take a walk.

"Grand game Smitty pitched to-day!" I says.

"What was grand about it?" says he. "Who couldn't beat that bunch? He'd ought to of been ashamed of himself for lettin' 'em score."

"He only give 'em two hits," says I.

"Sure!" says Fogarty. "And how was they goin' to get hits when he didn't throw nothin' near the plate?"

"Well," I says, "I don't see no harm in a few walks so long's a feller can get 'em over when he has to. It's pretty hard for a guy with all that smoke to control it right along."

"Yes," he says; "but I claim it takes a lucky bird to give eight bases on balls and get away with the ball game. It don't show no pitchin' on his part; all it shows is that the other club'd ought to try some easier game than baseball. All they had to do was go up there without their bats and they'd of trimmed us; but they didn't even make him pitch. It looked to me like as if their manager'd offered a prize to the one that could miss 'em the furthest. They looked like a vaudeville team rehearsin' a club-swingin' act. At that, Smitty's got a big advantage over most pitchers. He's so dam' homely that it scares a feller to look at him."

"If that's a advantage," I says, "nobody'd never even bunt one safe off o' you."

"You're kiddin' me now," he says. "I ain't stuck on my looks, but they wouldn't be no sense in me pretendin' that I didn't have him beat. I and him was together in the Central, y'know; and I was one o' the most pop'lar if not the pop'larest feller that ever played ball in Fort Wayne. It takes the skirts to judge if a man's good-lookin' or not; and I'm here to tell you without no boastin' that I could of married any dame in that burg. So far's Smitty was concerned, he couldn't get no girl to look at him."

"Fort Wayne girls ain't like the ones in Philly, then," says I.

"Girls is the same everywheres," says Fogarty. "You can't never make me believe that they'd chase him, unless it's out o' curiosity. You'll often see a crowd round a monkey cage, but it ain't 'cause the monkeys is handsome."

"Some girls likes them big, dark fellers," I says.

"Yes," he says, "and some people likes the smell o' garlic."

"I s'pose we'll get a lickin' to-morrow," I says. "Red ain't got nobody left to work, outside of a few bushers."

"This busher right here works to-morrow," says Fogarty; "and you can bet a month's pay that he won't give no eight bases on balls."

"Maybe you won't be in there long enough," I says.

"I'll be in there just nine innin's," says he; "and at the end o' that time the St. Louis Club won't have nothin' to show they been in a ball game."

"All you need to do," says I, "is to work as good as Smitty done to-day; but that's too much to look for from most bushers."

That stung him.

"They ain't no homely wop got nothin' on me!" he says. "If I can't do no better'n he done I'll quit pitchin' and peddle bananas, which is what he'd ought to be doin'."

Well, I kept him goin' till bedtime and all the next forenoon. He was out to the park and dressed before anybody, and he warmed up enough for three games. Red ast him oncet if he wasn't workin' too hard.

"Not me," he says. "I ain't delicate like some o' these here pitchers. Work's my middle name and you'll find it out before I get through."

Say, they wasn't no kick comin' on the way he done the job! One o' the St. Louis guys got as far as second base and was so surprised that Bill caught him off o' there flat-footed. Three little singles he give 'em and not a man did he walk. Bill told me afterward that it was fast one, fast, one, fast one, and hardly three hooks or spitters all through the game. Bill said them fast ones stung right through his big mitt like he'd been barehanded.

And Smitty, on the bench, acted just like Fogarty'd did the day before. He called them St. Louis hitters everything he could think of. When the big Turk whiffed the hull side in the seventh Smitty was so sore he kicked a hole in the ball bag and throwed away his chew.

The rest o' the bunch couldn't help noticin' the way he acted, and I seen where they'd be wise to the whole game before long.

That night Pat took Smitty to a bunch o' nickel shows and entertained him with conversation about Fogarty's grand performance. The result was that the wop got Red out o' bed at seven the next mornin' and ast him whether he could pitch the game. Red stalled him, 'cause he didn't know then how strong the both o' them was—him and Fogarty.

Anyway, it rained, so Smitty'd had two days' rest before we played again, and Red sent him in to wind up the serious. Gavvy saved St. Louis another whitewashin' by droppin' a fly ball with a guy on; but that run was all they got. Fogarty's game wasn't a bit better'n this second one o' Smitty's, and I kept rubbin' that into Fogarty all the way back to Philly.

They ain't no use goin' on and tellin' you about all the rest o' the games they pitched. They was both beat a few times, but it wasn't 'cause they didn't try. Every pitcher with a arm and a glove'd cop more'n two-thirds of his games if he'd work as hard as these babies done. Some o' the papers come out and said that Red was overworkin' 'em, but the reporters that wrote that didn't know what they was talkin' about. It was all Red could do to keep either o' them on the bench. If they'd of had their way about it they'd of both been out there in the middle o' the diamond every day, fightin' for possession o' the ball.

When Red sent Mayer or one o' the other boys in, the pair o' them'd sit on the bench growlin' and makin' remarks about each other. The minute the feller in their workin' showed any signs o' weakenin', Fogarty and Smitty'd both jump up and race down to the bull pen. And when Red got ready to take the guy out and sent for one or the other o' the two handsome birds the one he didn't pick would slam his glove on the ground and start kickin' it. Everybody on the ball club kept at 'em on the bench; but Red, figurin' they might get suspicious, give orders that nobody but I and Pat was to ride 'em in private.

We was right up on the Giants' heels by the first of August. Then Rixey and Alexander joined us, but all they was ast to do was fill in when Red could persuade Fogarty and Smitty to take a rest. We was about the only club that was beatin' New York, or else we'd of had the flag cinched long before we did. We was runnin' through the rest o' the league like soup through a sieve.

One day Smitty held the Brooklyn Club to six hits in a double-header and beat 'em both games. Fogarty ast me a hundred times in the next few days when we was goin' to have another double-header. And a week before it come off he made Red promise to let him tackle it alone. It was agin the Cubs and he beat 'em clean as a whistle; but they got a couple more hits than Brooklyn'd made agin Smitty. So the big Turk was just as discontented as though he hadn't did nothin' at all. You ought to of heard Hank rave, though! He couldn't figure how Red could get so much work out of a guy who'd been on his bench two or three months and hadn't did nothin' but sleep.

But you know what they done. What I set out to tell you was how I and Pat kept 'em goin'. We soon found out that they wasn't only jealous of each other's looks and their pitchin'. Neither one o' them would let the other have anything on him at all. If I'd make a remark about what a classy necktie Smitty was wearin', Fogarty'd go out and buy the loudest one he could find. If Pat mentioned to Smitty that Fogarty always kept his shoes shined up nice, Smitty'd sneak away to a shine parlor and make the boy work his fool head off for a hour. They just naturally hated each other and acted like a pair o' grand opery stars or a couple o' schoolgirls that was both tryin' to be teacher's pet.

I and Pat would get together and figure out different things to rile 'em up with. Pat was singin' The River Shannon in the clubhouse one day. Fogarty was standin' right by me.

"Pat's got a good voice," he says.

"Fair," says I; "but the best singer on the club is Smitty."

Now I hadn't heard Smitty sing—didn't know whether he could or not. Fogarty'd ought to of knew somethin' about it, as they'd been at Fort Wayne together a hull season; but, regardless o' the fact that neither one o' the two had a voice—as we soon learned—the Turk joined right in with Pat, and it wasn't two seconds before Smitty was whinin' too. Pat quit when he seen he had competition. Everybody stopped talkin' and listened.

I wisht you could of heard it! It was like as though all the ferryboats in East River had got into trouble at once. Their idea o' singin' was to see how many sour notes they could hit and how loud they could hit 'em. The bunch give 'em a hand when they got through, and each o' them figured it was on the square and was for him personally. Well, that was a big laugh with us for a while; but it got so's it was no joke when they done it every day and yelled different songs at the same time.

Another thing we done was to write letters to both o' them and sign a girl's name. The letters was just the same, and they said that she was a great fan and was pullin' for our club, and just loved to see them two pitch. We wound them up somethin' like this:

"I think you're so handsome and I would love to meet you. I've already met Mr. Smith." We said Mr. Smith in one and Mr. Fogarty in the other. "I think he's the handsomest man I ever seen, but maybe you're just as handsome when a person sees you up close. I sit in the third or fourth row o' the stand, right back o' your bench, every afternoon."

Say, you'd ought to of seen them birds fall for that! They rubbered for that dame every day we played at home for the last two months o' the season. Sometimes, when neither o' them was workin', they'd both get up and lean on the roof o' the bench and try to get a smile from every skirt in the place, thinkin' one o' them must be the girl who'd wrote.

On the road we'd get the telephone girls in the hotels to call up Smitty and ask him if he was Mr. Fogarty. When he'd say no she'd ring off; but she'd call him up again in about ten minutes and ask him the same question. We worked this on Fogarty, too, and both o' them pretty near went nuts 'cause the other was gettin' so many calls.

Pat pulled a hot one in Pittsburgh. He told Smitty that Fogarty was the most generous guy he'd ever met.

"Why?" says Smitty.

"He's so good to the waiters and bell hops," says Pat. "He gives the waiters a quarter tip at every meal and slips the boys two bits when they bring him ice water."

That started a battle that was pretty costly to the both o' them, but mighty sweet for the hops and waiters. If I'd of been Pat I'd of made 'em slip me a commission.

We had 'em both ridin' in taxis to and from all the parks on the last trip West. We had 'em gettin' their clo'es pressed every night, and buyin' new shirts and collars in every burg we blowed into, and gettin' shaved twicet a day, till Red made us cut some of it out, sayin' they was touchin' the club for too much dough. And all season I never seen 'em speak to each other, though neither one couldn't talk about nothin' else but the other when they was separated.

The pennant race was settled when we won a double-header in Cincy on the fifteenth o' September. When we got back to the hotel Red told us the lid was off for that night—that we could do anything we wanted to and stay out until breakfast. So they can't blame neither Pat nor I for what come off. One o' the other boys—I never found out who—told Fogarty that Smitty could hold more wine than a barrel. Then he pulled the same thing on Smitty about Fogarty.

I and Pat went to a show. When we blowed back, about eleven, they was a noise like New Year's Eve in the café. We went in to see what it was. They was a gang o' fellers at one table with Smitty, and another bunch at another table with Fogarty. They was four or five empty quart bottles in front o' each o' them. They'd had five or six more pints than they could carry comfortable and was hollerin' for more, but was broke. We got 'em both at one table and ast 'em to sing. Before they was halfway through the first verse o' whatever it was, the night clerk horned in and stopped 'em. Then we took 'em out in the street and told 'em to finish it, but they was too many coppers round.

Most of us was roomin' on the tenth floor and one o' the boys talked the pair into racin' upstairs instead of usin' the elevator. They both fell down at the first landin' and when they hit the floor they was all in. They'd of slept there for a week if we hadn't of carried 'em to the elevator and got 'em up the rest o' the way. Then what did we do but steer 'em both into Pat's room and put 'em to bed together. They was no danger o' them gettin' wise till the next day; they was dead to the world. I and Pat slept in my room and we was up bright and early so's not to miss nothin'. We walked in and found 'em both poundin' their ear. It must of tooken us fifteen minutes to get 'em roused.

"Well, boys," says Pat, "I'm glad to see you so friendly and lookin' so fresh."

They looked about as fresh as a old dray horse.

"How did you happen to be roomin' together?" I says.

It wasn't till then that they wised up. Smitty jumped out o' bed like the hotel was afire.

"I'll murder the guy that done this!" he hollered.

"What do you mean?" says Pat. "Don't you know who you went to bed with?"

"You must of been in bad shape," I says. "Fogarty was all right; he knowed what he was doin'."

Fogarty wanted to deny it, but he couldn't, 'cause if he had of he'd be admittin' that the wine was too much for him. So he just had to shut up and take it.

"I was all right too," says Smitty.

"Then what are you crabbin' about?" says Pat.

They wasn't no answer to that.

"I'm goin' to ring for some ice water," says Fogarty.

"Nobody never wants ice water at this time o' the mornin' unless they had a bad night," I says. "You don't hear Smitty askin' for no ice water."

Smitty'd of gave his right eye for a barrel of it, but he didn't have the nerve to say so.

Well, we made Fogarty get up and we stuck in there while they was dressin'. Fogarty had to go to his own room to get a clean shirt and collar, and we could hear him ringin' for water the minute he got in there. Fin'lly we took pity on Smitty and got him some too. He complained o' headache, and I says:

"That's a funny thing about Fogarty—no matter how much wine he laps up he don't never have no headache the next mornin'."

We didn't hear no more complaints from Smitty. They both went down to breakfast and tried to eat somethin', but it was hard work. And I noticed that neither o' them bothered Red with requests to pitch that day.

They went to bed—separated—right after supper and was as good as ever the followin' mornin'. I don't s'pose neither o' them had never drank no wine before, and, so far as I know, they didn't tackle it again. They both wanted to pitch in Chi, but Red was anxious to try out some kids; so he told both o' them, on the quiet, that they was the ones he was dependin' on for the World's Serious and he didn't want to risk gettin' 'em hurt.

Well, we wound up the season in Boston, and it was the next to the last day that we got into a awful jam! You remember readin' about Davis, the infielder Red bought from the New England League? Well, he'd got married the week before he joined us—married a Boston girl. He'd left her with her folks while he went West with us and she stuck to home till we hit Boston on that last trip. She was goin' to Philly with us to take in the serious.

Davis was a fast little cuss, not much bigger'n Maranville. Red had tried him out at short agin Pittsburgh and he'd looked good; but he was usin' the reg'lars most o' the time to keep 'em in shape for the big show. Davis had more nerve than any little feller I ever seen. He wouldn't break ground for none o' them Pittsburgh guys when they come into second base. In one o' the games there big Honus had told him to keep out o' the way or he'd get killed.

"It won't be no big slob like you that'll kill me!" says Davis.

Honus had a license to get sore at that, 'cause he was just slippin' the kid a friendly warnin'; but it shows you what a game little devil Davis was.

Well, as I was sayin', it was the next to the last day up in Boston that somethin' come off that pretty near cost us the big money. Mayer was pitchin' the game and we had the reg'lar club in agin 'em.

In one o' the boxes, right down next to the field, they was the prettiest girl I ever looked at. She was all alone and she was dressed up like a million bucks. She was sittin' where we could lamp her from our bench and all the boys had gave her the oncet over before the game ever started. Fogarty and Smitty wiped the dirt offen their faces and smoothed their hair the minute they piped her.

She was a lot more interestin' than the national pastime and I guess we was all gettin' a eyeful when, all of asudden, she smiled right at us. Our club was in the field and they was only a few of us on the bench—me and Pat and Davis and the pitchers, and one or two others. Well, I was one of a number that returned the salute; but after doin' it oncet I remembered I was a old married man and cut it out. But Fogarty and Smitty give a correct imitation of a toothpaste advertisement all the rest o' the time they sat there. Every three or four minutes she'd smile and then they'd smile back. They was wise to each other and it was a battle to see which one could give her the prettiest grin.

Just before the last half o' the eighth Fogarty ast Red whether he could go in and dress. He hadn't no more'n got permission when Smitty wanted to go too. I had 'em guessed right, and I and Pat was wonderin' which one'd cop. They raced to the clubhouse and Smitty beat him in. Now them two birds was usually awful slow about gettin' their clo'es changed, 'cause they was so partic'lar; but they beat the world's record this time. They was in their street clo'es and down in front o' that box just as the game ended.

Smitty was there first, but lots o' good it done him! He tipped his hat to the girl and got a cold stare. Then Fogarty come up and spoke to her. He was gave just as much encouragement as Smitty.

I begin to laugh, but I stopped quick. Before I knowed what was comin' off, little Davis grabbed a bat and started for the stand. Smitty was leanin' agin the box, with his left hand flat on the rail. Without a word o' warnin' Davis swung the bat overhand and it come down on poor Smitty's hand like a ton o' brick. Smitty yelled and fell over on the ground. Fogarty tried to duck, but he was too late. The little busher aimed the bat at his bean and catched him square on the right arm as he throwed it up to protect himself.

That's all they was to the bout. The first punch is a lot—'specially if you use a baseball bat. Neither o' them showed signs o' fightin' back. Besides, we was all on the job by that time and grabbed Davis. Little as he was, it took three of us to hold him. But, say, they was the devil to pay in the clubhouse! Red was goin' to shoot Davis till the truth come out."

"They went too far with it," says Davis. "They ain't no man can go up and talk to my wife without a introduction! I seen 'em tryin' to flirt with her. Them big bugs is so swell-headed that they think no girl could smile at nobody but them."

"You'd ought to of tipped 'em off," says Red.

"I hadn't ought to of did no such a thing," says Davis. "They'd ought to of knew by lookin' that she wasn't the kind o' girl that'd flirt. But I didn't feel in no danger o' havin' my home broke up, so I let 'em go."

Then Red jumped on me.

"That's what you get for eggin' 'em on," he says. "Where's our chancet in the World's Serious now?"

"Have some sense!" I says. "You wouldn't be thinkin' o' no World's Serious if I hadn't of egged 'em on."

We called a doctor for Smitty and Fogarty, and the news he give us didn't cheer us up none. He said he thought Smitty's hand was broke, but he'd have to take a X ray. The mitt was swole up as big as a ham. Fogarty's souper was hangin' limp as a rag, and the doc didn't believe he'd be able to raise it for a month. Afterward he found out that they was no bones busted in Smitty's hand, but it was in such shape that he couldn't hold a han'kerchief, let alone a baseball. There we was, three days before the start o' the serious, and our pitchin' staff shot to hellangone!

Red sent me and Pat and the trainer home that night with the pair o' cripples. We was to report up to the club's offices next mornin' and have all the doctors in Philly called in. Me and Pat was so sore that we couldn't talk to each other, and I don't think they was a word said on the trip. Yes, they was too; just before Smitty went to sleep he ast me a question:

"Who was that girl?"

"You'd ought to know by this time," I says. "That wasn't nobody but Davis' wife."

"Then what was she smilin' at me for?" he says.

Well, the Philly doctors told us they was absolutely no chancet o' havin' either o' them in shape for the serious and we was gettin' ready to count the losers' share. Red'd been figurin' on alternatin' the two, 'cause none o' the rest was in real shape; but now we didn't have nothin' that you could call a air-tight pitcher.

Rixey and Alexander and Mayer would of made 'em step some if they'd been right, but they wasn't.

I says to Pat:

"Looks like as though I and you and the bat boy would have to work."

"Looks that way," he says, "unless we can bring them two fellers round."

"How can we do that?" I says. "You heard what them doctors said."

"Yes," says Pat; "but they're the only hope we got, and I ain't goin' to give up till I have to."

Red and the bunch got in the next mornin', which was a Sunday. Most o' the gang went to church, and if the Lord'd never heard o' Fogarty and Smitty before I bet He knowed who they was when we got through prayin'. We practiced Monday and went over to Washin'ton that night.

Well, you know what come off. Johnson beat us there and Boehling beat us Wednesday in Philly. With Johnson to come back, twicet if necesary, it looked like a short serious.

And then it begin to rain. It's a wonder the District o' Columbia wasn't washed away. Four straight days of it, includin' Sunday; and I never seen it come down so hard. A cleanin' like that might do Pittsburgh or Chi some good, but it looked like wastin' it in Washin'ton. We was anxious to get the serious over with; and the more it rained, the worse we hated it. We never figured that it was the best thing that could of happened to us!

I'm the guy they'd ought to thank for coppin' the league pennant. And the rain and me together was what saved us from a awful lickin' for the big dough. On Sunday night, while we was still layin' round the hotel in Washin'ton, where we'd been stalled since Thursday, I got my hunch. I went to Red with it.

"Maybe one o' them fellers could help us out now," I says.

"What makes you think so?" says Red.

"Well," I says, "they've had time to get back in shape."

"No use," says Red. "I was just talkin' to Smitty in the dinin' room. He couldn't even hold his knife. He says his mitt feels just as bad as it did the first day."

"How about Fogarty?" I ast.

"He ain't no better off," says Red. "The worst of it is that neither one o' them seems to care."

"Maybe I can wake 'em up," I says.

"You got my permission to try," says Red.

Me and Fogarty wasn't roomin' together. The trainer was doubled up with him and they had another guy lookin' out for Smitty. Neither o' them had put on a suit, but they'd saw us get our two beatin's from the stand. I found Smitty first and took him into the bar.

"How does it look to you?" I says.

"We're licked," says he.

"Don't be too sure!" I says.

"What do you mean?" he ast me. "What chancet have we got with nobody to pitch?"

"We got somebody to pitch now," I says.

"Who?" says Smitty.

"Fogarty," says I. "The doctor says he's all right and Red's goin' to start him to-morrow."

"You're crazy!" says Smitty. "The doctor said he wouldn't be no good till next year."

"That was pretty near a week ago," I says. "Besides, that doctor didn't know nothin'. We had the best doctor in Washin'ton up to see him to-night—the doctor that looks after the President and all the congressmen. He says they's nothin' at all the matter with him."

I left Smitty then and went lookin' for Fogarty.

I found him in his room gettin' his poor souper rubbed. I spoke my piece over again. I told him Smitty'd been pronounced cured by the President's special surgeon and that he was goin' to start the next day's game.

An hour later I run into Red, and he was smilin' like Davis' wife.

"You've did it, old boy!" he says. "They both been after me till I had to duck out in the wet to get away from 'em. They both insist on workin' to-morrow, and I told 'em I wasn't goin' to decide on my pitcher till mornin'."

"I guess I don't know nothin'!" I says. "Which one are you goin' to start?"

"The one that can throw a ball with the least pain," says Red.

You know the rest of it. The sun shined on us next day, and Smitty shut 'em out and beat Johnson on the wettest grounds I ever seen! I don't know yet how he gripped a wet ball with that hand, but he done it. And Fogarty's game Tuesday was even better. If his arm hurt he kept it to himself.

Smitty come back agin Johnson Wednesday and pitched the prettiest game that was ever pitched. Milan and Gandil and them might just as well of used jackstraws as bats, for all the good their swingin' done. He whiffed plain sixteen men and Johnson's two-bagger was their only wallop. Nobody didn't grudge Walter that one, 'cause he pitched a grand game too.

Well, the honor o' coppin' the final pastime and winnin' the title went to Fogarty; and it pleased him about as much as a toothache. Do you know why? 'Cause the papers was full o' Smitty's two victories over Johnson and didn't say much about nothin' else. Fogarty told me afterward that if he'd thought at the time he'd of refused to pitch Thursday and made Red work him agin the big blond in the seventh game.

"But," I says, "s'spose Red had pitched Smitty right back and he'd of trimmed 'em and they hadn't been no seventh game anyway. Then where'd you of been at?"

"That's right!" he says. "That wop is just lucky enough to of did it, too, even if he can't pitch up an alley."

Well, I made a little speech in the clubhouse and collected a purse of a hundred and fifty bucks. I'm goin' to send it to Jack Barnett as soon as I can get his address. That'll fix him up on that bet he made with Punch Knoll and give him a little spendin' money besides. If he hadn't of told me that stuff in Dayton we'd of been fightin' the Cardinals for seventh place. And if he'd of told it to some guys they wouldn't of had sense enough to of tooken advantage of it.

One o' the Philly doctors told Red, and Red told me, that we'd prob'ly ruined both o' them guys for the next season by workin' 'em in the shape they was in. But I should worry! Between me and you, I ain't goin' to be with the Phillies next year. I'm goin' to manage the Mobile Club; and maybe I can play some in that climate. And I guess I don't know nothin' about managin' a ball club. No; I guess not!

Horseshoes

The Saturday Evening Post
AUGUST 15, 1914

The series ended Tuesday, but I had stayed in Philadelphia an extra day on the chance of there being some follow-up stuff worth sending. Nothing had broken loose; so I filed some stuff about what the Athletics and Giants were going to do with their dough, and then caught the eight o'clock train for Chicago.

Having passed up supper in order to get my story away and grab the train, I went to the buffet car right after I'd planted my grips. I sat down at one of the tables and ordered a sandwich. Four salesmen were playing rum at the other table and all the chairs in the car were occupied; so it didn't surprise me when somebody flopped down in the seat opposite me.

I looked up from my paper and with a little thrill recognized my companion. Now I've been experting round the country with ball players so much that it doesn't usually excite me to meet one face to face, even if he's a star. I can talk with Tyrus without getting all fussed up. But this particular player had jumped from obscurity to fame so suddenly and had played such an important though brief part in the recent argument between the Macks and McGraws that I couldn't help being a little awed by his proximity.

It was none other than Grimes, the utility outfielder Connie had been forced to use in the last game because of the injury to Joyce—Grimes, whose miraculous catch in the eleventh inning had robbed Parker of a home run and the Giants of victory, and whose own homer—a fluky one—had given the Athletics another World's Championship.

I had met Grimes one day during the spring he was with the Cubs, but I knew he wouldn't remember me. A ball player never recalls a reporter's face on less than six introductions or his name on less than twenty. However, I resolved to speak to him, and had just mustered sufficient courage to open a conversation when he saved me the trouble.

"Whose picture have they got there?" he asked, pointing to my paper.

"Speed Parker's," I replied.

"What do they say about him?" asked Grimes.

"I'll read it to you," I said:

"Speed Parker, McGraw's great third baseman, is ill in a local hospital with nervous prostration the result of the strain of the World's Series, in which he played such a stellar rôle. Parker is in such a dangerous condition that no one is allowed to see him. Members of the New York team and fans from Gotham called at the hospital to-day, but were unable to gain admittance to his ward. Philadelphians hope he will recover speedily and will suffer no permanent ill effects from his sickness, for he won their admiration by his work in the series, though he was on a rival team. A lucky catch by Grimes, the Athletics' substitute outfielder, was all that prevented Parker from winning the title for New York. According to Manager Mack, of the champions, the series would have been over in four games but for Parker's wonderful exhibition of nerve and—' "

"That'll be a plenty," Grimes interrupted. "And that's just what you might expect from one o' them doughheaded reporters. If all the baseball writers was where they belonged they'd have to build an annex to Matteawan."

I kept my temper with very little effort—it takes more than a peevish ball player's remarks to insult one of our fraternity; but I didn't exactly understand his peeve.

"Doesn't Parker deserve the bouquet?" I asked.

"Oh, they can boost him all they want to," said Grimes; "but when they call that catch lucky and don't mention the fact that Parker is the luckiest guy in the world, somethin' must be wrong with 'em. Did you see the serious?"

"No," I lied glibly, hoping to draw from him the cause of his grouch.

"Well," he said, "you sure missed somethin'. They never was a serious like it before and they won't never be one again. It went the full seven games and every game was a bear. They was one big innin' every day and Parker was the big cheese in it. Just as Connie says, the Ath-a-letics would of cleaned 'em in four games but for Parker; but it wasn't because he's a great ball player—it was because he was born with a knife, fork and spoon in his mouth, and a rabbit's foot hung round his neck.

"You may not know it, but I'm Grimes, the guy that made the lucky catch. I'm the guy that won the serious with a hit—a home-run hit; and I'm here to tell you that if I'd had one-tenth o' Parker's luck they'd of heard about me long before yesterday. They say my homer was lucky. Maybe it was; but, believe me, it was time things broke for me. They been breakin' for him all his life."

"Well," I said, "his luck must have gone back on him if he's in a hospital with nervous prostration."

"Nervous prostration nothin'," said Grimes. "He's in a hospital because his face is all out o' shape and he's ashamed to appear on the street. I don't usually do so much talkin' and I'm ravin' a little to-night because I've had a couple o' drinks; but—"

"Have another," said I, ringing for the waiter, "and talk some more."

"I made two hits yesterday," Grimes went on, "but the crowd only seen one. I busted up the game and the serious with the one they seen. The one they didn't see was the one I busted up a guy's map with—and Speed Parker was the guy. That's why he's in a hospital. He may be able to play ball next year; but I'll bet my share o' the dough that McGraw won't reco'nize him when he shows up at Marlin in the spring."

"When did this come off?" I asked. "And why?"

"It comc off outsidc the clubhouse after yesterday's battle," he said; "and I hit him because he called me a name—a name I won't stand for from him."

"What did he call you?" I queried, expecting to hear one of the delicate epithets usually applied by conquered to conqueror on the diamond.

"'Horseshoes!'" was Grimes' amazing reply.

"But, good Lord!" I remonstrated, "I've heard of ball players calling each other that, and Lucky Stiff, and Fourleaf Clover, ever since I was a foot high, and I never knew them to start fights about it."

"Well," said Grimes, "I might as well give you all the dope; and then if you don't think I was justified I'll pay your fare from here to wherever your goin'. I don't want you to think I'm kickin' about trifles—or that I'm kickin' at all, for that matter. I just want to prove to you that he didn't have no license to pull that Horseshoes stuff on me and that I only give him what was comin' to him."

"Go ahead and shoot," said I.

"Give us some more o' the same," said Grimes to the passing waiter. And then he told me about it.

Maybe you've heard that me and Speed Parker was raised in the same town—Ishpeming, Michigan. We was kids together, and though he done all the devilment I got all the lickin's. When we was about twelve years old Speed throwed a rotten egg at the teacher and I got expelled. That made me sick o' schools and I wouldn't never go to one again, though my ol' man beat me up and the truant officers threatened to have me hung.

Well, while Speed was learnin' what was the principal products o' New Hampshire and Texas I was workin' round the freighthouse and drivin' a dray.

We'd both been playin' ball all our lives; and when the town organized a semi-pro club we got jobs with it. We was to draw two bucks apiece for each game and they played every Sunday. We played four games before we got our first pay. They was a hole in my pants pocket as big as the home plate, but I forgot about it and put the dough in there. It wasn't there when I got home. Speed didn't have no hole in his pocket—you can bet on that! Afterward the club hired a good outfielder and I was canned. They was huntin' for another third baseman too; but, o' course, they didn't find none and Speed held his job.

The next year they started the Northern Peninsula League. We landed with the home team. The league opened in May and blowed up the third week in June. They paid off all the outsiders first and then had just money enough left to settle with one of us two Ishpeming guys. The night they done the payin' I was out to my uncle's farm, so they settled with Speed and told me I'd have to wait for mine. I'm still waitin'!

Gene Higgins, who was manager o' the Battle Creek Club, lived in Houghton, and that winter we goes over and strikes him for a job. He give it to us and we busted in together two years ago last spring.

I had a good year down there. I hit over .300 and stole all the bases in sight. Speed got along good too, and they was several big-league scouts lookin' us over. The Chicago Cubs bought Speed outright and four clubs put in a draft for me. Three of 'em—Cleveland and the New York Giants and the Boston Nationals—needed outfielders bad, and it would of been a pipe for me to of made good with any of 'em. But who do you think got me? The same Chicago Cubs; and the only outfielders they had at that time was Schulte and Leach and Good and Williams and Stewart, and one or two others.

Well, I didn't figure I was any worse off than Speed. The Cubs had Zimmerman at third base and it didn't look like they was any danger of a busher beatin' him out; but Zimmerman goes and breaks his leg the second day o' the season—that's a year ago last April—and Speed jumps right in as a regular. Do you think anything like that could happen to Schulte or Leach, or any o' them outfielders? No, sir! I wore out my uniform slidin' up and down the bench and wonderin' whether they'd ship me to Fort Worth or Siberia.

Now I want to tell you about the miserable luck Speed had right off the reel. We was playin' at St. Louis. They had a one-run lead in the eighth, when their pitcher walked Speed with one out. Saier hits a high fly to centre and Parker starts with the crack o' the bat. Both coachers was yellin' at him to go back, but he thought they was two out and he was clear round to third base when the ball come down. And Oakes muffs it! O' course he scored and the game was tied up.

Parker come in to the bench like he'd did something wonderful.

"Did you think they was two out?" ast Hank.

"No," says Speed, blushin'.

"Then what did you run for?" says Hank.

"I had a hunch he was goin' to drop the ball," says Speed; and Hank pretty near falls off the bench.

The next day he come up with one out and the sacks full, and the score tied in the sixth. He smashes one on the ground straight at Hauser and it looked like a cinch double play; but just as Hauser was goin' to grab it the ball hit a rough spot and hopped a mile over his head. It got between Oakes and Magee and went clear to the fence. Three guys scored and Speed pulled up at third. The papers come out and said the game was won by a three-bagger from the bat o' Parker, the Cubs' sensational kid third baseman. Gosh!

We go home to Chi and are havin' a hot battle with Pittsburgh. This time Speed's turn come when they was two on and two out, and Pittsburgh a run to the good—I think it was the eighth innin'. Cooper gives him a fast one and he hits it straight up in the air. O' course the runners started goin', but it looked hopeless because they wasn't no wind or high sky to bother anybody. Mowrey and Gibson both goes after the ball; and just as Mowrey was set for the catch Gibson bumps into him and they both fall down. Two runs scored and Speed got to second. Then what does he do but try to steal third—with two out too! And Gibson's peg pretty near hits the left field seats on the fly.

When Speed comes to the bench Hank says:

"If I was you I'd quit playin' ball and go to Monte Carlo."

"What for?" says Speed.

"You're so dam' lucky!" says Hank.

"So is Ty Cobb," says Speed. That's how he hated himself!

First trip to Cincy we run into a couple of old Ishpeming boys. They took us out one night, and about twelve o'clock I said we'd have to go back to the hotel or we'd get fined. Speed said I had cold feet and he stuck with the boys. I went back alone and Hank caught me comin' in and put a fifty-dollar plaster on me. Speed stayed out all night long and Hank never knowed it. I says to myself: "Wait till he gets out there and tries to play ball without no sleep!" But the game that day was called off on account o' rain. Can you beat it?

I remember what he got away with the next afternoon the same as though it happened yesterday. In the second innin' they walked him with nobody down, and he took a big lead off first base like he always does. Benton throwed over there three or four times to scare him back, and the last time he throwed, Hobby hid the ball. The coacher seen it and told Speed to hold the bag; but he didn't pay no attention. He started leadin' right off again and Hobby tried to tag him, but the ball slipped out of his hand and rolled about a yard away. Parker had plenty o' time to get back; but, instead o' that, he starts for second. Hobby picked up the ball and shot it down to Groh—and Groh made a square muff.

Parker slides into the bag safe and then gets up and throws out his chest like he'd made the greatest play ever. When the ball's throwed back to Benton, Speed leads off about thirty foot and stands there in a trance. Clarke signs for a pitch-out and pegs down to second to nip him. He was caught flatfooted—that is, he would of been with a decent throw; but Clarke's peg went pretty near to Latonia. Speed scored and strutted over to receive our hearty congratulations. Some o' the boys was laughin' and he thought they was laughin' with him instead of at him.

It was in the ninth, though, that he got by with one o' the worst I ever seen. The Reds was a run behind and Marsans was a on third base with two out. Hobby, I think it was, hit one on the ground right at Speed and he picked it up clean. The crowd all got up and started for the exits. Marsans run toward the plate in the faint hope that the peg to first would be wild. All of a sudden the boys on the Cincy bench begun yellin' at him to slide, and he done so. He was way past the plate when Speed's throw got to Archer. The bonehead had shot the ball home instead o' to the first base, thinkin' they was only one down. We was all crazy, believin' his nut play had let 'em tie it up; but he comes tearin' in, tellin' Archer to tag Marsans. So Jim walks over and tags the Cuban, who was brushin' off his uniform.

"You're out!" says Klem. "You never touched the plate."

I guess Marsans knowed the umps was right because he didn't make much of a holler. But Speed sure got pannin' in the clubhouse.

"I suppose you knowed he was goin' to miss the plate!" says Hank sarcastic as he could.

Everybody on the club roasted him, but it didn't do no good.

Well, you know what happened to me. I only got into one game with the Cubs—one afternoon when Leach was sick. We was playin' the Boston bunch and Tyler was workin' against us. I always had trouble with lefthanders and this was one of his good days. I couldn't see what he throwed up there. I got one foul durin' the afternoon's entertainment and the wind was blowin' a hundred-mile gale, so that the best outfielder in the world couldn't judge a fly ball. That Boston bunch must of hit fifty of 'em and they all come to my field.

If I caught any I've forgot about it. Couple o' days after that I got notice o' my release to Indianapolis.

Parker kept right on all season doin' the blamedest things you ever heard of and gettin' by with 'em. One o' the boys told me about it later. If they was playin' a double-header in St. Louis, with the thermometer at 130 degrees, he'd get put out by the umps in the first innin' o' the first game. If he started to steal the catcher'd drop the pitch or somebody'd muff the throw. If he hit a pop fly the sun'd get in somebody's eyes. If he took a swell third strike with the bases full the umps would call it a ball. If he cut first base by twenty feet the umps would be readin' the mornin' paper.

Zimmerman's leg mended, so that he was all right by June; and then Saier got sick and they tried Speed at first base. He'd never saw the bag before; but things kept on breakin' for him and he played it like a house afire. The Cubs copped the pennant and Speed got in on the big dough, besides playin' a whale of a game through the whole serious.

Speed and me both went back to Ishpeming to spend the winter—though the Lord knows it ain't no winter resort. Our homes was there; and besides, in my case, they was a certain girl livin' in the old burg.

Parker, o' course, was the hero and the swell guy when we got home. He'd been in the World's Serious and had plenty o' dough in his kick. I come home with nothin' but my suitcase and a hard-luck story, which I kept to myself. I hadn't even went good enough in Indianapolis to be sure of a job there again.

That fall—last fall—an uncle o' Speed's died over in the Soo and left him ten thousand bucks. I had an uncle down in the Lower Peninsula who was worth five times that much—but he had good health!

This girl I spoke about was the prettiest thing I ever see. I'd went with her in the old days, and when I blew back I found she was still strong for me. They wasn't a great deal o' variety in Ishpeming for a girl to pick from. Her and I went to the dance every Saturday night and to church Sunday nights. I called on her Wednesday evenin's, besides takin' her to all the shows that come along—rotten as the most o' them was.

I never knowed Speed was makin' a play for this doll till along last Feb'uary. The minute I seen what was up I got busy. I took her out sleigh-ridin' and kept her out in the cold till she'd promised to marry me. We set the date for this fall—I figured I'd know better where I was at by that time.

Well, we didn't make no secret o' bein' engaged; down in the poolroom one night Speed come up and congratulated me. He says:

"You got a swell girl, Dick! I wouldn't mind bein' in your place. You're mighty lucky to cop her out—you old Horseshoes, you!"

"Horseshoes!" I says. "You got a fine license to call anybody Horseshoes! I suppose you ain't never had no luck?"

"Not like you," he says.

I was feelin' too good about grabbin' the girl to get sore at the time; but when I got to thinkin' about it a few minutes afterward it made me mad clear through. What right did that bird have to talk about me bein' lucky?

Speed was playin' freeze-out at a table near the door, and when I started home some o' the boys with him says:

"Good night, Dick."

I said good night and then Speed looked up.

"Good night, Horseshoes!" he says.

That got my nanny this time.

"Shut up, you lucky stiff!" I says. "If you wasn't so dam' lucky you'd be sweepin' the streets." Then I walks on out.

I was too busy with the girl to see much o' Speed after that. He left home about the middle o' the month to go to Tampa with the Cubs. I got notice from Indianapolis that I was sold to Baltimore. I didn't care much about goin' there and I wasn't anxious to leave home under the circumstances, so I didn't report till late.

When I read in the papers along in April that Speed had been traded to Boston for a couple o' pitchers I thought: "Gee! He must of lost his rabbit's foot!" Because, even if the Cubs didn't cop again, they'd have a city serious with the White Sox and get a bunch o' dough that way. And they wasn't no chance in the world for the Boston Club to get nothin' but their salaries.

It wasn't another month, though, till Shafer, o' the Giants, quit baseball and McGraw was up against it for a third baseman. Next think I knowed Speed was traded to New York and was with another winner—for they never was out o' first place all season.

I was gettin' along all right at Baltimore and Dunnie liked me; so I felt like I had somethin' more than just a one-year job—somethin' I could get married on. It was all framed that the weddin' was comin' off as soon as this season was over; so you can believe I was pullin' for October to hurry up and come.

One day in August, two months ago, Dunnie come in the clubhouse and handed me the news.

"Rube Oldring's busted his leg," he says, "and he's out for the rest o' the season. Connie's got a youngest named Joyce that he can stick in there, but he's got to have an extra outfielder. He's made me a good proposition for you and I'm goin' to let you go. It'll be pretty soft for you, because they got the pennant cinched and they'll cut you in on the big money."

"Yes," I says; "and when they're through with me they'll ship me to Hellangone, and I'll be draggin' down about seventy-five bucks a month next year."

"Nothin' like that," says Dunnie. "If he don't want you next season he's got to ask for waivers; and if you get out o' the big league you come right back here. That's all framed."

So that's how I come to get with the Ath-a-letics. Connie give me a nice, comf'table seat in one corner o' the bench and I had the pleasure o' watchin' a real ball club perform once every afternoon and sometimes twice.

Connie told me that as soon as they had the flag cinched he was goin' to lay off some o' his regulars and I'd get a chance to play.

Well, they cinched it the fourth day o' September and our next engagement was with Washin'ton on Labor Day. We had two games and I was in both of 'em. And I broke in with my usual lovely luck, because the pitchers I was ast to face was Boehling, a nasty left-hander, and this guy Johnson.

The mornin' game was Boehling's and he wasn't no worse than some o' the rest of his kind. I only whiffed once and would of had a triple if Milan hadn't run from here to New Orleans and stole one off me.

I'm not boastin' about my first experience with Johnson though. They can't never tell me he throws them balls with his arm. He's got a gun concealed about his person and he shoots 'em up there. I was leadin' off in Murphy's place and the game was a little delayed in startin', because I'd watched the big guy warm up and wasn't in no hurry to get to that plate. Before I left the bench Connie says:

"Don't try to take no healthy swing. Just meet 'em and you'll get along better."

So I tried to just meet the first one he throwed; but when I stuck out my bat Henry was throwin' the pill back to Johnson. Then I thought: Maybe if I start swingin' now at the second one I'll hit the third one. So I let the second one come over and the umps guessed it was another strike, though I'll bet a thousand bucks he couldn't see it no more'n I could.

While Johnson was still windin' up to pitch again I started to swing—and the big cuss crosses me with a slow one. I lunged at it twice and missed it both times, and the force o' my wallop throwed me clean back to the bench. The Ath-a-letics was all laughin' at me and I laughed too, because I was glad that much of it was over.

McInnes gets a base hit off him in the second innin' and I ast him how he done it.

"He's a friend o' mine," says Jack, "and he lets up when he pitches to me."

I made up my mind right there that if I was goin' to be in the league next year I'd go out and visit Johnson this winter and get acquainted.

I wished before the day was over that I was hittin' in the catcher's place, because the fellers down near the tail-end of the battin' order only had to face him three times. He fanned me on three pitched balls again in the third, and when I come up in the sixth he scared me to death by pretty near beanin' me with the first one.

"Be careful!" says Henry. "He's gettin' pretty wild and he's liable to knock you away from your uniform."

"Don't he never curve one?" I ast.

"Sure!" says Henry. "Do you want to see his curve?"

"Yes," I says, knowin' the hook couldn't be no worse'n the fast one.

So he give me three hooks in succession and I missed 'em all; but I felt more comf'table than when I was duckin' his fast ball. In the ninth he hit my bat with a curve and the ball went on the ground to McBride. He booted it, but throwed me out easy—because I was so surprised at not havin' whiffed that I forgot to run!

Well, I went along like that for the rest o' the season, runnin' up against the best pitchers in the league and not exactly murderin' 'em. Everything I tried went wrong, and I was smart enough to know that if anything had depended on the games I wouldn't of been in there for two minutes. Joyce and Strunk and Murphy wasn't jealous o' me a bit; but they was glad to take turns restin', and I didn't care much how I went so long as I was sure of a job next year.

I'd wrote to the girl a couple o' times askin' her to set the exact date for our weddin'; but she hadn't paid no attention. She said she was glad I was with the Ath-a-letics, but she thought the Giants was goin' to beat us. I might of suspected from that that somethin' was wrong, because not even a girl would pick the Giants to trim that bunch of ourn. Finally, the day before the serious started, I sent her a kind o' sassy letter sayin' I guessed it was up to me to name the day, and askin' whether October twentieth was all right. I told her to wire me yes or no.

I'd been readin' the dope about Speed all season, and I knowed he'd had a whale of a year and that his luck was right with him; but I never dreamed a man could have the Lord on his side as strong as

Speed did in that World's Serious! I might as well tell you all the dope, so long as you wasn't there.

The first game was on our grounds and Connie give us a talkin' to in the clubhouse beforehand.

"The shorter this serious is," he says, "the better for us. If it's a long serious we're goin' to have trouble, because McGraw's got five pitchers he can work and we've got about three; so I want you boys to go at 'em from the jump and play 'em off their feet. Don't take things easy, because it ain't goin' to be no snap. Just because we've licked 'em before ain't no sign we'll do it this time."

Then he calls me to one side and ast me what I knowed about Parker.

"You was with the Cubs when he was, wasn't you?" he says.

"Yes," I says; "and he's the luckiest stiff you ever seen! If he got stewed and fell in the gutter he'd catch a fish."

"I don't like to hear a good ball player called lucky," says Connie. "He must have a lot of ability or McGraw wouldn't use him regular. And he's been hittin' about .340 and played a bang-up game at third base. That can't be all luck."

"Wait till you see him," I says; "and if you don't say he's the luckiest guy in the world you can sell me to the Boston Bloomer Girls. He's so lucky," I says, "that if they traded him to the St. Louis Browns they'd have the pennant cinched by the Fourth o' July."

And I'll bet Connie was willin' to agree with me before it was over.

Well, the Chief worked against the Big Rube in that game. We beat 'em, but they give us a battle and it was Parker that made it close. We'd gone along nothin' and nothin' till the seventh, and then Rube walks Collins and Baker lifts one over that little old wall. You'd think by this time them New York pitchers would know better than to give that guy anything he can hit.

In their part o' the ninth the Chief still had 'em shut out and two down, and the crowd was goin' home; but Doyle gets hit in the sleeve with a pitched ball and it's Speed's turn. He hits a foul pretty near straight up, but Schang misjudges it. Then he lifts another one and this time McInnes drops it. He'd ought to of been out twice. The Chief tries to make him hit at a bad one then, because he'd got him two strikes and nothin'. He hit at it all right—kissed it for three bases between Strunk and Joyce! And it was a wild pitch that he hit. Doyle scores, o' course, and the bugs suddenly decide not to go home just yet. I fully expected to see him steal home and get away with it, but Murray cut into the first ball and lined out to Barry.

Plank beat Matty two to one the next day in New York, and again Speed and his rabbit's foot give us an awful argument. Matty wasn't so good as usual and we really ought to of beat him bad. Two different times Strunk was on second waitin' for any kind o' wallop, and both times Barry cracked 'em down the third-base line like a shot. Speed stopped the first one with his stomach and extricated the pill just in time to nail Barry at first base and retire the side. The next time he throwed his glove in front of his face in self-defense and the ball stuck in it.

In the sixth innin' Schang was on third base and Plank on first, and two down, and Murphy combed an awful one to Speed's left. He didn't have time to stoop over and he just stuck out his foot. The ball hit it and caromed in two hops right into Doyle's hands on second base before Plank got there. Then in the seventh Speed bunts one and Baker trips and falls goin' after it or he'd of threw him out a mile. They was two gone; so Speed steals second, and, o' course, Schang has to make a bad peg right at that time and lets him go to third. Then Collins boots one on Murray and they've got a run. But it didn't do 'em no good, because Collins and Baker and McInnes come up in the ninth and walloped 'em where Parker couldn't reach 'em.

Comin' back to Philly on the train that night, I says to Connie:

"What do you think o' that Parker bird now?"

"He's lucky, all right," says Connie smilin'; "but we won't hold it against him if he don't beat us with it."

"It ain't too late," I says. "He ain't pulled his real stuff yet."

The whole bunch was talkin' about him and his luck, and sayin' it was about time for things to break against him. I warned 'em that they wasn't no chance—that it was permanent with him.

Bush and Tesreau hooked up next day and neither o' them had much stuff. Everybody was hittin' and it looked like anybody's game right up to the ninth. Speed had got on every time he come up—the wind blowin' his fly balls away from the outfielders and the infielders bootin' when he hit 'em on the ground.

When the ninth started the score was seven apiece. Connie and McGraw both had their whole pitchin' staffs warmin' up. The crowd was wild, because they'd been all kinds of action. They wasn't no danger of anybody's leavin' their seats before this game was over.

Well, Bescher is walked to start with and Connie's about ready to give Bush the hook; but Doyle pops out tryin' to bunt. Then Speed gets two strikes and two balls, and it looked to me like the next one was right over the heart; but Connolly calls it a ball and gives him another chance. He whales the groove ball to the fence in left center and gets round to third on it, while Bescher scores. Right then Bush comes out and the Chief goes in. He whiffs Murray and has two strikes on Merkle when Speed makes a break for home—and, o' course, that was the one ball Schang dropped in the whole serious!

They had a two-run lead on us then and it looked like a cinch for them to hold it, because the minute Tesreau showed a sign o' weakenin' McGraw was sure to holler for Matty or the Rube. But you know how quick that bunch of ourn can make a two-run lead look sick. Before McGraw could get Jeff out o' there we had two on the bases.

Then Rube comes in and fills 'em up by walkin' Joyce. It was Eddie's turn to wallop and if he didn't do nothin' we had Baker comin' up next. This time Collins saved Baker the trouble and whanged one clear to the woods. Everybody scored but him—and he could of, too, if it'd been necessary.

In the clubhouse the boys naturally felt pretty good. We'd

copped three in a row and it looked like we'd make it four straight, because we had the Chief to send back at 'em the followin' day.

"Your friend Parker is lucky," the boys says to me, "but it don't look like he could stop us now."

I felt the same way and was consultin' the time-tables to see whether I could get a train out o' New York for the West next evenin'. But do you think Speed's luck was ready to quit? Not yet! And it's a wonder we didn't all go nuts durin' the next few days. If words could kill, Speed would of died a thousand times. And I wish he had!

They wasn't no record-breakin' crowd out when we got to the Polo Grounds. I guess the New York bugs was pretty well discouraged and the bettin' was eight to five that we'd cop that battle and finish it. The Chief was the only guy that warmed up for us and McGraw didn't have no choice but to use Matty, with the whole thing dependin' on this game.

They went along like the two swell pitchers they was till Speed's innin', which in this battle was the eighth. Nobody scored, and it didn't look like they was ever goin' to till Murphy starts off that round with a perfect bunt and Joyce sacrifices him to second. All Matty had to do then was to get rid o' Collins and Baker—and that's about as easy as sellin' silk socks to an Eskimo.

He didn't give Eddie nothin' he wanted to hit, though; and finally he slaps one on the ground to Doyle. Larry made the play to first base and Murphy moved to third. We all figured Matty'd walk Baker then, and he done it. Connie sends Baker down to second on the first pitch to McInnes, but Meyers don't pay no attention to him—they was playin' for McInnes and wasn't takin' no chances o' throwin' the ball away.

Well, the count goes to three and two on McInnes and Matty comes with a curve—he's got some curve too; but Jack happened to meet it and—Blooie! Down the left foul line where he always hits! I never seen a ball hit so hard in my life. No infielder in the world could of stopped it. But I'll give you a thousand bucks if that ball didn't go kerplunk right into the third bag and stop as dead as George Washington! It was child's play for Speed to pick it up and heave it over to Merkle before Jack got there. If anybody else had been playin' third base the bag would of ducked out o' the way o' that wallop; but even the bases themselves was helpin' him out.

The two runs we ought to of had on Jack's smash would of been just enough to beat 'em, because they got the only run o' the game in their half—or, I should say, the Lord give it to 'em.

Doyle'd been throwed out and up come Parker, smilin'. The minute I seen him smile I felt like somethin' was comin' off and I made the remark on the bench.

Well, the Chief pitched one right at him and he tried to duck. The ball hit his bat and went on a line between Jack and Eddie. Speed didn't know he'd hit it till the guys on the bench wised him up. Then he just had time to get to first base. They tried the hit-and-run on the second ball and Murray lifts a high fly that Murphy didn't have to move for. Collins pulled the old bluff about the ball bein' on the ground and Barry yells, "Go on! Go on!" like he was the coacher. Speed fell for it and didn't know where the ball was no more'n a rabbit; he just run his fool head off and we was gettin' all ready to laugh when the ball come down and Murphy dropped it!

If Parker had stuck near first base, like he ought to of done, he couldn't of got no farther'n second; but with the start he got he was pretty near third when Murphy made the muff, and it was a cinch for him to score. The next two guys was easy outs; so they wouldn't of had a run except for Speed's boner. We couldn't do nothin' in the ninth and we was licked.

Well, that was a tough one to lose; but we figured that Matty was through and we'd wind it up the next day, as we had Plank ready to send back at 'em. We wasn't afraid o' the Rube, because he hadn't never bothered Collins and Baker much.

The two lefthanders come together just like everybody'd doped it and it was about even up to the eighth. Plank had been goin' great and, though the score was two and two, they'd got their two on boots and we'd hit ourn in. We went after Rube in our part o' the eighth and knocked him out. Demaree stopped us after we'd scored two more.

"It's all over but the shoutin'!" says Davis on the bench.

"Yes," I says, "unless that seventh son of a seventh son of a seventh son gets up there again."

He did, and he come up after they'd filled the bases with a boot, a base hit and a walk with two out. I says to Davis:

"If I was Plank I'd pass him and give 'em one run."

"That wouldn't be no baseball," says Davis—"not with Murray comin' up."

Well, it mayn't of been no baseball, but it couldn't of turned out worse if they'd did it that way. Speed took a healthy at the first ball; but it was a hook and he caught it on the handle, right up near his hands. It started outside the first-base line like a foul and then changed its mind and rolled in. Schang run away from the plate, because it looked like it was up to him to make the play. He picked the ball up and had to make the peg in a hurry.

His throw hit Speed right on top o' the head and bounded off like it had struck a cement sidewalk. It went clear over to the seats and before McInnes could get it three guys had scored and Speed was on third base. He was left there, but that didn't make no difference. We was licked again and for the first time the gang really begun to get scared.

We went over to New York Sunday afternoon and we didn't do no singin' on the way. Some o' the fellers tried to laugh, but it hurt 'em. Connie sent us to bed early, but I don't believe none o' the bunch got much sleep—I know I didn't; I was worryin' too much about the serious and also about the girl, who hadn't sent me no telegram like I'd ast her to. Monday mornin' I wired her askin' what was the matter and tellin' her I was gettin' tired of her foolishness. O' course I didn't make it so strong as that—but the telegram cost me a dollar and forty cents.

Connie had the choice o' two pitchers for the sixth game. He could use Bush, who'd been slammed round pretty hard last time out, or the Chief, who'd only had two days' rest. The rest of 'em—outside o' Plank—had a epidemic o' sore arms. Connie finally picked Bush, so's he could have the Chief in reserve in case we had to play a seventh game. McGraw started Big Jeff and we went at it.

It wasn't like the last time these two guys had hooked up. This time they both had somethin', and for eight innin's runs was as scarce as Chinese policemen. They'd been chances to score on both sides but the big guy and Bush was both tight in the pinches. The crowd was plumb nuts and yelled like Indians every time a fly ball was caught or a strike called. They'd of got their money's worth if they hadn't been no ninth; but, believe me, that was some round!

They was one out when Barry hit one through the box for a base. Schang walked, and it was Bush's turn. Connie told him to bunt, but he whiffed in the attempt. Then Murphy comes up and walks—and the bases are choked. Young Joyce had been pie for Tesreau all day or else McGraw might of changed pitchers right there. Anyway he left Big Jeff in and he beaned Joyce with a fast one. It sounded like a tire blowin' out. Joyce falls over in a heap and we chase out there, thinkin' he's dead; but he ain't, and pretty soon he gets up and walks down to first base. Tesreau had forced in a run and again we begun to count the winner's end. Matty comes in to prevent further damage and Collins flies the side out.

"Hold 'em now! Work hard!" we says to young Bush, and he walks out there just as cool as though he was goin' to hit fungoes.

McGraw sends up a pinch hitter for Matty and Bush whiffed him. Then Bescher flied out. I was prayin' that Doyle would end it, because Speed's turn come after his'n; so I pretty near fell dead when Larry hit safe.

Speed had his old smile and even more chest than usual when he come up there, swingin' five or six bats. He didn't wait for Doyle to try and steal, or nothin'. He lit into the first ball, though Bush was tryin' to waste it. I seen the ball go high in the air toward left field, and then I picked up my glove and got ready to beat it for the gate.

But when I looked out to see if Joyce was set, what do you think I seen? He was lyin' flat on the ground! That blow on the head had got him just as Bush was pitchin' to Speed. He'd flopped over and didn't no more know what was goin' on than if he'd croaked.

Well, everybody else seen it at the same time; but it was too late. Strunk made a run for the ball, but they wasn't no chance for him to get near it. It hit the ground about ten feet back o' where Joyce was lyin' and bounded way over to the end o' the foul line. You don't have to be told that Doyle and Parker both scored and the serious was tied up.

We carried Joyce to the clubhouse and after a while he come to. He cried when he found out what had happened. We cheered him up all we could, but he was a pretty sick guy. The trainer said he'd be all right, though, for the final game.

They tossed up a coin to see where they'd play the seventh battle and our club won the toss; so we went back to Philly that night and cussed Parker clear across New Jersey. I was so sore I kicked the stuffin' out o' my seat.

You probably heard about the excitement in the burg yesterday mornin'. The demand for tickets was somethin' fierce and some of 'em sold for as high as twenty-five bucks apiece. Our club hadn't been lookin' for no seventh game and they was some tall hustlin' done round that old ball park.

I started out to the grounds early and bought some New York papers to read on the car. They was a big story that Speed Parker, the Giants' hero, was goin' to be married a week after the end o' the serious. It didn't give the name o' the girl, sayin' Speed had refused to tell it. I figured she must be some dame he'd met round the circuit somewheres.

They was another story by one o' them smart baseball reporters sayin' that Parker, on his way up to the plate, had saw that Joyce was about ready to faint and had hit the fly ball to left field on purpose. Can you beat it?

I was goin' to show that to the boys in the clubhouse, but the minute I blowed in there I got some news that made me forget about everything else. Joyce was very sick and they'd took him to a hospital. It was up to me to play!

Connie come over and ast me whether I'd ever hit against Matty. I told him I hadn't, but I'd saw enough of him to know he wasn't no worse'n Johnson. He told me he was goin' to let me hit second—in Joyce's place—because he didn't want to bust up the rest of his combination. He also told me to take my orders from Strunk about where to play for the batters.

"Where shall I play for Parker?" I says, tryin' to joke and pretend I wasn't scared to death.

"I wisht I could tell you," says Connie. "I guess the only thing to do when he comes up is to get down on your knees and pray."

The rest o' the bunch slapped me on the back and give me all the encouragement they could. The place was jammed when we went out on the field. They may of been bigger crowds before, but they never was packed together so tight. I doubt whether they was even room enough left for Falkenberg to sit down.

The afternoon papers had printed the stuff about Joyce bein' out of it, so the bugs was wise that I was goin' to play. They watched me pretty close in battin' practice and give me a hand whenever I managed to hit one hard. When I was out catchin' fungoes the guys in the bleachers cheered me and told me they was with me; but I don't mind tellin' you that I was as nervous as a bride.

They wasn't no need for the announcers to tip the crowd off to the pitchers. Everybody in the United States and Cuba knowed that the Chief'd work for us and Matty for them. The Chief didn't have no trouble with 'em in the first innin'. Even from where I stood I could see that he had a lot o' stuff. Bescher and Doyle popped out and Speed whiffed.

Well, I started out makin' good, with reverse English, in our part. Fletcher booted Murphy's ground ball and I was sent up to sacrifice. I done a complete job of it—sacrificin' not only myself but

Murphy with a pop fly that Matty didn't have to move for. That spoiled whatever chance we had o' gettin' the jump on 'em ; but the boys didn't bawl me for it.

"That's all right, old boy. You're all right!" they said on the bench—if they'd had a gun they'd of shot me.

I didn't drop no fly balls in the first six innin's—because none was hit out my way. The Chief was so good that they was hittin' nothin' out o' the infield. And we wasn't doin' nothin' with Matty, either. I led off in the fourth and fouled the first one. I didn't molest the other two. But if Connie and the gang talked about me they done it internally. I come up again—with Murphy on third base and two gone in the sixth, and done my little whiffin' specialty. And still the only people that panned me was the thirty thousand that had paid for the privilege!

My first fieldin' chance come in the seventh. You'd of thought that I'd of had my nerve back by that time; but I was just as scared as though I'd never saw a crowd before. It was just as well that they was two out when Merkle hit one to me. I staggered under it and finally it hit me on the shoulder. Merkle got to second, but the Chief whiffed the next guy. I was gave some cross looks on the bench and I shouldn't of blamed the fellers if they'd cut loose with some language; but they didn't.

They's no use in me tellin' you about none o' the rest of it—except what happened just before the start o' the eleventh and durin' the innin', which was sure the big one o' yesterday's pastime—both for Speed and yours sincerely.

The scoreboard was still a row o' ciphers and Speed'd had only a fair amount o' luck. He'd made a scratch base hit and robbed our bunch of a couple o' real ones with impossible stops.

When Schang flied out and wound up our tenth I was leanin' against the end of our bench. I heard my name spoke, and I turned round and seen a boy at the door.

"Right here!" I says; and he give me a telegram.

"Better not open it till after the game," says Connie.

"Oh, no; it ain't no bad news," I said, for I figured it was an answer from the girl. So I opened it up and read it on the way to my position. It said:

"Forgive me, Dick—and forgive Speed too. Letter follows."

Well, sir, I ain't no baby, but for a minute I just wanted to sit down and bawl. And then, all of a sudden, I got so mad I couldn't see. I run right into Baker as he was pickin' up his glove. Then I give him a shove and called him some name, and him and Barry both looked at me like I was crazy—and I was. When I got out in left field I stepped on my own foot and spiked it. I just had to hurt somebody.

As I remember it the Chief fanned the first two of 'em. Then Doyle catches one just right and lams it up against the fence back o' Murphy. The ball caromed round some and Doyle got all the way to third base. Next thing I seen was Speed struttin' up to the plate. I run clear in from my position.

"Kill him!" I says to the Chief. "Hit him in the head and kill him, and I'll go to jail for it!"

"Are you off your nut?" says the Chief. "Go out there and play ball—and quit ravin'."

Barry and Baker led me away and give me a shove out toward left. Then I heard the crack o' the bat and I seen the ball comin' a mile a minute. It was headed between Strunk and I and looked like it would go out o' the park. I don't remember runnin' or nothin' about it till I run into the concrete wall head first. They told me afterward and all the papers said that it was the greatest catch ever seen. And I never knowed I'd caught the ball!

Some o' the managers have said my head was pretty hard, but it wasn't as hard as that concrete. I was pretty near out, but they tell me I walked to the bench like I wasn't hurt at all. They also tell me that the crowd was a bunch o' ravin' maniacs and was throwin' money at me. I guess the ground-keeper'll get it.

The boys on the bench was all talkin' at once and slappin' me on the back, but I didn't know what it was about. Somebody told me pretty soon that it was my turn to hit and I picked up the first bat I come to and starts for the plate. McInnes come runnin' after me and ast me whether I didn't want my own bat. I cussed him and told him to mind his own business.

I didn't know it at the time, but I found out afterward that they was two out. The bases was empty. I'll tell you just what I had in my mind: I wasn't thinkin' about the ball game; I was determined that I was goin' to get to third base and give that guy my spikes. If I didn't hit one worth three bases, or if I didn't hit one at all, I was goin' to run till I got round to where Speed was, and then slide into him and cut him to pieces!

Right now I can't tell you whether I hit a fast ball, or a slow ball, or a hook, or a fader—but I hit somethin'. It went over Bescher's head like a shot and then took a crazy bound. It must of struck a rock or a pop bottle, because it hopped clear over the fence and landed in the bleachers.

Mind you, I learned this afterward. At the time I just knowed I'd hit one somewheres and I starts round the bases. I speeded up when I got near third and took a runnin' jump at a guy I thought was Parker. I missed him and sprawled all over the bag. Then, all of a sudden, I come to my senses. All the Ath-a-letics was out there to run home with me and it was one o' them I'd tried to cut. Speed had left the field. The boys picked me up and seen to it that I went on and touched the plate. Then I was carried into the clubhouse by the crazy bugs.

Well, they had a celebration in there and it was a long time before I got a chance to change my clothes. The boys made a big fuss over me. They told me they'd intended to give me five hundred bucks for my divvy, but now I was goin' to get a full share.

"Parker ain't the only lucky guy!" says one of 'em. "But even if that ball hadn't of took that crazy hop you'd of had a triple."

A triple! That's just what I'd wanted; and he called me lucky for not gettin' it!

The Giants was dressin' in the other part o' the clubhouse; and when I finally come out there was Speed, standin' waitin' for some o' the others. He seen me comin' and he smiled. "Hello, Horseshoes!" he says.

He won't smile no more for a while—it'll hurt too much. And if any girl wants him when she sees him now—with his nose over shakin' hands with his ear, and his jaw a couple o' feet foul—she's welcome to him. They won't be no contest!

Grimes leaned over to ring for the waiter.

"Well," he said, "what about it?"

"You won't have to pay my fare," I told him.

"I'll buy a drink anyway," said he. "You've been a good listener—and I had to get it off my chest."

"Maybe they'll have to postpone the wedding," I said.

"No," said Grimes. "The weddin' will take place the day after tomorrow—and I'll bat for Mr. Parker. Did you think I was goin' to let him get away with it?"

"What about next year?" I asked.

"I'm goin' back to the Ath-a-letics," he said. "And I'm goin' to hire somebody to call me 'Horseshoes!' before every game—because I can sure play that old baseball when I'm mad."

Harmony

McClure's
AUGUST 1915

EVEN A BASEBALL WRITER must sometimes work. Regretfully I yielded my seat in the P.G., walked past the section where Art Graham, Bill Cole, Lefty Parks and young Waldron were giving expert tonsorial treatment to "Sweet Adeline," and flopped down beside Ryan, the manager.

"Well, Cap," I said, "we're due in Springfield in a little over an hour and I haven't written a line."

"Don't let me stop you," said Ryan.

"I want you to start me," I said.

"Lord!" said Ryan. "You oughtn't to have any trouble grinding out stuff these days, with the club in first place and young Waldron gone crazy. He's worth a story any day."

"That's the trouble," said I. "He's been worked so much that there's nothing more to say about him. Everybody in the country knows that he's hitting .420, that he's made nine home runs, twelve triples and twenty-some doubles, that he's stolen twenty-five bases, and that he can play the piano and sing like Car*us*'. They've run his picture oftener than Billy Sunday and Mary Pickford put together. Of course, you might come through with how you got him."

"Oh, that's the mystery," said Ryan.

"So I've heard you say," I retorted. "But it wouldn't be a mystery if you'd let me print it."

"Well," said Ryan, "if you're really hard up I suppose I might as well come through. Only there's really no mystery at all about it; it's just what I consider the most remarkable piece of scouting ever done. I've been making a mystery of it just to have a little fun with Dick Hodges. You know he's got the Jackson club and he's still so sore about my stealing Waldron he'll hardly speak to me.

"I'll give you the dope if you want it, though it's a boost for Art Graham, not me. There's lots of people think the reason I've kept the thing a secret is because I'm modest.

"They give me credit for having found Waldron myself. But Graham is the bird that deserves the credit and I'll admit that he almost had to get down on his knees to make me take his tip. Yes, sir, Art Graham was the scout, and now he's sitting on the bench and the boy he recommended has got his place."

"That sounds pretty good," I said. "And how did Graham get wise?"

"I'm going to tell you. You're in a hurry; so I'll make it snappy.

"You weren't with us last fall, were you? Well, we had a day off in Detroit, along late in the season. Graham's got relatives in Jackson; so he asked me if he could spend the day there. I told him he could and asked him to keep his eyes peeled for good young pitchers, if he happened to go to the ball game. So he went to Jackson and the next morning he came back all excited. I asked him if he'd found me a pitcher and he said he hadn't, but he'd seen the best natural hitter he'd ever looked at—a kid named Waldron.

"'Well,' I said, 'you're the last one that ought to be recommending outfielders. If there's one good enough to hold a regular job, it might be your job he'd get.'

"But Art said that didn't make any difference to him—he was looking out for the good of the club. Well, I didn't see my way clear to asking the old man to dig up good money for an outfielder nobody'd ever heard of, when we were pretty well stocked with them, so I tried to stall Art; but he kept after me and kept after me till I agreed to stick in a draft for the kid just to keep Art quiet. So the draft went in and we got him. Then, as you know, Hodges tried to get him back, and that made me suspicious enough to hold on to him. Hodges finally came over to see me and wanted to know who'd tipped me to Waldron. That's where the mystery stuff started, because I saw that Hodges was all heated up and wanted to kid him along. So I told him we had some mighty good scouts working for us, and he said he knew our regular scouts and they couldn't tell a ballplayer from a torn ligament. Then he offered me fifty bucks if I'd tell him the truth and I just laughed at him. I said: 'A fella happened to be in Jackson one day and saw him work. But I won't tell you who the fella was, because you're too anxious to know.' Then he insisted on knowing what day the scout had been in Jackson. I said I'd tell him that if he'd tell me why he was so blame curious. So he gave me his end of it.

"It seems his brother, up in Ludington, had seen this kid play ball on the lots and had signed him right up for Hodges and taken him to Jackson, and of course, Hodges knew he had a world beater the minute he saw him. But he also knew he wasn't going to be able to keep him in Jackson, and, naturally he began to figure how he could get the most money for him. It was already August when the boy landed in Jackson; so there wasn't much chance of getting a big price last season. He decided to teach the kid what he didn't know about baseball and to keep him under cover till this year. Then everybody would be touting him and there'd be plenty of competition. Hodges could sell to the highest bidder.

"He had Waldron out practising every day, but wouldn't let him play in a game, and every player on the Jackson club had promised to keep the secret till this year. So Hodges wanted to find out from me which one of his players had broken the promise.

"Then I asked him if he was perfectly sure that Waldron hadn't played in a game, and he said he had gone in to hit for somebody just once. I asked him what date that was and he told me. It was the day Art had been in Jackson. So I said:

"'There's your mystery solved. That's the day my scout saw him, and you'll have to give the scout a little credit for picking a star after seeing him make one base hit.'

"Then Hodges said:

"'That makes it all the more a mystery. Because, in the first place, he batted under a fake name. And, in the second place, he didn't make a base hit. He popped out.'

"That's about all there is to it. You can ask Art how he picked the kid out for a star from seeing him pop out once. I've asked him myself, and he'd told me that he liked the way Waldron swung. Personally, I believe one of those Jackson boys got too gabby. But Art swears not."

"That *is* a story," I said gratefully. "An old outfielder who must know he's slipping recommends a busher after seeing him pop out once. And the busher jumps right in and gets his job."

I looked down the aisle toward the song birds. Art Graham, now a bench warmer, and young Waldron, whom he had touted and who was the cause of his being sent to the bench, were harmonizing at the tops of their strong and not too pleasant voices.

"And probably the strangest part of the story," I added, "is that Art doesn't seem to regret it. He and the kid appear to be the best of friends."

"Anybody who can sing is Art's friend," said Ryan.

I left him and went back to my seat to tear off my seven hundred words before we reached Springfield. I considered for a moment the advisability of asking Graham for an explanation of his wonderful bit of scouting, but decided to save that part of it for another day. I was in a hurry and, besides, Waldron was just teaching them a new "wallop," and it would have been folly for me to interrupt.

"It's on the word 'you,'" Waldron was saying. "I come down a tone; Lefty goes up a half tone, and Bill comes up two tones. Art just sings it like always. Now try her again," I heard him direct the song birds. They tried her again, making a worse noise than ever:

"I only know I love you;
Love me, and the world (the world) is mine (the world is mine)."

"No," said Waldron. "Lefty missed it. If you fellas knew music, I could teach it to you with the piano when we get to Boston. On the word 'love,' in the next to the last line, we hit a regular F chord. Bill's singing the low F in the bass and Lefty's hitting middle C in the baritone, and Art's on high F and I'm up to A. Then, on the word 'you,' I come down to G, and Art hits E, and Lefty goes up half a tone to C sharp, and Cole comes up from F to A in the bass. That makes a good wallop. It's a change from the F chord to the A chord. Now let's try her again," Waldron urged.

They tried her again:

"I only know I love you—"

"No, no!" said young Waldron. "Art and I were all right; but Bill came up too far, and Lefty never moved off that C. Half a tone up, Lefty. Now try her again."

We were an hour late into Springfield, and it was past six o'clock when we pulled out. I had filed my stuff, and when I came back in the car the concert was over for the time, and Art Graham was sitting alone.

"Where are your pals?" I asked.

"Gone to the diner," he replied.

"Aren't you going to eat?"

"No," he said, "I'm savin' up for the steamed clams." I took the seat beside him.

"I sent in a story about you," I said.

"Am I fired?" he asked.

"No, nothing like that."

"Well," he said, "you must be hard up when you can't find nothin' better to write about than a old has-been."

"Cap just told me who it was that found Waldron," said I.

"Oh, that," said Art. "I don't see no story in that."

"I thought it was quite a stunt," I said. "It isn't everybody that can pick out a second Cobb by just seeing him hit a fly ball."

Graham smiled.

"No," he replied, "they's few as smart as that."

"If you ever get through playing ball," I went on, "you oughtn't to have any trouble landing a job. Good scouts don't grow on trees."

"It looks like I'm pretty near through now," said Art, still smiling. "But you won't never catch me scoutin' for nobody. It's too lonesome a job."

I had passed up lunch to retain my seat in the card game; so I was hungry. Moreover, it was evident that Graham was not going to wax garrulous on the subject of his scouting ability. I left him and sought the diner. I found a vacant chair opposite Bill Cole.

"Try the minced ham," he advised, "but lay off'n the sparrow-grass. It's tougher'n a double-header in St. Louis."

"We're over an hour late," I said.

"You'll have to do a hurry-up on your story, won't you?" asked Bill. "Or did you write it already?"

"All written and on the way."

"Well, what did you tell 'em?" he inquired. "Did you tell 'em we had a pleasant trip, and Lenke lost his shirt in the poker game, and I'm goin' to pitch to-morrow, and the Boston club's heard about it and hope it'll rain?"

"No," I said. "I gave them a regular story tonight—about how Graham picked Waldron."

"Who give it to you?"

Ryan," I told him.

"Then you didn't get the real story," said Cole, "Ryan himself don't know the best part of it, and he ain't goin' to know it for a w'ile. He'll maybe find it out after Art's got the can, but not before. And I hope nothin' like that'll happen for twenty years. When it does happen, I want to be sent along with Art, 'cause I and him's been roomies now since 1911, and I wouldn't hardly know how to act with him off'n the club. He's a nut all right on the singin' stuff, and if he was gone I might get a chanct to give my voice a rest. But he's a pretty good guy, even if he is crazy."

"I'd like to hear the real story," I said.

"Sure you would," he answered, "and I'd like to tell it to you. I will tell it to you if you'll give me your promise not to spill it till Art's gone. Art told it to I and Lefty in the club-house at Cleveland pretty near a month ago, and the three of us and Waldron is the only ones that knows it. I figure I've did pretty well to keep it to myself this long, but it seems like I got to tell somebody."

"You can depend on me," I assured him, "not to say a word about it till Art's in Minneapolis, or wherever they're going to send him."

"I guess I can trust you," said Cole. "But if you cross me, I'll shoot my fast one up there in the press coop some day and knock your teeth loose."

"Shoot," said I.

"Well," said Cole, "I s'pose Ryan told you that Art fell for the kid after just seein' him pop out."

"Yes, and Ryan said he considered it a remarkable piece of scouting."

"It was all o' that. It'd of been remarkable enough if Art'd saw the bird pop out and then recommended him. But he didn't even see him pop out."

"What are you giving me?"

"The fac's," said Bill Cole. "Art not only didn't see him pop out, but he didn't even see him with a ball suit on. He wasn't never inside the Jackson ball park in his life."

"Waldron?"

"No. Art I'm talkin' about."

"Then somebody tipped him off," I said, quickly.

"No, sir. Nobody tipped him off, neither. He went to Jackson and spent the ev'nin' at his uncle's house, and Waldron was there. Him and Art was together the whole ev'nin'. But Art didn't even ask him if he could slide feet first. And then he come back to Detroit and got Ryan to draft him. But to give you the whole story, I'll have to go back a ways. We ain't nowheres near Worcester yet, so they's no hurry, except that Art'll prob'ly be sendin' for me pretty quick to come in and learn Waldron's lost chord.

"You wasn't with this club when we had Mike McCann. But you must of heard of him; outside his pitchin', I mean. He was on the stage a couple o' winters, and he had the swellest tenor voice I ever heard. I never seen no grand opera, but I'll bet this here C'ruso or McCormack or Gadski or none o' them had nothin' on him for a pure tenor. Every note as clear as a bell. You couldn't hardly keep your eyes dry when he'd tear off 'Silver Threads' or 'The River Shannon.'

"Well, when Art was still with the Washin'ton club yet, I and Lefty and Mike used to pal round together and onct or twict we'd hit up some harmony. I couldn't support a fam'ly o' Mormons with my voice, but it was better in them days than it is now. I used to carry the lead, and Lefty'd hit the baritone and Mike the tenor. We didn't have no bass. But most o' the time we let Mike do the singin' alone, 'cause he had us outclassed, and the other boys kept tellin' us to shut up and give 'em a treat. First it'd be 'Silver Threads' and then 'Jerusalem' and then 'My Wild Irish Rose' and this and that, whatever the boys ast him for. Jack Martin used to say he couldn't help a short pair if Mike wasn't singin'.

"Finally Ryan pulled off the trade with Griffith, and Graham come on our club. Then they wasn't no more solo work. They made a bass out o' me, and Art sung the lead, and Mike and Lefty took care o' the tenor and baritone. Art didn't care what the other boys wanted to hear. They could holler their heads off for Mike to sing a solo, but no sooner'd Mike start singin' than Art'd chime in with him and pretty soon we'd all four be goin' it. Art's a nut on singin', but he don't care nothin' about list'nin', not even to a canary. He'd rather harmonize than hit one past the outfielders with two on.

"At first we done all our serenadin' on the train. Art'd get us out o' bed early so's we could be through breakfast and back in the car in time to tear off a few before we got to wherever we was goin'.

"It got so's Art wouldn't leave us alone in the different towns we played at. We couldn't go to no show or nothin'. We had to stick in the hotel and sing, up in our room or Mike's. And then he went so nuts over it that he got Mike to come and room in the same house with him at home, and I and Lefty was supposed to help keep the neighbors awake every night. O' course we had mornin' practice w'ile we was home, and Art used to have us come to the park early and get in a little harmony before we went on the field. But Ryan finally nailed that. He says that when he ordered mornin' practice he meant baseball and not no minstrel show.

"Then Lefty, who wasn't married, goes and gets himself a girl. I met her a couple o' times, and she looked all right. Lefty might of married her if Art'd of left him alone. But nothin' doin'. We was home all through June onct, and instead o' comin' round nights to sing with us, Lefty'd take this here doll to one o' the parks or somewheres. Well, sir, Art was pretty near wild. He scouted round till he'd found out why Lefty'd quit us and then he tried pretty near everybody else on the club to see if they wasn't some one who could hit the baritone. They wasn't nobody. So the next time we went on the road, Art give Lefty a earful about what a sucker a man was to get married, and looks wasn't everything and the girl was prob'ly after Lefty's money and he wasn't bein' a good fella to break up the quartette and spoil our good times, and so on, and kept pesterin' and teasin' Lefty till he give the girl up. I'd of saw Art in the Texas League before I'd of shook a girl to please him, but you know these left-handers.

"Art had it all framed that we was goin' on the stage, the four of us, and he seen a vaudeville man in New York and got us booked for eight hundred a week—I don't know if it was one week or two. But he sprung it on me in September and says we could get solid bookin' from October to March; so I ast him what he thought my Missus would say when I told her I couldn't get enough o' bein' away from home from March to October so I was figurin' on travelin' the vaudeville circuit the other four or five months and makin' it unanimous? Art says I was tied to a woman's apron and all that stuff, but I give him the cold stare and he had to pass up that dandy little scheme.

"At that, I guess we could of got by on the stage all right. Mike was better than this here Waldron and I hadn't wore my voice out yet on the coachin' line, tellin' the boys to touch all the bases.

"They was about five or six songs that we could kill. 'Adeline' was our star piece. Remember where it comes in, 'Your fair face beams'? Mike used to go away up on 'fair.' Then they was 'The Old Millstream' and 'Put on Your Old Gray Bonnet.' I done some fancy work in that one. Then they was 'Down in Jungle Town' that we had pretty good. And then they was one that maybe you never heard. I don't know the name of it. It run somethin' like this."

Bill sottoed his voice so that I alone could hear the beautiful refrain:

> " 'Years, years, I've waited years
> Only to see you, just to call you 'dear.'
> Come, come, I love but thee,
> Come to your sweetheart's arms; come back to me.'

"That one had a lot o' wallops in it, and we didn't overlook none o' them. The boys used to make us sing it six or seven times a night. But 'Down in the Cornfield' was Art's favor-ight. They was a part in that where I sung the lead down low and the other three done a banjo stunt. Then they was 'Castle on the Nile' and 'Come Back to Erin' and a whole lot more.

"Well, the four of us wasn't hardly ever separated for three years. We was practisin' all the w'ile like as if we was goin' to play the big time, and we never made a nickel off'n it. The only audience we had was the ball players or the people travelin' on the same trains or stoppin' at the same hotels, and they got it all for nothin'. But we had a good time, 'specially Art.

"You know what a pitcher Mike was. He could go in there stone cold and stick ten out o' twelve over that old plate with somethin' on 'em. And he was the willin'est guy in the world. He pitched his own game every third or fourth day, and between them games he was warmin' up all the time to go in for somebody else. In 1911, when we was up in the race for aw'ile, he pitched eight games out o' twenty, along in September, and win seven o' them, and besides that, he finished up five o' the twelve he didn't start. We didn't win the pennant, and I've always figured that them three weeks killed Mike.

"Anyway, he wasn't worth nothin' to the club the next year; but they carried him along, hopin' he'd come back and show somethin'. But he was pretty near through, and he knowed it. I knowed it, too, and so did everybody else on the club, only Graham. Art never got wise till the trainin' trip two years ago this last spring. Then he come to me one day.

" 'Bill,' he says, 'I don't believe Mike's comin' back.'

" 'Well,' I says, 'you're gettin's so's they can't nobody hide nothin' from you. Next thing you'll be findin' out that Sam Crawford can hit.'

" 'Never mind the comical stuff,' he says. 'They ain't no joke about this!'

" 'No,' I says, 'and I never said they was. They'll look a long w'ile before they find another pitcher like Mike.'

" 'Pitcher my foot!' says Art. 'I don't care if they have to pitch the bat boy. But when Mike goes, where'll our quartette be?'

" 'Well,' I says, 'do you get paid every first and fifteenth for singin' or for crownin' that old pill?'

" 'If you couldn't talk about money, you'd be deaf and dumb,' says Art.

" 'But you ain't playin' ball because it's fun, are you?'

" 'No,' he says, 'they ain't no fun for me in playin' ball. They's no fun doin' nothin' but harmonizin', and if Mike goes, I won't even have that.'

" 'I and you and Lefty can harmonize,' I says.

" 'It'd be swell stuff harmonizin' without no tenor,' says Art. 'It'd be like swingin' without no bat.'

"Well, he ast me did I think the club'd carry Mike through another season, and I told him they'd already carried him a year without him bein' no good to them, and I figured if he didn't show somethin' his first time out, they'd ask for waivers. Art kept broodin' and broodin' about it till they wasn't hardly no livin' with him. If he ast me onct he ast me a thousand times if I didn't think they might maybe hold onto Mike another season on account of all he'd did for 'em. I kept tellin' him I didn't think so; but that didn't satisfy him and he finally went to Ryan and ast him point blank.

" 'Are you goin' to keep McCann?' Art ast him.

" 'If he's goin' to do us any good, I am,' says Ryan. 'If he ain't, he'll have to look for another job.'

"After that, all through the trainin' trip, he was right on Mike's heels.

" 'How does the old souper feel?' he'd ask him.

" 'Great!' Mike'd say.

"Then Art'd watch him warm up, to see if he had anything on the ball.

" 'He's comin' fine,' he'd tell me. 'His curve broke to-day just as good as I ever seen it.'

"But that didn't fool me, or it didn't fool Mike neither. He could throw about four hooks and then he was through. And he could of hit you in the head with his fast one and you'd of thought you had a rash.

"One night, just before the season opened up, we was singin' on the train, and when we got through, Mike says:

" 'Well, boys, you better be lookin' for another C'ruso.'

" 'What are you talkin' about?' says Art.

" 'I'm talkin' about myself,' says Mike. 'I'll be up there in Minneapolis this summer, pitchin' onct a week and swappin' stories about the Civil War with Joe Cantillon.'

" 'You're crazy,' says Art. 'Your arm's as good as I ever seen it.'

" 'Then,' says Mike, 'you must of been playin' blindfolded all these years. This is just between us, 'cause Ryan'll find it out for himself; my arm's rotten, and I can't do nothin' to help it.'

"Then Art got sore as a boil.

" 'You're a yellow, quittin' dog,' he says. 'Just because you come round a little slow, you talk about Minneapolis. Why don't you resign off'n the club?'

" 'I might just as well,' Mike says, and left us.

"You'd of thought that Art would of gave up then, 'cause when a ball player admits he's slippin', you can bet your last nickel that he's through. Most o' them stalls along and tries to kid themself and everybody else long after they know they're gone. But Art kept talkin' like they was still some hope o' Mike comin' round, and when Ryan told us one night in St. Louis that he was goin' to give Mike his chanct, the next day, Art was as nervous as a bride goin' to get married. I wasn't nervous. I just felt sorry, 'cause I knowed the old boy was hopeless.

"Ryan had told him he was goin' to work if the weather suited him. Well, the day was perfect. So Mike went out to the park along about noon and took Jake with him to warm up. Jake told me afterwards that Mike was throwin', just easy like, from half-past twelve till the rest of us got there. He was tryin' to heat up the old souper and he couldn't of ast for a better break in the weather, but they wasn't enough sunshine in the world to make that old whip crack.

"Well, sir, you'd of thought to see Art that Mike was his son or his brother or somebody and just breakin' into the league. Art wasn't in the outfield practisin' more than two minutes. He come in and stood behind Mike w'ile he was warmin' up and kept tellin' how good he looked, but the only guy he was kiddin' was himself.

"Then the game starts and our club goes in and gets three runs.

" 'Pretty soft for you now, Mike,' says Art, on the bench. 'They can't score three off'n you in three years.'

"Say, it's lucky he ever got the side out in the first innin'. Everybody that come up hit one on the pick, but our infield pulled two o' the greatest plays I ever seen and they didn't score. In the second, we got three more, and I thought maybe the old bird was goin' to be lucky enough to scrape through.

"For four or five innin's, he got the grandest support that was ever gave a pitcher; but I'll swear that what he throwed up there didn't have no more on it than September Morning. Every time Art come to the bench, he says to Mike, 'Keep it up, old boy. You got more than you ever had.'

"Well, in the seventh, Mike still had 'em shut out, and we was six runs to the good. Then a couple o' the St. Louis boys hit 'em where they couldn't nobody reach 'em and they was two on and two out. Then somebody got a hold o' one and sent it on a line to the left o' second base. I forgot who it was now; but whoever it was, he was supposed to be a right field hitter, and Art was layin' over the other way for him. Art started with a crack o' the bat, and I never seen a man make a better try for a ball. He had it judged perfect; but Cobb or Speaker or none o' them couldn't of catched it. Art just managed to touch it by stretchin' to the limit. It went on to the fence and everybody come in. They didn't score no more in that innin'.

"Then Art come in from the field and what do you think he tried to pull?

" 'I don't know what was the matter with me on that fly ball,' he says. 'I ought to caught it in my pants pocket. But I didn't get started till it was right on top o' me.'

" 'You misjudged it, didn't you?' says Ryan.

" 'I certainly did,' says Art without crackin'.

" 'Well," says Ryan, 'I wisht you'd misjudge all o' them that way. I never seen a better play on a ball.'

"So then Art knowed they wasn't no more use trying to alibi the old boy.

"Mike had a turn at bat and when he come back, Ryan ast him how he felt.

" 'I guess I can get six more o' them out,' he says.

"Well, they didn't score in the eighth, and when the ninth come Ryan sent I and Lefty out to warm up. We throwed a few w'ile our club was battin'; but when it come St. Louis' last chanct, we was too much interested in the ball game to know if we was throwin' or bakin' biscuits.

"The first guy hits a line drive, and somebody jumps a mile in the air and stabs it. The next fella fouled out, and they was only one more to get. And then what do you think come off? Whoever it was hittin' lifted a fly ball to centre field. Art didn't have to move out of his tracks. I've saw him catch a hundred just like it behind his back. But you know what he was thinkin'. He was sayin' to himself, 'If I nail this one, we're li'ble to keep our tenor singer a w'ile longer.' And he dropped it.

"Then they was five base hits that sounded like the fourth o' July, and they come so fast that Ryan didn't have time to send for I or Lefty. Anyway, I guess he thought he might as well leave Mike in there and take it.

"They wasn't no singin' in the clubhouse after that game. I and Lefty always let the others start it. Mike, o' course, didn't feel like no jubilee, and Art was so busy tryin' not to let nobody see him cry that he kept his head clear down in his socks. Finally he beat it for town all alone, and we didn't see nothin' of him till after supper. Then he got us together and we all went up to Mike's room.

" 'I want to try this here "Old Girl o' Mike," ' he says.

" 'Better sing our old stuff,' says Mike. 'This looks like the last time.'

"Then Art choked up and it was ten minutes before he could

get goin'. We sung everything we knowed, and it was two o'clock in the mornin' before Art had enough. Ryan come in after midnight and set a w'ile listenin', but he didn't chase us to bed. He knowed better'n any of us that it was a farewell. When I and Art was startin' for our room, Art turned to Mike and says:

"'Old boy, I'd of gave every nickel I ever owned to of caught that fly ball.'

"'I know you would,' Mike says, 'and I know what made you drop it. But don't worry about it, 'cause it was just a question o' time, and if I'd of got away with that game, they'd of murdered some o' the infielders next time I started.'

"Mike was sent home the next day, and we didn't see him again. He was shipped to Minneapolis before we got back. And the rest o' the season I might as well of lived in a cemetery w'ile we was on the road. Art was so bad that I thought onct or twict I'd have to change roomies. Onct in a w'ile he'd start hummin' and then he'd break off short and growl at me. He tried out two or three o' the other boys on the club to see if he couldn't find a new tenor singer, but nothin' doin'. One night he made Lefty try the tenor. Well, Lefty's voice is bad enough down low. When he gets up about so high, you think you're in the stockyards.

"And Art had a rotten year in baseball, too. The old boy's still pretty near as good on a fly ball as anybody in the league; but you ought to saw him before his legs begin to give out. He could cover as much ground as Speaker and he was just as sure. But the year Mike left us, he missed pretty near half as many as he got. He told me one night, he says:

"'Do you know, Bill, I stand out there and pray that nobody'll hit one to me. Every time I see one comin' I think o' that one I dropped for Mike in St. Louis, and then I'm just as li'ble to have it come down on my bean as in my glove.'

"'You're crazy,' I says, 'to let a thing like that make a bum out o' you.'

"But he kept on droppin' fly balls till Ryan was talkin' about settin' him on the bench where it wouldn't hurt nothin' if his nerve give out. But Ryan didn't have nobody else to play out there, so Art held on.

"He come back the next spring—that's a year ago—feelin' more cheerful and like himself than I'd saw him for a long w'ile. And they was a kid named Burton tryin' out for second base that could sing pretty near as good as Mike. It didn't take Art more'n a day to find this out, and every mornin' and night for a few days the four of us would be together, hittin' her up. But the kid didn't have no more idea o' how to play the bag than Charley Chaplin. Art seen in a minute that he couldn't never beat Cragin out of his job, so what does he do but take him out and try and learn him to play the outfield. He wasn't no worse there than at second base; he couldn't of been. But before he'd practised out there three days they was bruises all over his head and shoulders where fly balls had hit him. Well, the kid wasn't with us long enough to see the first exhibition game, and after he'd went, Art was Old Man Grump again.

" 'What's the matter with you?' I says to him. 'You was all smiles the day we reported and now you could easy pass for a undertaker.'

" 'Well,' he says, 'I had a great winter, singin' all the w'ile. We got a good quartette down home and I never enjoyed myself as much in my life. And I kind o' had a hunch that I was goin' to be lucky and find somebody amongst the bushers that could hit up the old tenor.'

" 'Your hunch was right,' I says. 'That Burton kid was as good a tenor as you'd want.'

" 'Yes,' he says, 'and my hunch could of played ball just as good as him.'

"Well, sir, if you didn't never room with a corpse, you don't know what a whale of a time I had all last season. About the middle of August he was at his worst.

" 'Bill,' he says, 'I'm goin' to leave this old baseball flat on its back if somethin' don't happen. I can't stand these here lonesome nights. I ain't like the rest o' the boys that can go and set all ev'nin' at a pitcher show or hang round them Dutch gardens. I got to be singin' or I am mis'rable.'

"'Go ahead and sing,' says I. 'I'll try and keep the cops back.'

"'No,' he says, 'I don't want to sing alone. I want to harmonize and we can't do that 'cause we ain't got no tenor.'

"I don't know if you'll believe me or not, but sure as we're settin' here he went to Ryan one day in Philly and tried to get him to make a trade for Harper.

"'What do I want him for?' says Ryan.

"'I hear he ain't satisfied,' says Art.

"'I ain't runnin' no ball players' benefit association,' says Ryan, and Art had to give it up. But he didn't want Harper on the club for no other reason than because he's a tenor singer!'

"And then come that Dee-troit trip, and Art got permission to go to Jackson. He says he intended to drop in at the ball park, but his uncle wanted to borry some money off'n him on a farm, so Art had to drive out and see the farm. Then, that night, this here Waldron was up to call on Art's cousin—a swell doll, Art tells me. And Waldron set down to the py-ana and begin to sing and play. Then it was all off; they wasn't no spoonin' in the parlor that night. Art wouldn't leave the kid get off'n the py-ana stool long enough to even find out if the girl was a blonde or a brunette.

"O' course Art knowed the boy was with the Jackson club as soon as they was interduced, 'cause Art's uncle says somethin' about the both o' them bein' ball players, and so on. But Art swears he never thought o' recommendin' him till the kid got up to go home. Then he ast him what position did he play and found out all about him, only o' course Waldron didn't tell him how good he was 'cause he didn't know himself.

"So Art ast him would he like a trial in the big show, and the kid says he would. Then Art says maybe the kid would hear from him, and then Waldron left and Art went to bed, and he says he stayed awake all night plannin' the thing out and wonderin' would he have the nerve to pull it off. You see he thought that if Ryan fell for it,

Waldron'd join us as soon as his season was over and then Ryan'd see he wasn't no good; but he'd prob'ly keep him till we was through for the year, and Art could alibi himself some way, say he'd got the wrong name or somethin'. All he wanted he says, was to have the kid along the last month or six weeks, so's we could harmonize. A nut? I guess not.

"Well, as you know, Waldron got sick and didn't report, and when Art seen him on the train this spring he couldn't hardly believe his eyes. He thought surely the kid would of been canned durin' the winter without no trial.

"Here's another hot one. When we went out the first day for practice, Art takes the kid off in a corner and tries to learn him enough baseball so's he won't show himself up and get sent away somewheres before we had a little benefit from his singin'. Can you imagine that? Tryin' to learn this kid baseball, when he was born with a slidin' pad on.

"You know the rest of it. They wasn't never no question about Waldron makin' good. It's just like everybody says—he's the best natural ball player that's broke in since Cobb. They ain't nothin' he can't do. But it *is* a funny thing that Art's job should be the one he'd get. I spoke about that to Art when he give me the story.

" 'Well,' he says, 'I can't expect everything to break right. I figure I'm lucky to of picked a guy that's good enough to hang on. I'm in stronger with Ryan right now, and with the old man, too, than when I was out there playin' every day. Besides, the bench is a pretty good place to watch the game from. And this club won't be shy a tenor singer for nine years.'

" 'No,' I says, 'but they'll be shy a lead and a baritone and a bass before I and you and Lefty is much older.'

" 'What of it?' he says. 'We'll look up old Mike and all go somewheres and live together.' "

We were nearing Worcester. Bill Cole and I arose from our table and started back toward our car. In the first vestibule we encountered Buck, the trainer.

"Mr. Graham's been lookin' all over for you, Mr. Cole," he said.

"I've been rehearsin' my part," said Bill.

We found Art Graham, Lefty, and young Waldron in Art's seat. The kid was talking.

"Lefty missed it again. If you fellas knew music, I could teach it to you on the piano when we get to Boston. Lefty, on the word 'love,' in the next to the last line, you're on middle C. Then, on the word 'you,' you slide up half a tone. That'd ought to be a snap, but you don't get it. I'm on high A and come down to G and Bill's on low F and comes up to A. Art just sings the regular two notes, F and E. It's a change from the F chord to the A chord. It makes a dandy wallop and it ought to be a—"

"Here's Bill now," interrupted Lefty, as he caught sight of Cole.

Art Graham treated his roommate to a cold stare.

"Where the h—l have you been?" he said angrily.

"Lookin' for the lost chord," said Bill.

"Set down here and learn this," growled Art. "We won't never get it if we don't work."

"Yes, let's tackle her again," said Waldron. "Bill comes up two full tones, from F to A. Lefty goes up half a tone, Art sings just like always, and I come down a tone. Now try her again."

Two years ago it was that Bill Cole told me that story. Two weeks ago Art Graham boarded the evening train on one of the many roads that lead to Minneapolis.

The day Art was let out, I cornered Ryan in the club-house after the others had dressed and gone home.

"Did you ever know," I asked, "That Art recommended Waldron without having seen him in a ball suit?"

"I told you long ago how Art picked Waldron," he said.

"Yes," said I, "but you didn't have the right story."

So I gave it to him.

"You newspaper fellas," he said when I had done, "are the biggest suckers in the world. Now I've never given you a bad steer in my life. But you don't believe what I tell you and you go and fall for one of Bill Cole's hop dreams. Don't you know that he was the biggest liar in baseball? He'd tell you that Walter Johnson was Jack's father if he thought he could get away with it. And that bunk he gave you about Waldron. Does it sound reasonable?"

"Just as reasonable," I replied, "as the stuff about Art's grabbing him after seeing him pop out."

"I don't claim he did," said Ryan. "That's what Art told me. One of those Jackson ball players could give you the real truth, only of course he wouldn't, because if Hodges ever found it out he'd shoot him full of holes. Art Graham's no fool. He isn't touting ball players because they can sing tenor or alto or anything else."

Nevertheless, I believe Bill Cole; else I wouldn't print the story. And Ryan would believe, too, if he weren't in such a mood these days that he disagrees with everybody. For in spite of Waldron's wonderful work, and he is at his best right now, the club hasn't done nearly as well as when Art and Bill and Lefty were still with us.

There seems to be a lack of harmony.

Good For the Soul

The Saturday Evening Post
MARCH 25, 1916

BEFORE ME, a member of the Baseball Writers' Association of America, appeared this first day of February, 1916, one Robert Frederick Warner, alias Buck Warner, lately a professional player of the game known as baseball and now part owner of an automobile garage in Hopsboro, a suburb of Cincinnati, and voluntarily and without threat or coercion did dictate a confession, the full text of which follows:

I

THE WIFE SAYS that if I didn't quit grouchin' round the house she'd just plain leave me and go and live with her Aunt Julia. Well, the wife's a good scout and Aunt Julia's home is a farm twelve miles from Dayton, so I promised I'd try and cheer up.

"Yes, but you promised the same thing before," says Ethel;

that's the wife's name. "You promised the same thing before and that's all the good it done," she says. "It's your crazy old conscience that's botherin' you. You'd ought to go to the hospital and have it took out."

"Operations costs money," I says.

"Well," says Ethel, "I'd rather be broke than have old Sidney Gloom for a husband."

"I'll try and cheer up," I says again.

"You're the world's greatest tryer," says she, "but your attempts to make everybody miserable is the only ones that's successful."

It was at breakfast yesterday mornin' that she was payin' me these compliments. At supper she pointed out a piece in the evenin' paper and told me I should read it.

Seems like some old bird about seventy, worth a couple o' millions, had been a clerk in a grocery store when he was a kid, and one day he helped himself to twenty dollars out o' the till, and he was scared to death they'd learn who done it and send him over, but for some reason it wasn't never found out. So, as I say, he finally got rich and had everything that's supposed to make a man happy, but he hadn't been able to sleep good for several years on account o' thinkin' about his crime. So the minister o' the church where he attended at preached a sermon on what a good thing confession was for sinners, and the old boy couldn't even sleep through the sermon, so he got the drift and made up his mind to see if a confession would cure his insomnia and not bein' able to sleep. So he wrote one out, describin' what he'd did, and sent it to the minister to be read out loud in church, and that night he slept like a horse.

"Well," I says, when I was through readin', "what about it?"

"It's worth a try," says Ethel.

"You go in town to-morrow and find somebody that'll listen, and tell 'em all about your horrible crime. And then see if you can't come home to me smilin'."

"That'll be easy," I says, "if you'll leave me drink a couple o' beers."

"You can do that too," she says, "if you think it'll wash away the blues."

I thought she was kiddin' at first; I mean about the confessin'. But she made me understand she was serious.

"But I'd have to bring in the names of others that ain't entirely innocent," I says.

"Go as far as you like," says she. "You certainly don't think they're worth shieldin'; 'specially Carmody."

So here I am and she says I was to tell it all and not keep nothin' back.

It won't be necessary to start with where I was born and so forth. A year ago last August is where it really begins. Before that I'd been in the National League six years, and if they'd left me stick to short-stop all the time, they wouldn't of nobody had me beat. But they found out I could play anywheres they put me and they kept shiftin' me round like a motorcycle cop.

In the six years I'd did even worse than not save no money. I'd piled up pretty near four thousand dollars' worth o' debts. The biggest part of it I owed to fellas on the club that'd came through for me when I made a flivver out of a billiard hall in Brooklyn.

So, as I say, a year ago last August found me four thousand to the bad and that's when I met Ethel. We was playin' in Pittsburgh and she was visitin' some people I know there. She had eye trouble and liked me the first time she seen me. But she didn't like me nowheres near as much as I liked her. We both fell pretty hard, though, and the third evenin' we was together we got engaged to be married.

"I wisht I had more to offer you," I told her. "I'm flat outside o' my salary and I owe a plain four thousand."

"I don't care how much or how little you've got," she says. "Your salary'll keep us all right. But I don't want to marry you till you're clear o' debt."

"We'll do some waitin' then," I says. "A year from this fall is the best I can promise. I'll live on nothin' this winter and I won't spend nothin' next summer and I think I can just about get cleaned up. It'll be somethin' new for me to try and save, but you're worth starvin' for."

"And you're worth waitin' for," says she.

So we says good-by and I went to Chicago with the club. And the second day there I slipped roundin' first base and throwed my knee pretty near out o' my stockin'.

It wasn't no common sprain or strain. The old bird just simply flew out of his cage and flew out to stay. I seen two doctors there and two more back home. They all says the same thing; that I was through playin' ball.

"After it's had a rest," they told me, "just walkin' on it won't hurt nothin'. But the minute you run you're liable to get crippled up good and proper. And if you stooped quick or made a quick turn or if your leg got bumped into, you might serve a good long sentence on the old hair mattress."

I didn't want Ethel to find out how bad it was, so all that come out in the paper was that I had a Charley horse. Mac, o' course, knowed the truth, but he couldn't do nothin' except feel sorry for me. He knowed about the girl too.

"I wisht I had a place for you," he says, "but you wouldn't be satisfied scoutin', and with the low player limit we can't carry no men that ain't goin' to do us some good. You'll get paid, o' course, up to the end o' the season. But I can't offer you no contract for next year."

"That's all right," I says. "I just want it kept quiet till I find somethin' I can do."

And w'ile I was still half dazed over the shock of it I got a letter from the girl. She had some big news, she says. Her Aunt Julia'd been told about I and her bein' engaged and had promised her a present o' $2500 on the day we was married. And we was to put this money with another $2500 that her brother, Paul, was goin' to save up, and I and her brother was goin' to buy a garage in Hopsboro from a fella that'd promised Paul he'd sell it to him in a year.

And it was the only garage in Hopsboro and done a whale of a business. And Paul was a swell mechanic and I'd take care o' the business end. And I could quit playin' ball and never be away from home. It sounded mighty good to me just then. But they was still a little trifle o' four thousand that'd have to be took care of.

I'd just mailed back an answer, as cheerful as I could write, when a call come over the phone that Mr. A. T. Grant wanted to see me at the Kingsley Hotel. I'd saw his name mentioned in connection with a club in the new league, but I didn't know if he'd bought it or not.

Well, I went down there in a taxi and was showed right up to his room.

He shook hands with me and then ast me if I was signed up for next year. I told him I wasn't.

"I've just bought the club I was after," he says. "I wanted to know if you'd consider an offer."

I done some tall thinkin'. I made up my mind that it wouldn't do no harm to sign. If I found I couldn't play nobody'd be hurt. But if the old knee wasn't as bad as the doctors thought I'd probably get a better job here than anywheres else.

"Who's goin' to be your manager?" I ast him.

"Billy Carmody," he says. "He was the shortstop on the club this year."

"I never met him, but o' course I've heard of him," I says.

Then I done some more thinkin'.

"What's your offer?" I says.

"Five thousand," says Mr. Grant.

"Where would you want me to play?" I ast him.

"Where would you want to play?" says he.

That give me a hunch. I'd heard they was one or two short fences in the league. Maybe I could play an outfield position even if my legs wouldn't stand the infield strain.

"In the outfield," I told him.

"Which field?" he says, and then I knowed he was a bug.

"Right field," says I.

"That suits me," he says, and he sent for his secretary to fix up a contract.

So I signed to play right field, and nowheres else, for Mr. Grant's club for one year at $5000.

"This business is new to me," he says, "but I believe I'll get a lot o' pleasure out of it."

"What other men have you got signed?" I ast him.

"I'm not at liberty to tell you," he says. "But I may tell you that most o' them is young men that's as new to professional ball as I am. I believe in gettin' young fellas, for enthusiasm's more valuable than experience in a sport o' this kind."

"Oh, easy," I says.

Then we shook hands again and I beat it to a train for Dayton, where the girl was stayin'. And when I seen her I give her the whole story. It looked now like they was a little bit o' hope.

II

THE PAPERS I'd saw durin' the winter hadn't wasted no space on our club and I didn't know exactly who was my teammates till I blowed into Dixie Springs, the first week in March.

I landed in the forenoon. The clerk at the hotel told me the gang was all out to the grounds, practicin'. So I planted my baggage and washed up and then set out on the porch, waitin' for the boys to come back. The beanery was on the main street, but from the number o' people that went past you'd of thought our trainin' camp had been picked out by Robinson Caruso. About one bell I got sick o' lookin' at mud puddles and woke up the clerk again.

"What do you s'pose is keepin' 'em so long?" I ast him.

"They don't never show up till after four," he says.

"Don't they come back for lunch?" I ast.

"No," he says. "You see the ball grounds is over a quarter of a mile from here and Mr. Grant, who's the proprietor o' the nine, figured it would wear his men out to make the trip four times a day."

"So they don't eat at noon?" I says.

"Oh, yes," says the clerk. "We put up a nice lunch here and send it to 'em."

"I hope you don't send 'em nothin' that's hard to chew," I says. After a w'ile, I got up nerve enough to attemp' the killin' journey to the orchard.

It was an old fairgrounds or somethin', just on the edge o' what you'd call the town if you was good-natured. Waivers had been ast on a lot o' the boards on the fence and they was plenty o' places where a brewer could of walked through sideways. I was goin' in at the gate because it was handiest, but I found it locked. I give it a kick and it was opened from inside by a barber hater.

"You can't come in," he says through the shrubbery.

"Why not?" says I.

"I've got orders," he says.

"I don't wonder," I says. "You're liable to get anything in them dragnets."

"I'll fix you if you try to come in," he says.

"What'll you do?" says I. "Tickle me to death with them plumes?"

"Mr. Grant don't want no spies hangin' round," says Whiskers.

"O' course not," says I. "But I'm one of his ball players."

"Oh, no, you ain't," says the Old Fox. "If you was you'd be wearin' one o' them get-ups with the knee pants and the spellin' on the blouse."

"Look here," I says. "I don't want to cut my way through the undergrowth; they's too much danger of infection. You run along and tell Mr. Grant his star performer has arrived, and when you come back I'll give you thirty-five cents to'rds a shave."

So the old boy slammed the gate shut and locked her again and the minute it was locked I went to the nearest gap in the fence and eased in.

They was a game o' ball goin' on and I started over to where they was playin' to see if I recognized anybody. But I hadn't went more'n a step or two when Whiskers come dashin' up to me with Mr. Grant followin'.

"This is the man!" yells Whiskers. "And my suspicions was right or he wouldn't of snuck in."

Mr. Grant was gaspin' too hard to talk at first; when he catched his breath he lit into me. "A spy, eh!" he says. "Tryin' to learn our secrets, eh! That's a fine job for a big man like you! Whose stool pigeon are you?" he says. "Stop the game!" he says to Whiskers. "Don't let 'em show nothin' in front o' this sneak!"

But they wasn't no need of him givin' that order, because when the boys heard the rumpus they quit o' their own accord and come runnin' over to be in on it.

Leadin' the pack was Jimmy Boyle, that I'd busted into the game with, out in Des Moines. I'd noticed from the box scores the summer before that they was a Boyle in this league, but I hadn't never thought of it bein' Jimmy. In fac', till I seen him sprintin' to'rds me, I'd forgot they was such a guy. It was nine years since I'd saw him.

"Hello, Buck!" he hollers.

"Buck!" says Mr. Grant. "You ain't Buck Warner, are you?"

"That's me," I says, "and I guess if it hadn't been for Jimmy recognizin' me you'd of had me shot for a spy."

The Old Boy looked like he was gettin' ready to cry.

"I certainly owe you my apologies," he says. "I don't remember faces as good as I used to and besides, you're dressed different than when you and me met."

"Yes," I says, "I've changed my clo'es twice since September."

"I hope you'll forgive me," says Mr. Grant.

"I'll think it over," I says.

By this time the whole bunch was gathered round and I had a chance to see who was who. Outside o' Jimmy Boyle they wasn't only four out o' more'n two dozen that I knowed by sight. One o' the four, o' course, was Billy Carmody. Him and I hadn't never met; he'd always been in the American till he jumped. But I'd saw his picture of'en enough to spot him. Then they was Hi Boles that I'd knew in the Association. And they was Charley Wade that the Boston club had for w'ile, and Red Fulton, that had been with Philly. The rest o' them was all strangers to me and most o' them looked about as much like ball players as Mary Pickford.

I shook hands with Red and Charley and Jimmy and Hi Boles, and Mr. Grant introduced me to the gang.

"Now," he says. "I wisht you'd shake with me to show you don't bear no grudge. I wouldn't of had this thing happen for the world."

"I don't blame you at all, sir," I says. "A club owner's got to be careful these days, because if other owners will go as far as stealin' your ball players, they certainly wouldn't hesitate at hirin' spies to try and cop your club's hit-and-run signs. But," I says, "I think you're foolish not to plug them holes in the fence. A scout with a strong glass could stand way out there behind center field and find out how many fingers your catchers used to signal for a curve ball."

"Yes," he says, winkin', "but the signals we use now and the signals we're goin' to use when the season opens up is two different things."

"Oh! Deep stuff, eh!" says I. "Well, if that's the way you're workin' it you'd ought not to be scared of outsiders swipin' information. Leave as many of 'em as wants to come and look us over, and the more bum dope they take back home, the easier we'll beat 'em when we meet 'em."

"But I don't want nobody to even know my line-up," says Mr. Grant, "not till the boys runs out on the field for the openin' game. If they don't know who we got or what we got or our battin' order or nothin', they can't prepare for us, can they?"

"Ain't they no reporters along?" I ast him.

"I wouldn't have 'em," says Mr. Grant. "I don't want to have no advance news get out about this club. Takin' your enemies by su'prise is more'n half the battle."

"Yes," says I, "but after the first day they won't be no more su'prise. The whole country'll know who we are."

"But we'll be leadin' the league," he says. "They can't take that away from us."

"Not for twenty-four hours," says I.

By this time, Carmody'd took his men back to their practice. I wanted to see 'em in action and made a move to go over to where they was at, but the Old Boy flagged me.

"They'll be through in five minutes," he says. "You must be wore out with your long trip, so let's you and I walk back to the hotel and set and rest till the boys comes in. I want you to be fresh to-morrow."

So we come away together and the last thing I seen at the grounds was Whiskers. He had the gate open far enough so's his head could stick out and he could see the whole length o' the main street. They wasn't a chance for a spy to catch him off guard, unless the spy used unfair tactics and snuck up from some other direction.

"What do you think of our club?" says Mr. Grant.

"I don't know nothin' about it," I says. "Most o' them boys is strangers to me."

"But ain't they nice lookin' boys?" he says.

"Sure," says I, "but some o' the best ball players I ever seen was homelier than muskrats."

"But their bein' homely didn't make 'em good ball players," says he.

"No," I says, "but it helped 'em keep in the pink. They couldn't go girl-crazy and stay out all hours o' the night dancin'; they wasn't no girls that'd dance with 'em or be seen with 'em. And they couldn't lay against the mahogany all evenin', because all bars has got mirrors back o' them, and if a man didn't never open his eyes they'd think you'd fell asleep and throw you out."

"Your arguments may be all right for some teams," says Mr.

Grant, "but they don't hold as far as we're concerned. Bein' handsome won't hurt my boys, because they can't run round nights or drink neither one."

"Why not?" I ast him.

"Because they's a club rule against it," he says.

"Oh!" I says. "O' course that makes it different. How'd you ever happen to think o' makin' a rule like that? I bet when the other club owners hears about it, they'll follow suit and thank you for originatin' the idear."

"I hope they do follow suit," he says. "It's one o' my ambitions to perjure baseball of its evils."

"I wish you luck," says I.

"And another one," he says, "is to win the pennant, and between you and I, I believe I'm goin' to realize it."

"What year?" I says.

"This year," says my boss.

"Well," I says, "I'm new in the league and I don't know what it takes to win. But from what I seen of your club and from what I read about Chicago and St. Louis and some o' the rest, I'd say you had to strengthen some."

"I'm afraid you're pessimistical, Warner," he says. "I've got the winnin' combination—yourself and Carmody and Fulton and Wade and Boles and Boyle for experience and balance, and those youngsters o' mine for speed and spirit. We'll take the League off'n their feet."

"What does Carmody think about it?"

"The same as me," he says. "And he's a great manager."

"He must be," says I.

Well, when the crowd come in, Jimmy Boyle chased up to the clerk o' the hotel and had it fixed for me to room with him.

"They had me paired with one o' the kids," he says, "but I got to have somebody to laugh with. This is goin' to be the greatest season you ever went through. I don't know what I'll hit, but I bet I giggle .380."

"What is they to laugh at?" I says.

"What ain't they to laugh at?" says Jimmy. "Wait till you get acquainted with the old man! Wait till you've saw our gang in action! Wait till you watch Carmody managin'! Dutch Schaefer couldn't of got up a better club than this."

"What have we got, outside o' you and the other fellas I know?" I ast him.

"Say, if I told you, you wouldn't believe it," says Jimmy. "In the first place, there's old Grant. If he ain't got no relatives the county'd ought to look after him. He's goin' to keep us a secret till the season opens and then we're goin' to win the first game by su'prise. And somebody tipped him off that the club that wins the first game has got the best chance for the pennant. O' course they's eight clubs in the league and four o' them'll prob'ly win their first games, but he never thought o' that. And besides, the only chance we got o' winnin' the first game or any other game is to have the other club look at us and die laughin'."

"Ain't they no stuff in them kids?" I ast.

"Just one o' them," says Boyle. "They's a boy named Steele that must of took his name from his right arm. He can whizz 'em through there faster'n Johnson. He could win with any club in the world but our'n."

"Who's the other pitchers?" I ast him.

"They ain't none," says Boyle, "none that counts. All told, we got three right-handers and three cockeyes, but outside o' Steele, I'd go up there and catch any one o' them without a mask or glove or protector or nothin'. When the balls they throw don't hit the screen on the fly they'll hit the fence on the first hop."

"Where'd he get 'em all?" says I.

"He must of bought 'em off'n Pawnee Bill," says Jimmy.

"We seem to be long on catchers," I says.

"Wade and Fulton and myself," says Jimmy, "but some of us is goin' to get switched before the season's a week old. As I say, when Steele ain't pitchin' the club don't need no catcher, and it sure does need other things. Carmody's playin' short and Boles is the first sacker and you'll be somewheres in the outfield. That only leaves four positions without nobody to fill 'em. So I and Red and Charley's wonderin' which one of us'll be elected first. I wouldn't mind tacklin' right field; they's some short fences in the league. But Carmody's just crazy enough to stick me at third base where a man don't have time to duck."

"You lay off'n right field," I says. "I got a lien on that bird."

"You'll play where Carmody puts you," says Jimmy.

"You're delirious," says I. "You ain't seen my contract. I signed to play right field and nowheres else, and you couldn't get me out o' there with a habeas corpus."

"Mr. Fox, eh?" says Boyle.

"You know it," I says, "and between you and I, they's a reason. I'd just as soon tell you because they ain't no danger o' you spillin' it. My right knee slipped out on me last August, and when it went, it went for good. All the doctors I seen give me the same advice—to get out o' baseball. And I had my mind all made up to quit when old Grant stepped in with his offer. I took it, knowin' all the w'ile that it was grand larceny."

"Don't you worry about that," says Jimmy. "They'll be only one guy on this club that ain't a burglar. That's young Steele. The rest of us, includin' the M.G.R., is a bunch o' bandits. But I'm not frettin' over it. I figure that if he wasn't givin' me this dough somebody else'd be gettin' it, maybe somebody without as much license to it as me. If they wasn't nobody dependin' on me I might feel ashamed. But when you got a wife and two kids, and an old bug comes along and slips you a contract for three times what you're worth, it'd be cheatin' your folks to not take it."

"I ain't got no folks," I says.

"But you can never tell," says Boyle.

"I can tell," I says, "if you'll listen. I met a little lady the middle o' last July. The first week in August we got engaged. And the second week in August Mr. Knee blowed out. So when Grant come after me, along in September, I begin to believe in angels. But I ain't never felt right about it."

"How bad is the old dog?" says Jimmy. "Can you run on it at all?"

"I can run on it," I says, "but I can't get up no speed. And I don't know when she's goin' to slip again. I can't start quick. And I'm scared to stoop."

"You won't need to stoop; not with our pitchers," says Jimmy. "All that'll come out your way is line drives or high boys over the wall."

"And if I turn sudden, I'm gone," says I.

"That's easy," says Boyle. "Rest your spine against them boards and do all your runnin' to'rds the infield. You won't be the first outfielder that played that system."

"Carmody'll wise up to me," I says.

"You should worry your head off about Carmody," says Boyle. "He's pretendin' to take his job serious, but down in his heart he knows he's a thief. He's got just as much right to manage a ball club as that girl o' yours. You just stick it out and draw the old check every first and fifteenth, and remember that you got plenty o' company. Even if your two legs was cut off at the waist you'd be worth five times as much as some of us."

"Careful there, Jim," I says.

"You can hit, can't you?" he says. "And you can catch fly balls, and you can throw. There's three things you can do, and that's three more things than most of our gang can do. No, I'll take that back. They's one thing they can all do."

"What's that?" I ast him.

"Eat," says Jimmy, "and if you don't believe it come down in the dinin' room. The doors is supposed to open for supper at five-thirty, but after the first day we was here, the manager seen that the only way to save the doors was to keep 'em open all the w'ile. All the other ball clubs I was ever with talked about their hittin' and their bad luck, and all that. But this bunch don't talk nothin' but meats and groceries, and when they ain't talkin' about 'em it's because they got so many o' them in their mouth that they can't talk. The kid that was roomin' with me put what he couldn't eat in his pockets or inside his shirt, and after every meal he'd come straight to the room and unload on top o' the bureau. And if I went near his storehouse to brush my hair or look in the glass, he'd growl like a dog. He had himself trained so's he wouldn't sleep more'n three hours in a row. He'd go to bed at nine and get up at twelve and three for refreshments. But no matter how hungry he was at three, he always managed to save a piece o' cold hamburger or a little fricasseed veal for when he woke up in the mornin', so's he wouldn't have to go down to breakfast in his nightgown. Our second day here it was rainin' when I rolled out o' bed. Griffin, the kid I'm tellin' you about, was puttin' on his clo'es with one hand and feedin' himself with the other. 'Well, boy,' I says to him, 'it looks like we'd loaf to-day.' He must of thought I'd mentioned veal loaf or a loaf o' bread, because all the answer I got was more things to eat. 'Fruit and cereal,' he says, 'prunes and oranges and oatmeal, bacon and eggs straight up, small tenderloin medium, sausage and cakes, buttered toast, some o' them rolls, and a pot o' coffee.' 'Well,' I says, 'your dress rehearsal goes off all right; if you don't get scared and forget your lines in front o' the waiter, you'll be the hit o' the show.' But I might as well of been talkin' to a post hole. He didn't know I was speakin' unless I spoke like a bill o' fare."

"What position does he play?" I ast.

"Third base," says Jimmy, "and for the fear everybody won't know it, he always keeps one foot on the bag. But don't get the idear that he's a bigger eater than the rest o' them. They ain't no more difference in their appetites than in their ball playin'. When they got their noses in the feed-trough, though, they look like they was at home. And when they're out there on the field, you'd think they was It for blindman's buff."

I ast him about the Old Man havin' their lunch sent out.

"Even Carmody laughed at that," he says; "but Carmody's figured that the way to get along with old Grant is to agree with him in everything. So we're relieved from two changes o' clo'es, and a half mile walk that might help some of us get down to weight."

"Is it a regular lunch?" I ast him.

"All but the tools," says Jimmy. "And that makes it the favorite meal with Griffin and them. They can throw it in faster and without near as much risk. And all you have to do to start a riot is drop a bone or part of a potato on the grass."

"How is the grounds?" I says.

"Just as good as the club," says Boyle.

"Who picked out this joint?" says I.

"The same old bug that picked up these ball players," says Jimmy. "He was lookin' for a quiet place and he got it. The burg's supposed to have a population o' twelve hundred, but I haven't even saw the twelve. Dixie Springs they call it, but the only springs is in Carmody's bed. The town and the grounds is both jokes. The hotel's all right outside o' the rooms. I'll own up the eatin's good, but that's the one thing that don't make no difference to this bunch of our'n. They'd go to it just the same if it was raw mule chops."

"How much longer do we stick?" I ast him.

"Plain five weeks," says Jimmy. "We don't play no exhibitions nowheres because they might be spies from the other clubs watchin' us. We stay right here and do all our practicin' in a park that was laid out by a steeplechase fan, and then we go straight home and win the openin' game and the pennant by su'prise. You're lucky you come a week late. If I'd knew the dope in advance I wouldn't of never reported till the day o' the big su'prise party. But leave us hurry downstairs or it'll be too late for you to get a look at a fine piece of American scenery."

"What's that?" I ast.

"The Royal Gorge," says Jimmy.

Well, he hadn't lied when he told me about their eatin'. It was just like as if they knowed the league wasn't only goin' to last this one more season, and they all o' them expected to live to be over ninety, and was tryin' to get fixed up in a year for the next sixty-five. You remember how them waiters down South come one-steppin' in with their trays balanced on their thumb a mile over their head? Well, they didn't pull that stunt with the orders these here boys give 'em. Each fella's meal took two pall-bearers, with a couple o' mourners followin' along behind to pick up whatever floral pieces fell off when the casket listed.

I and Boyle and Fulton and Hi Boles had a table to ourself, and you ought to saw them Ephs quarrel over who'd wait on us. Besides our four orders together not bein' as big as one o' them other guys', we wasn't so exhausted at the end o' the meal that we couldn't dig down in our pocket and get a dime. Mr. Grant and Carmody and the secretary set next to our table and it seemed to worry the Old Boy that our appetites was so poor. He'd say:

"Warner, I'm afraid you ain't feelin' good. You don't eat hardly nothin'."

"I'm all right," I'd tell him; "but eatin' ain't no new experience for me. I ett for several years before I broke into baseball and I been gettin' regular meals ever since."

The lunch served out to the grounds was worth travelin' south just to look at it. It always come prompt at twelve, and for a half hour before that time every ground ball was a base hit because the fielders was all lookin' up at the sun. And when the baskets full o' nourishment was drug in, no matter if we was right in the middle of an innin', everybody'd throw away their bats and gloves and race for the front. Carmody'd follow along smilin', like it was a good joke.

I was hungry my first day out. I told Jimmy I felt like eatin' a big meal.

"Well," he says, "I bet you don't eat it when you see it."

He win his bet. I was the last fella up to the baskets. They was a couple o' sandwiches and one or two pieces o' fried chicken left, but it'd all be pawed over by the early birds, and amongst the other things the grounds was shy of was a place to wash your hands. Even if they'd been one, nobody'd of had time to use it.

So that day and the rest o' the time we was there I set out on the sidelines with Hi and Jimmy and Red durin' the noon hour, and watched the performance.

"This mayn't be a big league," says Jimmy, "but our club'll be big if they don't all get lockjaw."

"It'll take two engines to pull us home," says Red.

"If them boys could hit, they'd be heavy hitters," says Hi.

Well, they couldn't hit or they couldn't field; that is, the most o' them couldn't. They was a couple that had the stuff to make pretty fair ball players if they'd knew anything. Carmody couldn't learn 'em because he didn't know nothin' himself. I done what I could to help 'em, partly because I'm kind-hearted and partly so's I'd be doin' somethin' else besides riskin' my life in that outfield. It was rough enough so's a fella with two good legs would be scared to take a chance, and it wasn't no place for a cripple to frolic round in.

We put on two ball games a day between the regulars and yannigans. The only reason for callin' our team the regulars was on account o' Carmody playin' with us. We was licked most o' the time because young Steele done most o' the pitchin' against us. He sure could buzz 'em through and he had as good control as I ever seen in a kid. He was workin' the day that I and Carmody had our first and last argument. Carmody's whole idear o' baseball was "take two strikes." That was his instructions to everybody that went up to hit. It was all right when the other fellas was pitchin' because they was all o' them pretty near sure to walk you. But I couldn't see no sense doin' it against Steele; it just helped him get you in a hole.

This day it come up to the seventh innin' and Steele had us beat four to nothin'. We was all ordered to take two strikes and most of us was addin' one onto the order. But in the seventh, one o' the kids happened to get a base hit and they was a couple o' boots, and when it was my turn to go up there, the bases was choked and two out.

"Take two strikes," yells Carmody.

"Yes," I says to myself, "I'll take two strikes."

So Steele, thinkin' I'd obey orders, laid the first one right over in my groove and I busted it out o' the ball park.

When I come in to the bench Carmody was layin' for me.

"What kind o' baseball is that?" he says.

"It's real baseball," I says. "If you think it ain't you're crazy. When a pitcher's got as good control as him, and we're four runs behind and the bases is full, I'm goin' to crack the first ball I can reach."

He called me over away from the gang.

"It's a bad example," he says, "for you not to follow instructions."

"Maybe it is," says I, "but when the instructions is ridic'lous I'm goin' to forget 'em."

"I'm managin' this ball club," he says.

"You're doin' a grand job," says I. "When you take money for managin', it's plain highway robbery."

"I suppose you're earnin' yourn," says Carmody. "I suppose you got two good legs."

That kind o' shook me up.

"Listen," he says, "I got just as much license to draw a manager's salary as you have for takin' a ball player's. You're liable to be on crutches before the middle of April. But if I don't make no crack to Grant he won't know you was crippled when you signed; he'll think, when your knee goes back on you, that it's the first time and just an accident. So," he says, "if I was you I'd play the way the manager told me and not make no fuss."

"You win," says I. "But have a heart and forget once in a w'ile to give me orders. I don't mind if the rest o' the league knows I got a bum leg, but I don't want 'em to think my head's cut off."

They wasn't never such a long five weeks as I put in down to this excuse for a trainin' camp. After the first few days I got sick o' laughin' and sleepin' and everything else. I'd promised the girl I wouldn't take a drink, but all that kept me from breakin' the promise was lack of opportunity. The burg didn't even have a soda foundry.

Nights after supper I'd write a long letter to the future Missus and then I and Boyle'd set up in the room and wish we was somewheres else. Once or twice old Grant called on us and raved about our chances to win the pennant.

"If you boys finish on top," he says, "and if the European war's over by that time, I might give you all a trip acrost the pond next fall."

When he'd went out and left us after spillin' that great piece o' news, we was as excited as a couple o' draft horses.

"I wonder what they soak a man for a steamer trunk," says Jimmy. "It'd be a grand honeymoon for you," he says. "The lady'll love you better'n ever when she knows you're goin' to take her to see the Tower o' London and the Plaster o' Paris."

"I hope," says I, "that they'll be sure and have all the dead removed before we get there."

"We'll be right to home in the trenches after practicin' all spring on these grounds," says Jimmy.

Well, the time went by one way and another and the happiest day o' my life, bar one, was when us Wellfeds clumb aboard a rattler headed north. Our trainin' season was over and we was in every bit as good shape as if we'd just left the operatin' table. Our team was picked and they was ball players in every position except two, but Carmody and Wade was the only ones in the lot that was playin' where they belonged. The two kids that acted like they had a little ability was in the outfield with me. Jimmy Boyle'd been tried at second base and third base, but he was lost both places, so they'd stuck him on first and shifted Hi Boles, a first sacker, to third. Red Fulton, another catcher, was pretendin' to play second base. Carmody was at shortstop and it looked like Charley Wade was elected to catch whenever it didn't rain. That was the club that was goin' to take the pennant by su'prise and spend the winter in Monte Carlo.

But I was too happy over leavin' Dixie Springs to be worryin' about how rotten we looked.

"Lord!" I says to Charley Wade, "I guess it won't seem great to be in a real town!"

"I don't know," he says. "I'm afraid I'll be nervous when I get where they's people."

III

THEY WASN'T ENOUGH people in the park the day we opened to bother Charley Wade or anybody else. Old Grant had made such a success o' keepin' us a secret that only about eight hundred knowed we was goin' to perform; anyway, that's all that come out to watch us, and in his great, big new stands, they looked like a dozen fleas on a flat car.

It was a crime, too, that we didn't have a crowd, because we win the ball game. The records will show that; you don't have to take my word. The Old Boy had predicted a su'prise and his prophecy come true. And the ones that was most su'prised was us and the fellas we beat.

When that Buffalo bunch first come out and seen our line-up in battin' practice, they laughed themself hoarse. But they didn't do no laughin' after the game started and they got a sample o' Steele's stuff. The weather was twice as cold as any we'd ran into down South, but it didn't seem to make no difference to him. He was lightnin' fast and steady as Matty. He didn't give 'em one real chance to score.

We trimmed 'em two to nothin' and I drove in the both of our runs. Along with that I was lucky enough to make quite a catch o' the only ball they hit hard off o' Steele.

When we got in the clubhouse afterwards, Mr. Grant was there, actually cryin' for joy. He throwed his arms round Steele and was goin' to do the same to me, but I backed off and told him I was engaged.

O' course they was reporters lookin' us over this time and the next mornin' the population was informed that Grant and Carmody'd made quite a ball club out of a bunch of misfits. So when she started that afternoon, the stands was pretty near filled.

Our whole pitchin' staff, except Steele, was in there at one time or another. The Buffalo club hadn't been able to hit Steele. They didn't have to hit these other babies. I don't know how many bases on balls was gave, but I bet it was a world's record. Charley Wade, back o' the bat, did more shaggin' than all the outfielders. When Buffalo was battin' the umps could of left his right arm in the checkroom. Fourteen to nothin' it wound up and they was no spoonin' in the clubhouse after the game.

Steele was beat his next time out, but win his third start. And one o' the cock-eyes come acrost with a win in the second series, gettin' some valuable help from an umpire that'd been let out o' the Association for bein' stone blind. I think altogether we copped four games in April. Along the last part o' May or the first o' June we grabbed two in succession, but the streak was broke up when Jimmy dropped three pegs in the eighth and ninth innin's o' the third game.

Durin' the home series in May, four or five hundred people that was fond o' low comedy come out every afternoon to get our stuff. But we pulled the same gags so often that they quit us after a w'ile. We went round the western half o' the circuit in June and our split o' the gate wouldn't of tipped the porters. Then, we come home again and was welcomed by thirty-seven paid admissions, five ushers and two newspaper men.

The Old Boy cut the price to a dime for the bleachers. The ticket takers slept peaceful all afternoon. Then he hired a band to give a concert every day, so for a w'ile we was sure of an attendance o' thirty, except when the piccolo player got piccoloed.

When August come I was leadin' the league in hittin' and Mr. Grant thought I was the most valuable man he had. He overlooked a few things about my record that would of wised up any real baseball man. For instance, though I was battin' .420, my total o' stolen bases was three, and all three o' them was steals o' second that'd been made in double steals with Hi Boles goin' from second to third. And I didn't only have about ten extra base hits, o' which five was home run drives out o' the park. In other words, I wasn't doin' no more runnin' than I had to, and I didn't try to get nowheres where they was a chance that I'd have to slide. And under this kind o' treatment, Mr. Leggo had held up good. I'd felt him wabble two different times when I was chasin' fly balls, but he'd popped back into place without me even coaxin' him.

Then, in the middle of August, everything happened at once. Charley Wade broke an ankle, Carmody's right arm went dead, and the girl had a brawl with Aunt Julia.

We was in Indianapolis. We'd just got through carryin' Charley into the club-house when a boy come down to the bench and handed me a telegram. It says I was to come at once; she must see me.

"Carmody," I says, "I got to run down to Dayton to-night."

"What for?" he says.

"Somebody wants me," I told him.

"Not as bad as I do," he says.

"Well," says I, "it's somebody that makes more difference than you do."

"I'll talk to you after the game," he says.

It was our last bats and it didn't take 'em long to get us out.

"Now," says Carmody, "you can go to Dayton to-night if you'll promise to be back in time to play to-morrow."

"I can't make no promise," I says.

"Then you can't go," says Carmody.

"What's the matter with you?" I says. "Can't you stick a pitcher or one o' them kids in right field for one day?"

"You ain't goin' to play right field no more," he says.

"I ain't going to play nowheres else," says I. "Do you think I'm goin' to catch in Charley's place?"

"No," he says. "I'm goin' to put Boyle back there."

"And me go to first?" I says.

"No," says Carmody. "I'm goin' there myself and you're goin' to take my place at shortstop."

"You're maudlin," I says. "I signed a contract to play right field and that's where I'm goin' to stick. I'm awkward enough out there; I'd be a holy show on the infield. Besides, you never played first base in your life and one o' the pitchers or that big Griffin kid could do as good as you. What's the use o' breakin' up your whole combination just because one fella's hurt?"

"We couldn't make no change that'd be for the worse," says Carmody. "But I'll come clean with you and tell you where I'm at. I'm gettin' $1800 a month for this job. But my contract says I got to play the whole season out or he can cut $2500 off'n my year's salary."

"Well," I says, "what's the difference if you play first base or stay where you're at?"

"I can't stay where I'm at," he says. "My souper's deader'n that place we trained. She quit on me in the seventh innin' to-day. I couldn't stand on the foul line and throw to fair ground."

"You hurt it in action, didn't you?" I says.

"Yes, but he's sore at me," says Carmody, "on account of our swell showin'. And the way my contract reads, he could keep my dough if he wanted to."

"But you'll have to throw when you're playin' first base," says I.

"No, I won't," he says. "You watch me and see. If I've got the ball and they's a play to make anywheres, you'll see the old pill slip right out o' my hand and lay there on the ground."

"But I don't see why you should pick on me," I says. "Boles or Red Fulton or one o' them kids could do a whole lot better job o' shortstoppin' than me."

"Boles and Fulton is bad enough where they're at," he says, "without wishin' a new bunch o' trouble on 'em. You've played there and you'd know what you was doin' even if you couldn't stoop over or cover no ground. Besides," he says, "old Grant wants you to tackle it."

"When was you talkin' to him?" I says. "You ain't seen him since Charley got hurt and your arm went."

"That's more secrets," says Carmody. "Between you and I, my arm's been bad a long w'ile and I had the hunch it was goin' to do just what it done. So I told him a little story a couple o' weeks ago. I told him I wasn't satisfied with the way Boyle was playin' first base and I told him I was a pretty good first sacker myself and thought I'd move over there. So he ast me who'd play shortstop and I told him you'd make the best man and he says he thought so, too, but your contract read that you'd only play right field. So I told him maybe he could coax you to switch."

"It must be hard for you to shave with all that cheek," I says. "You can go and tell him now that you ast me would I play shortstop and I told you No, I wouldn't. So that's settled, and now I'm goin' to catch a train. If I can get back to-morrow I will. And if I do get back, I'll be in right field."

I left him bawlin' me out, but I knowed he couldn't do nothin' to me. I had as much on him as he had on me.

I run into a flood in Dayton, but it was salt water this time. The girl cried for two hours after I got there and couldn't quit long enough to tell me what it was about. I finally made like I was goin' away disgusted. Then she come through.

They wasn't goin' to be no $2500 from Aunt Julia. Aunt Julia'd fell in love with a G. A. R. that hadn't did nothin' since '65 but celebrate his team's victory. So Ethel, instead o' usin' her head, lost it, and ast Aunt Julia what she meant by tyin' up with a bird twenty years older than herself that hadn't shaved since Grant took Richmond. So they broke up in a riot and all bets was off.

"Well," I says, "maybe she'll get over it."

"No, she won't," says Ethel, "and even if she did, I wouldn't take her old money."

"Any high-class bank would give you new money for it," I says.

"It ain't no time for jokin'," she says. "Everything's all over. We can't get married this year; maybe not for ten years; maybe never."

"I don't have to pay all them debts right away," I says. "I can hold out $2500 and give it to Paul. The boys have waited this long for their dough; I guess they can wait a w'ile longer."

"You know what I've told you," she says. "We won't be married one minute before you're out o' debt."

"Well," I says, "it looks like they was no hurry about gettin' a license. They ain't goin' to be no post-season money for us guys."

"We'll just have to wait then," says the girl. "You'll have to save every cent o' your next year's pay."

"They ain't goin' to be no next year's pay," says I. "This league'll be past history in another season. And I couldn't carry bats anywheres else."

The more we talked the bluer things looked and I guess I'd of been cryin' myself in another minute if the big idear hadn't came to me.

"Wait a minute!" I says. "They's a chance that we can get out o' this all right."

"What's the dope?" she ast me.

But I wouldn't tell her; it wasn't clear in my own mind yet and I didn't want to say nothin' till I'd schemed it out.

"I'm goin' right back, back, back to Indiana," I says. "You'll get a wire from me to-morrow night. Maybe it'll be good news and maybe it won't. But you'll know pretty near as soon as I do."

I was up in Carmody's room at seven o'clock the next mornin'. I ast him if he'd said anything to Mr. Grant about me refusin' to play shortstop.

"No," he says. "I was hopin' you'd change your mind."

"Maybe I will," I says, "but not without he coaxes me."

Carmody didn't ask me what I was gettin' at. He dressed and went downstairs to find the Old Boy. And at half-past eight, in the dinin' room, the coaxin' commenced.

"Warner," says Mr. Grant, "Carmody's thinkin' about makin' a few changes in the team."

"Is that so?" I says. "What are they?"

"Well," he says, "he ain't satisfied with the way Boyle plays first base. And besides, now that Wade's hurt, he thinks Boyle should ought to go back and catch again. And he wants to try first base himself. So that would leave shortstop open."

"Maybe you could get a hold o' some semi-pro shortstopper," I says.

"I don't want none," he says. "I want a man that's had big league experience. I believe that with Carmody on first base and a good man at shortstop we could finish seventh yet. What do you think?"

"Very likely," I says, knowin' that they wasn't a chance in the world.

"I'd give a good deal to pull out o' last place," says he.

"Well," I says, "I'll see if I can't think o' some good shortstop that ain't tied up."

"You don't have to try and think o' one," says Mr. Grant. "I've got one in mind."

"Who's that?" I says.

"Yourself," he says. I pretended like I was too su'prised to speak.

"You can play the position, can't you?" he ast.

"Sure," says I. "That's where I was born and brought up."

"Well, then," he says, rubbin' his hands.

"Well, nothin'," I says. "I'm signed as a right fielder."

"We could make a new contract," he says.

"But listen, Mr. Grant," I says. "W'ile I know shortstop like a book, I don't want to play it. It's too hard. It keeps a man thinkin' and workin' every minute. One season at shortstop is pretty near as wearin' as two in the outfield. That's why I insisted on right field. I wanted to take things a little easier this year. That's why I was willin' to sign with you for $5000."

"What would you of wanted to play short?" he ast me.

"Oh," I says, "I wouldn't of thought of it for less than $9000."

He didn't say nothin' for a minute; a good long minute too. Finally he says:

"Well, Warner, they's only about six more weeks to go. But I'm wild to get out o' last place and I'll spend some money to do it, though spendin' money has been my chief business all season. I want to be fair with you, so if you'll finish out the season at shortstop I'll give you $2500 extra."

This time it was me that wanted to hug him. But I played safe. I considered and considered and considered and finally I give in.

"I'll do it, Mr. Grant," I says. "As a favor to you, I'll do it."

Out in the lobby Carmody was waitin' for me.

"It's fixed," I says. "He's a pretty good coaxer."

"What did you get?" he ast me.

"A November weddin'," says I.

I'd promised to wire Ethel by night, but the thing had been pulled a whole lot quicker'n I'd hoped for. I run right from Carmody to the telegraph office.

"All fixed," I says in my message. "I got $2500 extra."

At lunch time her answer come back:

"Good old boy. Did you hold somebody up?"

Well, sir, believe me or not, I hadn't thought of it that way before. But when I read her wire I had to admit to myself that she'd pretty near called the turn.

The less said about them last six weeks the better. I don't know how many games we was beat, but five was what we win. I felt worst about poor Steele. There he was, workin' his head off two to four games a week, worth four times as much as all the rest of us together, and drawin' a salary o' $400 a month. He's with a real club this year and you watch him go!

They'll always be a question in my mind about which was the biggest flivver, me at shortstop or Carmody at first base. I covered just as much ground as was under my shoes and if a ground ball didn't hop up waist high when it come to me, it kept right on travelin'.

I didn't take many plays at second base for the fear I'd get slid into. If I tagged anybody it was because they stuck out their hand

and insisted on it. And I was so nervous all the w'ile that I couldn't hardly foul one up at that plate.

Carmody's dead arm wasn't half his troubles. Findin' first base with his feet was what bothered him most. Everybody in the league was ridin' him.

"Tie a bell on the bag!" they'd holler. "Look out! You'll spike yourself! Get a compass! Who hid first base?"

It was lucky for me that the Old Boy's box was on the first base side and that he couldn't see far. He could take in a lot more o' Carmody's fox trottin' than he could o' my still life posin'. He knowed, though, that I wasn't a howlin' success as a shortstopper. When he give me my extra money, he says:

"Warner, you didn't come up to my expectations."

"Mr. Grant," I says, "playin' that outfield spoiled me for an infield job. I won't never tackle it again."

And for once I was tellin' him the truth.

I ast him what his plans was for another season.

"I ain't only got the one plan," he says. "That's to get out o' baseball."

"Well," I says, "I hope you can find somebody to buy the club."

"I ain't goin' to sell it," he says. "The next man that does me a dirty trick, I'm goin' to give it to him."

IV

Well, sir, I paid my debts first and then I sent the girl's brother a check for my share o' the dandy little garage. The marriage nuptials come off on schedule and I guess we wasn't su'prised when Aunt Julia showed up with a forgivin' smile and a check for $2500.

"You can't tell if it's old money or not," I says to Ethel.

"I guess we'll keep it anyway," she says.

"Maybe," I says, "I'll send it back to old Grant."

"Maybe you won't too," says she. "This money happens to belong to me and I never pretended I could play shortstop."

I feel better now that's off'n my chest. I know it was wrong, but as Jimmy Boyle pointed out, if one fella didn't take it some other fella would. And I think I got a better excuse than anybody else. Come out to the house sometime and see for yourself.

The Hold-Out

The Saturday Evening Post
MARCH 24, 1917

THREE PEOPLE not countin' myself, think I'm the greatest guy in the world. One o' them's my first and last wife, another's Mr. Edwards, and the other's Bill Hagedorn.

It'd be hard to pick three that I'd rather have cordial. If a person is livin' with their wife, it makes it kind o' pleasant to have her like you. Mr. Edwards, o' course, is the man I'm workin' for, so it don't hurt me at all to be his hero. And I'm glad to have Bill added to the list, because it means he'll play the bag better for me this year than he's done yet, and with a little pep on first base we're liable to be bad news to George Stallin's, Wilbert Robinson and John T. McGraw.

But listen. If Mr. Edwards ever got hold o' the truth o' the Hagedorn business, him and I'd be just as clubby as Lord George and the Kaiser. If he didn't drop dead when he found it out, he'd slip me the tinware, contract or no contract, and I wouldn't have the heart to fight it in the courts, because I admit I gave him a raw deal. My only alibi is that I left my feelin's get the best o' me, and that excuse wouldn't be worth a dime with him; they's no excuse that would be, where his pocketbook's concerned, like in this case. He just simply hates money!

The worst of it is that Hagedorn didn't deserve no consideration. I like to see a fella get all that's comin' to him, provided he goes after it in the right way and puts up a real fight. Hagedorn made a hog of himself and was tremblin' all the time he did it. If he was as yellow on the ball field as when he's makin' a play for more dough, I'd take away his uniform and suspend him for life; he wouldn't be no more use to me than a set of adenoids.

He's just as game a ball player, though, as you'll find. The minute he trots out there in the old orchard he's a different guy, afraid o' nothin'. All he's lacked so far is ambish, and I figure he'll show some o' that this year. He'll give me his best out o' gratitude. If he don't, it'll mean his finish on the big time, family or no family.

It's part o' my agreement with Mr. Edwards that I stick on the job all the year round, goin' to the league meetin's with him in winter, helpin' him sign up the boys, and so forth. Well, after we was through last fall, he called me up in the office and begin crabbin' about finances.

"Frank," he says, "we lost $18,000 this season. I pretty near wish I didn't have no ball club."

"You've pretty near got your wish," I says. "If some o' those bushers don't come through next spring, or if we don't swing a couple o' deals between now and then, the clubs that play against us won't even get good practice."

"Bad as we are," he says, "I bet we got the biggest salary list in the big leagues. It looks to me like not only one or two, but several of our men were bein' overpaid."

"Yes, sir," I says; "and on their showin' the last few months some o' them would be overpaid if they drawed a dollar a day."

"Well," he says, "I'm goin' to do some trimmin'. The boys'll kick, I suppose, but I'm dependin' on you to show 'em they deserve cuts."

"That's a nice little job for me," I says. "It's just as easy to convince a ball player that his pay ought to be trimmed as it is to score twelve runs off Alexander."

"I'd just as leave pay good prices for good work," he says, "but I'm not goin' to maintain no pension bureau. These ridic'lous Federal League contracts have all run out, thank heavens, and from now on my ball club'll be run on a sane basis. Look at Lefty Grant!" he says. "He got $7000 and pitched pretty near eleven full games, winnin' three o' them. And look at Hagedorn! A $6000 contract and no more life in him than a wet rag! What do you suppose ailed him?"

"Federalitis," I says. "He was gettin' soft money in the Federal, with no incentive to win and nobody to try and make him hustle."

"A $6000 salary," says Mr. Edwards, "for a man that hit round .220 and played first base like he was bettin' against us! Maybe we'd better just let loose of him."

"If I was you," I says, "I'd see what the recruits is like before gettin' rid o' Hagedorn. I'll admit he's been loafin', but he's a mighty good ball player when he tries."

"Maybe it'll wake him up to cut him," says he. "I'm goin' to send him a contract for $4000."

"Suit youself," says I. "He'll holler like an Indian, but if he sees you're in earnest I guess he'll come round."

"He lives here in town," says Mr. Edwards. "I'll have the girl call him up sometime and tell him I want to see him."

So we discussed a few others that was gettin' way more than they earned, and the boss says he wouldn't play no favorites, but would cut 'em all from ten to forty per cent. I knew they'd be plenty o' trouble, but I didn't care a whole lot. I figured that if everybody on the pay roll quit the game and went to work it'd strengthen the team.

Well, Hagedorn accepted Mr. Edwards' invitation to call and I was in the office when Bill come in.

"Mr. Hagedorn," says the boss, "Manager Conley and myself's been talkin' things over and we come to the conclusion that several o' you boys was earnin' less than we paid you. What do you think about it?"

"Well," says Hagedorn, "some o' the boys maybe deserve cuts. But I don't see how I come in on it."

"Why not?" says Mr. Edwards. "The unofficial averages gives you a battin' percentage o' .220."

"I can't help what them dam scorers do to me," says Bill. "I never did get fair treatment from the reporters."

"But when you was in the league before," says the boss, "you always hit up round .280, and it's a cinch the scorers didn't cheat you out o' sixty points."

"They'd cheat me out o' my shirt if they had a chance," Bill says. "But even if I did have a bad year with the wood, that ain't no sign I won't do all right next season."

"That's true enough," says Mr. Edwards. "Anybody's liable to have a battin' slump. But Manager Conley and myself wasn't thinkin' about your hittin' alone. We kind o' thought that your work all round was below the standard; that you was sort o' layin' down on the job."

Hagedorn began to whine.

"Mr. Edwards," he says, "you got me entirely wrong. I wouldn't lay down on nobody. I've give you my best every minute, and if I haven't it was because things broke bad for me."

"What things?" I ast him.

"Well," he says, "for one thing, I felt rotten all summer. My legs was bad."

"Well," I says, "you can't expect Mr. Edwards to pay $3000 apiece for bad legs."

"But they're all right now," he says. "I haven't had a bit o' trouble with 'em all fall. And I'm takin' grand care o' myself and next spring I'll be as good as ever."

"Why didn't you tell me about your legs?" I ast him. "I'd of let you lay off. You certainly wasn't helpin' us much."

"I'd of told you only I don't like to quit," he says. "And besides, my legs wasn't the whole trouble."

"What else was it?" I says.

"Well," he says, "the Missus was sick and in the hospital, and I had to pay out a lot o' money and it kept me worried."

"When was she sick?" I ast him.

"Let's see," he says, "it was while we was on our last Eastern trip."

"You never ast me to let you come home," I says.

"No," he says, "I didn't know nothin' at all about it till we got back."

"That's why you worried, I suppose," says I, "and I guess your wife's illness in September was what worried you in June and July."

"She was sick on and off all season," he says.

"I noticed," says I, "that she done most of her sufferin' in a grandstand seat. Her ailment," I says, "was probably brought on by watchin' you perform."

"She's full o' nerve," he says. "She wouldn't miss a ball game if she was dyin'. And besides, her sickness wasn't all of it."

"Let's hear the whole story at once," I says. "The suspense is fierce."

"Her folks kept botherin' us," says Hagedorn. "They live in Louisville, and they're gettin' old and they wanted that she should come down there and stay with 'em."

"Couldn't they come up here?" I ast him.

"No," he says, "they got their own home and their own friends and everything down there."

"Well," I says, "that'd probably be the square thing for you to do, just pack up and move to Louisville and live with 'em."

"We'd only be there in the winter," he says.

"No," says I, "I'll fix it so's you can be there all the year round."

"What do you mean?" he says.

"I mean that if you don't want to sign at our figures Louisville'd be the ideal spot for you," says I.

"What's your figures?" he ast.

"I'm willin' to give you $4000," says Mr. Edwards. Hagedorn swelled up.

"If you think I'll take a $2000 cut, you got me wrong," he says.

"All right," says I, "and I hope the Kentucky climate agrees with your legs."

We sent Lefty Grant a contract for $5000 and after a little crabbin' by mail he signed. Joe Marsh stood for a $1000 cut, and Bones McChesney, shaved from $3500 to $3000, refused to sign and got himself sold to Toronto. I didn't cry over losin' him; he'd always been fat from his neck up, and in the last two seasons the epidemic had spread all over his body.

Now it don't often happen that a seventh-place club begins lookin' like a pennant contender between October and February. But that's what come off with us. Our worst weakness last year was at shortstop and third base and back o' the bat. Well, I talked to a lot of Association men durin' the fall, and they told me that I had a second Schalk in this young Stremmle from Indianapolis. And I got swell reports on Berner, the shortstop we drew from Dayton. Both these guys, I was told, were ready. They wouldn't need no more seasonin'.

And then along come the league meetin' in New York, and I happened to catch the St. Louis gang when they were thinkin' about somethin' else, and they traded me Johnny Gould for Hype Corliss and Jack Moran, two guys that I'd kept down in the bull pen all summer so's the bugs couldn't get a good look at 'em. There was my third base hole plugged up and the ball club was bound to be a hundred per cent better, provided Hagedorn signed and give us his best work, or that young Lahey, the first sacker we bought from Davenport, made good. I wasn't worryin' much about him, as I figured right along that Hagedorn would take his $4000 when he seen we were in earnest.

O' course he had a little bit the best of us in the argument—that is, he would of had if he'd knew enough. Him and Lahey was the only candidates for first base, and no matter if he played the position in a hammock, he'd be better than an inexperienced kid from the Three Eye. Even if he wasn't never worth a nickel over $4000, here was a grand chance for him to hold us up. All he had to do was lay quiet at home, and when it come time for us to go South we'd of looked him up and met his demands. But no, he didn't have the nerve or sense to go at it the right way.

Instead o' keepin' us guessin', what does he do but hunt up excuses to come and hang round the office and try and get a hint o' whether we were goin' to stand pat or back down. I was alone the first time he showed.

"Hello, Bill," I says. "Did you bring your fountain pen?"

"What for?" he says.

"To sign that $4000 contract," says I.

"Oh, no," he says, "I wasn't thinkin' nothin' about the contract. I come up to see if they was any mail for me."

"Not now," I says, "but you may be hearin' from the Louisville club in a few days."

"What would they be writin' me about?" he says.

"Maybe they'll hear about you wantin' to move there," I says, "and they'll probably be askin' you if you'd care to take a job with 'em."

"Well," says Bill, "you won't catch me playin' ball with Louisville."

"Who was you thinkin' about playin' with?" I ast him.

"Nobody," he says. "I've decided to quit."

"That's fine, Bill!" I says. "Somebody left you money?"

"No," he says, "but I got some o' my own saved up."

"How much?" I ast him.

"Close to $2000," says Bill.

"Fine work!" says I. "You must of lived pretty simple to save $2000 in seven years."

"I never skimped," says Bill.

"Well," I says, "I don't know how you managed. But it's nice to feel that you won't never have to skimp again. If you can get six per cent for your money that'll mean $120 a year or $10 a month. That puts you on Easy Street. All you'll have to get along without is food, clothes, heat and a place to live."

He paid us another visit Christmas week, thinkin', maybe, that Mr. Edwards would be runnin' over with holiday spirits.

This was a bum guess. The old man's got more relatives than a perch, and when he was through buyin' presents for all o' them he wouldn't of paid a telephone slug for the release o' Ty Cobb.

"No mail yet," I says to Bill when he come in.

"I wasn't expectin' no mail," he says. "I was just wonderin' if I left a pair o' gloves here last time."

"A pair o' tan gloves?" I says.

"Yes," says Hagedorn.

"I didn't see 'em," I says. "I found some gray ones."

"How is everything?" he says.

"Fine!" says I. "It looks like we're goin' to have a regular ball club."

"Well, I hope you do," Bill says.

"Gould's goin' to help us a lot," says I, "and they tell me Stremmle and Berner's both good enough for anybody's team. And then, o' course, we got young Lahey."

"Who's young Lahey?" ast Bill.

"Can't be you never heard of him," I says. "He's the first sacker from Davenport that everybody was after. They say you can't hardly tell him from Hal Chase when he's in action. And he cracked the marble for about .340 last season."

"Hittin' .340 in the sticks and hittin' it up here is two different things," says Hagedorn.

"Not so different," I says. "A bird that can hit .340 anywhere can hit pretty good."

That's right, too. But the truth was that Lahey's figure had been eighty points shy o' what I credited him with. And from what I'd learned from some o' the Three Eye boys, Lahey was the eighth best first baseman in their league.

"Well," says Hagedorn, "if he makes good, you won't have no use for me."

"No," I says, "but I'd hate to see you go back in the bushes."

"Don't worry!" he says. "I'm goin' to stick right here in town."

"And live on your savin's?" I says.

"No," says Bill. "I'm just about signed up to play with the Acmes in the semi-pro league."

"How much are they givin' you?" I ast him.

"Fifty a game, and they only play Sundays," he says.

"Yes," says I, "and they're doin' well if they play twenty games a season. That nets you $1000, and you'll have somethin' like six days a week to spend it in."

"I can work at somethin' durin' the week," he says. "Maybe sell automobilies or somethin'."

"You could do that in the winter, too," I says, "if you didn't waste so much o' your time comin' for your mail and lookin' for your gloves."

"How's Mr. Edwards?" says Bill.

"Fine and dandy!" I says. "Want to see him?"

"What would I want to see him about?" says Bill.

"You might be able to sell him a car." say I. "He's right in the spendin' mood now. His nieces and nephews and Mr. Wilson's peace note has relieved him o' the few hundreds he had left after last season. I wouldn't be surprised if he'd reconsider cuttin' your contract—maybe give you a bonus just for the devil of it."

While we was talkin' Mr. Edwards come out from his private office.

"Hello, Hagedorn," he says. "Ready to sign?"

"At my own figure," says Bill.

"That's good," says Mr. Edwards. "Conley and myself was afraid you might accept the cut, and we couldn't hardly afford to keep an extra first baseman at $4000 a year."

"It's best all round," I says. "Bill's goin' to make more dough than we could possibly give him; he's goin' to sell cars durin' the week and play semi-pro ball Sundays. And maybe he can master the barber trade and pick up a few extra hundreds Saturday nights. But even if he don't make a nickel, he's got $2000 hoarded up."

"That's fine!" says the boss. "I like to see thrift in a young man. And it always seems like a pity that so many boys squander their earnin's and have to keep on slavin' as ball players till they're thirty years old and past the prime o' life."

For three or four days early in January they was an epidemic o' lockjaw in Washington, and the market come up enough for Mr. Edwards to take a trip to New Orleans. He left me in charge o' things, and my job consisted o' makin' up stories for the newspaper boys and entertainin' Hagedorn about once a week.

Once he dropped in to find out Joe Marsh's address; it'd of been impossible, o' course, to inquire by telephone. Another time he just happened to be passin', and happened to remember that he was carryin' a letter that his wife had ast him to mail, and wanted to know if I had a stamp.

I entertained him every time with dope on Lahey and what a whale of a man he was goin' to make us. But one day he come up loaded with some real facts about the guy I'd been boostin'.

"I thought you told me Lahey hit .340 with Davenport," he says.

"I did tell you that," says I.

"Well," says Bill, "somebody was stringin' you. I seen the Three Eye records the other day and they give Lahey .262."

"That don't mean nothin'," I says. "The scorers probably had it in for him."

"And he made more boots than any first baseman in the league," says Bill.

"That shows he was hustlin'" I says. "The more ground you cover, the more you're liable to kick 'em round. Besides," I says, "he was so perfect that the scorers probably thought he'd ought to make plays that would be impossible for a common first sacker."

"Another thing," says Hagedorn: "I happened to run acrost Jack Wells that played in the league with him, and he tells me Lahey's a left-hand hitter. Well, Gould's a left-hand hitter and so's young Berner, and you already had two left-hand hitters amongst the regulars. Your club's goin' to be balanced like a stew on a wild broncho. McGraw and them'll left-hand you to death."

"What do you care!" I says.

"It's nothin' to me," says Bill.

"Well, what do you suppose we better do about it?" I ast him.

"If I was you," he says, "I'd try and get myself a first baseman that hits right-handed."

"It's too late to get anybody," says I. "I guess we're just plain up against it. I wisht you hadn't made up your mind to retire."

"I'd play for you," says Bill, "if you'd meet my price."

"That's up to the old man," I says, "but I know he won't back down. He wouldn't give in to one man when he's stood pat on all the rest o' them."

"It won't be just one man," says Bill.

"What do you mean?" I ast him.

"He'll be lucky if he's got anybody when the showdown comes," says Bill. "The fraternity's give orders that nobody's to sign till you hear from them, and you won't hear from them till the leagues meets its demands."

"That don't affect our club," I says. "We got every man already signed up except yourself."

"Yes," says Hagedorn, "but signed up or not signed up, they won't report till the fraternity tells 'em to."

"You've been playin' long enough to know better'n that," says I. "If you think any ball player's goin' without his prunes to help out some other ball player, you got even less brains than I figured."

"They'll have to strike if the fraternity says so," says Bill. "They're goin' into the Federation o' Labor and be like any other union. And if they don't strike when they're ordered to they'll be canned out o' the fraternity."

"Well," I says, "suppose you was Ty Cobb, draggin' down a measly $16,000 a year, or whatever he's gettin'. Which would you do if the choice come up, go without the $16,000 or go without the fraternity?"

"I'd certainly stick with the fraternity," says Hagedorn. "if I didn't, I'd be a traitor."

"If I make you out a contract for $6000, will you sign it?" I ast him.

"Sure," he says. "I always told you I'd sign for my price."

"Well, Bill," I says, "I won't give you the contract. I'd hate to think I'd made a traitor out o' you."

"I don't want no contract anyway," says Bill. "I'm through. I'm goin' into business."

"What business?" I says.

"Somethin' pretty good," he says. "I and a friend o' mine's goin' in partners in a garage.

"That's a great idear!" says I. "You won't have no competition and it won't cost nothin' to start, and besides that, it's a game you know more about than any other, unless it's dressmakin'."

"My friend knows all about it," says Bill. "and I can pick it up from him."

"You better stick to pickin' up low throws," I says. "It takes years to learn the mechanism of a car when you don't know nothin' to start, not even what makes the front wheels run. But o' course you won't be the only one in the garage business that has to learn, and so long as it's other people's cars you wreck while you're learnin', why what's the difference!"

"They's good money in a garage," says Bill.

"I know it, and a whole lot of it's mine," I says. "They's good money in any business like that—smugglin' or counterfeitin' or snatchin' purses. But it must be hell on a man's conscience, even worse'n drawin' $6000 per annum for takin' a six months' nap on the old ball field."

The first thing Mr. Edwards ast me when he got back from the South was what was the latest dope on Hagedorn.

"He's surprised me," I says. "I thought he'd give in long before this. But nothin' doin'."

"What will we do about it?" says the boss.

"Mr. Edwards," I says, "you're the man that's payin' me my money and it's my business to look out for your interests. If Hagedorn had of kept away from here all winter, if we hadn't heard nothin' from him from the day he first turned down the contract, I'd say give him his $6000. But him comin' round here once a week shows that he needs us as much as we need him, and that he'll stand for the cut, if he's got to. Besides, he's showed a mighty poor opinion o' me by expectin' me to believe all that junk about him goin' into business, and so on—stuff that was old in the Noah's Ark League. He couldn't earn a dime a day in anything outside o' baseball. If he had a factory that made shells out o' lake water, he'd be bankrupt in a month. Now they's probably four better first basemen than him in the league, but I doubt if more'n one o' them's drawin' $6000. O' course with him on the ball club it looks like we'd be somewheres up in the race, and we ain't got a chance with a busher playin' the position.

"If it was a case o' givin' him his dough or gettin' along without him, I'd rather see him get the money even if it's a holdup. But if I'm any judge of a ball player, he'll come round here on his hands and knees the day before we start for the Springs, and he'll sign at whatever price you offer him."

"It's a shame," says Mr. Edwards, "when everything else looks so good for us, to have to be worryin' about a man like him, that loafed on us all last summer and that I'd get rid of in a minute if I had somebody in his place. I suppose they's no chance o' tradin' for a first baseman at this stage."

"Oh, yes, they's a chance," I says. "I suppose Matty'd let us have Chase if we'd give up our pitchin' staff and half a dozen infielders and $40,000 or $50,000 in cash. Then we'd have Chase and nothin' with him."

"Maybe young Lahey'll surprise us," says the boss.

"It won't hurt us to hope," I says, "but from what I can learn Bill Doyle was mad at you when he recommended him. And besides," I says, "Lahey's a left-hand hitter, and that'd mean five o' them in the game every day. We'd be a set-up for fellas like Schupp and Smith and Tyler. Take Hagedorn, and he can murder a left-hander even when he ain't hittin' his weight against a regular pitcher."

"Well, all we can do is wait," says Mr. Edwards.

"And I don't think it'll be long," I says.

But when the night come for us to start South, Hagedorn was still a hold-out, though he did show one more sign o' weakenin'. He was down to the station to shake hands with the boys and see us off, and he looked like he was ready to cry. I called him off to one side.

"Would you like to be goin' along, Bill?" I ast him.

"Oh, I don't know," he says.

"Why don't you take your medicine and hop aboard?" I says. "Your missus can pack up your stuff and send it after you."

"I'll go if you say the word," he says.

"You're the one that must do the talkin'," says I.

"Why couldn't I go along without signin'?" he says. "Maybe the old man would meet my figure when he seen how hard I'd work to get in shape."

"No," says I, "this ain't no charity excursion we're runnin'. We pay nobody's fare that ain't signed up and a member o' this ball club. If you want to sign at $4000, they's a contract right there in my grip. If you don't, why you can spend the rest o' the winter countin' snowflakes and cursin' the coal trust."

"Well," he says, "I'll freeze to death before I'll be robbed; starve to death, too, before I'll let old Edwards bull me out o' what's comin' to me."

"I'm sorry, Bill," I says. "But anyway, good luck to you."

"Good luck to you too," says Bill. "You'll need it."

"Oh, I don't know," I says. "I got a hunch that it's goin' to be a great year for everybody in baseball."

"Well," says Hagedorn, "I know some fellas that'll have a great year."

"Who do you mean, Bill?" I ast him.

"All the left-handers that pitches against your ball club," he says.

About half the baseball reporters on our papers know somethin' about the game. The other half's kids that can write cute stories, but don't know a wild pitch from a hit and run sign. This was the half that went on the spring trip with us. The old heads was sent with the Americans, because they'd made a fight for the pennant last year and the public was strong for 'em.

Well, I took advantage of our gang bein' green and made 'em perjure themself to their papers every day. When they'd come to me for the dope, I'd rave to 'em about what a world-beater young Lahey was, and how he'd burn up the league as soon as I'd learned him a few o' the fine points o' first-base play. If they'd been wise they could of told with one look that Mr. Lahey wouldn't do. But they were just kids and they ate it up. I bet if any o' the fellas that had played with Lahey read what I was sayin' about him in the papers they must of thought I was crazy.

My idear, o' course, was to worry Hagedorn. I knew he'd be readin' everything he could find about us, and I didn't want him to get the impression that the ball club was goin' to bust up without him.

I thought Mr. Edwards would have sense enough to get this. But no; he fell just as hard as the reporters. And when he joined us after we'd been at the Springs two weeks, he was all smiles.

"Well," he says, "I been readin' some mighty encouragin' news."

"What news?" I says.

"About Lahey," says he. "I told you he might surprise us."

"He's surprised me in one way," I says. "I'm surprised that he ever had the nerve to come on this trainin' trip. I always thought pretty well o' the Three Eye League till I seen him," I says.

"You're jokin'," says Mr. Edwards. "I've read nothin' but good reports of him."

"I'm responsible for the reports," I says, "but I thought you'd guess that I was fakin' for Hagedorn's benefit."

"Well, if you've fooled Hagedorn, he's got company," says Mr. Edwards. "I thought our troubles was all over."

"Our troubles won't never be over if Hagedorn don't give in," I says.

"But Lahey must be some good, the way he was recommended," says the boss.

"Doyle probably seen him just once," I says, "and that must of been the one good day he had. But even at that, Doyle couldn't of never watched him handle his feet and thought he was a ball player."

"Is it just his feet that's the trouble?" ast Mr. Edwards.

"No," I says, "but they'd be plenty without outside help. We've had infield practice about nine times since we been here, and that means he's got nine hundred self-inflicted spike wounds. And they must of kept first base in a different place down to Davenport. Anyway he can't find it here. And when he does happen to stumble onto it, it's always with the wrong foot. Besides that, every time Gould or Berner makes a low peg Lahey loses a tooth. Gould ast him one day why he didn't wear a mask. But you ought to see him field bunts! If experience counts for anything, he'd ought to be the most accurate thrower in the world, from a sittin' posture."

"How about his hittin'?" the boss ast me.

"He's a consistent hitter," I says. "They's a party from Kansas City stoppin' at the hotel. They come out to every practice and always set in the same place right back o' the plate, behind the grandstand screen. Well, every ball Lahey's hit so far has made 'em duck."

"Does he act like he had stage fright?" says the boss.

"Not him!" says I. "Nobody but the gamest guy in the world could cut off a few toes every day and come out the next day for more. And nobody without a whole lot o' nerve could keep diggin' after low throws when he knows that they're goin' to uppercut him in the jaw. No, sir! You can't scare Charley!"

"Charley!" says Mr. Edwards. "I thought his name was Mike."

"Gould's nicknamed him Charley," I says, "after Charley Chaplin."

Well, the boss wasn't what you could call tickled to death with my dope on Lahey, but he cheered up a little when I told him about Gould and the rest o' them. Gould was goin' even better than when he was with St. Louis. He was hustlin' like a colt and hittin' everything they throwed up there. And he kept coachin' young Berner like he'd been hired for that job. He put real pep in the infield, and I knew it was tough for him to keep it up when Lahey gummed pretty near every play that was pulled.

Berner cinched his job the first day out. He's the kind of a kid that just won't stay on the bench, as lively and full o' fight as little Bush, at Detroit, or Buck Weaver, or Rabbit Maranville. And Stremmle come up to everything they said about him. Then Joe Marsh seemed to of got over the Federal League and acted five years younger than he is. And our outfield was workin' hard. O' course this young Sheppard showin' up so good helped a lot and made the rest o' them hustle.

I told Mr. Edwards, I says:

"Outside o' first base, I wouldn't trade this ball club for McGraw's. These boys have got more spirit than any team I ever managed. They're the kind that's liable to upset the whole league. If we only just had a good reliable man on that bag, I'd almost guarantee to finish one-two-three."

"And do you still think Hagedorn's goin' to join us?" the boss ast me.

"I certainly do," I says. "I wouldn't be surprised to get a wire from him any day."

But we went along another week without hearin' from Bill. Mr. Edwards kept gettin' more and more nervous. And I guess I was beginnin' to get nervous too.

About the second day o' the third week down there, a letter come to me from Hagedorn's wife. It hit me right in the eye.

Bill, she told me, didn't know she was writin' and would probably kill her if he found it out. She'd been beggin' and beggin' him all winter to take what we offered, and she'd just about had him coaxed when the papers begin printin' the swell reports about

Lahey. Those reports had took all the zip out o' Bill. Instead o' frightenin' him into signin' at our figure, they'd convinced him that he wasn't wanted on our club. And Bill was worse than broke. He was over three months behind with the rent and the meat bill and so forth, and coal was a hundred dollars a ton, and they wasn't no coal even at that price, and she was afraid he'd do somethin' desperate. And she thought if I'd just send Bill a wire and tell him that we'd carry him as an extra man, or if I'd try and trade him somewheres where he could make some kind of a salary, he'd be so tickled that he'd come to us or go wherever we sent him at whatever price he could get. And she begged me to not tell anybody that she'd wrote.

Mr. Edwards had just left us to run down to Dallas for a few days. O' course I wouldn't of let him know about the letter anyway. But him bein' away give me the idear o' keepin' Bill's comin' a secret. I was goin' to surprise him by havin' Bill blow in unexpected, because it was a cinch the old man'd be back before Bill could get there. So I didn't wire Dallas, but just sent a telegram to Bill, sayin', "If you'll sign for $4000, first-base job is yours. Answer."

The answer come the same night. It said all right, that he'd join us the followin' Thursday.

On Wednesday Mr. Edwards come back to the Springs. And that afternoon Charles C. Lahey give the funniest exhibition I ever seen on a ball field. The whole practice was a joke, because Gould and Berner and Marsh and the rest o' them was laughin' so hard they couldn't do nothin'. But the wind-up come near not bein' a joke. It'd of been a tragedy if Lahey wasn't the awkwardest guy in the world.

We was tryin' the double play, first base to second base and back. I hit a ball pretty close to the bag and it took a nice hop, so they wasn't no chance for Charley to boot it. He pegged down to Berner, and then turned round and started lookin' for his own bag. Berner took the throw and sent it back as fast as I ever seen a ball pegged. Well, sir, Lahey found out where first base was by trippin' over it. But just before he tripped he turned his head to look for the throw. If he hadn't tripped and went sprawlin', that ball would of cracked him right in the temple, and if it had, good night! To show you how much Berner had on it, it hit the grandstand on the short hop and made a noise like somewheres in France.

"That'll do, boys!" I hollered to them. "We'll quit. The express rates on caskets between here and Davenport is somethin' fierce."

I walked back to the hotel with Mr. Edwards. I never seen a guy so blue.

"He's impossible," he says.

"Never mind," says I. "He won't be with us long. One o' these days his luck'll desert him and he'll get killed."

"I think we'd better send for Hagedorn," says the boss.

"Oh, no," I says. "He'll show up before long."

"Yes," says Mr. Edwards; "but he'd ought to be here right now to get used to playin' with Gould and Berner. And I ain't so sure he'll show up, neither."

"I'd like to make you a little bet," I says. "I'd like to bet you five that we hear from him before the end o' the week."

"I'll just take that bet," says Mr. Edwards, "and I'll be glad to pay if I lose."

Well, knowin' him pretty well, I didn't hardly believe that. But I told him the bet was on.

The first train into the Springs from the North is supposed to arrive at nine in the mornin' and it don't hardly ever get in later than 3 P.M. On this Thursday it come at one-thirty. I snuck down alone to meet it, and there was Bill. "Mighty glad to see you, Hagedorn," I says.

"I'm glad to get here," says Bill.

"You don't need to work to-day if you don't want to," says I, "but we want you out there as soon as you feel like it."

"Why, what's happened to this wonderful Lahey?" says Bill.

"Not a thing," I says; "but as you pointed out, he's a left-hand hitter, and we're overloaded with 'em."

"I suppose you'll play him when they's right-hand pitchin' against us," says Hagedorn.

"No," I says, "I don't believe in switchin' on the infield. Still, you'll have to keep hustlin' to hold him on the bench. He's one o' the most remarkable first sackers in baseball."

"I'm just as good as he is," says Bill.

"You'll have to show me," I says.

"That's just what I'm goin' to do," says Hagedorn.

"And how's everything at home?" I ast him.

"Well, Frank," he says, "it's been a tough winter—the toughest I ever put in. I'm in debt so far that it scares me to think of it."

"Where was that $2000 you had saved?" I says.

"I was just stringin' you about that," says Bill. "I never had a nickel saved. But $2000 is just about what I'm behind."

"Good lord, Bill!" I says to him. "What have you done, bought a limousine?"

"No, sir," he says. "I ain't bought nothin' only clothes and food and not much o' that. But I was way in the hole before, and just this week they've ran up about $200 more on me."

"What for?" I ast him.

"Well, Frank," he says, "the wife presented me with a little boy last Sunday mornin'. If it hadn't been for that, and the way she worried about things, I'd of never been down here to sign for $4000. It was a case of have to, that's all."

I'd left orders for the boys to be out for practice at a quarter to two, and I knew Mr. Edwards would be out there with 'em. I and Bill was pretty near to the hotel by this time, but I stopped him short.

"Bill," I says, "you ain't givin' me no bull like that $2000 fortune, are you?"

"No, Frank," he says, "I'm tellin' you the truth."

"All right, Bill," I says; "I'm takin' your word. They's a northbound local train leavin' here at three bells. You go down and get aboard it and ride to Silver Creek. That's a station about twenty miles up the line. They's a hotel there, and that's about all. You go there and stay till I send for you."

"What's the idear?" he says.

"You'll find out later," I says. "I just tell you now that it's to your interest to do what I say."

"I can't go nowheres," he says. "I've got just forty cents."

"I'll stake you," says I, "and you'll hear from me in three or four days."

"But I want to get out there and see this here Lahey," says Bill. "I want to get busy showin' him up."

"He'll tend to that end of it himself," I says. "But you're on this ball club and I'm manager of it, and if you want to stick on this ball club you'll obey the manager's orders."

So Bill took the local for Silver Creek and I beat it out to the orchard to see that nobody got killed.

I set down with the boss at supper that night.

"Mr. Edwards," I says, "I've changed my mind about Hagedorn."

"What do you mean?" he says.

"I mean that I think he's through with us," I says.

"But good lord!" says the boss. "We can't get along without him."

"Well," says I, "we can get him by givin' him $6000."

Mr. Edwards shook like he had a chill.

"Give in to him now!" he says. "When he's tried to hold us up! And I thought you was so sure he'd come round."

"I did think he would," says I, "but I'm sure now that he won't. He's stuck this long, and he'll stick forever. He's gamer'n I figured."

"But I'd rather lose another $18,000 than let him hold us up," says the boss.

"Well," I says, "that's up to you. But you'll lose $18,000 all right, and maybe then some, if you don't get him. Because without him on first base we'll be the worst ball club in the league."

Mr. Edwards didn't say nothin' more for maybe five minutes. Then he give up.

"I got a lot o' confidence in you, Frank," he says. "I'll go by what you tell me. If you want to you can wire Hagedorn. Tell him we'll meet his terms, and tell him to get here on the first train."

"I think it's the best thing to do," I says. And I went out and pretended to send Bill a wire.

It takes two days and a half to get to the Springs from home. So I called Bill up at Silver Creek and had him blow into camp on the Sunday train. I met him and tipped him off. He fell all over himself thankin' me and says he was goin' to name the boy Frank. And then he made a request.

"Keep this a secret from my missus," he says. "I want her to think that I got what I was after because I insisted on it. Because she kept tellin' me all winter that I wouldn't never get it and was a sucker to try."

"Don't worry," I says, "I want it to be kept a secret from certain people myself, and I certainly ain't goin' to spill it to no woman."

Mr. Edwards was on the walk in front o' the hotel when I and Bill showed up.

"Well, Hagedorn," he says, "you got what you wanted and I hope you'll try and earn it."

"I'll earn it all right, Mr. Edwards," he says, "and I'm mighty grateful to you for comin' acrost."

The boss turned to me.

"How about our little bet?" he says.

"What bet?" says I.

"You bet me five," he says, "that we'd hear from Hagedorn before the week was over. And this is another week."

"So you want me to pay you that five?" I ast him.

"I certainly do," he says.

Well, I give him the five, and afterwards Bill told me he'd make that up to me as soon as he could. But I can't accept it from him. I'd feel like I was takin' candy from a baby, a baby named Frankie Hagedorn.

The Crook

The Saturday Evening Post
JUNE 24, 1916

TO-MORROW MORNIN' you'll see a statement in the papers, signed by Ban, sayin' that it's been learned that they was some excuse for Bull doin' what he done, and that the charge of him bein' pickled on the field wasn't true, and that he's been took back on the staff. But they won't be nothin' printed about who was the dandy little fixer; my part in it is a secret between you and I and one or two others.

I don't suppose they's a ball player in the League that Bull's chased as often as me. I don't suppose they's anybody he's pulled as much of his stuff on. I can't count the times I've got cute with him, but the times I got the best o' the repartee I can count 'em on the fingers of a catcher's mitt. Just the same, it was me that went to Ban with the real dope and was the cause of him gettin' rehired, and it was me that got him his girl back, though he don't know about that yet.

I wouldn't of took no trouble in the case if it was any other umps but Bull. But I come as near likin' him as a man could like a guy that never give a close one any way but against you. And he's a good umps, too; he guesses about a third of 'em right, where the rest o' Ban's School for the Blind don't see one in ten. And another thing: I felt sorry for him when he told me the deal he got. And besides that, he's gave me too many good laughs for me to stand by and see him canned out o' the League. Many's the time I've made a holler just to hear what he'd say, and he always said somethin' worth hearin', even if it stung; that is, up to day before yesterday, when the blow-off come.

I noticed he wasn't himself when I was throwed out at the plate in the second innin'. I wanted to stop at third, but Jack made me keep goin', and Duff Lewis all ready to shoot with that six-inch howitzer he wears in his right sleeve. Cady and the ball strolled out to meet me and I couldn't get past 'em.

"You're out!" says Bull.

"He didn't tag me," I says.

And Bull didn't say a word.

In the fourth innin' Hooper was on third base and somebody hit a fly ball to Shano. Hooper scored after the catch and big Cahill run out from the bench and made a holler that he'd left the bag too quick. The ball was throwed over to third base, but Tommy wouldn't allow the play. Then Cahill went to Bull and ast him hadn't he saw it. O' course Bull says he hadn't.

"No, I guess not!" says Cahill. "Us burglars stick together." And then, on the way back to the bench, he turned to Bull and says: "You're so crooked you could sleep in a French horn."

Bull was just puttin' on his mask, but he throwed it on the ground and tore after Cahill. He nailed him right on the edge o' the dugout, and what a beatin' he give him! It took eight or nine of us to drag him off, and he managed to wallop everybody at least once durin' the action. Some o' the boys picked Cahill up and carried him to the club-house. He was a wreck. Bull stood there a minute, starin' at nothin'; then he turned and faced the grand stand.

"Anybody else," he yelled—"anybody else that thinks I'm a crook can come down and get a little o' the same."

Well, they wasn't no need of extra police to keep the crowd back. But Ban was settin' in the stand and o' course he wasn't goin' to just set there and not do nothin'. It was too raw. So he give orders for the cops to grab Bull and get him out o' the way before he committed murder. They led him to his dressin' room and stuck with him w'ile he changed clo'es. Then they called the wagon and give him a ride. Tommy handled the rest o' the game alone and we was beat just as bad as if nothin' had happened.

Right after the game the witnesses was examined. Cahill's lips was so swelled he couldn't hardly talk. But several of us had heard the whole thing and could testify they hadn't been no profanity. Cahill hadn't no license to call Bull crooked, but if an umps was goin' to fight for a little thing like that, every ball game'd wind up in a holycaust. Besides, "a crook" was one o' the mildest things Bull'd ever been called, and till this time nobody'd ever knew him to lose his temper.

As I say, his specialty was conversation. When they was a kick made, he'd generally always pull some remark that got a laugh from everybody but the fella that was crabbin', and sometimes from he himself. He'd canned plenty o' guys out o' the ball game for tryin' too hard to show him up, but he'd did it as part o' the day's work and without displayin' any venoms. I'd heard 'em tell him he was yellow, and blind, and a jellyfish, and a "homer," and a thief, and a liar; and that he'd steal the cream off'n his mother's coffee; and that his backbone was all above the neck. I'd heard 'em call him fightin' names and saw him take it smilin'. And now, because a fella made an innocent remark about him bein' crooked, and no naughty words along with it, he'd went off his bean and all but destroyed a good Irish citizen, besides intimidatin' five or six thousand o' the unemployed.

It wasn't no wonder everybody thought what they thought, though Bull hadn't never been known to touch a drop between April and October.

"I'll uphold my umpires when they're right," Ban says to the reporters; "but when they're wrong, they got to suffer for it. They's only just the one explanation for Bull's actions. So he's discharged from the staff."

"What about Cahill?" ast somebody. "Goin' to suspend him?"

"No," says Ban. "Bull saved me the trouble."

Well, Tommy fixed it up to have Bull let out o' jail and took him back to the hotel where the two o' them was stoppin'. When Tommy told him he was canned he didn't make no comments only to say that they was one good thing about the umpirin' job—you didn't feel bad if you lost it.

On my way home from the game I got to thinkin' about Bull and what a shame it was to have him let out for just the one slip, and wonderin' what he'd do with himself, and so on. So when I'd had supper I rode down to the umps' beanery to try and find him, and maybe cheer him up.

He'd went out. Tommy told me he'd disappeared after askin' for his mail and not gettin' none.

"He'll come back with a fine package," says Tommy.

"Do you know what made him fall off?" I says.

"He didn't fall off," says Tommy. "That's the funny part of it. I and him was right up in my room readin' the papers all mornin'; then we had lunch and went out to the park together and got dressed and went on the field. I noticed he was grouchin', but I was with him every minute o' the day up to game time and I know for a fact that he didn't have nothin' to drink only his coffee at breakfast. Somethin's happened to him, but I don't like to get inquisitive because we haven't only been teamin' together a couple o' weeks."

I and Tommy didn't have nothin' else to do, so we set down in the writin' room and chinned. Bull, o' course, was the subject o' the conversation. You could talk about him all week and not tell half o' the stuff.

The first game he umpired in our League was openin' day in Chi, four or five years ago. It was our club and St. Louis. I guess he was about twenty-six years old then, but he didn't look more'n twenty. So the boys was inclined to ride him. Arnold, the St. Louis catcher, started on him in the first innin'.

"Did you ever see a ball game, kid?" he ast him.

"No," says Bull, "but if I make good these four days, I'm goin' to stay here for the Detroit series."

Arnold come up with the bases full and two out in the fourth or fifth. He took three healthy lunges and fanned. I led off in our half and Bull called the first one a ball. It was pretty close and Arnold, peeved about strikin' out in the pinch, slammed the pill on the ground.

"You're a fine umpire!" he says.

"I can't be right all the time," says Bull. "Even the best of us misses 'em sometimes. But I'll have to miss the next two in succession to tie your score."

We was one run ahead when the ninth begin. We got two o' them out and then Hank Douglas made a base hit and stole second. The next fella made another base hit, but Shano fielded it clean and Hank was called out at the plate.

"That's right," he says to Bull. "Favor the home team. You wouldn't be umpirin' in this league if you wasn't yellow."

"No," says Bull, walkin' away, "and you wouldn't be in the League at all if you wasn't a Brown."

In one o' the Detroit games Cobb was on second base with a man out and Crawford hit a slow ground ball between short and third. The ball was fielded to first base and Cobb kept right on for home. Parker was catchin' for us and he was a little spike-shy, especially with Cobb. So when the ball was relayed to him from first base he backed off in an alley somewheres and give Tyrus the right o' way. Somebody hollered from the bench that Cobb hadn't touched third.

"Yes, I seen it," says Parker to Bull, lookin' for an alibi. "He cut third base."

"I don't know about that," Bull says, "but it's a safe bet that he'll never cut you."

Bull went with us for our first series in Cleveland that year.

They was a fly-ball hit to Lawton in the third and he muffed it square, lettin' in a couple o' runs. As soon as he'd dropped the ball he looked up in the sky and then stopped the game till he'd ran in and got his glasses, though it was so cloudy that we was hurryin' to beat the rain. Right afterward, when Lawton come to bat, Bull called a strike on him.

"Too high! Too high!" says Lawton.

"Maybe it was," says Bull. "I lost it in the sun."

A little w'ile later the Cleveland club had a chance to tie us up. It was some left-hand batter's turn to hit, but they was a cockeye pitchin' for us, so they sent up a kid named Brodie, a right-hander, to pinch hit. He swung at the first one and missed it. The next one was called a strike, and w'ile he was turned round, arguin' with Bull about it, another one come whizzin' over and Bull says:

"You're out!"

"It wasn't a legal delivery," says Brodie.

"Why not?" says Bull. His feet was on the slab and you wasn't out o' your box."

"You got a lot to learn about baseball," says Brodie.

"I'm learnin' fast," says Bull. "I just found out why they call your club the Naps."

He didn't put nobody out of a game till along in the middle o' that season. We was playin' Washin'ton and Kennedy was in a battin' slump. He was sore at the world and tryin' to take it out on the umps. He'd throwed his glove all over the field and tossed his cap in the air and beefed on every decision, if it was close or not. He struck out twice, and when Bull called a strike on him his third time up, he stooped over and grabbed a handful o' dirt.

"A yard outside!" he says, and tossed the dirt to'rds Bull.

"Well, Mr. Kennedy," Bull says, "if there is a yard outside, that's where you better spend the rest o' the afternoon."

"Am I out o' the game?" says Kennedy.

"Hasn't nobody told you?" says Bull. "You been out of it pretty near two weeks."

"You're about as funny as choppin' down trees," says Kennedy.

"Go in and dress," Bull told him. "Maybe you'll find your battin' eye in your street clo'es."

The next day Bull was umpirin' the bases. Kennedy didn't get suspended, and when he come to bat in the first innin' and seen that Bull had switched, he yelled to him: "Congratulations! You ought to do better out there. It's a cinch you couldn't do worse."

"Walter," says Bull to Johnson, who was pitchin', "give Kennedy a base on balls. I want to talk to him."

In the last game o' the series Kennedy finally did get a hold o' one and hit it for two bases.

"Now it's my turn to congratulate you," Bull says to him.

"Oh," says Kennedy, "I can hit 'em all right when they's a good umps behind that plate."

W'ile he was still talkin', whoever was pitchin' wheeled round and catched him a mile off'n the bag. Bull waved him out and he started to crab.

"Go on in to the bench, Kennedy," says Bull. "The game must look funny to you from here anyway."

Big Johnson worked against us in Chi one day and he had more stuff than I ever seen him have. Poor little Weber, facin' him for the first time, was scared stiff. He just stood there and took three. Next time, he struck at one and let the next two come right over. Bull, who was back o' the plate, couldn't help from laughin' and the kid got sore.

"Why don't you call 'em all strikes!" he says.

"I would," Bull says, "only they's just a few o' them I can see."

Well, Weber's third trip up there was just like his first one. He didn't even swing. And after Bull had called him out for the third time, he says:

"Fine work, umps! You ought to go to an oculist and get the dust took out o' your eyes."

"Yes," says Bull, "and you ought to go to a surgeon and have the bat removed from your shoulder."

One afternoon Jennin's started a kid named Sawyer against us. He was hog wild and he throwed ten balls without gettin' a strike.

"It looks like a tough day for us, Bull," says Stanage.

"Well, anyway," Bull says, "my right arm needs a good rest."

When two fellas had walked and they was two balls on the next one, Sawyer pitched a ball that you could of called either way. Bull called it a ball.

"What was the matter with that one?" says Sawyer.

"You pitched it," says Bull.

He was base umpire once when Walsh caught Carney flat-footed off o' third base. It was in the ninth innin' and they was only the one run behind us, so Carey begin to whine.

"Kind o' drowsy, eh?" says Bull. "I'll bet your mother was up all night with you."

Before the end of his first season he had the boys pretty well scared o' that tongue of his'n and they weren't none o' them sayin' much to him. But o' course, durin' the winter, they forgot how he could lash 'em, and when spring come again he was as good as ever. It's been that way every season since. Along about this time, and up to July, they're layin' themself wide open and takin' all he can give. Then, from July on, they're tired o' bein' laughed at and they see they can't get the best of him, so they lay off.

Not me, though. I beef on every decision he makes against me all season long. I can get as good a laugh when it's me that's the goat as when it's somebody else.

He's pulled some pippins on me. I wisht I'd wrote down even half o' them, but anyway they don't sound as good when I tell 'em as when he sprung 'em on me.

I remember we was playin' our last series with the Boston club in 1912. They'd cinched the pennant already and nobody cared a whole lot how our games come out. I've got plenty o' friends in Boston, and the first night we was there I neglected to go to bed. So the next afternoon I was kind o' logy.

I dropped a couple o' thrown balls at first base and was off the bag once when I had all the time in the world to find it. Well, Bull had three or four close ones to guess and he guessed 'em all against us.

"Are you goin' to work in the World's Series?" I ast him.

"I haven't heard," he says.

"If you do," I says, "I'm goin' to bet my season's pay on the Red Sox."

"If you're lookin' for easy money," says Bull, "why don't you go ahead and bet your season's pay on the Red Sox, and then sign with the Giants to play first base?"

In 1914 I'd been havin' a long spell o' bad luck with my hittin' and they was just gettin' ready to bench me when one day, in St. Louis, I got one safe. I tried to make two bases on it, but overslid the bag and Bull called me out.

"Oh, Bull!" I says. "Have a heart."

"They won't bawl you for this," says Bull. "You ain't been here in so long it's no wonder you forgot where the station was. I think you done pretty well to remember my name. I been umpirin' the bases for two weeks."

Then they was once in Boston, just last year. We still had a chance yet and we was crazy to take a fall out o' that bunch. I was overanxious, I guess. Anyway, it was a tight game and in the sixth or seventh innin' I got caught off o' first. "Bull," I says, "if you're with the home club, why don't you wear a white suit?"

"Larry," says he, "you ought to play ball in your pyjamas."

And in New York one day I give somebody the hit and run, and the ball fooled me and I didn't swing. The fella was throwed out at second base, and Bull called it a strike on me.

"Why, Bull!" I says. "He was wastin' that ball."

"Sure he was," says Bull. "All the good balls is wasted on you."

And once in Washin'ton, we was two runs to the good in the ninth and had two men out and it looked all over. The next man—Milan, I think it was—hit a fly ball straight up and I hollered I was goin' to take it. Well, it just missed beanin' me and Milan pulled up at second base. The next fella hit a ground ball between I and the bag. I missed it clean. Milan scored and the other fella stopped at second. Then somebody made a three-base hit. The score was tied and the winnin' run was on third base.

A slow ground ball was hit down to'rds me. I seen that Doran, who was pitchin', was goin' for the ball instead o' the bag and I seen that the ball was mine and I'd have to get it and chase back with it myself. I done it as fast as I could and the play was mighty close. Bull called the man safe. It meant the game and we was all sore, but me especially, on account o' them two flivvers.

"You blind owl!" I says to Bull. "Who told you you could umpire?"

"Who recommended you to Griffith?" says Bull.

That's the way he was. You could set up all night and figure out what you was goin' to say to him next day, and then when you said it, he'd come back with somethin' that made you wish you hadn't. That is, unless you was like me and kept after him just for the laughs he give you.

I and Tommy set there talkin' till pretty close to midnight. Then we decided they wasn't no more use waitin' for Bull. So Tommy went up to his room and I moseyed out the front door and onto the walk. I hadn't took more'n a couple o' steps when I seen the guy we'd been fannin' about. He was just goin' in to the hotel bar. I followed him.

"Hello, Bull!" I says, when we was both inside.

"What's the idear?" he says. "Did you come clear down here to tell me that Cady didn't tag you?"

"No," I says. "He tagged me all right. But I'm taggin' you to find out what's got into you."

"I guess I got plenty into me now," says he. "When a man that's cold sober gets fired from his job for bein' lit, they's only the one thing to do. I've been tryin' my best all evenin' to deserve the reputation they've wished on me."

I give him the double O. He could walk straight and he could talk straight. But he was kind of owl-eyed and his face looked like a royal flush o' diamonds.

"Let's have somethin'," he says.

"You've had enough," says I.

"That's no sign I ain't goin' to have more," he says.

"You better go to bed," I says.

"What for?" says he. "I got nothin' to do to-morrow or any other to-morrow. I'm through."

"They's other leagues," says I. "You won't have no trouble gettin' a job."

"I don't want no job," says Bull. "I haven't no use for a job."

"What are you goin' to live on?" I ast him.

"I don't want to live," he says.

"Aw, piffle!" says I. "You'll feel better for a good night's sleep."

"Well," says Bull, "they's just as much chance o' me gettin' a good night's sleep as they is o' them playin' part o' the World's Series in Peoria."

"Bull," I says, "I believe they's somethin' botherin' you outside o' losin' your job."

"You're too smart to be playin' ball," he says.

O' course I knowed then that Tommy'd been right—that the old boy had had a blow o' some kind. And I was mighty curious to learn what'd came off. But I realized it wouldn't get me nothin' to ask.

We h'isted three or four together without exchangin' a word. Then, all of a sudden, I seen a big tear streakin' down Bull's cheek and in another minute I was listenin' to his story.

Bull's parents is both dead—been dead five or six years. He never had no brothers or sisters or aunts or uncles or nothin'. He was born down South somewheres and didn't have no use for cold weather, but his old man moved to Buffalo when Bull was about sixteen, so from that time till his mother and father died he spent his winters, and the summers before he went to umpirin', up North. They wasn't no reason why he shouldn't suit himself after the old people passed out, so back South he went for his winters. He stayed in New Orleans the first couple o' years, but it cost him a pile o' money. Then he tried Montgomery, and that's where he met the lady.

Her name's Maggie, Maggie Gregory. Bull described her as the prettiest thing he ever seen, and so on. The Gregorys didn't have so much dough that they didn't know how to spend it. In fact, they was kind o' hard up. The head o' the house worked in a hardware store for somethin' like fifteen a week. He had a son named Martin; yes, sir, the same Martin Gregory that Connie Mack let go last week and we got signed up now.

Martin and Maggie was twins. Maggie was learnin' the milliner trade, but at the time Bull met 'em Martin wasn't workin' at all, except durin' meals. He was one o' the kind o' guys that'd rather go to the electric chair, where he could be sure o' settin' down, than attend the theater and take a chance o' havin' to stand up w'ile they played the Star-Spangled Banner. If he'd lived in a town where they wasn't no letter carriers he wouldn't never got no mail. He'd of starved to death in a cafeteria with a pocket full o' money.

He treated the whole of his family like they was waiters, and they treated him like he was the Kaiser. His mother was crazy over him, and Maggie used to split fifty-fifty with him on her princely salary. The old man never called him, and seemed to just take it for granted that Martin was born to have the best of it.

Bull landed in Montgomery the same time that the Gregorys made up their mind to take a boarder. They put an ad. in the paper and Bull answered it. He answered it in the evenin', when Maggie was home. After gettin' a look at her, he'd of stayed there if they made him sleep in the sink and give him nothin' to eat but catnip.

Maggie and Martin was eighteen then. They ain't no use o' me tryin' to give you Bull's description of her. Martin, accordin' to Bull, was a handsome kid and had the best clo'es his sister's money could buy. He was built like an ath-a-lete and his features was enough like the girl's to make him good-lookin'. Bull fell for him this first night; he didn't know nothin' then about the feud between Martin and Work.

Well, they all treated Bull like he was an old friend and made him feel more like it was his own house than just a place to board. Maggie smiled at him every time she seen him, though it wasn't no case o' love at first sight on her part; she was just tryin' to be friendly. The old lady worried if he didn't take nine or ten helpin's o' whatever was on the table, and kept his room as neat and clean as Martin's. The old man played rummy with him three or four times a week and give Bull good laughs on all his quick stuff. And Martin took kindly to him, too, figurin' probably that the dough Bull paid for board would mean more dude clo'es in the wardrobe. Bull says he never knowed what this here Southern hospitality was till he went to live with the Gregorys.

It wasn't till Bull had been there about three weeks that he told 'em what he done for a livin'. Well, the old people and Maggie didn't know nothin' about baseball except that Martin, when he was a kid, had been the best player in the school where he attended at. He'd told 'em so. But Martin himself, it turned out, was a nut on the national pastime. He knowed who Cobb was and who Matty was and their records, right down to little bits o' fractions. Not only that, but he went to see the Montgomery bunch perform whenever they had the courage to face the home crowd. So Bull was a hero to him, in spite of his profession.

At meals, Martin wouldn't talk nothin' but baseball, and Bull had to talk it with him. I suppose the proud parents and Maggie felt kind o' sorry for Bull, figurin' that the kid, bein' perfect, was gettin' all the best of him in the arguments. The old boy was foxy enough to see that the easiest way to win Maggie was by helpin' to make Martin look good. So when they'd got about so far in a fannin' bee, Bull'd stop dead and say, "By George! You're right," even if Martin was arguin' that Walter Johnson ought to learn to throw left-handed and play third base.

Bull thought he was just a fresh kid. He thought the reason he wasn't workin' was probably because he'd lost a job and hadn't found another. He liked Martin O. K. till he begin to suspect that he was too proud to toil. It was the old lady that give him the hunch, when she says somethin' about the kid's delicate health.

"Yes," Bull says to himself, "he's awful delicate lookin', like Frank Gotch."

Before the winter was half over, Bull was givin' 'em the time o their lives, takin' 'em somewheres every other night. It was a pipe that Maggie liked him, and it was a bigger pipe that she had him on her reserve list, with no chance to get away. But he was too shy to talk to her about anything but the climate; he says she was the first girl he was ever scared of.

Along in March, some o' the Montgomery ball players showed up for their trainin'. Bull always took some work in the spring to get himself hard and fix up his windpipes, so that year he joined the local bunch and done stunts with them. Martin ast to go along with him the third or fourth day. So out they went together to the Montgomery orchard and Bull got the biggest su'prise of his life.

Instead o' settin' up in the stand and lookin' on, Martin peeled down to his shirtsleeves and busted right into the practice. He tackled the high-low game first, and Bull says to see him at it you wouldn't of never believed it was the same boy that wouldn't drink coffee unless you held the cup to his mush. Baseball wasn't work to him—it was fun. And that made the whole difference.

Well, Martin showed so much life the first day that Bull borrowed a suit for him and fixed it with the Montgomery gang to leave him frolic round their park as much as he liked. And he wasn't no joke with the ath-a-letes. He didn't know nothin', but he had as much mechanical ability as you ever see in a kid. He could whip the ball round like a shot, and he was good on ground balls and he swung the old stick like it was a lath. Bull give him a lot o' pointers and so did the rest o' the boys, and by the time Bull was ready to go North, Martin was good enough to hold down an infield job somewhere in the brush.

Maggie and old Gregory was as proud as peacocks. The old woman was proud too, but she was scared to death that the pet would get beaned or stepped on and killed. Bull finally convinced her that baseball was as safe as ridin' in a rockin'-chair, and Martin was allowed to keep on with the only exercise he'd took in years, outside o' puttin' on his pyjamas at night and pullin' 'em off in the mornin'.

Bull left Montgomery with the understandin' that he could

have his room when he come back in the fall. Maggie squeezed his hand when she told him good-by, and that, Bull says, along with the post cards she sent him, was all that kept him alive that summer.

In June the Gregorys sent him a clippin' from a Montgomery paper. Martin had been signed by the Montgomery club to play second base, and he looked like the best thing that had broke into the Southern League in years.

The second off-season that Bull spent with the Gregorys he was still too shy yet to make any play for the lady, outside o' blowin' all his loose change in showin' she and her folks a time. But last fall, after they'd gave him his bit for workin' in the big series, and he felt like he had enough financial backin' to justify the plunge, he wired her to meet his train and he pulled his speech on her w'ile his nerve was still with him.

She didn't say yes or she didn't say no. She told him she liked him a whole lot bettern'n anybody except Brother Martin, and she appreciated his kindness to all o' them, and so on. But it would take a lot o' thinkin' to decide the question, and could he wait? So he says he could do anything for her and they left it go at that.

As soon as they was off'n the subject, she begin to talk about Martin and what he'd been doin' in baseball. She admitted that he was the greatest ball player south of Alaska, but o' course the Montgomery club didn't give him a fair show on account o' bein' jealous, and the manager kept him on the bench half the time for the fear some big league scout'd see him and steal him away from Montgomery. What she wanted Bull to do was tell some manager in our league about him, and have him bought. Martin would do the rest; he'd show 'em if he ever got the chance.

Well, Bull told her it was against the rules for an umps to recommend a ball player to a club in his own league. It wouldn't be fair to the Boston club, for instance, if Bull give Detroit first whack at a second Cobb. O' course Bull knowed that plenty o' scouts must of saw Martin and passed him up, and that the Montgomery club wasn't tryin' to conceal a man for who they could get a big price.

She ast him if he couldn't get some friend to do the recommendin' if he couldn't do it himself. He told her he was scared his part in it would be found out. Then she says that he must care a lot about her if he was afraid to take a little risk like that. He told her he'd try and think of a way to swing it, but she must give him time.

He found Martin more of a dude than ever and as modest as a wrestler. He couldn't talk about nothin' but how much better he was than the Southern League, and it was easy to see from his clo'es that he wasn't contributin' nothin' to the family except conversation and his personal attendance at meals.

Hatin' yourself, though, ain't nothin' against a ball player. Take most any real star and when the dialogue ain't about him he's bored to death, and if he has a bad day, pitchin' or hittin' or whatever it is he does, it's plain tough luck or rotten umpirin'. So Bull didn't think none the less o' Martin's ability on account o' the size of his chest, even if he did get good an' sick o' hearin' nothin' but Martin, Martin, Martin, all day and half the night.

Bull would of gave anything if Maggie and the rest o' them had forgot their scheme to land the pet in the big menagerie. But they wasn't a chance. When he'd rather of been hearin' that she cared somethin' about him, she was eggin' him on to hurry up and think of a way to bring Brother to the attention o' the real people.

In December Bull read in the paper that Ted Pierce, the manager o' the Montgomery club, was in town. He made a date to meet him and find out just how good Martin was.

"He's just good enough to of pretty near drove me wild," Ted told him. "If we're ten runs ahead and he comes up with the bases full, he'll hit one from here to Nashville. Or if we're fifteen runs behind in the last half o' the ninth, with two out, it's fifty to one that he'll get to first base. But put him up to that plate when everything depends on him and you'd think he had paralysis o' the arms. He'll take three in the groove and then holler murder at the umps."

"Plain yellow, eh?" says Bull.

"I don't like to say that about nobody," Ted says. "But if the old

U.S. called for volunteers, I'd bet on Benedict Arnold to beat him to the front."

"Ain't they no chance of him gettin' over it?" ast Bull.

"I've tried everything," says Ted. "I've called him all the names I could think of. I've tried to jolly him too; I've told him the pitchers was all scared of him and all he'd have to do was swing that club. But he's just as bad as when he broke in."

"He's a kid yet," says Bull. "It may be just stage fright."

"It may be," says Ted. "He certainly is cocky enough most o' the time; it's only in a pinch that he loses it."

"I'm a friend of his family," says Bull. "I'd like awful well to see him move up."

"You wouldn't like it no better'n me," says Ted. "I'd like to see him move anywheres. I'm sick o' lookin' at him. If you can sell him for any kind of a price, I'll give you half of it."

"You know I couldn't sell him," says Bull. "But if somebody else recommended him to somebody and I was ast about him, I'd do my best."

"Well," says Ted, "I ain't goin' to recommend him nowheres, unless it's to a fella I got no use for. I'm goin' to try him again in the spring, and if he don't quit chokin' to death every time he's got a chance to be a hero, I'll tie a can on him whether he's a friend o' yours or Woodrow Wilson's."

"Outside o' that, he's a good ball player, is he?" says Bull.

"They ain't no man I ever seen with more natural advantages," Ted told him. "His record shows that he hit .329 and stole thirty-two bases and fielded as good as any second baseman in the league. But he didn't make none o' those base hits when we'd of gave a thousand dollars apiece for 'em, and when he could of pulled a pitcher out of a hole with a swell piece o' fieldin' he simply booted the ball all over the infield."

"They's just the one hope for him, then," says Bull, "and that's to go out and get some o' the old nervine."

"If you can make him do that," says Ted, "I'll guarantee to sell him to any club you name."

So Bull, that night, told Maggie that Martin was still shy of experience and needed at least another year in minor league ball before he could hope to stick up with the E-light. He figured that he could work on the kid all the rest o' the winter and maybe succeed in stingin' him enough with hot conversation to get that streak out of him.

But Maggie right away wanted to know where Bull'd got his information and Bull had to tell her.

"No wonder!" says Maggie. "Pierce never did have a good word for him. Him and all the rest o' them's jealous."

"You're mistaken," says Bull. "Pierce wouldn't like nothin' better than to sell him for a good price."

"All right," says Maggie, "if you think I'm mistaken, that shows you don't care nothin' about me."

So Bull didn't have no answer to that swell argument only to beg her pardon and say she was probably right.

Well, it finally come to a kind of a showdown: Bull was either to see that Martin got his chance this spring or he'd have to worry along without Maggie. She didn't come right out and say that the way I've put it, but she made it plain enough so's they wasn't much chance to misunderstand.

Bull kicked the sheets round for a few nights and then got his idear. O' course the first thing was to pick a club that was tryin' to build up, and if possible to pick one that had a manager who'd pay the right kind of attention to a kid. Bull chose Connie as the best bet. The next thing was to persuade Connie to give Martin his trial. Bull wanted to be perfectly square, as you'll see by the deal he put through. He got a fella there in Montgomery with a good Irish name to write to Connie and recommend the boy, and if Connie didn't believe Martin was a good prospect he was to ask Bull about him, and if Martin didn't make good he wouldn't cost Connie nothin', not even his railroad fare to the trainin' camp and back. Bull framed it up with Ted Pierce as a matter o' friendship to leave the boy go on trial, and if he did su'prise 'em all and make good, the Montgomery club was to get whatever Connie was willin' to pay.

Well, the letter was sent and Connie wrote back to Bull, and says a boy named Gregory had been mentioned to him, and ast Bull was he worth a trial. Bull answered that Gregory was a kid with great natural ability and one or two faults that'd have to be overcome. Then Connie fixed it with the Montgomery club, and Bull thought he'd finished his job.

But he found out different. W'ile Maggie consented to becomin' engaged, she wasn't in no hurry to get married. She says her parents was gettin' old and she didn't want to leave 'em all summer, and besides, she didn't have no clo'es, and besides, it would be a whole lot nicer to wait till fall and spend the honeymoon where they'd first met each other and when Bull was just startin' his vacation instead of endin' it. Bull coaxed and coaxed, but her rules was just like his'n—she couldn't change a decision on a question o' judgment.

In the three weeks before Martin was to report in Jacksonville, Bull done nothin' but try and shoot him full o' confidence.

"The pitchers down here have got everything you'll see in the big league," he told him. "You don't need to be afraid o' none o' them. A man that handles a bat the way you do can hit anything in the world if he'll just swing. Connie or any other manager don't care how many times you strike out in the pinch, provided you strike out tryin'. You got the stuff in you to make Cobb and Baker and them look like a rummy. Don't get scared; that's all."

Bull pulled that talk on him right up to the day the kid left Montgomery. Down at the train, Bull says to him:

"Remember, they's nothin' to be scared of. Make us all proud o' you! Make good!"

"I'll make good if they give me a square deal," he says.

"Yes," Bull says to himself, "it's a cinch it'll be somebody else's fault if he falls down. It always is."

Well, in a little w'ile it come time for Bull to leave too. And here's what the girl sprung on him at the partin':

"You'll help him all you can, won't you?" she says.

"They's not a chance for me to help him," says Bull. "A man in my place can't favor nobody."

"A man could," she says, "if a man knowed it would please the girl he was stuck on."

Now if it'd of been me that she made that remark to, I'd of ast for waivers. But you know what they say about love bein' blind. And when it's a combination o' love and an umpire—well, how can you beat it!

Bull kept close tab on the papers and he seen that Martin was at second base in the lineup o' the Ath-a-letics' regular club. This was w'ile they was still South. Then, in one o' their last exhibitions before the season started, Martin's name was left out. He wrote to the kid and he wrote to Maggie, tryin' to find out what was doin'. Maggie wrote back that she didn't know and Martin didn't answer at all.

The season begin and Bull was workin' in the West. Every mornin' he grabbed the papers and looked to see if Martin was back in. Four times in three weeks the kid went up to bat for somebody, but without doin' no good. Then come the second week in this month and the first series between the Eastern clubs and us.

Bull had the Detroit-Philadelphia series. Just before the first game he run into Connie outside o' the park. They shook hands and then Bull says:

"Didn't you ask me about a ball player this winter?"

"Yes," says Connie, "a boy named Gregory."

"How's he comin'?" says Bull.

"I don't think he's comin'," says Connie. "I think he's just gettin' ready to go."

"What's the trouble?" ast Bull.

"Well, says Connie, "once in a w'ile our club happens to not be more'n two or three runs behind, happens to have a chance to tie or win. Gregory's one o' the kind o' ball players that spoils them chances. In practice down South he looked like a find. He hit everything and fielded all over the place. But we got into some tight exhibitions on the way up and when the opportunities come to him to do somethin' big he faded away. He ain't there in a pinch; that's all."

"Is he with you yet?" Bull ast him.

"He's with us," says Connie; "he's with us for one more trial. If they's a place in this series where I can use a substitute hitter, Gregory's goin' to be the man. And if he don't swing that club the way he can swing it when it don't mean nothin', I'll hand him his transportation back to Montgomery."

"Does the kid know that?" ast Bull.

"Yes," says Connie, "and if they's any stuff in him the knowledge that this is his last chance should ought to bring it out."

"You mean," says Bull, "that if he strikes out again in a pinch he's through?"

"No, I don't," says Connie. "I mean he's through if he doesn't try to murder that ball. I don't care if he strikes out on three pitches, just so he swings."

"But suppose," says Bull—"suppose they don't throw him nothin' he can hit; suppose they walk him."

"O' course," says Connie, "if the count gets down to two and three, I'd want him to pass the ball up if it was bad. But if it was where he could reach it, I'd want him to take a wallop, just to show me he ain't scared."

So that's how Martin stood with Connie at the beginnin' o' the series between the Ath-a-letics and Detroit.

The thing didn't happen the first day. The game wasn't close and Martin watched it all from the bench. Bull talked to him, but didn't get what you could call a cordial welcome. Bull wasn't su'prised at that; they ain't no ball player that'll kid with an umps when his dauber's down. He refused Bull's invitation to come round to the hotel that night and have supper with him. And Bull decided that the best play was to leave him alone.

They was a letter from the girl waitin' for Bull that evenin'. She'd heard from her brother and she knowed that he wasn't burnin' up the League; but he'd confessed that Connie hadn't treated him good and the umpires had robbed him blind. She knew, she wrote, that Bull wouldn't cheat him; if Bull really cared for her, he'd help him if he got a chance. And it would kill her and her father and mother besides if Martin had to face the disgrace o' not makin' good.

Bull went to bed and dreamt that Martin was up in a pinch, and he was umpirin' behind the plate, and Martin turned round and looked at him just before the ball was pitched, and Bull smiled at him to encourage him, and Martin took an awful wallop at the pill and give it a ride to the fence in right center. That's what Bull dreamt before the second game o' that series. And here's what really come off:

Big Coveleskie and Bush was havin' a whale of a battle. They wasn't nobody scored till the eighth. Cobb got on then, with only one out. So that give Detroit a run. The ninth looked to be all over. Two o' the Ath-a-letics was out. Then somebody got hold o' one and lit on it for three bases, and what was left o' the crowd decided to stick round a w'ile.

Bull says he knowed Martin was comin' up before he ever looked. And he smiled at him when he announced himself as the batter.

Coveleskie come with a fast ball. Martin had to duck to keep from gettin' hit. Coveleskie come with a curve. Martin made a feeble swing and missed it. Jennin's hollered from the bench:

"Run out with the water! The boy's goin' to swoon!"

Another curve ball that broke over, and Martin left it go.

"Strike two!" says Bull.

"It was inside," says Martin.

"You'll never drive in that run with a base on balls," says Bull.

Coveleskie come with a curve that was high and outside. It was the second ball. He come with another curve, in the same spot. It was three and two.

"Give him all you got!" yelled Jennin's. "Get it over there! He's too scared to swing!"

Bull told me that w'ile Coveleskie was gettin' ready for that next pitch he could see Maggie and the old folks in front of him just as plain as if they was there, and a voice kept sayin' to him, "Call it a ball! Call it a ball!"

The ball come—a fast one. Bull knowed what it was and where it was comin', and he bit his tongue to keep from sayin' "Swing!" Right across the middle it come, as perfect a strike as was ever pitched. And Martin's bat stayed on his shoulder.

"You're out!" says Bull. "It cut the heart!"

The heart o' the plate, and Bull's too, I guess.

Bull met Connie again next day, outside o' the park.

"I've canned your friend Gregory," says Connie.

"Do you know," says Bull, "I come near callin' that last one a ball?"

"If you had," says Connie, "the kid would of been let out anyway and you'd of fell, in my estimation, from the best umpire in the league to the worst in the world."

Now what does dear little Brother Martin do next? Instead o' goin' back to Montgomery like a man and tryin' to get a fresh start with the club that he'd been borrowed off of, he sets down and writes Maggie that Connie would of kept him only for Bull callin' him out on a ball that was so low and so far outside that the Detroit catcher had to lay down to get it, and that Bull done it because he didn't like him, and if Maggie didn't tie a can to Bull, Martin was through with her and with the old man and old lady too.

Well, the girl wrote back to Bull callin' off the engagement, sayin' how sorry her and her parents was to find out that he would stoop to such meanness and askin' him not to communicate with her no more. And Bull's bull-headed enough so as he wouldn't make a move to square things.

He got that letter from her day before yesterday, just before he left his hotel to come out to the yard. Is it any wonder he didn't say nothin' when I claimed Cady didn't tag me, and went entirely off'n his nut when Cahill called him a crook?

W'ile he was spillin' me the story I got enough into him to make a good sleepin' potion, and then helped him to the hay. The first thing yesterday mornin' I seen Ban and fixed that end of it by repeatin' the romance. But don't never breathe that Ban knows all about it. Bull thinks he's takin' him back because it was his first offense. And he's comin' back; Ban says he's promised to be in there to-morrow.

And right here in my pocket I got somethin' to show him that'll be better news than gettin' back his job. As luck would have it, I was the first guy to get to the park yesterday, and when I blowed into the clubhouse, who was settin' there but young Mr. Gregory himself! He told me his name and wanted to know was they any chance of him gettin' a try-out with us?

"Yes," I says, "they's one chance and you'll get it if you do as I say. Connie couldn't of gave you the Montgomery club again if we hadn't waived. But I'll fix it for you to join us to-morrow and try your luck again on these conditions: In the first place, you got to go right out now and wire your sister and tell her that the ball you was called out on was right through the middle o' the plate and the best strike you ever seen, and that Connie would of released you anyway, and that if your sister don't wire right back to Bull, in my care, statin' that she's reconsidered and it's still on between she and him, you won't never recognize her as your sister."

"And what if I won't do that?" he says.

"You won't get no chance of a job here," says I, "but you'll get the worst lickin' that was ever gave."

He sent the telegram and I got a night letter this mornin'; addressed to Bull it was, but I read it. I've been tryin' to locate him all day and he's goin' to call up as soon as he gets back to his hotel. Everything's fixed and to-morrow he'll feel so good that he's liable to forget himself and give us somethin' but the worst of it.

As for Martin, if he don't make good with our club it'll be because he can't hit and not because he's too scared to try. I'll have him too scared o' me to be scared of anything else.

The Yellow Kid

The Saturday Evening Post
JUNE 23, 1917

I

THE FIRST THING we found out about Crosby was that he couldn't read. The next thing was that he was scared to death o' women and girls. It was Buck Means that give us the info, and he done it out o' spite.

You see, Buck and Crosby was with the Dallas Club together year before last, and Buck was sore because Crosby got drafted, while Buck was overlooked. And Buck didn't like to see a kid with only one year's experience go up, when Buck himself had been in the sticks four or five seasons and nobody'd paid any attention to him.

Crosby was recommended to us by Jake Atz. Jake wrote up along in July and ast if we could use the fastest young left-hander he ever seen. So the old man put in a draft and we got him.

Well, Jake was right about the kid's speed. I've faced 'em all, from Rube Waddell down, but I never hit against nobody that could zip 'em through there like Crosby. If he ever beaned a man they'd have to get along afterwards without no head. O' course that wouldn't be no hardship to most o' them. It wouldn't affect the work o' nobody on our club.

Our first exhibition game last spring was in Dallas. Buck Means was talkin' to Gilbert and I before the practice.

"How's Crosby comin'?" he ast us.

"I'm glad he's on our club," I says, "so I don't have to hit against him all season."

"He's faster'n Johnson," says Gilbert. "If he was only a little wild with it they'd all be swingin' from the bench."

"They's no doubt about his smoke," says Buck; "but he's got nothin' besides, not even a noddle. He can't even read."

"Can't read!" I says. "Why, he looks brighter'n that."

"Sure!" says Means. "He's a good-lookin' kid. But, from the shoulders up, he's unimproved property."

"Not bein' able to read won't hurt him," I says. "He won't be bothered if the newspaper boys handle him a little rough once in a while."

"But if you got a joker on your club," says Buck, "Crosby'll be pie for him. McGowan, one of our outfielders, made a monkey of him all last year. He'd buy a paper and come and set down somewheres near Crosby and make up stuff that was supposed to be in there, and read it out loud. And he didn't read no compliments, neither, except when it come to Crosby's looks. You see, that's another thing about the poor simp: He's afraid o' skirts. He's so bashful that if they's a girl under ninety stoppin' at the same hotel he'll duck out and buy a meal at his own expense rather'n take a chance o' havin' her look at him in the dinin' room. And McGowan, while pretendin' that the papers was knockin' him as a pitcher, pretended, besides, that they were always printin' how handsome he was and how all the girls was wild about him. And, to make it good, Mac'd write fake love letters to him and he'd get somebody to read'em, and then good night! He'd lock himself up in his room for a week and never come out, only to get to the ball park. We had him believin' they was a girl in Austin that was crazy to marry him, and he was weak and sick all the times we was there, for the fear she'd call him up or he'd run into her on the street."

Well, when I and Gilbert was alone, I says that maybe we'd better keep this dope to ourself, or somebody might take advantage o' the kid and maybe spoil him as a pitcher. Gilbert was agreeable—that is, he told me he was. But he didn't lose no time spillin' the whole thing to Harry Childs, and he couldn't of picked out a worse one to tell it to.

Harry'd rather kid somebody than hit one on the pick, and him and Joe Jackson hates their base hits just alike.

So as soon as he got a chance he went after Crosby.

We was ridin' to Fort Worth and Childs had a Chicago paper. He flopped down in the seat beside Crosby.

"Well, kid," he says, "do you want to read what the reporters has sent up about you?"

"No," says Crosby, "I ain't interested in no newspaper talk. As long as I give the club the best I got, they can write anything they please."

"Yes, says Childs; "but this is a nice little boost and they's no man can tell me he don't like encouragement."

"But readin' papers on the train always puts my eyes on the bum," says the kid."

"I'll read it to you," says Harry. "I don't think your ears'll be hurt."

So Childs pulled somethin' about like this:

"One o' the most promisin' recruits is Lefty Crosby, that was drafted from the Texas League last fall. Though this boy only had one year's experience in the minors, he already handles himself like a veteran. His speed is terrific and his control a whole lot better than the average young left-hander's.

"Manager Cahill's only fear about him is that the female fans o'

Chicago and New York will bother him to death with telephone calls and sweet notes. In appearance, Crosby is a great deal like Francis X. Bushman. It is a certainty that he will take the fair sex by storm, provided he gives them the slightest encouragement."

Crosby was redder'n an undershirt.

"That's bunk!" he says. "Who wrote that?"

"The guy didn't sign his name," says Childs.

"I shouldn't think he would," says Crosby.

"I don't know why not," says Childs. "He was tellin' the truth. A fella as handsome and young-lookin' as you can just about take his pick of any dame in New York or Chi."

"I wasn't thinkin' about gettin' married," says Crosby, "I'm satisfied the way I am."

"Cahill'd rather have you married, though," says Harry. "He figures a man's liable to behave himself better if he's tied down."

"I'll behave all right," says the kid. "I got no bad habits."

"But if they's a beautiful bride for you to support, you'll work harder and improve faster," Childs says.

"I always work as hard as I can," says the kid.

"Maybe you already got a girl here in Texas," says Harry. "Maybe it's some little black-eyed peacherita from acrost the Border."

"I haven't no girl at all, and don't want none," says Crosby. "I don't see why a man can't get along without thinkin' about girls all the while."

"But," says Harry, "the Lord wouldn't of made you so beautiful if he thought you was goin' to be a woman hater."

"I ain't beautiful or nothin' o' the kind," says Crosby, blushin' harder'n ever.

Childs started to tell him he was too modest; but the kid got up and moved away.

In the hotel at Fort Worth, Harry got one o' the telephone girls to call up Crosby's room and tell him she'd love to meet him. He hung up on her. In Oklahoma City, Childs had one o' the local papers print a picture o' Crosby in action. He brought the paper into the dinin' room and flopped down at the same table with the kid.

"Did you see this?" he ast him. "It's pretty fair; but it don't hardly do you justice."

"What do I care!" says Crosby.

"I'd care a whole lot if I was you," says Harry. "If I had your looks I wouldn't allow no picture to be printed that didn't give me a square deal. And you ought to read what it says under it. But maybe it affects your stomach to read while you're eatin'. I'll read it to you."

"I don't care what it says," says Crosby.

"It's only a few words," says Childs. "I don't mind readin' it at all." And he handed him this kind o' stuff: "Above is showed a likeness o' Lefty Crosby, one o' Manager Cahill's recruits from Texas. They expect him to not only break a few strike-out records in the big circuit, but also the hearts of all the girls that gets a good look at him. Crosby promises to be the Adonis o' baseball."

I guess the kid didn't know Adonis from Silk O'Loughlin; but that didn't keep him from blushin' like a beet. Childs leaned over and whispered to him.

"They's a queen over there by the window," he says, "and she's done nothin' only look at you for five minutes. Maybe if I leave you alone she'll come over and introduce herself."

"I don't feel like eatin' no more lunch," says Crosby; and he beat it out o' the room. He hadn't hardly gargled half his soup.

From then on the kid tried to duck Harry all he could. But he didn't have the nerve to offend nobody, and lots o' times Childs'd corner him where he couldn't escape without makin' it too raw.

Crosby's best pal on the club was Joe Martin. Joe's always the bushers' friend because he don't believe in ridin' 'em. Crosby tried to set with Joe at the same table on the diners and in the hotels, because Martin'd read pretty near the whole bill o' fare out loud and Crosby could pick out what he really wanted to eat. Martin, o' course, done this on purpose, knowin' Crosby couldn't read and was generally always hungry.

It's pretty tough on a kid with a good appetite to not be able to tell what's listed unless somebody reads it off to him.

But Joe couldn't spend all his time makin' things easy for Crosby, and whenever Childs could manage to set with the kid he was meaner to him than a snake. For instance, after we'd had a tough work-out and everybody was starvin', Childs'd pick up the bill and begin crabbin' about how many things had been scratched offen it.

"We're gettin' a fine deal," he'd say. "They's nothin' left only salad and ice cream." Then he'd say to the waiter: "Bring me salad and ice cream."

And Crosby'd have to say that he'd take the same. Childs was willin' to go hungry himself for the sake o' puttin' it over.

The last day we was on the spring trip, Harry bought a rule book and brought it on the train.

"They've certainly made some radical changes this year," he says to Crosby. "A left-handed pitcher can't throw to first base without turnin' round twice before he pegs. And a left-handed pitcher can't throw more'n two curve balls to the same left-handed hitter durin' one time at bat. They're tryin' to increase the hittin'. And only the first foul counts a strike. And the pitcher and catcher ain't goin' to be allowed to work with signs. And when it's a pitcher's first year in the Big League, he ain't only allowed two strikes up there at bat. That's to hurry the game. And you got to get four men out instead o' three. And you can't pitch nothin' only new balls. The minute a ball's even tipped by a bat, the umps throws it away and gives you a brand-new one. And a pitcher ain't allowed to warm up the day he's goin' to pitch. And a pitcher can't wear a glove. And a pitcher can't wind up unless they's a runner on first or second base. Then he's got to. And if a pitcher's taken out three times in three months, he's automatically released, and either he's got to go to a Class E league or quit playin' baseball."

I don't know if Crosby fell for all o' that or not; but, anyway, I got him alone a while later and told him Childs was just kiddin' and the rules was the same as ever. It'd probably been hard enough for him to learn 'em in the first place without ringin' in no long list o' changes for him to try and master.

The train was late pullin' into Chi next mornin' and Harry got one more crack at the kid before we come to Englewood.

"Well, Lefty," he says, "you're goin' to have a real try-out right away. I was talkin' to Cahill and he says he's goin' to start you Friday o' this week."

Crosby looked tickled to death.

"The reason for it," says Childs, "is because Friday is Lady's Day at our park. The womenfolks all comes in free and the boxes and stand is always full o' them. And the old man wants to get 'em well pleased with the club right from the jump. He figures that if they see you once, they'll make their husbands and sweethearts bring 'em every time you pitch."

"I don't know if I'm goin' to be right to pitch Friday or not," says the poor boob. "The old souper felt kind o' numb when I worked yesterday."

"On Fridays," says Childs, "the boxes right back of our bench is always saved for showgirls. And the ball players that looks good to them, they always talk to."

"If Friday ain't a nice hot day," says Crosby, "I'm goin' to ask him not to work me. My arm feels rotten."

II

Well, Cahill didn't ask the kid to pitch Friday's game; never had no intention o' doin' it, o' course! But he did start him the followin' Monday, against the Cleveland gang.

For five innin's he pitched as pretty a game o' ball as I ever seen and we had 'em licked 3 to 0. Then Childs, who was warmin' the bench, got after him, either because he was sore on havin' been took out o' the outfield or just naturally couldn't resist a chance to pull somethin'.

While Cahill was coachin' at first base, Childs called Crosby up to one side o' the shed.

"Did you see her yet?" he ast him.

"See who?" says the kid.

"I guess you know who," says Childs. "They's a peach right behind the middle o' this bench. I noticed her lookin' at you ever since you warmed up. And while you was out there pitchin' last innin', she ast me your name. I told her and she says you was the handsomest man she ever looked at. So then she ast me would I introduce her to you when the game's over."

"I won't have no time," says Crosby.

"But, man," says Harry, "I promised I'd do it."

Just then the innin' was over and we went out. You never seen such a change in a pitcher. He couldn't get one near the plate. He acted like he was scared stiff. He was so wild that he had the ushers duckin'.

Cahill left him in there a few minutes to give him a chance to steady himself. But they wasn't nothin' to do but take him out after he'd walked four o' them without pitchin' a strike. Cahill was ravin' mad.

"Another yellow dog!" he says. "The next time Jake Atz recommends a man to me, I'll wire him at his own expense to take a dose o' bichloride. What do you think o' this stiff? We give him a three-run lead and they can't hit him with a board, and he's only got four innin's to go! And he blows higher'n a kite! Sixteen balls without a strike! And once he pretty near missed the whole grand stand! Go climb in the shower so you'll be clean when you start back for Texas."

Crosby was glad to sneak to the clubhouse and get out o' the park. But I and Martin was suspicious that somethin' had come off, and next time we come in we ast Childs.

"Yes," says Harry, "I suppose it's my fault. But if the poor boob is as simple as that, he'd ought to lose out."

"What did you pull on him?" ast Joe.

"I just told him," says Harry, "that they was a pretty girl settin' right back of our bench that ast to meet him after the game."

"That ain't right, Harry," says Martin. "He looks as good as any left-hander in the league, and we can't afford to spoil him. Just lay offen him. You know he's scared o' women; but that ain't the worst fault in the world, and you got to admit that he didn't look scared o' them Cleveland boys till he blowed up. Leave him alone and he'll win a lot o' ball games for us."

"Why should I leave him alone?" says Harry. "Since they got me settin' on the bench, they's nothin' left for me to do only kid somebody."

"All right," says Joe, "if you won't do it for me I'll put it up to Cahill."

And sure enough, in the clubhouse after the game, Martin told the M. G. R. just what had come off.

"Look here, Childs!" says Cahill. "That'll be enough o' that. I don't care how much fun you have with him offen the field, but when we're playin' a game, lay off! If you don't think I'm in earnest you may soon be takin' a trip to Texas yourself!"

So Childs laid offen him entirely for a while, not even tryin' to pester him when we went on our first trip. But I knew it wouldn't never last. While it did last, though, Crosby done better work than any o' the rest of our pitchers and had the whole league stood on their heads with that fast one o' his.

III

We left Cleveland one evenin', goin' to St. Louis, and the boys started a game o' cards. Childs was in it and Crosby was leanin' over the back of a seat, watchin'. I was settin' in the game, too, right where I could look at Crosby.

Well, Gilbert win three pots in a row, with aces one time, aces up the next time, and the third time he beat Childs with three o' the big bulls.

"Come on, Gil!" says Harry. "Give the aces a chance to roam round the deck once in a while."

"I can't spare 'em, Harry," says Gilbert.

"You put 'em in the deck!" says Childs, just kiddin'.

"You make me put 'em in the deck!" says Gil.

Well, Harry had a gun on his hip, with nothin' in it but blanks, and he pulled it out and laid it on the table in front of him, just for a joke.

But Crosby didn't see the joke. I happened to be lookin' at him when Childs showed the gun. He turned white as a sheet and I thought for a minute he was goin' to keel over. Then he grabbed the top o' the seat to steady up, and the next thing we knew he was beatin' it for the other end o' the car as fast as he could navigate.

"What's the matter with him now?" says Harry.

"Looks like he objected to the firearms," says Gilbert.

"What the hell ain't he scared of?" says Childs.

"Well," I says, "Ty Cobb for one thing and Bob Veach for another."

"Did he think I'd be monkeyin' with a loaded gat?" says Harry. "I'll have to try him out and see which he likes best, women or artillery."

"Oh, leave him alone!" says I. "As long as he keeps winnin' ball games for us, what's the difference if he's scared o' wild cats or fishworms?"

But Harry'd been good long enough. The next mornin', when we was crossin' the bridge into St. Louis, he finds Crosby in the washroom. Without sayin' nothin' he just simply laid his gun on one o' the sills, pointin' it straight at the kid. And Crosby begin shakin' like a leaf and staggered out o' the room without even waitin' to grab his collar.

Childs told us about it and seemed to think it was the funniest thing ever pulled off. But some o' the rest of us didn't think it was so funny, especially when we had to put Crosby to bed the minute we got to the hotel, and then get along without him all through the series with the Browns.

And Cahill made the remark, so as Childs could hear him, that the next guy that pulled a gun where Crosby was, or left one where he would see it, was through with our ball club for life.

IV

For a while after that, Harry was satisfied to just pull the girl stuff on his victim. He begin writin' fake love letters, like the guy'd done down in the Texas League. Some o' them was wonders. I know, because I read 'em to Crosby myself, he tellin' me that the different handwritin's was so funny that he couldn't make 'em out. But this wasn't much joy for Childs, because you can bet he wasn't never ast to read 'em.

Crosby wouldn't only let me get so far when he'd make me stop, and then he'd take the letters and tear 'em up.

"I wisht all girls would leave me alone," he'd say.

"What have you got against 'em?" I'd say to him.

"Bill," he'd say, "I'd just as lief own up to you. I don't feel comfortable round 'em. I'm just plain bashful. That's what my sister used to tell me. She was the only one I could ever talk to without pretty near faintin'."

"You'd get over that soon enough, if you'd try," I'd tell him. "You won't never know what livin' is till you get married and have a home o' your own. And they's nothin' about girls to be scared of, especially for as nice a lookin' guy as you are. They wouldn't never make fun o' you."

"I ain't afraid o' that," he'd say to me. "I wouldn't mind talkin' to 'em if I thought they'd just laugh and joke with me or talk baseball. But girls is liable to get personal and begin makin' eyes; and if they done that with me, I'd run a mile."

"Wasn't they no girls in the town you come from?"

"Too many o' them," he says. "They was only about two hundred people in the town and half o' them was girls, seemed like to me."

"How'd you get away from 'em?" I says.

"Just by runnin'," he says. "I beat it from home when I was twelve years old and that's why I didn't get no schoolin' to speak of. I joined in with a minin' gang up North, where I was sure they wouldn't be no skirts to bother me."

"You was young to be mixed up with a crowd like that," says I.

"Yes; but they treated me fine," says Crosby. "I'd of been in that game yet only for somethin' happenin'."

"What happened?" I ast.

"Oh, you'd think I was crazy if I told you," he says. "They was too rough for me. I can fight as good as the next guy when it's just usin' your fists. But I can't stand guns. Between you and I, I'm scareder o' them than I am o' girls. It started, I guess, one night when they was a scrap in a saloon. Everybody was lit up and, first thing you know, they had their gats out and was pluggin' away. And the guy that had took care o' me, when I first come to the camp, was shot dead right in front o' my eyes. I got sick at that time, watchin' it, and ever since then I get sick every time I see one o' the damn things."

"You're gunshy and girlshy," I says. "Anything else you're scared of?"

"Yes," he says; "a fast ball that's comin' at my bean. But I guess I got plenty o' company there."

"Well, Lefty," I says, "I can say one thing for you: You're brave enough when it comes to pitchin' against a .400 hitter in a pinch. And that's more than can be said for some o' the rest of our beautiful pitchers."

V

One o' the prettiest girls I ever seen was a telegraph operator at the hotel where we stop at in Detroit. Her name was Mary Lloyd. All the single guys on the ball club was more'n half crazy about her, and even the married ones was never heard objectin' when she give 'em a smile. To see us in that hotel, you'd of thought we was the greatest bunch o' telegram senders in the world.

Harry Childs had probably fell for her stronger than any o' the rest. When he wasn't busy talkin' base hits or kiddin' Crosby, he was tellin' somebody what a pippin she was, like nobody else had suspected it. And I guess he'd sent her enough cards from round the circuit to start a pinochle deck.

"Bill," he'd say to me, "she's the only one I ever met that I felt like I wanted to marry her."

"Go ahead!" I'd tell him. "I'd want to marry her, too, only I kind o' feel my own Missus might make a holler."

"Go ahead!" he'd say. "It's all right to say 'Go ahead'; but every time I start she says 'Back up!' She's worse'n a traffic cop."

"Keep tryin', Harry," I'd say to him. "Maybe she's heard about you bein' the world's champion joker and thinks you're just triflin' with her."

"She does all the jokin' when I'm round," he says. "She makes a regular monkey out o' me."

"Oh, I wouldn't blame that on her!" I says.

Now Mary wasn't no flirt, but she didn't mind bein' admired. She never give one guy more encouragement than another; she didn't play no favorites, or she didn't never let nobody on the club get the idear that she was to be had for the astin'. But she wasn't never too busy to talk to any of us, or to smile back when we smiled at her.

I and Gilbert was standin' there kiddin' with her the first time she seen Crosby. We'd just got in that mornin', and when he come out from breakfast he beat it through the lobby past her desk and out on the front walk.

"Who's that handsome wretch?" she ast us.

"That's the guy that made a sucker out o' Cobb and Veach over home," says Gilbert.

"Maybe if I ast him not to," she says, "he'll leave our team win a game or two this series."

"You got a sweet chance of astin' him anything," says I, "unless you got a megaphone."

"Is he deef?" says Mary.

"When they's girls round he's deef and dumb and blind," I says.

"He must of been disappointed in love," she says.

"Not him," says Gil. "The only time he was ever disappointed was when they postponed the game he was goin' to pitch."

"What's the trouble between him and girls?" says Mary.

"He just naturally don't like 'em—that's all," I says.

"Well," says Mary, "I don't think that's hardly fair to our sex. They ain't so many handsome men in the world that we can afford to have 'em woman haters."

"No," I says; "and they ain't so many good pitchers on our ball club that we can have him scared to death by gettin' a smile from you. So when you happen to run into him, face to face, kindly act like you didn't see him."

"I'm much obliged," she says, "for bein' told that my smile is terrifyin'. I'll keep it to myself after this."

"Not at all," says I. "I'd pretty near rather miss a hit-and-run sign than that smile o' yours. But this kid is just plain bashful; he ain't no woman hater; he's too backward to hate anything. He wants to be left alone—that's all. If a girl looks at him cross-eyed it takes him a week to get so's he can pitch again."

"I believe I'll go right out now," says Mary, "and look at him cross-eyed. You know I ought to be loyal to the Tigers."

"You ought to be loyal to this here beanery," says I; "and if you put him out o' commission, why, we'll just pass up this hotel."

"All right," she says. "I won't pay no attention to him, because I know I'd simply die if you boys stopped somewheres else and gave me a chance to do a little work."

"Has Childs been round yet?" says Gilbert.

"Foolish Question 795!" I says. "He was here even before he went in for his prunes."

"What's the matter with Harry Childs?" she ast us. "Why ain't he playin?"

"We like to win once in a while," says Gilbert.

"The reason Harry ain't playin' " I says, "is a young outfielder from the Coast, named Patrick."

"Why," says Mary, "Harry told me he was out of it with a Charley Horse."

"Yes," I says; "and a battin' average last year o' .238."

Crosby pitched the first game for us and win 2 to 1 in eleven innin's. He was goin' to wind up the series, but it begin to pour rain at noon o' the last day and the battle was off before we went out to the park. We wasn't startin' home till nine o'clock that night; so we had a lot o' time to kill. Naturally they was a reception all afternoon round Mary's desk. I and Joe Martin happened to be left there alone with her while Childs was gettin' shaved and some o' the others was celebratin'.

"Well," says Mary, "now that they ain't no more chance o' me spoilin' your trip, I think you might bring Mr. Shy round."

"She means the kid," I says to Joe. "I told her all about him."

"Have you seen him?" Joe ast her.

"O' course I seen him," she says.

"What do you think of him?" says Joe.

"Well, gentlemen," she says, "I don't want to hurt the feelin's o' the present company, so I'll just keep still."

"He is a pretty kid," says Martin, "and he's a whole lot better-lookin' since I coaxed him into some decent clothes. But he don't want to meet no girls."

"They's no sense to it," I says. "It wouldn't hurt him a bit to mingle a little with the dames. It'd do him good. And he'd get along O. K. when he found out they wasn't all tryin' to steal him."

"I'll promise not to steal him," says Mary.

"Well, it's up to Joe, here," I says. "He's his best pal."

"I guess he'd come if I ast him," says Martin. "But I don't know if I want to take a chance."

"Oh, come on!" says Mary. "I don't feel comfortable when they's one o' your boys I ain't acquainted with."

"Well," says Joe, "maybe he's up in his room takin' a nap."

"If he is in his room," says I, "that's probably what he's doin'. It's a cinch he ain't readin."

"Why not?" says Mary.

Joe give me the wink.

"He hates books," I says.

It was just then that the kid come across the lobby, toward the front windows. He looked like he was goin' to cry.

"My! He needs cheerin' up," says Mary. "Do you suppose he's sick?"

"You bet he's sick," says Martin. "He was goin' to give your Tigers another lickin' to-day, and the rain beat him out of it."

"Well, how about callin' him over?" I says.

So Martin went up to him and made the proposition. I could see the poor kid blush and then start like he was goin' to run out in the rain. Then Joe grabbed ahold of his arm and begin arguin' with him.

And finally the pair o' them come toward us. Nobody only Joe could of done it.

"Miss Lloyd," says Martin, "this is another o' the boys, Mr. Crosby. He's disappointed about the rain and I thought maybe you could cheer him up."

Mary give him her best smile.

"I'm glad to meet you, Mr. Crosby," she says. "You're the first ball player I ever seen that was disappointed about the rain."

"Except when it didn't fall," I says.

The kid didn't say nothin'; didn't even look at her. I caught him moistenin' his lips, tryin' to get a word out. But he couldn't. He seen her put her hand out to shake and he finally managed to meet it. But he done it with the one he uses in pitchin'. And then, the minute Martin left go his arm, he backed away, pivoted on a pillar and dashed for the elevator.

"Good night!" says Mary. "Well, of all the rummies!"

"We warned you," says Martin.

"You certainly cheered him up," I says—"all the way up to his room."

"He can stay there, for all o' me," she says "I won't never try to force my acquaintance on nobody again."

"I bet he's offen me for life." says Joe.

"You ought to be glad if he is," she says.

"But you got to admit he's a handsome brute," says I.

"Yes," says Mary; "and I'd like to scratch his handsome face to pieces."

When we got on the train that night Harry Childs come up to me.

"Bill," he says, "I believe I'm goin' to win out."

"Win out what?" I ast him.

"With Mary," he says. "I took her out to supper. It was the first time she ever let me do it. And she acted like she really was fond o' me."

"Here's luck, Harry!" I says.

I didn't tell him the reason she was so friendly. It was because she'd been stung. And Harry's attentions was salve.

We was in Detroit again the first week in July. Harry took her out to supper or a picture show, or somethin', every night. I never heard her mention Crosby, and I was scared to mention him in front of her.

I did see her try to get even though. She come out from behind her desk one mornin', just as he was walkin' in from outside. She got right in his way, so as he either had to run into her or dodge. And he couldn't help lookin' at her. She looked him right in the eye and didn't speak.

And the kid looked like he was mighty glad of it.

VI

Young Patrick got hurt and Childs was back in the game when we went East in August. Harry was full o' pep.

"I'll show 'em I can hit," he says to me. "I never felt luckier in my life."

"You don't need no luck to hit if you take care o' yourself," I says.

"Don't worry about that," he says. "I got to keep in shape. I'm tryin' to save the coin."

"What for?" I ast him.

"Well, Bill," he says, "I'm kind o' figurin' on gettin' married."

"Nice work, Harry!" I says. "I didn't know you'd gone as far as that."

"They's nothin' settled," he says. "But she's writin' to me, and when we strike Detroit next month I'll make her say yes."

Harry started to paste that pill in Philly. He broke up two games for us there and got seven blows in three days. He was the pepper kid when we got to Washington and he couldn't resist takin' some of it out on Crosby.

They set at lunch together the second day.

"Lefty," he says, "looks like we're goin' to fight Germany. I was down to the White House this mornin' to call on a friend o' mine, a Mr. Wilson, and he says he don't think we can hold out much longer."

"Well," says Crosby, "let 'em fight, as long as they leave us guys out of it."

"Who says they'd leave us out of it?" Harry ast him.

"They'll leave me out of it, all right," says Crosby. "I never shot a gun in my life."

"It ain't guns they want you to shoot. It's Germans," says Childs. "And if the President called for volunteers I bet you'd be one o' the first to go."

"You'd lose your bet," says the kid. "I can't take no chance o' gettin' my left arm shot off."

"Good Lord! That reminds me o' somethin'," says Harry. "I seen in the papers this mornin' that most o' the guns this country's got is left-handed guns. And they'll probably call for all the left-handed men in the United States to handle 'em."

Crosby didn't wait for no desert.

In New York, a couple o' days later, Childs was at him again.

"War's gettin' closer every minute," he says to Crosby.

"The Germans torpedoed the City o' Benton Harbor yesterday and sunk eleven bootblacks without even givin' 'em a chance to take their stands with 'em. And the Kaiser went fishin' in the mornin' and caught an American sturgeon. The President says if that kind o' thing keeps up he's offen the Kaiser and we'll all have to enlist—that is all the able-bodied guys."

"That lets me out," says the kid. "My ankles wouldn't hold up a minute if I was to try and march."

"They'd stick you in the calvary and leave you ride a motorcycle," says Childs.

"I don't know how," says Crosby; "and, besides, a man couldn't ride no motorcycle acrost the ocean."

"Oh, yes, they could," says Childs, "if the tires was blowed up tight enough. And, anyway, they's lots of us would have to do our fightin' here in this country, to keep the Germans from breakin' up the League."

I went in to breakfast with the kid the mornin' we landed in Boston. I had a paper myself and they was a piece in it sayin' that this country was thinkin' about callin' on all the young men o' nineteen and twenty, to train 'em for war—that is, all the ones that wasn't married. Childs, settin' at the next table, read it and couldn't get over to us fast enough.

"Crosby," he says, "how old are you?"

"Twenty," says the kid.

"You're in tough luck, old boy!" says Childs; and he begin readin' out loud. It was a cinch this time, because the readin' matter was really there.

"Congress," it says, "is considerin' a proposition to start universal military trainin' on account o' the strained relations with Germany and the prospects o' war. The plan is to draft every unmarried man in the United States o' the ages o' nineteen and twenty, and make 'em fit for war."

Anyway, it was somethin' like that.

"It looks like your baseball career was pretty near over," Harry says to the kid. "It's a crime too! You've had a great year, and without knowin' nothin' about pitchin' at that. But still, it ain't hard to learn to shoot and duck bullets; and they's a whole lot o' satisfaction in knowin' that you're workin' for the Stars and Stripes."

"When does this business come off?" says Crosby.

"Oh, not for a couple months," says Childs. "They'll probably leave you stick with us through the city series."

Then Childs got up and left us.

"Bill," says Crosby to me, "they ain't no kiddin' about this, is they?"

"No, Lefty," I says. "It's there in the paper, all right. But it just says they're thinkin' about it. If I was you I wouldn't start worryin' yet."

"Bill," he says, "before I'll join a army I'll walk out in Lake Michigan till my hat floats."

"Quit frettin' over it," says I. "You won't be able to pitch in this series, and you know we want some o' these games."

"But they're goin' to draft all the twenty-year-olds," he says, "and I just broke into that class. I wisht to the devil I was your age."

"Yes," I says; "or married."

"Married!" says Crosby. "That's right! It's just the single fellas that's gone."

"They ain't nobody gone," says I. "But if you don't quit worryin' you'll be just as good."

Childs spoiled whatever chance the Kid had to quit worryin' by sayin' to him, just before we started the game:

"Well, Lefty, they's one pipe: You'll be the handsomest guy in the army."

Before Crosby was taken out, Harry probably regretted that remark; because in the five innin's he pitched our outfielders must of ran back to the fence fifty times.

VII

Joe Martin told me about the kid bracin' him in the hotel that night.

"Joe," Crosby says to him. "I'd kind o' like to get acquainted with a girl."

"Good Lord!" says Joe. "What girl?"

"It don't make no difference," says the kid. "Some girl that ain't married, but might like to be, and ain't liable to want to spoon or make eyes or nothin' like that."

"Are you thinkin' o' gettin' married?" Joe ast him.

"Yes; only keep it quiet," says Lefty.

"And do you expect a girl to marry you for your money?" says Joe.

"You know I got no money," Crosby says.

"Well," says Joe, "if you got no money and you want to get married, you got to find a girl that's fond o' you. And a girl that's fond o' you might want to hold hands some time."

"Ain't they no sensible girl that might take me?" says the kid.

"What girls do you know?" Joe ast him.

"Joe," he says, "I ain't met a girl since I was fifteen or sixteen years old."

"Oh, yes, you have," says Joe. "How about that girl you was so nice to in Detroit?"

"Do you mean that girl you introduced me to?" says Crosby.

"Sure!" says Martin. "Mary Lloyd, the telegraph operator."

"Do you think she'd like me?" ast the kid.

"Well," Joe told him, "she ast to meet you, and she certainly was broke up the way you treated her."

"But what kind of a girl is she?" he says. "She ain't too soft?"

"I never caught her at it," says Joe.

"But she's probably sore at me," says Crosby.

"You can apologize to her," says Martin.

"But we won't be in Detroit for ten days," says the kid.

"Write her a letter," says Joe.

"I don't like to write letters," Crosby says. "Joe, will you write her a letter for me?"

"That'd make her sorer than ever," says Martin. "Besides, I don't know what you're tryin' to pull off."

"I'm on the square," says the kid. "If she'll marry me—why, I'll take her."

"That's damn' sweet o' you!" says Joe. "But what's your idear in gettin' married?"

"Never mind, Joe," says the kid. "I just feel like I want to."

"Well," says Joe, "if you want to square it with Mary, and you don't feel like writin' to her, why not send her a night letter?"

"What's that?" says Crosby.

"It's a telegram that goes at night, and you can say about fifty words for fifty cents," Joe told him.

"But I don't know no fifty words to say," says the poor kid.

To make it short, Joe done it for him, either because he was sorry for the kid or because he thought it was a joke or because he ain't none too good friends with Harry Childs. The telegram said that the kid was sorry he'd froze her, that he'd been feelin' tough that afternoon, that he apologized, and would she please forgive him, because he thought a whole lot of her.

The answer come next day, at noon. Mary wired that she'd pay more attention to him if he said all that to her face.

VIII

HARRY CHILDS' lucky spell ended when we stopped over for a game in Cleveland on the way home. He changed his mind at the last minute about makin' a slide to the plate, and they carried him off with a busted leg.

So Harry Childs didn't make the last trip to Detroit.

Young Mr. Crosby did, though he was so scared leavin' Chi that

I and Gil and Martin was afraid he'd throw himself offen the train in the night.

The three of us talked it all over.

"He'll fall down, sure!" says Gil. "She'll give him an unmerciful pannin' and he'll faint dead away."

"But suppose he don't," I says. "Suppose he goes through with it and wins. Are we bein' fair to Harry?"

"Why not?" says Martin. "Childs played jokes on him all season. It's pretty near time the kid got back."

"I'm for helpin' him," says Gilbert.

"Me too," says Joe.

"All right; you're on!" I says; and we begin discussin' how to go about it.

We finally fixed it up that we'd get a taxi to come to the hotel at Mary's lunchtime. Then we'd coax 'em into it and slam the doors, and tell the driver to break all the laws o' Michigan.

Because, as Joe said, if we put 'em together where Crosby could get away, he'd get away sure!

They's nothin' more to it. They were back from their ride at one o'clock, both o' them as red as an open switch. But the smile Mary give us was an inch or so wider than we ever got before.

Crosby come blushin' acrost the lobby.

"Well?" we says.

"Well, boys," he says, "it wasn't bad."

"What do you mean—wasn't bad?" says Martin.

"Her," says the kid.

"Not half as bad as one o' them German centipede guns," says I.

"Not half!" says Crosby.

I suppose by this time she's got him through the First Reader.

III

Reds 5, Black Sox 3

Gents: Lardner Says the Umpires Interfere With His 'Dope' on Big Series

You Never Can Tell What They Are Going to Do Declares Expert Who Compares Players of Both Teams and a Few Who Are Not

Cincinnati, Sept. 28—Gents: In doping out a conflict like the threatened world serious, an expert like myself works under a heavy strain as they's no way of telling what those d—m umpires is going to do and in the case of a couple of even matched ball clubs like the White Sox and Reds neither 1 of which has ever lose a world serious why some finicky notion of some umpire is libel to raise havioc.

An expert's 1st duty then is to make a study of the umpires that has been chose to rule or ruin the comeing serious and a comparison between the 4 of them in this case shows the advantage to be all in their favor. Suppose for inst. Heinie Groh was to hit a high fly and nobody catched it, but the umpires got it in their head to play a practical joke on the big Dane and call him out why they wouldn't be no recourses for Heinie only to walk off the field and join the New York Yanks. So as I say a man that is not in the umpires confidents and trys to make predictions may make a monkey of himself instead.

But wile it never settled a world serious 1 way or the other to figure out whether Limbo has it all over Bimbo as a bench warmer or vice versa why still and all its a habit amidst the experts, and one that don't do it lays himself open to the abuse that is always heaped onto a reformer, so I may as well try and remember who is on the different clubs and set down the facts about them in Black and White and plain water.

Reds Pitching Staff Savors of the Bible

STARTING OFF with the cathers, Bill Rarideh was born in Bedford, Ind., and Ray Schalk was born in Litchfield, Ill., so neither one of them is libel to be dazzled by the big crowds. The edge, if any, belongs to Bill; as he has lived more different places than Ray. As for Ivy Wingo and Byrd Lynn, why Byrd has more ys in his 8 letters, but when it comes to slideing home they's very few people afraid of a Byrd wile the White Sox don't know but maybe Ivy is poison. Both clubs will miss Larry McLean.

Coming to the pitchers, I had to buy a paper to see who was the regulars on the Reds and the only name that pitched for them that day was Luque, but I suppose the others is Mathew, Mark and John. Mathew is probably Mathewson's old man and has got some of the family traits, which means he will have about as much luck in a world serious as the crown prince at Verdun. Mark, of course, has got a unfortunate name, but that don't seem to make no differents in a pitcher, as you take Ruth for inst. and you wouldn't never think it was a girl. I looked up John's record and about the only place where he mentions athaletics is where he outrun Peter and you can't judge nothing by that, as Peter may of triped over his beard or something.

It's an Even Break Between Hoblitzel and Isbell

None of the White Sox pitchers has ever wrote a gospel and any way they's only 2 of them to hear some people tell it. The 2 is Wms. and Cicotte, of which Cicotte is 1 of the most baffling pitchers in baseball, as you can't never be sure 2 days in succession how he is going to be pronounced. Wms. was baptized Claude, but has growed up normal outside of being a left hander. Of the others in the list Dick Kerr throws left handed and hits the same way, while Grover Lowdermilk throws right handed and hits seldom.

It looks like a even break between Hoblitzell and Isbell on the initial sack, as I have nicknamed 1st base, and at second base the rivals appears to be peers on paper, though they tell me Morris Rath is going to get marred this fall, but on the other hand you take a bird like Collins and they's no telling what he will do under fire, as a man like he is liable to blow sky high in a pinch. For inst. in the last game vs. the Giants 2 yrs. ago he lose his head completely and run home backwards from 3d base though Heinie Zimmerman that was chasing him is 1 of the fastest men in the Natl. League and can beat his own throws.

Moran and Gleason Widely Different Types

The shortstops can be past over, as they seldom never cut any figure in a event of this kind, and that brings us to Weaver and Groh at 3d. base both of which is the greatest 3d. baseman in the game today. Comparisons is obvious but they tell me Heinie is libel to quit as for inst. when he was first born his old man said Heinie Groh and Heinie started but soon give it up.

The least said about the 2 outfields the better as they are about equally bad and the only chance for a argument is who has got the cutest nickname Shoeless Joe Jackson or Greasy Neale.

The rival mgrs. is widely different types as Moran gets his results by rough houseing wile Gleason is the soft spoken effeminate kind that a person would think to hear him talk that he was secretary of war or something. In the off season Moran is a Deutscher Artz at Fitchburg, Mass., wile the big Greek runs a handkerchief store in Philly. Neither 1 of them is hardily out of their teens you might say.

As far as the utility men is conserned it looks to me like it was a exageration to call them that.

Lardner Finds Cincinnati Baseball Mad, But Purse Is Out of Danger

Our Expert Delivers Presentation Speech at Reds' Banquet and Delves Into Players' Past

Cincinnati, Sept 29—Well, gents! Several times dureing the past month I have heard people say that if Cincy win the pennant the old burg would go crazy but I didn't know how nuts they really was till they called me up and said they would pay me money to come down there and make a speech. This was after the flag was win and it seems the town wanted to give the boys some reward for their grand fight and they had decided to give them Rookwood vases and needed somebody to come down there and explain why.

Well before I went I read somewheres that this was the 1st. time Cincinnati had ever win a pennant since they's been agonized baseball but when I got there I seen plainly that it was the 1st. time any town had ever done it. The old burg was raving mad but it hadn't went to their purse and when I mentioned the jack I had on me that the boys in Chi had sent down to bet at evens why all as I could hear was 7 and 8 to 5.

Well Geo. Golde that owns a bunch of stock in the Reds give a dinner at the Business Men's Club for the athaletes and I and they had a prune colored orchestra that sung parodys about the different stars that nobody had ever heard sung before includeing the orchestra. Well I asked Sherwood Magee if the team was all there and he said all but Jake Daubert and Charley See a young outfielder and Pitcher Luque. So I says "That's one for the minstrels." So he says what did I mean. So I said well you say to me, you say: "Mis' Lahdnah, who am the playahs that isn't heah outside of Mis' Daubert"? Then I say to you "Well Mr. Magee, who are the absent players besides Mr. Daubert"? Then you say "Luque and See."

After the dinner they took us over to Music Hall that don't only hold 4 or 5000 people and they was all there and I and the ball players and Mayor Galvin set up on the stage amidst the pottery and I was as cool as a waffle iron and finely the mayor introduced me in a few well chose words quite a few of them and I got up there to talk and for the benefit of those that wasn't there to hear me as well as those who was I will tell you what I said in part.

"Ladies and Cuckoos: I hadn't no idear I would be called on for a speech tonight, but I generally always keep one in my pocket so I will read it to you. I don't know a whole lot about your ball club but I do think that while some of the ball players had something to do with the winning of the championship the greater portion of the credit should be given to the management of William A. Phelon and Pat Moran. (Applause.)

Neither Club Ever Lost a World's Series

"I PRESUME A GREAT MANY of you is wild to know how I think the serious is going to come out as I picked Willard down at Toledo. Well, cuckoos, it is impossible to tell in this case as neither of the 2 clubs ever lose a serious of this kind though back in 1843 Cincinnati played for the world's championship but it didn't count on acct. of the Natl. Commission not getting nothing out of it and I have even forgot how the games resulted though I can remember rideing out to the opening clash in a go cart pushed by Hugh S. Fullerton. (Laughter.)

"A great many of you cuckoos may resent me being here as I am supposed to be from Chicago but I want to assure you that I am so strong for the Reds that before I left old Chi I went to Ban Johnson and got him to promise that he wouldn't suspend none of your pitchers till the serious was over. (Applause.)

"The other day somebody told me they was going to be a world serious and that I was going to write something about it so I thought I better go out to a ball game and see how many men they was on a side. The game I seen was between the Cubs and Philadelphia and Philadelphia looked just like a club that Pat Moran got canned for manageing them. (Applause.)

"Well, cuckoos, when I landed here this A.M. I called up the man that had asked me to make this speech and asked him what was I to talk about and he said the Reds and I said who is on the Reds so he give me a list and I looked them over and only found 4 of them that I knowed personly outside of Pat Moran and Sallee who I give him the nickname of Slim, but I would like to meet Ring as he must be a grand fellow. The 4 I know best is Dutch Reuther and Bill Rariden and Sherwood Magee and Morris Rath. Bill Rariden was with the Boston club when I use to pretend to work there and his club use to tie up the score every day in the 9th. inning with a pop fly over the right field fence and lose out in the 13th. Bill started the season with a brand new glove and at the end of the season the glove was brand new as none of the other pitchers could throw a ball that far. (Shouts of laughter.)

Morris Proves He Must Have Been Sick

"MORRIS RATH WAS WITH THE White Sox and 1 day we was playing in Washington and it was Walter Johnson's turn to pitch so at 11 A.M. Morris said to Manager Callahan I am sick but Manager Callahan said I don't believe it so he made Morris play and Morris got three hits off of Walter and then Cal knowed he must of been telling the truth. (Applause.)

"I bumped into Mr. Reuther in the spring of 1913 in San Francisco when he was pitching for St. Mary's College and the White Sox played them a exhibition game and murdered Dutch with a total of 1 hit which was a couple ft. foul and as for Sherwood Nottingham Magee why it was in 1872 when the Cubs was parked in Philly over Sunday and arranged a exhibition game at Atlantic City and Mac was then with the Philadelphia club and use to spend the Sabbath on the Boardwalk. Well we went down there the Saturday night before and I and Frank Schulte and Harry Steinfeldt was walking along the walk and a guy from N. Y. come along and stopped us and asked if we was members of the Cubs. So Schulte says yes this is Harry Steinfeldt the best 3d. baseman in the country. So the N. Y. bird said Arthur Devlin is the best 3d. baseman in the country so Frank hit him and knocked him for a gool. Well wile the poor bird was still laying in the ditch along come Sherwood and says what is the matter Frank are you in trouble? No trouble said Frank I just had a little fight. I will take it off your hands said Mac. (No laughter.) That is all there is to that story. (Applause).

Mayer and Mitchell Surprise of Season

"I DON'T KNOW the rest of the Reds very well outside of Gary Herrmann and I read in the paper the other day where he had decided to make the serious go 9 games this yr. instead of 7 so that more people would get a chance to enjoy it but personally I think his motive was to give more of Gleason's pitchers a chance to pitch. (No applause.)

"This brings us to the business of the evening. Most presents gave to baseball players on occasions like this is absolutely useless but the gifts presented to the Reds tonight will keep them busy all winter wondering what to do with them. Gents of the Reds I take great pleasure in presenting to you on behalf of whoever is giveing them away these beautiful Rookwood vases which you should ought to pronounce vases on acct. of them being $2000.00 worth of them."

Several times dureing the speech I was interrupted by crys of Lauder on acct. of people not knowing how I pronounce my name or else they was trying to convey the idear that I am as funny as the other great Scotch comedian. Well when it was over I slipped out the stage entrance and catched an obscure train for Indianapolis and here I am safe in sound.

As for my personal feelings about the serious I have lived in Chi a No. of yrs. but always recd. fine treatment in Cincinnati so I only wished both clubs could win 5 straight and now they'se nothing more to be said till Pat and the Kid pulls the surprise of the season and sends Erskine Mayer and Roy Mitchell out to warm up for the opening of the fray.

Well, Gents: The Chisox Won't Forfeit the Series

Lardner Finds Chicago Team Diving Into Grapefruit; Then Interviews Umps.

Cincinnati, Sept. 30.—Gents: The world series starts tomorrow with a big surprise. A great many people figured that the White Sox would be scared out and would never appear. But sure enough, when we woke up this morning and came down to breakfast, here was the White Sox as big as life and willing to play.

The first bird I seen amidst them was Ray Schalk, the second catcher.

"Well, Cracker," I said, "I never expected to see you down here, as I had been told that you would quit and would never appear."

"Well, Biscuit," was his reply, "here we are and that's the best answer." So after all that is said and done the White Sox is down here and trying to win the first 2 games on their merits, so it looks like the series would not be forfeited after all.

Most of the experts went to the 2 different managers to try and learn who was going to pitch the opening game. So to be different from the rest of them as usual I passed up the two managers and went to the umpires. The first one I seen was Cy Rigler and I have known him all my life.

"Who is going to win, Cy?" I asked. "I don't know," was his ample reply. You can take that tip or leave it. Personaly I am betting on his word. He will give them the best of it if possible.

The next umpire I seen was Quigley. "My system," he said, "is to call everybody out." The two American League umpires could not be seen as they were both up writing their stuff, but you can be sure that neither of them will give anybody the best of it.

It Looks Like a Free Hitting Game

THAT BRINGS US TO THE hotel accommodations. A large Chicago newspaper has got the price rm. of the lot, namely the smoking rm. off the ball rm. in the Gibson. This means that if anybody wakes up at 3 in the morning and wants to smoke why they can do so without moving out of their rm. and they want to dance why all as they have to do is go in the next rm. and look for a pardner.

A great many people have written in to this hotel to ask how I am going to bet so they can do the opposite and make big money. Well, Gents., I might as well tell you where I stand. I don't believe either club can win as neither one of them has got a manager. But I do know both of the so called managers personally, and I have asked them who is going to pitch the opening game and they both say everybody on the staff so it looks like a free hitting game with Gerner and Mayer in there at the start and Mitchell and Lowdermilk to relieve them, but neither has made any provisions in regards to who is going to relieve us newspaper guys.

The other day as you may remember, I tried to make a comparison of the two clubs man for man, and when I come to the shortstops why, I said the logical thing, which is, that no shortstop can win the serious as nobody ever hits to the shortstops in a big event like this. But thousands of birds wrote in personal letters to know what I thought of the two shortstops anyway, so I suppose I have got to tell them.

Two Stars of Series Have Been Overlooked

WELL, OF THE TWO SHORTSTOPS mentioned, Risberg and Kopf, will be in there at the start of the serious but they will both be took out before the serious is 9 games old. Comparing the both of them, Risberg is a Swede but on the other hand Kopf hits from both sides of the plate. Both of them is tricky and is libel to throw a ball to a different base than expected. Kopf is the better looking, but Risberg is the tallest and if they ever try to drive a high line drive over his head they will get fooled.

The two stars of the coming serious has both been overlooked by the experts, and I refer to Sherwood Magee and John Collins, whom a lot of you think won't be in there. Even if they are not they are both good fellows.

Another question the public keeps asking we experts is who get the advantage out of having the serious nine games instead of seven. Well, gents, all I can say is it isn't the newspaper men. Further and more I wouldn't be surprised if neither ball club liked the new regime as I have nicknamed it, as it looks to me like both mgrs. would use up all the pitchers they have got tomorrow and wouldn't know what to do next.

All together, it looks like a long serious and whoever made it nine games had it in for us.

Daubert Fools Lardner

Refuses to Stay Down
Sox Lack "Strategem"

Cincinnati (O.), Oct. 1.—Gents: Up to the eighth innings this pm we was all setting there wondering what to write about and I happened to be looking at Jake Daubert's picture on the souvenir program and all of a sudden Jake fell over and I thought he was dead so I said to the boys:

"Here is your story. Jacob E. Daubert was born in Shamokin, Pa., on the 17 of April, 1886, and lives in Schuykill Pa. and began playing with the Kane, Pa., Club in 1907. With Cleveland in 1908 and Toledo for two years. Joined the Brooklyn Club in 1910 and remained there until this season. Then joined the Cincinnati Reds and fell dead in the 8th inning of the 1st game of the World Serious."

So everybody got up and cheered me and said that was a very funny story but all of a sudden again Jake stood up and looked at the different pts of the compass and walked to 1st base and wasn't dead at all and everybody turned around and hissed me for not giving them a good story.

Well Gents I am not to blame because when a man has got a fast ball like Grover Lowdermilk and hits a man like Jake in the temple, I generally always figure they are dead and the fact that Jake got up and walked to 1st base is certainly not my fault and I hope nobody will hold it vs me.

That was only 1 case where Mr. Gleason's strategy went amuck. His idear there was to kill the regular 1st baseman and then all Mr. Moran would have left to do would be to either stick Dutch Reuther on 1st base where he couldn't pitch or else stick Sherwood Magee over there where he couldn't coach at third base. But Jake gummed it all up by not dying.

Well another part of Mr. Gleason's strategy was dressing the White Sox in their home uniforms so as they would think they was playing on the home grounds in front of a friendly crowd but the trouble with that was that the Reds was all dressed in their home uniforms so as you couldn't tell which club was at home and which wasn't and it made both of them nervous. Then to cap off the climax Mr. Gleason goes and starts a pitcher that everybody thought he was going to start which took away the element of surprise and made a joker out of the ball game.

If he had of only started Erskine Mayer or Bill James or any of the other boys that I recommended why the Reds breath would have been took away and even if they had of hit they couldn't of ran out their hits.

The trouble with the White Sox today was that they was in there trying to back up a nervous young pitcher that never faced a big crowd in a crux before and when he got scared and blowed why it was natural for the rest of them to also blow up. But just give these young Chicago boys a chance to get use to playing before a big crowd with money depending on it and you will be surprised at how they get on their ft and come back at them.

Nobody should ought to find fault with Mr. Gleason, however, for what happened today. As soon as it was decided that they would have 9 games in this serious why the Kid set down and figured that the rules called for 9 men on a side and if 1 Red was killed per day and the serious run the full 9 games why they would only be 1 man left to play the final game and 1 man cant very well win a ball game even vs the White Sox the way they looked. But Daubert didn't die as expected and they will know better next time then to hit a left handed 1st baseman in the egg.

As for the game itself they has probably never been a thriller game in a big serious. The big thrill come in the 4th innings when everybody was wondering if the Sox would ever get the 3rd man out. They finely did and several occupants of the press box was overcome. The White Sox only chance at that pt was to keep the Reds in there hitting till darkness fell and made it a illegal game but Heinie Groh finely hit a ball that Felsch could not help from catching and gummed up another piece of stratagem.

Before the game a band led by John Philip Sousa played a catchy air called the Stars and Stripes Forever and it looks to me like everybody would be whistling it before the serious runs a dozen more games.

It now looks like the present serious would be 1 big surprise after another and tomorrow's shock will occur when the batterys is announced which will be Rube Bressler for the Reds and Lefty Sullivan for the Sox. This will be the biggest up set of the entire fiasco.

I seen both managers right after today's holy cost and Moran said hello old pal, and Gleason said hello you big bum so I am picking the Reds from now on.

'Ballyhoo' Foils Gleason

Score Board Balks
'Happy' Felsch Is Lucky

Cincinnati (O.), Oct. 2.—Gents, the biggest scandal of a big year of baseball scandals was perpetrated down here this afternoon when the American League turned against itself and beat the White Sox out of the second game of the present horror.

Whoever is running the serious went and hired Mr. Announcer at the Washington ball park to come and announce for this serious thinking he was a fair minded American Leaguer, and what does he do today but announce Mr. Ivy Wingo as the catcher for the Reds and fool a Mr. Gleason into thinking Mr. Ivy was going to catch and he hits left-handed, so Mr. Kid started a left-hand pitcher instead of going through with his original plan, which was to pitch Mr. Red Faber.

Before the mistake could be rectified Mr. Game started.

If I was running an event as big as this I would try and get a loyal Mr. Announcer who would announce the right Mr. Catcher and not cross up his own league, and as far as that is concerned I could of got down there and told the people the right Mr. Catcher who was going to catch, and maybe nobody could of heard me, but at least they wouldn't of had to go to the expense of getting a Mr. Man from Washington to announce the wrong catcher, as some other goof is paying my expenses down here.

That was the first break of the game, and the second was the trick Mr. Score Board, which could not register strikes. This was fatal.

For instance, in the fourth inning up come Mr. Morris Rath, and Mr. Williams kept pitching to him and pitching to Mr. Rath and had him struck out at least a dozen times, but Mr. Evans would look up at Mr. Score Board and no strikes was registered there, so Mr. Evans finally got sick of looking at the left side of Mr. Morris' profile and said, "You walk, Mr.," so Mr. Morris had no choice only to walk and say thank you, Mr. Umpire, as an umpire is a czar in a event of this kind.

The next bird up, who I have forgot his name, and anyway it don't make no differents, and besides that he got out. But a man named Mr. Groh and a man named Mr. Roush kept their bat on their shoulder and watched the score board, and next thing you know they was both misters on base, and then Mr. Larry Kopf popped one up between Messrs. Felsch and Jackson for three bases and Mr. Me took a long nap, and the next time I looked at Mr. Score Board some club had three runs, which I have nicknamed Mr. Tallies.

From a baseball standpoint, if there is any such thing, the thing that impressed me most was Mr. Felsch, who I have decided that the minute we get back to old Chi we will have his first name changed from Mr. Happy to Mr. Lucky.

The first three or four times Mr. Felsch came up Mr. Felsch sacrificed, and then all of a sudden Mr. Felsch popped up a fly to Mr. Roush while Mr. Weaver was loitering on Mr. Third Base, and Mr. Roush seems to have caught it while facing Kentucky, and if he hadn't of why Mr. Felsch could of scored three times, which would of tied up the game.

Later, in Mr. Eighth Inning, up come Mr. Lucky again with Mr. Jackson on the keystone sack and knocked down Mr. Groh, but when Mr. Groh finally got up Mr. H. Groh had the baseball in his hands and threw it over to this First Mr. Baseman, who I have forgot his name. But speaking of names, it will be Mr. Lucky Felsch hereafter far as Mr. Me is concerned.

In the seventh inning a effigy was threw out of a airship and landed on the middle of Mr. Diamond, and for a minute I hoped it was me, but it turned out different.

I don't know who was playing, but I think it was Columbus and Ohio. Anyway I think Mr. Ohio won. Pay your war tax as you pass out.

Lardner Aids Chisox

Keeps Off 'Em
Little "Dick" Does Rest

Chicago (Ill.), Oct. 3—Gents, credit, if any, for beating the Reds today belongs to Dick Kerr and I, Dick on account of his pitching and me for not betting on the White Sox.

The very instant I made up what is left of my mind not to lay a bet on Gleason's birds, I knowed they would win and if I had of went a step further and bet on the Reds the score would of been 6 to nothing instead of half that amount.

In the place of going up in the press coop where I would of had to set next to Bud Fisher or who knows what I set this time in a box right close to the White Sox bench and as soon as the boys come out to warm up I told them I was not wagering, which gave them the added confidents needed to win.

Another advantage of me setting down there is that I could keep my ears open and overhear a lot of witty remarks which certainly would never happened up in the press coop, even setting next to Mr. Fisher.

For instants, when Heinie Groh came out to practice, a bird in the next box hollered "Hellow, you big egg," which is certainly a vivid description of Heinie, who is pretty near as big as Dick Kerr and looks more like a cucumber than an egg though he may resemble Mr. Egg in one respect, namely, being worth a whole lot of money.

On another occasion somebody hit a foul ball out in left field and Pat Duncan couldn't get to it a bird setting a couple of boxes away yelled "You couldn't catch nothing you big bum." Pat is bigger than Heinie all right but I have met him and never seen any evidents on him that he is a bum and when the man said he couldn't catch nothing he was telling a fib about him, as I seen him catch several baseballs down in Cincy.

Now, you take Charlie Risberg and Jimmie Smith and Heinie himself and if they had been calling each other eggs or bums, why it would have been just a laughing matter instead of them getting all het up and pretty near coming to blows but it must of been something else they was calling each other and I am sorry I wasn't in a position to hear all of their conversation so I could tell you birds what it was all about but the only remark I heard was when Heinie said to Charley "You will be setting on the bench next yr."

Well he shouldn't ought to say a thing like that if he don't know if its true or not and I don't believe that Mgr. Gleason has been confiding his plans for next summer to no Cincinnati ball player, even if Heinie is their captain.

From where I set I could see every decision Billy Evans made and I am pleased to state that he was right on every occasion and I wished I could say the same for the rest of the umpires but I wasn't close enough to watch them with the naked eye but will try and give a report on them later.

It looked at the start of the battle like the Reds was going to try and play a bunting game on Dickie and I guess maybe it was because perhaps they had heard that he was the best fielding pitcher in the American League and wanted to find out if it was true. Towards the finish they quit trying to bunt and some of them even went so far as to swing their bats all the way around and hit line drives to the catcher.

I suppose a great many of the other experts will criticise Ray Fisher for how he pitched, but I will say nothing about him as I expect to move down to Connecticut as soon as this holy cost is over and he teaches school down there in the winter and I might meet him some day when he had his switch on him or he might even stoop so low as to lick my kids if they happened to be wished onto his school.

So I will hafe to heap my verbal abuse on somebody else and I guess it better be Adolfo Luque, as I understand he don't read many words of English. Well then it Luques to me like he should of went to Fisher's relief earlier in the day and the score might of been 1 to 0 or 2 to 1 instead of disgraceful figures like 3 to 0.

The only unsportsmanlike thing I seen occur was in the third innings when Buck Weaver came up with Collins on first base and the Reds expected him to bunt but he hit a single over Kopf's kopf and I don't know what Cincinnati will think of Chicago's hospitality after that.

I know of no more fitting way to close than by giveing a report of the inning Luque pitched in pure Cubanola. El Lieboldo whif-foed. Si si senor Collins was outo Jako Dauberto to Adolfo. Bucko Weavero outo Ratho to Dauberto. No runos. No hittos, no bootos.

Rings Are Much Alike

Jim Has More Speed
Nine Games Hit Moran

Chicago, Oct. 4.—Gents! There is a strong family resemblance between the Rings. Both of them is tall and handsome and has beautiful curves. Both of them is inclined to be a trifle wild. Jim has a bit more speed. Neither of them has much luck, at least they told me down in Cincy that Jim was the jinx bird of the National League all summer, as the Reds never batted much behind him.

As for me, the boys has been batting around me only a trifle. Jim pitches better than I write and I pitch better than he writes. Jim is a decided blonde wile I am a kind of a dapple gray since the serious opened up.

On acct of Jim's complexion he don't look so bad when he don't have a chance to shave. Jim got a lot of praise today wile all I got was insults. For inst I was down in the hotel before the game and a Chicago man and a man from Cincy was trying to bet but they couldnt find no one to put it up with and finely the Chicago man spots me and introduces me to the Red bird and the latter said he wouldn't bet under such conditions.

As for today's game they was a scribe down town this am that 2 men asked him who was going to pitch today and the scribe said Cicotte and 1 of the men said you are crazy as Cicotte has such a sore arm that he cant wash the back of his neck so when we come out to the park this scribe told me about it and I said they wasn't nothing in the rules of Monday's game that required Cicotte to wash the back of his neck or any of the newspaper men neither.

"Well," said the other expert, "the man was just speaking figurative and meant that Eddie had a sore arm."

"Well," I said, "if he has only got one sore arm he can still wash the back of his neck as I only use 1 even when I am going to a party."

"The back of your neck looks like it," said the other expert.

"Yes," I said, "but what is the differents or not about Cicotte only having 1 sore arm as he only pitches with 1 arm."

"Yes you bum but that is the arm that the man said was sore." That is the kind clever repartee that goes on between the experts and no hard feelings on neither side.

No gents it wasn't no sore arm that beat Eddie today but just the other member of the Ring family finely getting some of the breaks and the way I seen the games you couldn't make me believe that either of the 2 birds had any impediment in the old souper as I have nicknamed it. Eddie had a sore heart when it was all over but theys other seasons comeing and may be another game in this serious which dont look like it would end for a month as I look for another 1 of them 40 day rains to begin early tomorrow am.

Gents do you remember when they decided to have the serious go 9 games instead of the conventional 7 and a whole lot of people said that was soup for the Reds as Mr. Gleason didn't have the pitchers to go 9 games.

Well now it looks like the disadvantage was vs P. J. Moran as if the serious had of only been skedoodled to go 7 games why by now he would of only had 1 more to win by now where as on the other hand Mr. Gleason has still got the same pitchers he had to begin with. The only people therefore that gets the advantage is the athaletes themselfs as they get paid for 5 games instead of 4 and I beg to assure the public that the newspaper men wishes they had kept it 4 games as we dont even get the priviledge of talking back to the umpire.

Tomorrows game will be postponed till the 4th day of November and I hope before that time they will give me a rm with bath.

Ring's Right on Rain

Even with Soothsayer Finds Hurlers Immune

Chicago, Oct. 5.—Gents: Well Gents I guess the experts who have been sniggering in their sleeve at me because maybe once in a while I make a little mistake about who is going to win a ball game or something will do their laughing on the other ft. After the little trick I showed them yesterday when I come out in print and said today's game would be postponed on account of rain.

The prediction is all the more wonderful when you set down and figure out that this is the first Sunday it ever rained in old Chi when there was a ball game skedooled at Comiskey Park, so me coming out and saying it would rain today puts me on a par with that old guy in Rome that told Caesar he was going to croke on the ideas of March and sure enough he did and it was first time in his life that he ever done it in that month or any other month in the calendar you might say.

The first thing I done when I woke up this morning was look

outside of the window and the instant I looked out I seen it drooling so I ordered up the morning paper and laid down and turned to the humorous column called "Today's Weather."

Well, who ever writes it said "Probably showers with lower temperature and versatile winds." But he didn't mention nothing about postponing no ball game so if he comes forwards with the claim that he is in the same class as myself and that old Rome guy why he will get himself laughed out of the league.

Now the next thing is to predict what effect will the rain be on the remains of the worlds serious. Well, theys several ways of looking at it and a man that jumps into conclusions and says this and that the other thing about setting down and giving the matter careful thought is libel to become the Philadelphia of predicters.

So during the sermon this morning I leaned back and kind of half closed the old eyes and studied the matter from all angles and here is some of the conclusions I reached and I will give the way I arrived at them so you fans will have some idear on how a great man's mind works.

Well then to begin with there is the effect on the R. R. Companys was had their trains all fixed to start for Cincinnati tonight and either they will have to go empty or else call up all the porters and say "George, you don't need to show up tonight." This problem is out of my lines and up to the R. R. Administration.

Question No. 2—Is which club gets the benefits out of the rain. To answer this a man has got to know how rain effects the different pitchers. For inst Grover Lowdermilk always gets taller after a heavy rain. Dick Kerr usually gets cross and mean. Lefty Williams, just kind of half smiles and makes the best of it. Eddie Cicotte plays a lot of practical jokes on the rest of the boys. Bill James simply lets things take their course and waits for the clouds to roll by.

I have not yet became acquainted with Mr. Wilkinson but as they tell me he runs a farm down east I suppose he hasn't no objection to a little rain providing it dont have no heavy wind with it.

Now take the Cincinnati staff and a man stumbels on to some

startling facts. On a rainy day in the regular season Slim Sallee generally most always goes to the races and the way he feels the next few days depends on who wins.

Well they wasn't no races here today or race riots neither one so I haven't no idear if Sol will be sunny and gay or morose. As for Dutch Reuther they was 1 day last summer when the Reds was supposed to play here but they was a regiment of Chi soldiers going to be welcomed home that same day so of course it poured rain and I was wading along Clark st. and met Dutch and he was wearing a rain coat so the Red fans neednt have no fear that he will come down with a heavy cold.

I never seen Jimmy Ring after a rainstorm but if he is like the rest of the Rings he will probably look like he ought to get his clothes pressed. Personally I never carry a bumbershoot and always look worse than usual when I come in out of the wet and when I look bad I get mad and bark like a dog. The one who is libel to be the most surprised is Luque as they tell me it never rains in Cuba. Eller, Fisher, Mitchell and Gerner is all good natured boys that dont allow a little thing like a rain to ruffle them up.

So all in all it looks like the rainy day would have absolutely no effect on neither club and it only remains to be seen how the umpires will take it. It will probably make them all more anxious to get the serious over in a hurry and they will begin striking everybody out.

The game was called off about 11 bells this a.m. after a consultation between Managers Gleason and Moran which run something like as follows: Moran—"Hello, is this you Bill? They tell me the grounds are too wet to play on them."

Gleason—"Well the outfield is pretty wet but we had the infield covered and we could play the game on that."

Moran—"Oh no we wont or happy and lucky Felsch might get an extra base hit."

Gleason—"Well godby old pal."

Moran—"Good luck old chum."

Ring Denies 'Hod' Rumor

Didn't Fall Down
Moran Meets Mr. Rigler

Chicago, Oct. 6.—Gents: Well, they asked me what was the feature of this game and I says I thought I heard a rumor that Hod Eller come down for breakfast this a. m. in the stead of ordering it up in his rm and wile he was struggling to get through the lobby he fell on the pavement and broke his right arm at the elbow.

Well, evidently he went and seen a dr and the next time I seen him he was out on the mound or box or what they call it pitching for the defeated Reds and I couldn't see his elbow from the where I set but dont ever let that bird brag about strikeing out 6 birds in succession because once I was pitcher for the Niles High School against New Zealand and I whiffed the whole ball club.

But speaking about the roomer of Hod Eller toppling over in the hotel lobby if he had of been a roomer at my hotel he wouldn't of never fell over because they wasnt no rm. in our lobby because the minute you try and walk through the lobby in our hotel a million bugs from Cincinnati and old Chi grabs you by either arm and ask you how to bet on the rest of the series.

Thus you get through the lobby. Now let us get back to Hod Eller. If he did fall down in the hotel lobby and break an arm it must of been the arm he pitched with because I never seen such nonsenical pitching in all my born days to use a new expression and I have seen a whole lot of pitching in my born days.

But as a matter of fact gents, you cant tell me that that bird ever fell down in a hotel lobby this morning or any other morning because he didnt fall down in a much larger place this P.M.

Please don't believe that Hod fell down either morning or afternoon either one though it was a Cincinnati baseball writer that gave me a story about him falling down which makes it exclusive between I and you and the world.

The Cincinnati baseball writer give it to me in confidence and any time they do that to me I tell it. But I really did strike out more birds the day we played New Zealand than Hod did after falling down.

Well, that disposes of the ball game and brings us to the business of the evening. A great many Cincinnati fans may think that today's game was won its merits but I ask them to consider the umpires. Why I know of a whole lot of umpires that could of win that game for the White Sox in less innings than it took to play it.

Now as for the details of the game the other experts can tell you what was visible on the field but very few can tell you what really happened in the Reds' fourth. I suppose a whole lot of you wondered what come off when Pat Moran dashed up from the first base coaching line and stopped what ever game there was going on. Well, here is the actual conversation that occurred.

"Mr. Rigeler," said Pat, "I don't believe I know you."

"I guess you don't," said Mr. Rigler, "as you have spelled my name wrong."

"Well," said Pat, "I just wanted to know if you was one of the Riglers from Crystal Falls?"

"No," said Mr. Rigler.

The game then went on as usual.

The most interesting thing I could find about the game was in the program and here is what it said in part "So and So beer has the largest sale of any beer in the loop."

"So and So beer is a case of good judgment."

Well, gents, that makes a man wonder which beer is going to advertise next.

But on the other hand it says "The pitcher who wins the game must be in perfect physical condition and the same applies to the game of life. We respectfully refer you to the following patrons, Mr. Charles A. Comiskey, Hon. Geo. Carpenter, Mr. Ban B. Johnson and Bishop C. P. Anderson"

So that puts me all up in the air again as I dont know who is going to pitch tomorrow whether it will be Charles A. Comiskey or Mr. Ban B. Johnson or Bishop Anderson, but I know it won't be a carpenter as he charges too much per hr.

Ring Tells Umps' Secret

Kerr an Oil Magnate
Schalk Right With Ban

Cincinnati, Oct. 7.—Gents: Instead of going to the Latonie today I sent my Jack over by a messenger and told him to throw it through the gate and in the meanwhile I went to the so-called national pastime. My first experience was trying to get into the park without showing a ticket and the guy stopped me and says where is your ticket brother?

Well I never seen this bird before in all my born days but I have got 3 perfectly good brothers so I gave him a keen glance to see maybe he was 1 of them but if he was he had changed a whole lot so I said "Which of my brothers is you?" and he kind of fumbled and stalled and couldn't answer nothing back so I simply passed it up by showing him my ticket and going into the ball park.

Up on the runway I met a lady from Philadelphia who says "Well the series will be all over today" and I asked her how did she know and she said because Cincinnati is a one night stand as all they have got to see here is Fountain Square and the Ohio River and Garfield Statue so I quit talking to her as I have seen more than that and I know for a fact that theys a whole lot more to be seen here than is visible to the nude eye if you stick around here a while which it looks like we would do so now.

After leaving the lady from Philadelphia much to her regrets I went in the banquet hall and who should I run into but the presidents of the other league. "Well Ban" I said, "are you going to suspend Cracker Schalk for what he done yesterday?"

I call Schalk Cracker because he calls me biscuit.

"What did he do?" says Ban.

"Why," says I, "he hit an umpire and didn't kill him."

"I didn't see it," says Ban, and I asked him if he was out to the game and he said he was so that makes 2 people that can go to the game and not watch them not including the umpires.

A great many of you gents may wonder why I keep bragging the umpire like this. Well I don't really mean it and the real purpose is kind of subtle but I would just as leaf tell you birds what it is.

The other day I met Bill Evans and he said, "Keep putting my name in the paper," so I have to sort of pan them or how could I do it but at that I was kind of wondering around amidst the bugs in the 9th inning this pm and Bill called a strike on whoever was up to the bat and a lot of maudlins around me begin to pan Bill so i stepped up and said, "Do you know why they have the umpires down there on the field?" and one bird said "No," so I said "It's because they can see the plays much better than if they was up in the grandstand." That silenced them.

But to get back to Ban I said "If you arent going to suspend Cracker why dont you suspend Carl Mays as you ought to live up to your reputation as a suspender?" Its a wonder he didnt give me a belt in the jaw.

After banqueting on a special brand of ham recommended by Garry Herrmann but I wont mention its name in pure reading matter why I went up in the press coop and looked down on the field and some birds from Texas was just presenting Dickie Kerr with a bunch of oil stock. The differents between a bunch of oil stock and a bunch of flowers which they usually wish on a pitcher is that a bunch of oil stock waits 2 days instead of one before it withers and dies.

Well in the 5th, they was a man on third and second and first and very few out and Cocky Collins hit one by his drives which dont never seem to go safe and somebody caught it and whoever was on third scored an waffles Schalk stuck on second base but Dickie was still thinking about this here oil stock yet and he run down to second and found that somebody else had a lease on that property and along come Sheriff Groh and tagged him and said you are it you cant expect a left hander with oil stock to respect other peoples leases on bases.

Between that inning and the subsequent inning Dickie took off his shoe to rest his dogs and it took him such a long while that I was going to walk out and leave the ball game flat as I though the serious was over any way and I got down on the next floor and first thing you know Dutch Reuther wasn't in there pitching no more as Happy Go Lucky Felsch had finely got one and Pat said to himself if a man is unlucky enough to let Felsch get a base hit he is better in the clubhouse than here anyway.

I looked out there to see who was pitching and it was the other member of the Ring family, so that is why I stayed through the ball game and pretty soon I was parked right beside Dutch Reuther himself and he said "Well it ought to be over by now but I lost my stuff."

So I said let us go to the races tomorrow and he said that was my intentions but now I have got to come back here again, he acted kind of disappointed over not winning but great heavens when he gets to be my age he will be glad to be alive let alone mournin over one ball game.

Well along come the tenth inning and the Sox got a couple birds on the bases and Dutch said goodbye as I dont want to see this whatever happens as I cant stand no more strain so he left me and I promised to tell him how the game come out and I will as soon as I see him.

They tell me that the Reds went out on 3 pitched balls in their half of the tenth and that is all I would pitch in any inning if I was doing it but any way I didn't see the Red part of the tenth as I was looking up at a sign on the fence which says "Vote your protest. Vote wet November 4th." so it looks like we would be here a long while and even then I will protest by voting dry.

Lardner Has Shine Ball

Present From Ump
Kopf Couldn't Hit It

Cincinnati, Oct. 8.—Gents: This is the most scandalous and death dealing story ever wrote about a world serious ball game. They have been a whole lot of talk in this serious about one thing and another and it finely remained for me to get at the facts.

Well, those of you who was out at todays game dont have to be explained to that in the fifth inning Eddie Cicotte pitched a baseball to Larry Kopf and Larry missed it and turned around to Mr. Quigley who was supposed to be umpiring behind the plate and asked this bird to let him (Kopf) see the ball.

Well, Mr. Quigley give Mr. Kopf the ball and he looked at it and Mr. Quigley said "Larry do you want the ball," and Larry said "No I dont want it." So Mr. Quigley said "All right throw the ball back to the pitcher. I cant stop this ball game all day to let an infielder look at a ball." Then I stepped in and said "Give me the ball" so they did.

Well, they give me the ball and here it is laying in front of me and I want to say to all infielders who of course never kep a ball long enough to look at it just what a baseball looks like and if I was an infielder I would catch a ball some time and hold on to it till after the game was lost and then I would study the ball.

Well, here is the ball right in front of me as I try to write. I will describe to you guys as I see it. Well this ball looks to me like a National League ball. That is what probably deceived them.

Well you see the reason that an infielder dont know what a baseball looks like is because the minute he gets it he has to throw it somewhere. Well as I said before here is what the baseball looks like. The National League baseball is nearly round.

This baseball which I am going to keep and give to my oldest child is a baseball that needs further description. It is the same baseball that Larry Kopf looked at and I only wished I was as nice looking as him and I wouldn't be writing this horrible stuff or working at baseball.

Well, then here is about that baseball. It is nearly round and looks nearly like an American League baseball except it has more seams and to be exact it has got 126 seams and if you take an American League ball why it has got 140 seams so why shouldnt you hit them.

But at that you take any ball and start counting seams on it and you can count all night and get innumerable seams. Well to distinguish this ball from its brothers it says John A. Heydler on it which makes it a cinch that it is a National League ball as it is a certainty that John wouldnt sign a ball that belonged to the other league.

Well as for the rest of the ball it looks soiled on the northwest side and I will worry my life away wondering who put a dirty finger on that ball which I have got and my children will still have it after me.

Now we have wrote almost a whole story about a ball. Now let us take a different angle about the game and start in on Morris Rath. At one stage of the game Morris hit a ball and broke his bat and the man setting next to me said that is the only time Morris ever broke a bat in a world's serious.

Another funny thing I heard was as follows.

A man named Wingo come up to the bat and the bird setting next to me said come on Wingo get a bingo.

Pitchers Puzzle Lardner

Why Are They Plural?

Ban Suspends Flingers

Chicago, Oct. 9.—Gents, the special train for Cincy wiil leave tonight at 11:30, new time, and I would advise everybody to be there with their tooth brush and typewriter. The train will leave out of the Pennsy station, and immediately on arriving in old Cincy it would be a great idear to try and get a room somewheres so as you can get shaved.

The game tomorrow will be the crucial game of the serious and it looks to me like it would be between Grover Lowdermilk and Rube Dressler. Neither mgr. dares to pitch anybody else.

Today's game here was just a exhibition between the White Sox and Reds and believe me it was some exhibition. It looked like both sides were having a battle to see which could get 3 men out the slowest. Finely Joe Jackson hit a pop fly into right field seats and broke up the game as far as I am concerned.

The first two White Sox pitchers was Williams and James, and I can't tell you why they either of them is plural, and if I was running it I would call them William and Jane. I wouldn't plural neither one of the both of them. If I was manager I would pitch a guy with a singular name like Lowdermilk. Another thing Manager Gleason did today was to change the outfield around to deceive the newspaper men. The scheme worked perfectly and I do hope he is satisfied. I know I am.

Speaking about this world serious, I will have to join the statisticians and tell you the different records I seen broke. It was the first world serious that Morris Rath ever broke a bat in. It is the only world serious which Sherwood Magee ever got a base hit. It is the only world serious that Umpire Nallin ever called a strike on Jake Daubert. It is probably the last world serious I will ever see. So much for the records.

Now to get down to facts. Here is quotations from a letter received just before the game by a Chi baseball writer:

"I have been a follower of athletics for yrs. and have taken part in athletics in my younger days. I have been greatly amused during the present series in reading the ifs, ands and buts explaining Chicago's defeat from day to day. It looks like a case of sour grapes to me. In fact, it borders on rowdyism. I suppose if you lose another game or two you will mob the Cincinnati team."

Well I know this here Chi baseball writer that the letter come to and he never mentioned sour grapes in his life or ordered them neither and as for mobbing the Cincinnati Ball Club, why this same baseball writer was standing with me when the Clubs come out of the clubhouse and Sherwood Magee come up and spoke to the both of us. If that don't prove how we stand I don't know what will or care neither one.

Now personly I don't think they will be a game tomorrow and if there is I don't know who will pitch, as I seen Ban Johnson after today's alleged game and he said he had suspended all the pitchers on both clubs.

Wile being exhausted at the game I finely set down and read the following in the afternoon paper:

"The names of the early Dukes of Normandy, as well as their

family history, are known but very dimly, and it may be as well that it should be so, for their descent does not seem to have been as Orthodox as it might. Thus William 1 of England (William 2 of Normandy) was the illegitimate son of his predecessor Robert the Devil," and so on. How can a man pay attention to a ballgame like that when they's such good stuff to read in the paper.